DEMOCRACY IN AMERICA?

DEMOCRACY IN AMERICA?

*What Has Gone Wrong and What
We Can Do about It*

BENJAMIN I. PAGE

MARTIN GILENS

The University of Chicago Press   Chicago and London

The University of Chicago Press, Chicago 60637

The University of Chicago Press, Ltd., London

© 2017 by The University of Chicago

Published 2017

Printed in the United States of America

26 25 24 23 22 21 20 19 18 17   1 2 3 4 5

ISBN-13: 978-0-226-50896-2 (cloth)

ISBN-13: 978-0-226-50901-3 (e-book)

DOI: 10.7208/chicago/9780226509013.001.0001

Library of Congress Cataloging-in-Publication Data

Names: Page, Benjamin I., author. | Gilens, Martin, author.
Title: Democracy in America? : what has gone wrong and what we can do about it / Benjamin I. Page and Martin Gilens.
Description: Chicago ; London : The University of Chicago Press, 2017. | Includes bibliographical references and index.
Identifiers: LCCN 2017015527 | ISBN 9780226508962 (cloth : alk. paper) | ISBN 9780226509013 (e-book)
Subjects: LCSH: Democracy—United States. | United States—Politics and government—21st century. | Pressure groups—United States. | Rich people—Political activity—United States.
Classification: LCC JK275.P344 2017 | DDC 320.973—dc23
LC record available at https://lccn.loc.gov/2017015527

♾ This paper meets the requirements of ANSI/NISO Z39.48-1992 (Permanence of Paper).

CONTENTS

PART FOUR: HOW TO DO IT

ILLUSTRATIONS

PART ONE

Introduction

ONE

More Democracy

Today the United States faces a number of daunting problems. Economic inequality has reached levels not seen for a hundred years. While the wealthy keep piling up riches, many Americans are hurting from job losses, low wages, high health-care costs, and deteriorating public services. Whole communities have been devastated by factory closings. Our public schools are neglected. Our highways and bridges are in disrepair.

Well-designed government policies could help deal with these problems. Large majorities of Americans favor specific measures that would be helpful. Yet our national government often appears to ignore the wants and needs of its citizens. It pays more attention to organized interests than to ordinary Americans, and it gets bogged down in gridlock and inaction.

No wonder many Americans are angry and alienated. No wonder there have been populist rebellions on both the Left and the Right: the Tea Party, Occupy Wall Street, Bernie Sanders, Donald Trump.

In this book we argue that gridlock and inaction in Washington result from two main causes: clashes between our two sharply divided political parties and obstructive actions by corporations, interest groups, and wealthy individuals. The many "veto points" in our complex political system (that is, the many opportunities for one or another political actor to thwart policy change) are used to prevent the enactment of policies that most Americans want.

The nonresponsiveness and dysfunction of government are closely related to *undemocratic* features of our political system.

Our laws and institutions make it hard for ordinary citizens to have an effective voice in politics. They permit corporations, interest groups, and the wealthy to exert a great deal of influence over what the government does. And they allow donors and highly ideological political activists to dominate the parties' nominations of candidates for office, so that the two parties are pushed in sharply contrasting directions—contributing to gridlock. *Both* parties often stray from what majorities of Americans want them to do.

It follows that our problems can be more effectively addressed if we reform our political system to achieve *more democracy*: more equal opportunity for all citizens to shape what their government does and policies that better address the needs of all Americans.

If the political parties are democratized, for example, so that each of them is forced to appeal more to the voters and less to the party's donors and activists, they will differ less sharply from each other. That will reduce gridlock. Both parties will be more responsive to the citizenry and more likely to adopt solutions that Americans favor for the problems we face.

Similarly, if we reform elections so that all citizens have an equal voice, and if we mute the influence of political money and organized interests, public officials will more faithfully reflect what ordinary Americans want.

Again, if the Congress and other political institutions are reformed to represent all citizens equally, those institutions will be more harmonious—less prone to clashes with each other that result in gridlock—and more responsive to the citizenry as a whole.

Some impediments to democracy have been with us for a long time. Others have grown worse in recent years. But most, we think, are fixable.

In the course of American history, the health of democracy and the extent of economic equality have tended to rise and fall together. Each has affected the other. In the late nineteenth-century Gilded Age, for example, extreme inequalities of income and wealth—inequalities not unlike those that afflict us today—empowered the wealthy few and undermined democracy. Yet that same extreme economic inequality provoked protests and social movements, which in turn helped bring about reforms that advanced both political and economic equality. Through such efforts, the United States has enjoyed periods of relatively democratic, harmonious, and effective government, and widely shared prosperity.

We believe that we can once again enjoy more vigorous democracy and more widely shared prosperity, if enough citizens mobilize and work hard for effective reforms that promote both economic and political equality. The two types of reform go together. Each facilitates the other. Neither is likely to get very far alone.

In the following chapters we show precisely how undemocratic U.S. government policy making has become. We do our best to diagnose exactly what has gone wrong. Based on that diagnosis, we explain how certain specific political reforms could greatly increase democratic responsiveness. Finally, we explore how the formidable obstacles to reform might be overcome.

Why Democracy

We define *democracy* as *policy responsiveness to ordinary citizens—* that is, popular control of government. Or simply "majority rule."[1]

This commonsense definition reflects the foundation of our Constitution in the will of "we the people of the United States." It embodies the fundamental value of *political equality*, insisting that in a democracy all citizens should have an equal opportunity to influence the making of public policy. It reflects the assertion in the Declaration of Independence that all men (we would now say all human beings) are "created equal." It corresponds to Abraham Lincoln's espousal of government "of the people, by the people, and for the people."

Yet the fact is that this sort of "majoritarian" democracy— which is widely embraced by ordinary Americans—has been rejected by a number of political theorists and by many social and political elites.[2] So we need to explain why we think majoritarian democracy is desirable.

ELECTIONS ALONE DO NOT GUARANTEE DEMOCRACY. Some theorists have argued that all that is needed for democracy is elections that create a competitive struggle for citizens' votes.[3]

To us, however, a core element of democracy is *political equality*—
an equal voice for each citizen. Just holding elections does not guarantee that citizens will have equal influence. For example, even if
we formally allow each adult citizen one and only one vote, some
people may be left out because they are deterred or excluded from
voting. (We will see that voters in the United States tend to be quite
*un*representative of the citizenry as a whole.) Other people may, in
effect, get *many* votes—if they provide money or organizational
support that is essential to running political campaigns and getting
a party's supporters to the polls. Moreover, election outcomes may
not reflect the real preferences of the voters if the choices on the
ballot are severely restricted. And policy may diverge sharply from
the desires of the public if officials ignore those who elected them
and pay attention to lobbyists instead.

One way in which elections can go wrong is if voters' choices
are circumscribed. A stark example: Iran's Guardian Council, a
twelve-member body of jurists and theologians appointed by Iran's
"Supreme Leader," decides which candidates can get onto the ballot. In Iran's 2013 presidential election, the Guardian Council dis-
qualified the vast majority of would-be candidates—including all
thirty women and the reformist former president. So even though
many Iranians (72 percent of them) voted and could exercise a
"free" choice among the six candidates on the ballot—and even
though the winner of the most votes peacefully took office a few
weeks later—we would not want to call that election democratic.[4]

In the United States today, no body of theologians controls who
can and who cannot run for office. Yet—as a result of much more
subtle and indirect processes—we may actually have something like
our own Guardian Council. In today's America, a relatively small,
unelected set of people exerts a great deal of influence over who
appears on the ballot and who has a realistic chance to win: those
who supply the money. When the members of this group agree with
one another, they have the power to determine that certain kinds of
electoral choices are essentially off-limits for voters.

In our electoral system, private money plays a huge part. Neither
major party can function without many millions of dollars. And the
parties generally select their candidates in obscure, low-visibility

primary elections, in which only a small, atypical set of voters participates. This process limits the influence of rank-and file voters. It empowers a few highly ideological activists, organized interest groups, and donors. In this and many other ways, our system differs from those of most other advanced countries.

Since Republican and Democratic activists and donors typically disagree sharply with each other about a number of issues, there are usually very real differences between Republican and Democratic candidates. But the megadonors of *both* parties tend to agree in opposing certain policies that most Americans favor. These include important policies related to government budgets, international trade, social welfare spending, economic regulation, and taxes (as will be discussed in chapter 4). On these issues, big-money political donors can act rather like a Guardian Council. They can keep off the ballot candidates, ideas, and policies they disagree with, by giving or withholding the money that is needed to put on a serious campaign.

THE MONEY PROBLEM. A crucial part of this picture is that both parties need enormous amounts of money, but—under our current system—that money mostly comes from a very small set of megadonors. In 2012, for example, a tiny sliver of the U.S. population—just *one-tenth of one-tenth of 1 percent* of Americans—provided *almost half* of all the money spent in federal elections.[5] Even more remarkably, just 132 donors to huge political action committees (PACs) known as "super PACs," giving an average of almost $10 million each, accounted for more money than all of the 3.7 million small donors to the Barack Obama and Mitt Romney campaigns combined.[6]

It is extremely difficult to win a major government office without the backing of affluent campaign donors. The "preapproval" process by America's "Guardian Council" of potential donors seems to be remarkably effective at screening out candidates who fundamentally disagree with the preferences of well-funded interest groups and well-to-do contributors. The result: U.S. government policy often reflects the wishes of those with money, not the wishes of the millions of ordinary citizens who turn out every two years to choose among the preapproved, money-vetted candidates for federal office.

To be sure, the 2016 "outsider" campaigns of Bernie Sanders and Donald Trump seemed to demonstrate that—at least under certain circumstances—huge contributions from the usual millionaire and billionaire donors may not be necessary to compete. But of course Sanders did not win the Democratic Party nomination, let alone the general election. Trump was an extremely unusual case: his celebrity and communication skills markedly lowered his campaign costs by giving him an enormous amount of free media exposure. And Trump had his own fortune to fall back on, if necessary, which also helped make him unusually independent of megadonors.

We will have much more to say in later chapters about the distorting effects of money in politics. For now, the main point is that we should not think about democracy in terms of the mere existence of elections. If we want true majoritarian democracy, what really matters is whether—and to what extent—ordinary citizens can control what their government does. Elections can effectively ensure democratic control only if a representative set of citizens votes, and only if election outcomes are not excessively influenced by party activists, interest groups, or financial donors.

But *do* we want true, majority-rule democracy? Not everyone thinks so.

IS THE GENERAL PUBLIC WORTH PAYING ATTENTION TO? The most important objection to majoritarian democracy is that ordinary citizens may be too uninterested in politics, too ill informed, too capricious in their political opinions, too selfish, and too subject to demagoguery to have their views taken seriously. What if most Americans do not really know which public policies would be good for them or for the country? Why should we pay any attention to what they think?

In the nation's early days, James Madison and Alexander Hamilton worried about alleged "extreme fluctuations," "passions" and "temporary errors and delusions" of the public. Walter Lippmann bemoaned "stereotypes" or "pictures in [the] heads" of ordinary citizens, who (he said) often fail to comprehend world realities. Subsequently, decades worth of polls and surveys have shown that most Americans are not much interested in or informed about politics. Again and again, many or most Americans have failed quizzes about basic political facts, such as which party controls the House of Representatives or how long a term senators have in office. Most people have trouble identifying or locating foreign countries. Acronyms and abbreviations that are coin of the realm in Washington, DC—NATO, ICBM, MFN, and the like—are mysteries to many Americans.[7]

Moreover, many Americans are confused or uncertain about exactly what kinds of government policies they favor or oppose. "Don't know" responses to poll questions are fairly common, at least when survey researchers don't make it too embarrassing to give them. Repeated surveys of the same individuals over time have showed that their stated opinions about political issues tend to vary from one year to another—sometimes back and forth, for no easily discernable reason. Researchers have talked of "non-attitudes" and have called into question the very existence of meaningful public opinion.[8]

Right up to the present day, scholars continue to write that "widespread political ignorance" is a profound problem for democracy and (in effect) to counsel political leaders to pay no heed to what ordinary citizens say they want.[9] An important recent book on "democracy for realists" seems to cast doubt on the idea that the public has meaningful views that should shape government policy.[10]

There are good reasons for low levels of political information, reasons that can be summed up in the phrase "rational ignorance."[11] Most people—unless they happen to enjoy being political junkies—have little reason to devote a great deal of time or energy to most political matters. To most people, work, family, and leisure are higher priorities than most aspects of politics. Why make a big investment in acquiring political information? Especially since the odds of one individual having a pivotal effect on a major electoral outcome are usually vanishingly small.

"Rational ignorance" notwithstanding, a few members of the public are indeed political junkies who enjoy learning about politics. And a larger portion are concerned with and knowledgeable about specific issues such as education, health care, or Middle East politics, depending on their particular occupations or interests. Whereas most people lack clear preferences on most issues, many people do have informed views about the few issues that they care about most.[12] And still more have general notions about what sorts of policies are likely to suit them.

Critics of democracy are certainly right that most *individual* Americans lack fully informed opinions about most issues. But it does *not* follow that the *collective* or aggregate, survey-measured policy preferences of all Americans—such as the percentages of Americans that polls show favoring or opposing various public policies—have the same characteristics as the preferences of a single typical individual. The notion that whole entities must have the same characteristics as their individual parts is a fallacy, known as the "fallacy of composition."

THE STRENGTH OF *COLLECTIVE* POLICY PREFERENCES. There is plenty of evidence that public opinion as a *collective* or aggregate phenomenon is very different, much more worth paying attention to, than the day-to-day opinions of a typical *individual* citizen.

How can this be?

There are two main reasons. The first involves *collective deliberation*: a society-wide process in which experts and leaders debate public policies, their views are reported in the media, attentive Americans pick up cues from those they trust, and the attentive citizens communicate those views to their families, friends, and coworkers.[13]

The second reason involves the *aggregation process* itself: when many uncertain expressions of opinion are combined into a collective whole (for example, into the percentage of Americans favoring a particular policy), random errors and uncertainties among individuals tend to get averaged out. Survey measures of collective preferences cannot overcome *systematic*, nonrandom errors (we will have more to say about that later), but they do cancel out random variations that occur in "doorstep" opinions offered to survey interviewers. In most cases, the results of well-designed surveys fairly faithfully reflect longer-term, underlying tendencies of collective opinion.[14]

The process of forming collective opinions about politics is akin to the processes that tend to make verdicts by twelve-person juries, or market judgments by thousands of consumers or investors, much more reliable than the opinion of a typical individual. Each is an example of what can be called the "wisdom of crowds."[15]

Most Americans do not devote a great deal of thought to politics. But they do have easy, direct access to some information that is highly relevant to public policy: the size of their Social Security checks; what is happening to their jobs and wages; the (perhaps crumbling) condition of roads they drive on; price rises or declines in grocery stores or at gasoline pumps. On some of these day-to-day pocketbook concerns—and on such matters as neighborhood crime, the challenge of holding down a job with no paid sick leave, the difficulty of finding affordable child care, or the (un)reliability of public transportation—ordinary Americans may actually have better firsthand information than elites who live more rarefied, sheltered lives.

When it comes to many abstract, complex, or distant matters, however—including precisely what sorts of public policy might be best for reducing layoffs and wage cuts, or for curbing price inflation, improving air quality, or avoiding war casualties—collective deliberation becomes crucial. Experts debate the merits of alternative public policies. Commentators and politicians express their views through various media. A set of relatively attentive citizens—without having to memorize a lot of facts—can figure out what sorts of policies are favored by leaders whom they trust to have expertise and to share their own values. (This works only if such leaders exist, can be heard, and deserve the trust bestowed upon them.[16]) Attentive citizens adopt those policy preferences for themselves, and—again without needing to learn or recite a lot of facts—communicate them to friends, families, and coworkers who also share similar values.

As a result, most Americans—on most major issues—are able to form a general idea about what they want the government to do. They develop underlying *tendencies* of opinion. When the uncertain beliefs and opinions of millions of people are combined, the random noise is reduced. Collective preferences tend to be solid. They tend to reflect the underlying needs and values of the whole body of citizens, in light of the best available information from experts and commentators.

This is not just a theory. It is supported by evidence drawn from close examination of Americans' actual collective policy preferences, as expressed in many polls and surveys conducted over many years. An exhaustive study of thousands of survey questions that had been asked over a fifty-year period found that Americans' *collective* policy preferences do not in fact suffer from the alarming defects that are often attributed to them. "Violent fluctuations" in collective opinion are a myth. The proportions of Americans favoring or opposing a given policy generally stay *stable* over time, except that they *react in sensible ways* to such big events as an armed attack or a nuclear reactor meltdown. And they gradually change to take account of new realities or new information. As unemployment declines, for example, public support for unemployment assistance declines as well; when tax rates are lowered, public support for tax cuts declines.[17]

Americans as a group make many definite *distinctions* among policies (for example, which countries should receive economic aid; under what conditions abortions should be allowed; which kinds of assistance to the poor should be expanded or curtailed). Collective policy preferences are generally *coherent*: they are seldom inconsistent or mutually contradictory.[18] Well-designed polls and surveys typically do a good job of revealing collective policy preferences that *reflect the worldviews, values, and interests* of the average American.

In a word, public opinion is generally *deliberative*—it generally reflects the best available information and the values and interests of the citizenry. It does so not because most individuals are deliberative or aware of the best information but because individuals form their opinions through a collective social process that brings deliberation and information to bear on the issues of the day.

We need to add certain caveats. First, poll results—especially those based on confusing, biased, or inept questions—have to be interpreted with care. But even poorly worded questions, properly interpreted, can often help reveal the contours of collective opinion.[19] Another problem is that tabulated poll responses can underrepresent the interests of respondents who are uncertain and give arbitrary answers or say "don't know." Such effects (which, however, are not generally large) should be taken into account when possible.[20]

The more important caveat is that collective opinion sometimes does not reflect the best available information because individuals' errors do not always "cancel out." This is particularly true if systematic misinformation is fed to many Americans at once and is not effectively contradicted. Examples include "fake news" transmitted by social media or misleading claims about events abroad (e.g., alleged "weapons of mass destruction" in Iraq) by presidents or executive branch officials who have a near-monopoly on intelligence sources.

Our view is that successful manipulation of public opinion is not common, at least not concerning the domestic policy issues that we focus on in this book. On such issues, personal experience and competing elites can usually be counted on to help people figure out the truth.[21] In later chapters, however—when we describe concrete policies that majorities of Americans favor, and advocate that the public's wishes should be heeded—we need to be alert for any cases in which public opinion may have been manipulated or misled.

As a general matter we believe that the expressed preferences of the American people deserve much more respect from policy makers than they currently get. *Respect* does not mean slavish adherence. The public is certainly not infallible, and majorities are sometimes shortsighted or misguided in ways that policy makers must try to recognize and resist. But in most cases, we believe that majority rule—even when we ourselves happen to disagree with the majority—tends to produce public policies that benefit the largest number of people and promote the common good. We believe that more democracy in the United States today would yield better policies: "better" in the sense that they would advance the interests and preferences of more Americans.

This conclusion is strengthened when we consider the rather

bleak alternatives. Who, exactly, should rule if the people do not? Most modern societies have, for good reasons, rejected rule by hereditary monarchs, landed gentry, dictators, party cadres, or theocrats. Even rule by the best-educated, most successful Americans— if it could somehow be arranged—would suffer from serious flaws. Our political and economic elites—who have recently stumbled into costly and futile wars, neglected economic inequality and wage stagnation, caused devastating financial crashes, and snarled up the functioning of government—appear to suffer from their own defects of judgment. Our *wealthiest* elites, though highly educated and knowledgeable about many things, often seem to know or care rather little about the needs of ordinary citizens. (We will have more to say about this in chapter 4, when we discuss the enormous political clout wielded by wealthy Americans.)

In short: citizens are not perfect guardians of their own values and interests. But they are pretty good guardians.[22] And they are the best we are likely to find.

WHAT ABOUT MINORITY RIGHTS? Even if majority rule does good things for most citizens, a serious problem remains: how to protect minorities.

We are not much moved by Madison's fear that the masses might use democratic control of government to seize property from a well-to-do minority, through such "wicked schemes" as the printing of paper money.[23] In our view, U.S. history and, in recent years, survey data have demonstrated that most Americans have no desire to confiscate the property of the wealthy. They have never come close to doing so. In fact, wealthy Americans have been highly successful at resisting or rolling back even mildly redistributive threats to their property, such as the progressive income tax.

But other minorities—especially racial, ethnic, and religious minorities, and those who have distinctive political interests or hold unpopular views—deserve protection.

Surely Madison, the French political observer Alexis de Tocqueville, and others were right that under certain circumstances (fear of terrorism comes to mind), majorities can threaten the rights and interests of minorities who live in their midst. We are not absolutist democrats. We accept the desirability of providing minorities with special protections in case majorities of Americans might want to use the power of government against them. We believe the framers of the U.S. Constitution were wise to append a Bill of Rights, including protection for freedoms of speech, assembly, religion, and the press; guarantees of due process; and protection against arbitrary arrest or unreasonable searches and seizures—all provisions that help safeguard minorities from unfair treatment.

The tricky part is how to guarantee that these freedoms are actually protected. The record of the U.S. Supreme Court is mixed, at best. Until relatively recently the court did little or nothing for enslaved or abused African Americans and Native Americans. It has frequently permitted harsh treatment of political dissenters, especially during wartime—or amid foreign policy crises or "red scares." As recently as World War II (1939–45), the Supreme Court went along with the shameful incarceration of Japanese Americans in prison camps, without any evidence that they represented a threat. The court swims in the same political sea as the rest of us. It cannot always be counted on to protect minorities whom majorities of Americans are willing or eager to oppress.

Still, we cannot think of a superior system of legal protection. The Supreme Court and the Constitution—helped along by vigilant civil liberties lawyers—are probably the best we can do.

But we believe that minorities should also be protected in ways that go beyond bare-bones constitutional rights. As we will note in our discussion of democratic reforms of the U.S. Senate, it is worth maintaining certain institutional protections for minorities of any sort who hold intense political views. Even the much-despised filibuster, if properly reformed, might be turned into a tool for preventing unjust government actions against minorities—instead of preventing action of almost any kind, as it does now. But that is a topic for a later chapter.

How This Book Unfolds

In the next chapter we note certain patterns in American history, from Alexis de Tocqueville's 1830s onward. Democracy has tended to flourish in times of relative economic equality but has withered when there are big gaps between rich and poor. Yet periods of very high economic inequality have sometimes provoked social movements that have fought for and won amelioration of both economic and political inequality. (The same thing may be starting to happen today.)

In part 2 of the book we examine more closely what has gone wrong and what is obstructing democratic responsiveness now.

Chapter 3 shows how undemocratic the United States is today. Ordinary citizens have little or no influence on public policy, while affluent and wealthy Americans and organized interest groups—especially business groups—often get their way. When large majorities of Americans want policy changes that would improve their jobs, wages, retirement pensions, or health care—or that would combat climate change, reduce gun violence, improve public schools, or rebuild bridges and highways—they are often thwarted by gridlock and inaction.

In chapter 4 we examine just how much political clout wealthy Americans have (a great deal), what techniques they use to exercise it, and what sorts of government policies they want and get.

Chapter 5 documents the substantial political influence of organized interest groups and explains how they exercise it. Corporations and business associations do particularly well, while "massbased" groups have relatively little clout.

Chapter 6 explores the vexing problems of highly polarized political parties, gridlock, and policy inaction. It discusses how polarization has increased with geographical and racial realignments, demographic and economic changes (especially the great increase in economic inequality), and certain features of our electoral system. It notes how polarization interacts perniciously with our separation of powers and our multiple "veto points" to produce gridlock and inaction.

We then turn, in part 3, to the question of what sorts of political reforms might be effective for making government policies more responsive to ordinary citizens.

Chapter 7 discusses a number of "equal voice" reforms that would move all citizens toward equal political influence. Campaign finance regulation—or (even without such regulation) public funding—could greatly reduce the power of private political money. Other reforms could curtail the impact of interest groups. Still others could encourage voting by citizens who are currently not well represented in the electorate—especially lower-income people and racial and ethnic minorities.

Chapter 8 considers how to overcome policy gridlock and, more generally, how to make our political institutions more democratic. It notes undemocratic features of Congress that our legislators could easily improve if they felt sufficient pressure to do so. It also discusses undemocratic electoral arrangements that will be harder— but far from impossible—to change. And it mentions certain particularly difficult but important-to-address problems, including the extremely unrepresentative, rural-heavy nature of the Senate, and the tendency of the Supreme Court to overturn (without, in our opinion, sound justification) certain policies backed by large majorities of Americans.

Part 4, the final section of the book, addresses the difficult question of whether and how major democratic reforms can actually be enacted. Big obstacles stand in the way, especially the need to persuade, pressure, or replace officials who have been elected in an undemocratic system and would be happy to keep it that way. Major changes will likely take a long time and a lot of work. But we are optimistic that they can be achieved.

Chapter 9 addresses the idea of a social movement for Democracy.[24] Some important improvements can be accomplished through simple changes in rules or laws that policy makers might be pushed to adopt through conventional political pressure. Ultimately, however, we believe that the most important major reforms can probably be won only by means of something new: a large-scale, long-term social movement for Democracy. The chapter draws lessons from past social movements—especially the Populists, the Progressives, the labor movement, and the civil rights movement—to suggest what sorts of strategies and tactics might lead to success. And it points to groups that are already beginning to work together toward democratic reforms and might help form the core of a Democracy movement.

Chapter 10 highlights democratic reforms that are currently being achieved on the state and local level. By building on these efforts, we believe that a successful social movement for more Democracy can eventually transform America, enhancing both the quality of our politics and the quality of our lives.

Now we turn to concrete discussions of what has gone wrong and what we can do about it.

TWO

Unequal Wealth Distorts Politics

Among the new objects that attracted my attention during my stay in the United States, none struck my eye more vividly than the equality of conditions. . . . The social state of the Americans is eminently democratic. It has had this character since the birth of the colonies; it has it even more in our day. . . . It is of the very essence of democratic governments that the empire of the majority is absolute . . . there is nothing that resists it.

ALEXIS DE TOCQUEVILLE, *Democracy in America*, 1835[1]

To understand what has gone wrong with American democracy, it is helpful to look back at how our economy and our politics have changed since the early days of the United States. One historical pattern stands out. Economic inequality—the concentration of wealth and income in a few hands, with a big gap between rich and poor—has risen and fallen at various times. And democracy—popular control of government—has tended to move in the opposite direction. When citizens are relatively equal, politics has tended to be fairly democratic. When a few individuals hold enormous amounts of wealth, democracy suffers.

The reason for this pattern is simple. Through campaign contributions, lobbying, influence over public discourse, and other means, wealth can be translated into political power. When wealth is highly concentrated—that is, when a few individuals have enormous amounts of money—political power tends to be highly concentrated, too. The wealthy few tend to rule. Average citizens lose political power. Democracy declines.

This pattern underlies a key theme of this book: that the extreme economic inequality afflicting the United States today is a major cause of our loss of democracy. Only if we reduce economic inequality—and/or break the links between money and political power—can we hope to make our government responsive to the citizenry.

In this chapter we take a quick look at the historical relationship between economic inequality and political inequality in the United States. When Americans have been relatively equal economically—as they were in the early years of our country and were again during our post–World War II "golden age"—democracy has generally flourished. But when the gaps between the rich and everyone else have grown too great—as in the Gilded Age of the 1890s and again during recent decades of low, stagnant wages for most Americans but soaring wealth at the top—democracy has suffered.

American history also shows, however, that we are not helpless in the face of impersonal forces that exacerbate economic inequality. Public policy matters. At several key moments in American history, extreme economic inequality has led to anger, protests, social movements, and government action to remedy the situation. Average citizens, working together, have been able to make important strides toward moderating economic inequality and enhancing democracy.[2]

Tocqueville's Relatively Equal America

In 1831, when the young French aristocrat Alexis de Tocqueville visited the newly founded United States, he was deeply impressed by the high level of economic and social equality among Americans. He was also struck by the extent to which government policies—especially in the states—were responsive to the will of the majority of citizens. He called the majority "omnipotent" and declared that nothing could resist it.[3]

From today's vantage point, the America of the 1830s was certainly no utopia. Equality and democracy were far from complete. As Tocqueville was well aware, the slave system in the South treated most African Americans as property, exploited their labor, deprived them of personal freedom, and excluded them from any voice in politics. Women were stuck in a patriarchal society, with subordinate status and no right to vote. Native Americans were being driven from their lands, conquered, and killed—under the leadership of (among others) the democratic hero Andrew Jackson.[4]

No utopia, for sure.

Still, *among white males*, equality and democracy were indeed highly advanced during the Jacksonian period—much more so than in any European country at that time, and much more so than in the United States today.

In the 1830s many white male Americans were farmers who owned a small piece of land and grew or raised their own food. These farmers, along with craftsmen and small merchants who lived in towns and cities, enjoyed fairly similar standards of living and had much the same modest levels of wealth. Only a few big merchants, manufacturers, and (especially) Southern plantation owners stood out as notably more affluent, while slaves and landless urban laborers stood out as deprived.

Economic historians calculate that U.S. inequalities of income and wealth were substantially lower in Tocqueville's time than they are today—though there was a sharp distinction between the highly equal North and the very unequal South, and much depends on how the calculations treat slaves. For the country as a whole in 1810, if one considers only the *free* (nearly all white) population, some estimates indicate that the top 1 percent of wealth holders owned less than 15 percent of all the wealth, much less than the 35 percent figure for the United States in 2010.[5] Consider those numbers for a moment. Today, *1 percent of* Americans hold fully *one-third* of all the wealth in the country. The distribution of wealth in early nineteenth-century America was much more equal than today. Indeed, it was much more equal than in most other times and places.

If slaves—who owned virtually nothing—are included in the population, and if the market value of slaves is attributed to their owners (a grim but useful calculation), Tocqueville's America looks considerably less egalitarian—but still more equal than Europe at that time or the United States now.[6]

Much the same was true of *incomes*. In colonial times (and

presumably in the Jacksonian period as well), U.S. incomes were distributed much more equally than those in England or Holland, and much more equally than in the late nineteenth-century United States.[7]

THE RISE OF DEMOCRACY IN THE UNITED STATES. As to politics, we cannot be sure exactly how responsive the state or federal governments were to citizens in the 1830s. (There were no opinion polls to tell us which policies citizens favored or opposed.) But the judgment of most historians, bolstered by evidence on voting turnout and other matters, is that among white men, American politics were in fact relatively democratic in the age of Jackson.

In the earliest years of the United States, the right to vote had been severely restricted. The U.S. Constitution provided direct elections only to the House of Representatives. Presidential candidates were to be proposed and winnowed down by "electors," who were chosen "in such manner as the [state legislatures] may direct"; House congressional delegations were expected to do the final picking of presidents. Senators were chosen "*by*" (emphasis added) state legislatures, and Supreme Court justices were appointed.

Only a small minority of Americans could vote at all. The states controlled voting qualifications. Most states allowed only white males who were owners of substantial amounts of property to vote, and some states imposed religious or other qualifications as well. As a result, in 1790 only about two-thirds of adult white men—and few others—were legally eligible to vote.[8] And far fewer did so.

By 1828, however, when Andrew Jackson won his first term as president in an outburst of popular participation, presidential and House elections had become more democratic. All but two states let their voters choose presidential electors, who were generally pledged to back a particular candidate—in effect allowing citizens a more or less direct vote for president. And more white males could take part. Several of the original states had loosened their voting restrictions, and many new, more democratically oriented states had joined the union, so that in 1830 only eight of the then-total twenty-four states imposed property requirements for voting.[9]

Levels of voting turnout rose markedly. Turnout for the first election for the U.S. House of Representatives, in 1788—as a proportion of the people who were potentially eligible to vote in terms of their age, sex, race, and citizenship—was only about 12 percent, an astoundingly low figure. It rose to 38 percent by 1812 and, after a decline, jumped up to about 56 percent in Jackson's two elections of 1828 and 1832.[10]

The establishment of political parties and active campaigning made a big difference, by offering citizens choices and mobilizing them to get to the polls. The highly democratic society that Tocqueville observed reflected strong popular mobilization for the 1828 election, when frontiersman and military hero Andrew "Old Hickory" Jackson of Tennessee, and his key ally, Martin Van Buren of New York, assembled a broad political coalition drawn from much of the Northeast, South, and West. A sophisticated party committee worked with Van Buren's congressional caucus in Washington, DC, to set up state campaign committees, local Hickory Clubs, and a vigorous network of partisan newspapers around the country. Rallies, parades, and get-out-the-vote efforts delivered a large, enthusiastic popular vote for Jackson, who defeated the incumbent president, John Quincy Adams.[11]

In office, Jackson set a tone for popular democratic control of government. His inauguration brought an outpouring of people from hundreds of miles around Washington, who lined the route to the Capitol. Jackson opened his White House reception to citizens of modest background, who were scornfully described by a society matron as "a rabble, a mob, of boys, negros [sic], women, children, scrambling, fighting, romping. What a pity, what a pity." Conservative Supreme Court Justice Joseph Story wrote to his wife that "the reign of KING MOB seemed triumphant."[12]

At least in electoral and symbolic terms, then, the American politics of Tocqueville's time were relatively democratic.[13]

Inequality after Tocqueville

As the nineteenth century proceeded, however, the relatively equal, small-farm, agrarian America of Tocqueville's time turned into something else. Settlers moved West. Millions of immigrants arrived from Ireland, Germany, and then southern and eastern Europe. The U.S. population doubled, doubled again, and then nearly doubled once more, from thirteen million in 1830 to ninety-two million in 1910.[14] Millions of people moved into big cities.

While agriculture continued to expand and move westward, manufacturing surged, with more and more big mills and factories coming into existence, owned by wealthy individuals and—increasingly—by large corporations. Economic productivity soared. The United States launched into a post–Civil War "special century" of rapidly increasing standards of living. Railroads and (later) automobiles provided swift transportation. Electricity lit up people's evenings and later began to power remarkable new consumer appliances. The telegraph, telephone, and national newspapers (and, in the twentieth century, radio and television) revolutionized communications. Nutrition, medical care, and life expectancies all improved.[15]

At the same time, however, millions of urban workers suffered from dismal living and working conditions, while the owners and managers of big businesses thrived. Inequality of wealth and income grew markedly.

In a prescient chapter on "How Aristocracy Could Issue from Industry," Tocqueville himself foresaw that industrialization and economic development might well undermine the high level of equality that he had observed among Americans. Increased division of labor would do it. Workers, he said, become "weaker, more limited, and more dependent," while very wealthy men come forward to exploit industries. "At the same time that industrial science constantly lowers the class of workers, it elevates that of masters."[16]

Yes, indeed. As industrialization proceeded, the U.S. population became more and more sharply divided between a few very wealthy captains of industry and millions of low-wage workers. During the Gilded Age of the late nineteenth century, inequality of income and wealth reached extreme heights. Government policies that placed the interests of businesses above those of citizens, along with Supreme Court decisions that rejected progressive taxation or regulation of business, contributed to economic inequality. Extreme economic inequality, in turn, created a wealth-dominated, undemocratic politics.

The English scholar James Bryce, who retraced some of Tocqueville's steps in the 1870s and 1880s (and wrote a lengthy tome on

American government) found that the inequality of material conditions in the United States had become greater than that of Europe. The United States had more "gigantic fortunes" than anywhere else in the world and a remarkable "crowd of millionaires."[17]

By 1910, the top 10 percent of U.S. wealth holders owned the vast bulk—fully 80 percent—of all the wealth in the country. That left only 20 percent of the wealth to be divided among the whole other 90 percent of Americans. Nearly *half* of all the wealth (45 percent of it) was owned by the top *1 percent* of Americans.[18]

Americans' annual incomes were quite unequal as well. The top *1 percent* of U.S. income earners got almost one-fifth of all the income in 1910, and almost one-quarter of it at the end of the 1920s. These numbers are worth thinking about. They imply big differences between the lives of people at the top and everyone else.[19]

During the Gilded Age of the late nineteenth century that laid the groundwork for those early twentieth-century economic disparities, the huge, unregulated "trusts" that dominated many industries extracted monopolistic prices from consumers and paid enormous profits to stockholders. Meat-packers sold adulterated food. Rapacious railroads charged farmers exorbitant rates to ship their grain to market. Workers labored long hours for low wages. Even professionals and people running small to-middle-size businesses resented the conspicuous consumption of the "plutocrats."

An emblem of Gilded Age excess was Cornelia Bradley Martin's lavish Waldorf-Astoria costume ball in the midst of the depression of 1897. While many Americans were struggling to make ends meet, six to seven hundred wealthy New Yorkers joined Cornelia—who was dressed as a queen and greeted her guests from a raised dais under a canopy of rare tapestries—to display their jewels, silks, and brocades, and to enjoy the Versailles-like scene of mirrors and tables laden with food.[20]

THE DECLINE OF DEMOCRACY. The extreme economic inequality of the Gilded Age brought with it a high degree of *political* inequality. Democracy declined. "Muckraker" journalists wrote of the "treason of the Senate"; they showed that key senators were on the payrolls of wealthy bankers or industrialists and did the bidding of their employers. The Senate became a graveyard for popular reforms. In an eerie foreshadowing of today's politics, wealthy individuals, business firms, and institutional gridlock combined to prevent Congress from passing laws that large majorities of Americans undoubtedly wanted them to pass.[21]

The decline in democracy was also manifested in a sharp decline in voter turnout. After the pivotal election of 1896—in which the industrial conservatism of William McKinley decisively defeated the agrarian populism of William Jennings Bryan—a series of changes in election laws curtailed citizens' participation: new, onerous requirements for personal registration; disenfranchisement of working-class immigrants; barriers against party labels on ballots or party mobilization of voters. (Many of these "reforms" were supported by Progressives, who sought to reduce corruption and shift power away from the wealthy toward middle-class professionals, not ethnic urban masses.) Also, voters were discouraged by a narrowing of political choices under the business-dominated politics of the day.[22] The high, 80 percent or so presidential-election turnout levels of most of the nineteenth century fell sharply, to just 59 percent in 1912.[23]

THE REBIRTH OF EQUALITY AND DEMOCRACY. The extremely high levels of economic and political inequality during and after the Gilded Age were eventually moderated, however. Inequality itself provoked protests and social movements that pressed for reforms and—after a long struggle—enjoyed considerable success. The Populist and Progressive victories of the early twentieth century (which are discussed further in chapter 9) included two fundamental democratic reforms: direct election of U.S. senators (rather than selection by corrupt state legislators) and the right of women to vote. They also brought more popular participation in party nominations; government regulation of business monopolies; limits on long working hours and bad working conditions; and the beginnings of a progressive federal income tax.

After a relapse into economic and political inequality during the 1920s, the Great Depression led to the political mobilization of millions of citizens and to Franklin Roosevelt's New Deal policies of the 1930s, which more closely regulated business, imposed more progressive income taxes, and provided social welfare programs including Social Security. Most important for reviving democracy, the New Deal facilitated the organization of workers into unions that could mobilize their members and exert countervailing power against business.[24] New Deal policies, together with the economic leveling effects of World War II and its aftermath, produced a "great compression" (much more equality) of income and wealth and a substantial restoration of democracy.[25]

THE "GOLDEN AGE." For a period of twenty to thirty years after World War II (from about 1946 to 1973)—which is sometimes referred to as a "golden age," though it was certainly not golden in every respect—income and wealth were much more widely shared.

By 1950, the share of wealth owned by the top 1 percent of wealth holders had fallen from 45 percent to 30 percent. The *income* share of the most affluent Americans was also down markedly from the late-1920s peak.[26] As the economy grew rapidly during the 1950s and 1960s, the American Dream seemed realizable. Average workers could expect ever-increasing prosperity for themselves and their children. Real incomes were doubling each generation. Living standards soared.[27] The most economically successful Americans did not seem to be impossibly far ahead; one could imagine that—with hard work and luck—one might possibly join them.

As to democracy: we cannot be sure exactly how responsive to the citizenry the federal government was during the 1950s. (Available survey data are too scanty to judge how well public policies reflected citizens' preferences.) But indications are that policy making was much more democratic during the Eisenhower administration (1953–61) than it is today. Certainly the political parties were less polarized; there was more bipartisan cooperation, less gridlock, more legislative accomplishment—including clearly popular measures like the development of the interstate highway system and the maintenance or expansion of a number of social programs.[28]

Today's Explosion of Inequality

Then, in the 1970s, things began to go badly wrong. Already during the golden age, other countries had started to undermine the global economic dominance of the United States. Germany and Japan recovered from the ravages of World War II and built vigorous new economies. Volkswagens and then Hondas began to undersell Detroit cars in the U.S. market, and inexpensive Japanese electronic goods began to appear on our shelves.

Suddenly, in 1973–74, an embargo by the Organization of Petroleum Exporting Countries (OPEC) doubled the price of oil. Wages, salaries, and the U.S. economy as a whole stagnated, while prices rose. At first nearly all Americans suffered. Then the wealthiest began to leap ahead while nearly everyone else stayed stuck, and a period of sharply rising inequality began.

WAGE AND INCOME STAGNATION AMONG AVERAGE AMERICANS. American workers' wages stopped rising. Since 1973—including many years of substantial economic growth—median hourly wages have barely risen at all. (Half of all workers earn more than the median, while half earn less. The *median* wage tells more about typical workers than does the *mean* or average wage, which can be misleadingly high because of a few extremely high-wage earners. If Bill Gates walks into a bar, the "average" income of the customers jumps way up in terms of the mean, but there is little or no effect on the median income, nor—unless Gates buys the drinks—on anybody's actual welfare.)

Even now, median wages remain stuck around $16 per hour, where they have been (in "real," inflation-adjusted terms) ever since the early 1970s. *Wage stagnation* is a fundamental feature of contemporary America.[29]

For a while, family incomes (though not necessarily families' well-being) did a bit better than wages, but only because more family members began working harder and for longer hours. And soon family incomes stagnated too. Between 1947 and 1979, in terms of real dollars, the total incomes of American families in the bottom two thirds of the income distribution more than doubled. But since 1979, they have stayed nearly flat.[30]

Pundits and pontificators sometimes attribute this wage and income stagnation to workers' alleged lack of skills or effort. Nonsense. American workers did not suddenly lose their ambition, their energy, or their skills at the end of the golden age. They continue to work hard and work well. Their productivity rose markedly for many years. Between 1979 and 2011, in fact—while wages were staying flat—average productivity nearly doubled, from $36.03 of goods produced per hour worked, to $60.83.[31]

The problem is not that the typical American worker is not working hard enough or not producing enough; it is that factors beyond his or her control—chiefly labor-saving technology and wage competition from low-wage countries—have reduced the *market value* of that work. A bigger share of revenue now goes to managers and stockholders. So a small number of wealthy people with very high incomes now get most of the gains from increased production.

No wonder that many Americans feel that they have been marching up a steep hill but getting nowhere. No wonder that many resent those who seem to have leapt ahead—whether they focus on wealthy corporate executives and hedge fund managers or on immigrants and minorities. Wage and income stagnation tell us something about why there were so many antiestablishment Trump and Sanders voters in the 2016 elections.[32]

Americans can no longer take much consolation from hopes and dreams of *upward mobility*, even in relative terms. The American Dream promises that hard work, creative thinking, risk taking, and thrift can get anyone—or at least anyone's children—to the top of the heap. In actual fact, however, Americans who are born into lower-income families tend to stay in the lower income ranges all their lives. So do their children. Those born at the top mostly stay near the top.

For example, a recent study found that about half of Americans who had been in the bottom fifth of income-earning households in 1987 and were aged thirty-five to forty at the time remained in the bottom fifth twenty years later, despite the normal expectation of rising earnings over the life cycle. Those who did move generally did not move far. Fewer than one out of twenty made it into the top fifth, and fewer than one in forty into the top tenth.[33]

Americans enjoy somewhat more mobility *between* generations than within them, but less than we might like to think. High-earning parents tend to have high-earning children, and low earners tend to have low earners. The sons of fathers in the bottom tenth of income earners have just a paltry 4.5 percent chance of making it into the top fifth. (If parents' income did not matter, everyone would have a 20 percent chance of making it into the top fifth.)[34] A moment's thought about the importance of family in early childhood nurturance and in schooling, personal networks, college attendance, and financial help with homes and businesses helps us understand why it is rare to leap from the bottom to the top.

More startling is the fact that the United States now appears to have *less*, rather than more, intergenerational mobility than several other countries that we sometimes sneer at as stultified: especially the egalitarian Scandinavians (Denmark, Norway, Finland, Sweden), but also Australia, New Zealand, Germany, and Japan. The most striking contrast is with our neighbor Canada, which resembles us in many ways but has some government policies that are very different from ours. Canada enjoys one of the highest rates of intergenerational mobility among advanced countries, while we suffer from one of the lowest.[35]

Unfortunately, intergenerational mobility in the United States could well worsen in the future, due to increasing income inequality. Economic researchers have discovered that countries with higher levels of income inequality tend to have lower levels of intergenerational mobility. As the gap between economic tiers increases, the ability of people to enter higher tiers is diminished.[36]

This lack of mobility between the top and the bottom, combined with stagnant wages and incomes for typical Americans, means that for most of us, the American Dream of increasing prosperity is now an illusion.

INCREASING AFFLUENCE AT THE TOP. While the incomes of typical American families have stagnated, the highest income earners have been doing quite well.

Putting together the wage and income stagnation suffered by most Americans and the huge upward leap enjoyed by the affluent, there has been what economist Thomas Piketty calls an "explosion" of income inequality.[37] The share of all income going to the richest Americans now matches the previous peak of inequality back at the end of the 1920s and substantially exceeds the income inequality of post–Gilded Age 1910.

In terms of international comparisons, over the years the United States has managed to reverse a contrast between itself and Europe that we Americans once used to celebrate. In Tocqueville's day, and during most of the nineteenth century, we were much more egalitarian than the hierarchical societies of the Old World. Now we suffer from far greater income and wealth inequality than most of the countries of Europe.[38]

Much of the U.S. explosion of income inequality—which contrasts so markedly with other advanced countries—is due to a big increase in "capital gains" from the sale of stocks, bonds, art, and the like that belong to affluent Americans. Some of the explosion has resulted from the rise in the United States of "supersalaries" (including stock-based compensation), particularly among the top managers of large firms.[39]

A study of CEOs at the top 350 U.S. firms found that their total compensation in 2014 averaged *$16.3 million*. It had grown *997 percent* since 1978—almost double the amount of stock market growth, and far more than the painfully small growth in a typical worker's pay. The $16.3 million figure amounted to *303 times* the annual compensation of the typical worker, far above the 20-to-1 ratio of 1965 or even the 87-to-1 of the middle 1990s.[40]

A 2015 *Wall Street Journal* report on CEO salaries argued that in recent years—under strong pressure from stockholders—CEO pay has been tied more closely to performance. It claimed that the old system of profligate rewards by board compensation committees that were cozy with management has been modified. But the link to performance still appears to be a loose one. True, the *Journal* found that the CEOs of the best-performing firms nearly all got raises. But so did almost everyone else, including CEOs whose firms actually *lost* money for stockholders in the course of the year, including Phillipe Dauman of Viacom and Jeffrey Immelt of General Electric.[41]

The big story about high U.S. incomes concerns the masters of *finance*. These include the heads of major investment banking firms such as JP Morgan Chase (where titan Jamie Dimon received a $20 million package in 2015) and Goldman Sachs (where, despite a tough year, Lloyd Blankfein got a small raise to $24 million.)[42] But the financial sector also includes the less visible heads of private equity firms and hedge funds, some of which are secretive private partnerships[43] not required to report their compensation levels. In a single year, a leading hedge fund manager can actually earn *$1 billion (one thousand million dollars)*. That is roughly twenty thousand times the income of a typical American family. Even in 2015, a weak year for hedge funds, Kenneth Griffin of Citadel and James Simons of Renaissance Technologies each got $1.7 billion. And Raymond Dalio of Bridgewater Associates (which, like Renaissance, relies partly on high-speed, computer-based trades) took home $1.4 billion.[44]

These enormous sums of money can exert a powerful force in politics. A few million dollars—pocket change to a hedge fund manager—can mean life or death to the career of an aspiring politician.

EXTREME CONCENTRATION OF WEALTH. *Wealth* is distributed even more unequally than income—much more unequally. Most Americans have little or no wealth at all—that is, little or no surplus of assets over debts. Any wealth they have usually takes the form of equity in a home. In 2014, a typical (median) white family had just $142,000 in net worth, down from $192,500 before the earlier twenty-first-century financial crash and the Great Recession. The median wealth of black families had fallen even further, to a meager $11,000.[45] By contrast, in 2013 *each one* of the top 1 percent of U.S. wealth holders—a group that held nearly 20 percent of total U.S. wealth—had at least $7.8 million.[46]

Far above the rest of the top 1-percenters stand the four hundred wealthiest Americans—listed annually by *Forbes* magazine—who have astronomically large fortunes. In autumn 2016, Bill Gates topped the *Forbes* list with $81 billion (*billion*, not million)—more than the entire gross domestic product (GDP) of Lithuania, Jordan, Uganda, Panama, or Bolivia, not to mention some 150 other countries.[47] Next came Jeff Bezos ($67 billion), Warren Buffett ($65.5 billion), Mark Zuckerberg ($55.5 billion), Larry Ellison ($49.3 billion), Michael Bloomberg ($45 billion), Charles and David Koch ($42 billion each), Larry Page ($38.5 billion), Sergey Brin ($37.5 billion), three members of the Walton family (two male, one female, $35.5 billion each), Sheldon Adelson ($31.8 billion), Steve Ballmer ($27.5 billion), and 385 others—on down to lowly Gail Miller, with just $1.7 billion. A mere one billion dollars is no longer enough to make the list.[48]

Of course many of these wealthy people and their firms have provided goods and services that are greatly appreciated by millions of Americans: sophisticated software (Microsoft and Oracle), efficient and inexpensive retailing (Walmart, Amazon), business news (Bloomberg), search engines (Google), social media (Facebook). *Forbes* likes to celebrate much of this wealth as "self-made"—it classifies all of the ten richest Americans as self-made—and today's great fortunes may indeed reflect more personal creativity and hard work at building businesses, and less pure inheritance of assets, than did big fortunes in the recent past.[49]

Still, most U.S. billionaires have enjoyed significant head starts in life, beginning with a fortunate choice of parents. It can help a lot to have parents who raise their offspring in pleasant, nurturing neighborhoods; teach them skills and ambition at an early age; introduce them to helpful personal networks; educate them in exclusive private schools and elite colleges; and provide them with business start-up money. Other kinds of luck also play a part in many spectacular economic successes. Most of the "founding generation" of high-tech billionaires, for example, are people born in the right place (the United States) at just the right moment (1955 or so) to ride the strong wave of technological development that crested around 1975.[50]

Opportunities and legacies outside the control of individuals can be crucial. Donald Trump began accruing a $12,000-per-year income from a trust fund while he was still in diapers. Trump also received lots of business tutoring and numerous loans (amounting to at least $14 million) from his father, Fred. These resources came in addition to extremely valuable but more difficult to quantify forms of assistance that Fred provided, such as cosigning on large loans and connecting his son with the right people. And—although exact figures are elusive—the construction business that Trump eventually inherited was so valuable that if he had simply invested that money passively in a stock market fund, he might have a larger fortune today than he actually does, without any need for astute deals or decisions at all.[51]

To take a possibly more sympathetic case: Bill Gates was the son of a wealthy Seattle lawyer who sent him to elite Lakeside School, where (in 1968, when most high schools had barely heard of computers) the Mothers Club bought a time-sharing computer terminal and started a computer club. The club soon hooked up with an early computer firm, one of whose founders had a son at Lakeside. Gates wangled free computer time at the nearby University of Washington and—again with help from a personal connection—learned advanced programming at TRW. All this before he finished high school, just in time to help lead the software revolution.[52]

Great fortunes nearly always draw on many resources of the society as a whole—schools, infrastructure, skilled workers, the ideas and inventions of others. Great fortunes often do reflect the energy, talent, and creativity of exceptional individuals, but they are also the products of many thousands of other people's work.

We believe that the contributions of extremely productive people such as Steve Jobs merit handsome material rewards. But we also believe that it makes sense for them to *share* their rewards with the broader society that helped make their successes possible.

To their great credit, Bill Gates, Warren Buffett, and a number of other billionaires have given much of their fortunes to philanthropic causes. They have urged all billionaires to do likewise by signing the "Giving Pledge" that at least half their wealth will eventually go to philanthropy.[53] But it has become clear that most billionaires—more than two-thirds of them, at recent count—have no interest in signing up. Why should we rely on this voluntary arrangement? Moderately higher taxes on top incomes and on multimillion-dollar estates could help ensure that more of our nation's economic gains are shared among all Americans. Also, that way the gains would be shared according to priorities determined by our elected representatives, not by unelected foundations or wealthy individuals. There is no credible evidence that America's billionaires would work less hard or less creatively if their taxes went up a bit.[54]

THE ISOLATED RICH. With a few striking exceptions,[55] today's superrich Americans do not generally engage in extreme cases of conspicuous consumption like Cornelia Bradley Martin's Gilded Age costume ball. They do spend a lot of money on multimillion-dollar homes (often several homes), and many fly in private jets around "the circuit" of parties, art shows, sporting events, and political and economic confabs at exclusive resorts.[56] But they mostly avoid tasteless public displays of wealth.

America's superrich do want to be seen and be part of a community—but mostly with each other, not with average Americans. Many live in gated communities or private spots in the mountains, on the seashore, or on islands. The "Mansions" section of the *Wall Street Journal* has reported that the market for homes with fifteen or more bedrooms is booming: some sell for more than $100 million, as wealthy buyers seek privacy and security for numerous visiting friends and relatives.[57] With much of their social life enjoyed at home or on the wealthy-only "circuit," superrich Americans tend not to be exposed to the day-to-day life of most Americans, especially not to those who are struggling economically.

This situation has important political implications. Isolation from ordinary Americans makes it easy for the wealthy to be unaware of the suffering of others or of the importance of government programs in helping them out.[58] Isolation makes it easy to accept convenient but incorrect beliefs—that programs like Social Security are "wasteful" or "bankrupt" or "don't work," for example. If one has no firsthand knowledge of anyone who is trying to get by on meager Social Security retirement benefits, it is easy to think of Social Security as a doomed Ponzi scheme rather than as a lifeline for millions of elderly people. The federal Food Stamp Program (now the Supplemental Nutrition Assistance Program, or SNAP) can be stereotyped as doling out unhealthy snacks to wastrels rather than providing essential nutrition for many poor children and disabled adults—who together constitute nearly 70 percent of the recipients. The Earned Income Tax Credit (EITC), which provides crucial wage supplements for lower-income people, can be stigmatized as "welfare."[59]

Particularly relevant to our concern about the distorting effect of concentrated wealth on politics is the ominous trend toward political kingmaking by billionaires.[60] Money can buy McMansions and private jets, yes, but it can also purchase political influence. We will have more to say in chapter 4 about exactly how that works.

LIVES OF THE FAR-FROM-RICH. After glancing at the lives of the wealthy, it is useful to contrast the day-to-day struggles of lower-income Americans. For her classic book, *Nickel and Dimed: On (Not) Getting By in America*, journalist Barbara Ehrenreich undertook some firsthand research and chronicled her own and her coworkers' struggles to make a living by waiting on tables, cleaning houses, selling big-box retail, and providing care in nursing homes—the kinds of low-end service jobs that millions of Americans must rely on. Even when she took the best-paying jobs available in those fields and kept costs to a minimum, Ehrenreich found that she could barely support herself by the sweat of her brow. And the working conditions were appalling: Frustrating scrambles to land job interviews. Degrading urine tests. Long, intense working hours, with sore feet and few breaks. Intrusive surveillance and petty tyranny by supervisors. Ehrenreich herself could ultimately return to a comfortable middle-class life, but her coworkers were stuck. Their lives were precarious, prone to disaster if they suffered a broken ankle, a transportation breakdown, or the loss of a spouse or roommate. One might think that the world's richest country could do better for its less-fortunate citizens.[61]

Plenty of middle-class Americans are struggling as well, as a recent study of Ohio residents makes clear. Buffeted by backbreaking work, workplace injuries, layoffs, factory closings, medical bills, and home foreclosures, many of them are surprisingly resilient—but they need help. The government has not seemed to do much for them.[62]

The Roots of Inequality

Public policy matters. American history—as well as the experience of other countries—makes clear that *policy choices* have contributed greatly to the current extremely high level of inequality in the United States.

"Market based" incomes are in fact heavily influenced by government laws and policies that *create the rules* under which markets operate. Strong or weak antitrust policies help determine whether or not big monopoly profits go to wealthy business owners. Lax financial regulation can permit banks to accumulate huge, risky profits that ordinary taxpayers may have to pay for after a financial crash. Union-busting labor laws cut workers' wages. Bankruptcy laws that offer no escape from home- or student-loan debts can sentence people to financial insecurity for much of their lives.[63] (In contrast, corporate bankruptcy laws allow business owners to walk away from bad investments intact—or even leverage their losses to avoid taxes for years to come.) Loose laws on fraud can allow well-to-do businesspeople to cheat their lower-income brethren while enforced arbitration rules prevent those who were cheated from suing. These and many other policy decisions can severely exacerbate economic inequality. In the United States, they have definitely done so.[64]

By the same token, however, the opposite sort of government policies—strict regulation of business; people-friendly laws on fraud and bankruptcy; high-quality, universal education; encouragement of unionization and collective bargaining; government-provided job training and direct job provision at good wages—these and other policies can greatly reduce "market-based" inequalities in people's incomes and wealth.

Postmarket redistributive policies can also make a big difference. Wage supplements; children's allowances; generous old-age pensions; free child care, health care, and other services; and *progressive taxation* (taxes that take a higher percentage of income from high-income people than low-income people) can significantly counteract economic inequality. Yet while other countries have been actively pursuing such policies, the United States has not. In fact, we have repeatedly cut taxes on the highest incomes.[65]

It is quite possible for public policies to act effectively against the ills of economic inequality. Other countries do it. And many such policies are favored by large majorities of Americans. Yet in the United States, all too few of them get enacted. Why?

One reason is that the same economic inequality that most Americans want to ameliorate through democratic politics brings with it highly unequal political resources that undermine democracy. Economic wealth can produce political influence. When wealth is highly concentrated, a relatively small number of very wealthy people—who tend to be happy with their positions at the top of the heap and generally do not want to pay higher taxes to help others—have the power to thwart the majority and prevent egalitarian actions. Economic inequality begets political inequality, which, in turn, makes it harder to address economic inequality.[66]

We believe that—with clear thinking and hard work—we can break this vicious circle of economic and political inequality. To do so, however, we need to understand other roots of contemporary economic inequality, including certain powerful forces that may seem beyond our control but in fact are not. (Both their origin and their ultimate impact depend heavily on what public policies we choose.) Two major contributors to inequality are increased global wage competition and the expansion of labor-saving technology.

THE EFFECTS OF ECONOMIC GLOBALIZATION. One fundamental cause of our recent upsurge of economic inequality has been *economic globalization*: the great increase, during recent decades, in the flow across national borders of goods, capital investments, technological know-how, and workers. The world economy has opened up. Transportation and communication are much quicker and cheaper. Billions of dollars can be instantly transferred to Asia with the click of a computer mouse. Enormous new markets for trade and investment became available after the fall of communism in Europe and the opening of China. Tariffs and other economic and political barriers to trade have been much reduced through the World Trade Organization (WTO) and various multilateral and bilateral negotiations.[67]

Economic globalization has brought great benefits to hundreds of millions of formerly impoverished people in developing countries, who have experienced rapid economic growth, rising wages, and ever-increasing standards of living. In China, for example, average wages have leapt up, tripling between 2006 and 2015.[68] American consumers have benefited too; we buy inexpensive clothing, electronics, and other goods from Asia. As economists are fond of pointing out, there are always "gains from trade": free-market buyers and sellers would not agree on a transaction unless it made both of them better off. The total gains from international trade are huge. These gains are so enormous, in fact, that *in principle*—if they were widely shared—they could actually make every woman, man, and child on the planet economically much better off than they have been. Then trade would be unambiguously a good thing.[69]

But the gains from international trade have *not* in fact been shared by everyone. Economic globalization has produced losers as well as winners. Unfortunately for us, the losers include millions of ordinary workers in the United States and other advanced countries.

The problem is that under free-market conditions, gains from trade are only guaranteed to accrue to the *direct parties* to economic transactions—such as the owners of a U.S. textile firm that moves production to China (getting lower labor costs and higher profits) and the Chinese workers they hire (who get new jobs at higher wages). "Externalities" from trade—that is, effects on people who are "external" to (not parties to) a contract—can be highly negative.

When a company closes a U.S. textile plant and moves production to China, the company can produce textiles more cheaply and efficiently. But the shutdown may have a devastating impact on the local community where the plant was once an important employer. American workers who lose their jobs may find that their accumulated skills have suddenly become worthless. They may have to accept other work at much lower wages or endure years of unemployment. True, American consumers as a group are likely to gain something from the opportunity to buy cheap imported sneakers or T-shirts, but displaced workers are likely to suffer income losses that far exceed anything they gain in their role as consumers. These losses appear to have played an important part in voters' support for Donald Trump in 2016.[70]

It is difficult to calculate the precise magnitude of the negative effects of globalization, but they are clearly very large. One estimate is that globalization-associated increases in international *trade* alone have led to a 5.5 percent average reduction in earnings for all U.S. workers and have, over the 1979–2011 period, widened the wage gap between college-educated and non-college-educated Americans by 7.3 percent.[71] The full effects of economic globalization, including flows of capital and workers as well as trade in goods, have almost certainly been much greater.

We cannot know exactly how many Americans have lost how much from economic globalization. The important point is that there have been many losers. It is not even clear that more Americans have gained than have lost. Many of the gains have gone into higher profits for a rather small number of business owners and managers. The fact of stagnant median wages and incomes over recent decades suggests that *most* Americans may have lost out, at least in the sense of failing to make much economic progress—even while the U.S. economy, workers' productivity, and the wealth of the wealthiest have been growing.

GLOBAL WAGE COMPETITION. How is this possible, when trade is supposed to be a good thing? The short answer is that the *global labor market* responds to supply and demand. Free trade and investment across national boundaries mean, in effect, that workers in all countries who supply labor have to compete with one another. So long as transportation costs are not too high, a firm with a factory in a poor country with hourly wages equivalent to, say, one U.S. dollar an hour can sell goods much more cheaply than one with a U.S. factory that pays wages of fifteen dollars per hour. In the long run, it becomes impossible for the U.S. firm to pay that fourteen-dollar difference. It cannot sell the expensive products that result. It must either sharply cut wages and benefits or close the U.S. plant and move production to a low-wage country.

In a global labor market where workers in many countries all compete with one another, the long-run equilibrium result will be essentially *equal wages* for equal work by any worker anywhere in the world. This economic principle seems to imply severe downward pressure on U.S. wages, in a world in which workers in some poor countries were earning the equivalent of only fifty cents a day, while U.S. workers doing similar jobs were earning more than one hundred times as much.[72]

Movement toward wage equalization does not necessarily mean that there must be an actual drop in wages for workers in high-wage countries. In theory, most or all of the action might come from wage rises in the low-wage countries. And indeed, the lot of workers in China, India, Indonesia, Bangladesh and elsewhere seems to have been improving rapidly, while workers in the United States and Europe have not been totally impoverished. World wages may be converging more toward the top than toward the bottom.

Still, the *stagnation* of Americans' wages is a big problem, particularly given the American Dream of constant material improvement, and given the reality that our average incomes used to *double* nearly every generation during the century that ended with the "golden age."[73]

LABOR-SAVING, DIGITAL-BASED TECHNOLOGY. Besides global wage competition, another important contributor to downward wage pressures on American workers and the hollowing out of the middle class is the rapid development and use of labor-saving technology, often involving computers and robotics. Computers have increasingly automated and taken over tasks of manufacturing and assembly that used to be done by well-compensated factory workers.[74]

During the "golden age" of the 1950s and 1960s, for example, large numbers of U.S. automobile workers held rather prestigious, high-paying jobs. Through the United Auto Workers union, they constituted the progressive heart of the U.S. labor movement. Now auto parts are largely made by low-wage workers abroad and are put together by robots on automated assembly lines. Far fewer workers are employed. It now takes less than *one-tenth* the former number of workers to produce the same number of cars. Years of employer-forced contract givebacks have depressed wages and benefits. Much the same thing is true in a whole array of rust belt industries.[75]

Even in aircraft production—a great global success story for the United States—economic viability has come at the cost of ever-increasing levels of automation, downward pressures on wages and benefits, and severe contraction of the workforce. At the Boeing Corporation (our star builder and exporter of aircraft), robots have taken over jobs that many machinists used to do, such as drilling holes and adding fasteners to join fuselage sections of the Dreamliner and the 777X. They do these tasks faster and more accurately than any human could. Robots have also taken over the formerly dangerous and dirty job of painting planes. Digital design programs that automatically update drawings have displaced technicians who used to make new drawings of every part of a plane affected by a design change. The authors of a careful study of how Boeing workers and managers weathered decades of global economic competition and automation aptly titled their book *Turbulence*.[76]

The job-eroding impact of technology goes well beyond manufacturing. It includes jobs in agriculture and services, even high-end services.[77] Many thousands of typists have been replaced by do-it-yourself word processing. Retail sales clerks have declined in the face of web-based sales by Amazon and others. Farm workers have dwindled as agribusinesses have used more and more sophisticated agricultural machinery. Telephone operators have practically vanished. (At its peak, AT&T used to employ three-quarters of a million people. Now Google, with about the same market value, employs only 55,000 people worldwide. YouTube, when purchased by Google, employed only sixty-five workers—mostly engineers. Instagram, bought for $1 billion by Facebook in 2012, had just thirteen employees.)[78] Soon drones and autonomous, self-driving vehicles may replace delivery workers, truckers, and taxi drivers.

At first, labor-saving technology mostly hit relatively low-skill jobs held by blue-collar or middle-class white-collar workers. A big "skills gap" emerged: the wages of low-skill workers—especially those who had not finished high school—fell farther and farther behind the pay of people with more formal education and more sophisticated skills. This skills gap is still very much with us.[79] It began to look as if only workers with advanced education and high-tech skills could do well in the future. Some pundits argued that more education was the panacea for American workers; that if everyone went to college they would all be better off, and inequality would be much reduced.

Increasingly, however, it has become clear that practically *everyone*—except the owners and managers of certain big businesses—may be at the mercy of technological change, including upper-income professionals. Accountants have been hard-hit by business-planning and tax-preparation software such as TurboTax. Lawyers and paralegals have lost jobs to software such as e-Discovery, which instantly analyzes millions of pages of documents to locate relevant legal concepts and precedents. Travel agents are an endangered species. Quill software generates business reports that highly skilled experts used to write. Highly trained engineers are being put out of work by software and computers empowered with artificial intelligence that design electrical circuits, mechanical systems, optics, and much more. College professors feel the hot breath of superstar-lecturer videos, computerized instruction programs, and computerized essay grading. Stock market traders have given way to computer trading systems, which now make some 70 percent of all stock trades. Medical doctors are under pressure from computerized diagnosis and treatment programs.

Many well-educated, highly skilled, high-tech Americans are now losing jobs or suffering downward pressure on their salaries.[80]

Talk about "a jobless future" or "a world without work" may be overstated. But one observer foresees "an era of technological unemployment, in which computer scientists and software engineers essentially invent us out of work, and the total number of jobs declines steadily and permanently."[81] Even if the number of *jobs* does not actually decline sharply (if desperate people are willing to work for a pittance), *wages* may go way down.[82]

GLOBALIZATION AND TECHNOLOGY INTERACT. Labor-saving technology and economic globalization have both had devastating effects on American workers. But their effects are not independent. (Efforts to sort out their "separate" impacts generally founder.) They reinforce each other.

Neither technological advances themselves nor their effects are handed down by the gods. Technology is invented and is applied (or not) by human beings. The Egyptians invented steam power, for example, but did not bother to use it because they had slaves to do the work. Today's leaps forward in the use of labor-saving technology partly reflect the different incentives created by global economic competition. Now that the globalized labor market has put hundreds of millions of low-wage foreign workers into competition with much more expensive American workers, if a firm wants to—or has to—stay in the United States and is unable or unwilling to cut wages to the bone, it has strong incentives to use labor-saving technology to lower labor costs by shedding jobs. Computer scientists and engineers (and those who hire them), in turn, have strong incentives to develop ever-better new technology. The vastly increased supply of cheap labor abroad accelerates the adoption of labor-saving technology in advanced countries, which adds to the pressure on U.S. jobs and wages.

THE IMMIGRATION PIECE OF GLOBALIZATION. Still another cause of wage stagnation applies to those who provide hard-to-automate services in purely local markets. They are relatively insulated from technology or international competitive pressures based on trade or investment, but many of them (house cleaners, gardeners, haircutters, home health aides) are vulnerable to another aspect of globalization: competition from immigrant workers who are willing to work for pay that is low by U.S. standards but higher than in their home country.

Competitive pressure from immigrants probably does not account for a substantial part of our overall wage stagnation and inequality, but it does affect quite a few American workers who might otherwise enjoy a higher standard of living.[83]

Perhaps the only Americans who are truly safe from the negative effects of global labor markets, capital flight abroad, immigration, and labor-saving technology are the affluent owners of stock in multinational corporations. They unambiguously profit from all these forces. Here we see a major cause of the extreme increase in economic inequality. It is a tough time to be an American worker but a great time to be an owner of capital.

IT'S NOT THE WORKERS' FAULT. The forces that produce job losses and stagnant or declining wages are almost entirely beyond the control of individual workers. Unemployment due to automation, for example, should not by any means be considered a worker's own fault. An automobile worker displaced by robotics, who suddenly finds that a lifetime's worth of accumulated skills have become nearly worthless, cannot do much about it. "Retrain yourself!" some pundits urge. But do we seriously expect a fifty-five-year-old former auto worker to take computer programming courses and wrest a job away from young hotshots who grew up with video games and computers?

None of this means that labor-saving technology is a "bad thing." The total economic gains from advanced technology, like the gains from international trade and investment, are enormous. These gains—if properly shared—are sufficient to make every American better off. So why not ensure that we share them? Why let millions of people lose out?

AGAIN: PUBLIC POLICY MAKES A DIFFERENCE. Even though the vast, impersonal forces of economic globalization and technological innovation lie at the root of our explosion of inequality, it still does not follow that this inequality is inevitable. On the contrary: political choices concerning *public policy* can make a big difference to peoples' incomes and their material well-being. Bad policy choices have contributed to our problems. Good choices can make things better.

Policy decisions—free-trade agreements without much worker protection; public investment in high technology rather than focusing on, say, environment-protecting jobs; and especially *financial liberalization*, allowing virtually unlimited freedom to send capital abroad (exacerbated by permitting "race to the bottom," low-tax and deregulatory policies abroad)—all have contributed to economic globalization and job-reducing technology.

But suppose we take globalization and technological change as mostly given. All other advanced countries have faced the same pressures as the United States has. But nearly all of them have done much better than we have at avoiding extreme increases in inequality. They have done so by using a range of egalitarian public policies to spread the gains from trade and technology more widely, allowing many more of their citizens to benefit.

Most other advanced countries have pursued "active labor market" policies (job training, employment services, wage supplements, direct provision of jobs); strong collective bargaining; and egalitarian policies such as the minimum wage, all of which produce much better *market-based earnings* for low-income people than the United States does. A comparison of how much the lowest one-tenth of earners get relative to the typical (median) worker, across twenty-one advanced countries, revealed that the United States ranks dead last: most unequal.[84]

Moreover, the U.S. *poverty rate* is significantly higher than the poverty rate in any other of twenty-three advanced countries studied. The U.S. relative poverty rate of 17 percent is three times that of Denmark and nearly twice the average of all the countries.[85] The U.S. *child poverty* rate is far higher than in any other advanced country: at 23 percent in 2009, it was almost *five times* the rate in Iceland and more than twice as high as in the average country.[86] In most other advanced countries, such policies as family allowances, free or inexpensive medical care and day care, food and housing assistance, and the like have big effects on reducing poverty and inequality. The United States lags far behind.

In the United States it is often said that government policies "don't work." But our own history makes clear that that is incorrect.

It is common, for example, to assert that the 1960s War on Poverty "failed," or that—as Ronald Reagan famously put it— "poverty won." This bromide may seem to be supported by the fact that the official U.S. poverty rate, which dropped significantly between 1964 and 1969, has not shown any appreciable downward trend in the years since then. As policy expert Christopher Jencks points out, however, that comparison is quite misleading. If one corrects for certain obvious errors in the official poverty measure, the actual U.S. poverty rate in 2014 was only *4.8 percent*, down dramatically—by about *75 percent*—since 1964, largely as a result of such public policies as Social Security (which has greatly reduced poverty among the elderly); food stamps; rent supplements; and the EITC, a program that makes work pay by supplementing the incomes of low-wage workers.[87]

What are these obvious errors in official poverty rates? One is that the official statistics overcorrect for increases in the cost of living, so that the real value of the official "poverty threshold" (the amount of income a family is officially said to need to avoid poverty) keeps rising and leaving more people below it. Another error is an exclusive focus on cash income, entirely ignoring non-cash benefits such as food stamps. Still another is the omission of income from tax credits such as the EITC, which by 2013 provided a helpful $3,250 per year to low-wage workers with two or more children. (Why do we put up with such errors? Jencks suggests that conservatives are happy with data that seem to demonstrate a policy failure, while liberals are content to overstate the poverty problem in hopes that someone will do something about it.)[88]

The point here is not that America's low-income families are actually well off. They are certainly not; they suffer from a great deal of financial anxiety and deprivation. The original poverty threshold was set very low. Further (as our cross-national comparison indicated) a substantial 17 percent of Americans—and an even higher proportion of our children—still suffer from *relative* poverty, receiving less than half the income of the typical family. We could certainly do more. We *should* do more. The point is that in the United States, too, public policy can make—and has made—a big difference to families' incomes.

All advanced countries entered the 1970s with average wages much higher than those in poor countries. As globalization and automation advanced, all advanced countries faced the same relentless downward pressures on jobs and incomes. But while the United States was cutting taxes for the wealthy, letting the minimum wage fall behind inflation, and doing little for the unemployed, most other countries were vigorously using public policies to protect their citizens. These policies included various combinations of active labor market measures (the star here being Denmark); strongly unionized workforces or other forms of collective bargaining (especially prominent in Sweden); and webs of social benefits, including family allowances, affordable day care, generous unemployment insurance, and universal health care.[89]

Most advanced countries have, in effect, used public policies to ensure that the economic gains from advanced technology and international trade are widely shared. We have not.

In the United Kingdom—like the United States—tightfisted public policies have left workers highly vulnerable to global pressures.

The distinguished British economist Anthony Atkinson has laid out a carefully designed set of policy proposals that would move the United Kingdom closer to the much lower levels of poverty and inequality found in most European and other countries in the Organization for Economic Cooperation and Development (OECD). Many of these proposals could be applied straightforwardly to the United States: more progressive taxation; a big increase in family, unemployment, and retirement benefits; guaranteed minimum-wage public jobs for the unemployed; new rights for organized labor; a national savings program; and "inheritance for all," with a capital endowment assigned to each young adult reaching the age of eighteen. As Atkinson has shown in detail, such programs are affordable. They would have a tremendous impact.[90]

Former U.S. Secretary of Labor Robert Reich would go further, ending policy-driven "upward pre-distribution" of supposedly market-based incomes by shortening the duration of patents, pursuing vigorous antitrust policies, forbidding all insider trading, favoring labor agreements in bankruptcies, preventing forced arbitration, forbidding abusive reselling of franchises, and the like.[91]

Reich would also "reinvent the corporation," returning firms to the model of benefiting workers and customers rather than purely pursuing short-term shareholder profits. Reich argues that progressive taxes and redistributive transfers—even a global wealth tax—could only go so far. To make sure that future wealth is widely shared, Reich proposes a "citizen's bequest" akin to Atkinson's "inheritance for all": a basic minimum monthly income to all Americans starting when they reach age eighteen. Payments would be only enough to ensure a minimally decent standard of living. But even if present trends continue—so that robots end up doing almost all the work and the owners of companies that make robots get all the profits—average people can reap some benefits.[92]

Of course opinions differ concerning exactly what (if anything) to do about economic inequality. But—as we will see in chapters 3 and 4—many polls and surveys indicate that a number of egalitarian proposals would meet with approval from large majorities of Americans. If we live in a democracy, why don't such policies get adopted? Why does U.S. public discourse barely even *mention* such sweeping ideas?

The problem, we believe, is *political*. Our political system has institutional features (such as separation of powers and multiple veto points) that contribute to gridlock, inaction, and nonresponsiveness to average citizens, especially when the parties are polarized. Furthermore, American politics is fundamentally corrupted by money, which wealthy people can deploy to block any major egalitarian actions and even discourage serious talk about them.

Economic Inequality and Democracy in Conflict

Opinion surveys make clear that large majorities of Americans are unhappy about extreme inequality and want to do something about it. Most do not resent the rich and do not want to "level" incomes, but they dislike what they see as *excessive* or *undeserved* wealth— including the current ultrahigh compensation of CEOs and hedge fund managers. Most Americans want the wealthy to pay a fair share of taxes, in order to fund programs that will ensure equal opportunity for all Americans.[93]

In a spring 2015 poll, for example, two-thirds of Americans declared that "the money and wealth in this country should be more evenly distributed among more people." About the same proportion said the gap between rich and poor "needs to be addressed *now*" (emphasis added). Large majorities favored requiring employers to provide paid sick leave and paid parental leave; raising the federal minimum wage from $7.25 to $15.00; raising taxes on people earning more than $1 million per year; and raising taxes on the sale of stocks or bonds.[94]

In a democratic political system, one might think that such popular policies would quickly become law. But they did not. One of the main reasons is that big political money comes from wealthy individuals and organized interest groups (especially business firms) that are opposed to paying more taxes themselves and uninterested in spending public money on programs to benefit average citizens. The "money primary" that we compared to Iran's Guardian Council ensures that wealthy-friendly candidates can run for office, while most others are shut out.[95]

The extreme economic inequality that we suffer from today has led to demands for government help. But increased inequality has also brought weaker unions, a political right turn by business firms, and greater concentration of wealth among those opposed to egalitarian policies. Extreme economic inequality undermines the very democratic political processes that ordinary citizens rely on to ameliorate economic inequality.

In short, economic inequality and democracy are in serious conflict.

One might imagine a downward *spiral*, in which ever-increasing economic inequality continually erodes democracy and leads to public policies that accelerate, rather than ameliorate, the increases in economic inequality. That might further damage democracy, produce even more antiegalitarian policies, and on and on. There is some evidence that exactly that sort of downward spiral is in fact occurring.[96] But it is not inevitable.

The next four chapters of this book show that the political wishes of average Americans are often being thwarted; that wealthy individuals and corporate interest groups tend to get their way; and that polarized political parties and our multiple veto points contribute to gridlock and prevent the enactment of policies that large majorities of Americans want.

But then the book takes a more positive turn. Chapters 7 and 8 describe reforms that would help defang the political power of the wealthy and business groups, give a more equal voice to average citizens, and overcome gridlock. Finally, chapters 9 and 10 discuss how such reforms can actually be achieved.

PART TWO

What Has Gone Wrong

THREE

Thwarting the Will of the People

It seems obvious to us that in a democracy, the government should pay attention to what policies its citizens want. In chapter 1 we noted some of the reasons why. The policy preferences of the American public as a collective whole—unlike the opinions of many individuals—tend to be stable, coherent, consistent, and reflective of the best available information. They generally reflect people's true values and interests. They are worth heeding.

In a country with free elections, one might expect that the government *would* generally respond to the wishes of its citizens. If large majorities of Americans favor a higher minimum wage, one might expect the U.S. Congress to raise the minimum wage.

Yet, as we will see in this chapter, the best evidence indicates that the wishes of ordinary Americans actually have had little or no influence at all on the making of federal government policy. Wealthy individuals and organized interest groups—especially business corporations—have had much more political clout. When they are taken into account, it becomes apparent that the general public has been virtually powerless.

The will of majorities of Americans is often thwarted by the affluent and the well organized, who block popular policy proposals and enact special favors for themselves. Frequently, gridlock in Washington—resulting from sharply divided parties and undemocratic features of our political system—prevents the adoption of new policies that large majorities of Americans want.

For example, majorities of Americans favor specific policies designed to deal with such problems as climate change, gun violence, an untenable immigration system, inadequate public schools, and crumbling bridges and highways. Yet Congress has mostly failed to act on them. The government has also failed to do much to ameliorate economic inequality. Large majorities of Americans favor various programs to help provide jobs, increase wages, help the unemployed, provide universal medical insurance, ensure decent retirement pensions, and pay for such programs with progressive taxes. Most Americans also want to cut "corporate welfare." Yet the wealthy, business groups, and structural gridlock have mostly blocked such new policies. Why?

What Has Gone Wrong

To understand what has gone wrong and how it could be fixed, it is useful to consider how elections *might* bring about democratic responsiveness if our political system were properly organized.

The United States has made a good start. Most adult Americans are legally eligible to vote. Our Constitution guarantees the rights of free speech and free assembly. We have open competition between political parties that put up candidates and debate their merits. Winners are generally determined by majority rule. And we have a long tradition of peacefully allowing the winners to take office.

Yet all those admirable features of our political system are not sufficient, by themselves, to ensure popular control of what the government does. More is needed.[1]

To ensure democratic outcomes, it is also important that *all citizens*—or at least a truly representative group of citizens—*actually vote*. Voters need to have *attractive choices* to vote for, not be forced to pick the lesser evil. *Good information* should be available concerning what the candidates would be likely to do if they took office. *Only voters*, not financial donors or party activists, should affect the outcomes of elections. After elections, *only citizens' preferences*, not pressure from lobbyists (or anticipation of lucrative job opportunities after leaving office), should affect what officials do. *Political institutions* should give an *equal voice* to all citizens, and should be *able to act* on their wishes.

The realities of American politics do not live up to these ideal conditions. Problems include the following:

- *The power of wealthy individuals.* U.S. parties rely on private money to fund primary and general election campaigns, buy advertising, and encourage their supporters to turn out, which means that wealthy donors have big effects on what sorts of candidates run and are elected.
- *The clout of corporations and organized interest groups.* Organized interest groups too can have major effects on who runs and who is elected, which tends to tilt election results away from what average citizens want.
- *Extreme activists and polarized parties.* Party activists often hold extreme views about public policy. Their special influence in primary elections tends to produce extreme nominees—and extreme officials—who poorly represent their constituents and are highly polarized by party.
- *Restricted choices.* Party donors and activists can strongly affect what sorts of candidates run for office and win party nominations, especially in one-party districts, which limits the choices that voters have and frees parties from having to appeal to the median voter or the majority of citizens.
- *An unrepresentative electorate.* Democratic outcomes depend on all citizens being represented equally. But many citizens do not vote. Those who do vote tend to be different from those who do not— more affluent, older, more white; they are quite unrepresentative of the citizenry as a whole.[2]
- *Manipulated turnout.* Our election laws have kept turnout low and unrepresentative by making it burdensome for people to vote and by holding elections at obscure times and places. This barrier tilts election results away from what majorities of all Americans want. Parties mobilize supporters and discourage opponents from voting, sometimes using unsavory tactics.[3] Such manipulation gives political power to the vote mobilizers: party activists and donors of money, who often seek different policies than the average citizen does.
- *Misinformation in elections.* Candidates, parties, and the media often provide distracting, confusing, misleading, and just plain false information about the state of the country, what policies the candidates

stand for, and what their personal characteristics are. "Fake news," spread through social media, can deceive voters or make them distrust any information they encounter. Such misinformation can make it difficult for citizens to vote on policy grounds and can mislead them about which party or candidate would best satisfy their wants and interests. The need for money to buy media coverage further empowers campaign donors.

- *Unrepresentative institutions.* Our political institutions do not faithfully represent the citizenry. The U.S. Senate represents states, not people (each state, no matter how small, gets two senators), so urban and suburban Americans are badly underrepresented. Minorities concentrated in urban areas are particularly likely to get left out. One-party rule in the House of Representatives disenfranchises the minority party and deflects results away from what the average citizen wants. The unelected Supreme Court sometimes overturns the work of lawmaking majorities. The electoral college disadvantages large states and can lead to the candidate with fewer votes winning the presidency (as has happened twice in the past five elections).

- *Lobbying by the affluent and well-organized.* After elections, wealthy individuals, organized interest groups, and party activists continue to push against many policies sought by majorities of citizens.

- *Fragmented authority.* In office our parties do not act as unified "teams" that do exactly what they promised to do. Different parties, or different factions within a party, often control different institutions in the executive, legislative, and judicial branches of government.

- *Gridlock.* The separation of powers, together with highly polarized parties that command different institutions or "veto points," means that attempts at policy making are often bogged down in gridlock. Gridlock is exacerbated by obstructive rules and procedures such as the Senate's "hold" and filibuster and the House's disenfranchisement of the minority party. These institutions and rules produce a strong bias against action and toward the "status quo." They often thwart policy changes that majorities of citizens want.

Each of these factors undermines democratic control. In later chapters we will discuss the political power of wealthy individuals, organized interest groups, and political party activists, as well as certain structural and institutional barriers to democracy—bad election rules, polarized parties, institutional gridlock, and the like. We will describe political reforms that could help deal with each of these problems, and we will discuss how we can actually make such reforms come about.

In this chapter we consider two problems that directly involve ordinary citizens: (1) the unrepresentativeness of who votes, and (2) false, misleading, or distracting information that is provided to voters in elections.

The Unrepresentative Electorate

Today, nearly all adult U.S. citizens have the legal right to vote.[4] But only a rather small—and quite unrepresentative—fraction of our population actually does vote in most elections, which has profoundly negative consequences for democracy. This problem could easily be fixed, however, if we were to summon the political will to do it.

In today's U.S. presidential elections—big national spectacles, where the stakes are very high—some media pundits sound pleased when just 65 percent or so of eligible citizens cast ballots. The figure is often closer to 60 percent, and in 2016 it was only about 59 percent.[5] That is, in the most important elections we hold, more than *one-third* of eligible Americans *do not vote*. U.S. turnout rates are lower than those of many other countries, including such developing nations as Nicaragua, Sri Lanka, and Ghana. We ranked number thirty-one in turnout among the seventy-six countries that held presidential elections between 2004 and 2014.[6]

Turnout is even lower in "off-year" elections for the U.S. Congress, when no presidential candidates are around to generate media coverage and focus people's attention. In nonpresidential years, only about 40 percent of eligible Americans vote. This rate is far lower than the typical turnout for parliamentary elections in other countries. Off-year turnout in the United States ranks near the bottom for parliamentary elections around the world, among poor countries as well as rich ones. Between 2004 and 2014, we came in nearly dead last: *113th* out of *114* countries.[7]

It gets worse. As we suggested in connection with Iran's Guardian Council, *primary* elections that pick party candidates for Congress and other offices are crucial: they play a big part in deciding what choices the voters have and who will take office. Most congressional elections are held in heavily one-party districts, where the stronger party is almost sure to win the general election, so the primary election generally decides who will become a member of Congress. Yet typically only *10 to 20 percent* of eligible voters turn out at the polls for these important elections. During the 2014 midterm elections, for example, nearly 123 million Americans were eligible to vote in states that held primaries, but only about 18 million—15 percent of them—actually voted.[8] So a very small minority of voters—often dominated by the most intense and most extreme party activists—can, in effect, choose that district's next member of Congress.

Many state and local elections are held on obscure dates—when neither the president nor members of Congress are being chosen—so that they are barely visible to the citizenry. In those cases turnout is often even lower, sometimes falling below 15 percent. Even elections for big-city mayors, which are sometimes hotly contested, average a turnout of only about 25 percent, and some mayors are elected with a single-digit turnout.[9] In short, extremely small factions of voters—who tend to be quite unrepresentative of American citizens as a whole—often make key political decisions for everyone.

To be clear: Low turnout is not inevitable. States including Washington and Oregon have passed laws to raise turnout, first by allowing county auditors to hold all-mail elections for off-cycle elections and expanding citizens' access to permanent absentee voting; then by holding only all-mail elections.[10] Better yet are automatic, universal voter registration (recently adopted by California and Oregon) and Election Day holidays.

THE BIG PROBLEM WITH TURNOUT IS *UNREPRESENTATIVENESS.* Low turnout in itself might not be a serious problem if American voters were representative of the whole population of citizens—if they were highly similar to the whole population in their life cir-

cumstances, interests, values, and policy preferences. Then the results of elections would be about the same as if everyone had voted.
We might still deplore the fact that many Americans missed the
chance to be active and engaged, but in terms of democratic control of public policy, we might conclude that low turnout was not
so bad.

The problem is that American voters are *not* representative of
the citizenry as a whole. This is even true in presidential elections,
which come closest to engaging all Americans. It is much truer
of lower-turnout elections—off-year congressional elections and
especially party primaries. Moreover, unrepresentativeness is even
greater with respect to electoral activities beyond the vote—wearing
a button, persuading others, working for a campaign—with those
who donate money being the most unrepresentative of all.

Americans with lower incomes, less formal education, and less
prestigious occupations—including many Latinos, African Americans, and other minorities—are considerably less likely than other
Americans to vote or to engage in other political activities, in large
part because they are not mobilized to do so.[11] For example, when
a team of political scientists separated survey interviewees into five
socioeconomic status groups based on the level of their family income and educational attainment, they found that 89 percent of
the top group but only 55 percent of the bottom group reported
voting in a presidential election. Nearly half (44 percent) of the
top group engaged in at least one national political activity beyond
the vote, but only 14 percent of those at the bottom of the income
and education groupings did so. The biggest difference involved
contributing money. People who have a lot of money are more
likely to donate some of it. In the top income and education group,
38 percent reported making a political contribution, while only
8 percent of the bottom group did so.[12]

Does this matter? We believe it matters a great deal. Some scholars have suggested that the partisan outcomes of elections would
not be much different if everyone voted because nonvoters have
sometimes reported similar party loyalties and similar candidate
preferences to those of voters.[13] But these findings mostly concern
high-visibility presidential or senatorial elections, where turnout

is relatively high. The problem is much worse in other elections. Moreover, these researchers do not deal with the possibility that if all Americans were engaged in politics over the course of *several* elections, their party attachments might change as the parties changed. The parties would have more reason to appeal to lower-income Americans, to pay attention to the issues they care about, and to mobilize them to vote in harmony with their interests. Elections might produce quite different results.

In any case, it is now clear that the *political needs and circumstances* and the *policy preferences* of voters tend to differ in key ways from those of nonvoters, particularly on class-related economic issues. In 2008, for example, "inactives" (who did not vote or give money or work in a campaign) were nearly twice as likely as voters to lack health insurance. They were significantly more likely to favor universal health care. More inactives than voters reported that they had had to cut back on paying basic bills for food, rent, and the like, and nearly three times as many reported that they had received means-tested government benefits. Politics would be different if these currently uninvolved Americans were engaged in politics.[14]

An analysis covering a number of U.S. presidential elections adds to this picture. In surveys from the first decade of the twenty-first century, nonvoters tended to be less Republican than voters by about 16 percentage points. They were also more favorable than voters toward increasing the minimum wage, making it easier to organize unions, giving federal aid to schools, and providing health insurance to workers and children.[15] Nonvoters were also more favorable than voters toward government job guarantees (by 10 points) and government health insurance (by 12 or 13 points). Similar differences over jobs, health care, and government services occurred in every one of the ten presidential elections between 1972 and 2008.

Our point here is that *both parties* would pay more attention to the distinctive policy preferences of lower-income citizens if these citizens participated at the same rates as the well-to-do. We might end up with different public policies—policies more reflective of what majorities of all Americans want.

WHY PEOPLE DON'T VOTE. Many researchers have tried to sort out exactly which personal characteristics lead some people to go to the polls and some not. Is it income, or education? Does age, or gender, or ethnicity make a difference? Interesting questions, but more important to us are the *election rules and procedures* that contribute to such low, unrepresentative turnout in U.S. elections as compared with elections in other countries. If we can identify rules or institutions that make our electorate unrepresentative and undemocratic, we can work to change those rules or institutions.

Our system of personal registration. One culprit is obvious. The United States is unusual among modern democracies in requiring its citizens to make a personal application and *register* to vote, usually well before Election Day. This requirement puts a substantial burden on people. They have to think about registering before politics is in the air. They have to figure out where to go and when. They need to find time (not during working hours) and transportation to get there.[16]

Why do we do this? Most democracies register their citizens automatically. We did not impose registration requirements during the high-turnout years of the nineteenth century.

Recently some states have made it easier to register—in some cases allowing registration right at the polling place on Election Day. This change makes a difference. When registration is easier, turnout rises. If this easier registration process is done right, the electorate becomes more representative as well. Studies have shown that Election Day registration raises overall turnout and also significantly reduces biases in turnout between the wealthy and the poor, especially in places where the bias is biggest.[17]

A major improvement would be a system of *automatic* registration, in which all citizens were automatically eligible to vote—as is true in most advanced countries. We might or might not want to take one more step and make voting compulsory (perhaps with a small fine for nonparticipation), as twenty-eight countries do—including Australia, Brazil, Singapore, and Turkey. The evidence indicates that compulsory voting raises turnout substantially, by 10 or 15 percentage points.[18]

Additional barriers and burdens. Registration requirements are not the only barriers and burdens that the United States puts in the way of voting. Many countries hold elections on the weekend or on a special public holiday. We hold them on a workday (usually a Tuesday), when voters in places that require Election Day turnout must either make a special effort to get to the polls very early or late in the day or get permission to leave work. Employers are legally required to grant that permission, but most don't make it easy to ask. It is not clear exactly how much effect on turnout the workday scheduling of elections has, but why not change our election day and find out?

A step backward in recent years has been the imposition by a number of states of burdensome "voter identification" laws that require the presentation at the polls of an official form of identification (ID) that includes a photo. This requirement may sound simple; a driver's license will do the trick. But many lower-income people—especially in big cities—do not drive, and it can be a hassle to get an alternative photo ID. These laws also deter some Latino citizens from voting out of fear that they will be mistaken for undocumented immigrants. There is little or no evidence that the laws actually serve their ostensible purpose of curtailing vote fraud— which is seldom a serious problem. When fraud occurs, it is mostly perpetrated by campaigns or vote counters, not voters themselves, and virtually never through attempts to impersonate a voter at a polling place.[19]

Another problem: many would-be voters, especially in urban areas, face long lines and delays due to inadequate numbers of voting machines and limited voting hours. In some cases the delays may be created deliberately for partisan reasons.[20]

Many states deny voting rights to ex-felons, even those convicted of minor drug infractions, and even after they have done time in prison and paid their debt to society. This restriction not only makes the electorate less representative (it disproportionately affects lower-income people and African Americans) but also produces political apathy and alienation that affects whole neighborhoods.[21]

All these burdens on voting result from laws, regulations, or practices that can be changed easily, if we insist on changing them.

The nature of the electoral choices offered to Americans also contributes to our low and unrepresentative turnout. Many of our elections–especially elections in one-party states or one-party congressional districts—are not competitive between the two major parties. The results are a foregone conclusion: the dominant party is sure to win. So why bother to vote? Little wonder that turnout is so low in our off-year congressional elections, when there is a sure-thing winner in most contests.

Our two-party system itself also tends to depress turnout, especially among lower-income citizens who feel that neither the Republicans nor the Democrats pay much attention to them. When citizens hold many combinations of values and interests but are forced to choose between just two alternative packages of policies, many are bound to feel that they have no good choice. For example, many working-class Americans are economic liberals but social conservatives; for decades they had no clear home in either major party. Evidence from around the world indicates that multiparty systems—with Green, Libertarian, Social Democratic, and Conservative parties of many sorts—generally have much higher turnout than two-party systems do.[22]

In chapter 7 we will discuss what sorts of reforms would best help solve the problem of an unrepresentative electorate. Here we now turn to another obstacle to democracy that directly involves ordinary citizens—the problem of political *misinformation* in elections, which makes it harder for citizens to control policy making.

Misinformation in Elections

We noted earlier that "rational ignorance" about politics is widespread. Most citizens have little desire—and little reason—to invest a lot of time and energy learning detailed facts about politics.[23] It is sensible for most people to stay poorly informed. But this makes them—and the country as a whole—vulnerable to distracting, biased, or downright false information that may distort voting decisions, shifting decisions away from what they would be if citizens were fully informed.[24]

Providing false or misleading information, therefore, becomes one pathway for exerting unequal power in politics.[25] Wealthy individuals, corporations, and interest groups often have millions of dollars at stake in a single policy decision. So they (unlike most citizens) *do* often have material incentives to keep close track of what is happening in politics and to act on their knowledge. Using their money and connections, and working through political advertising, think tanks, and the media (including media that they own), they can deliberately confuse citizens about what the government is doing, what the parties and candidates stand for, and what sorts of policies would advance the common good. Big money can produce a lot of misinformation, which can sometimes overwhelm the truth.

Political appeals do not confine themselves to debating the merits of an opposing candidate's policy stands; they often attack the opponent on spurious personal grounds. He or she is said to be "unpatriotic," "weak," or "corrupt." How is the poorly informed voter supposed to be sure that such charges are false? Especially if they come in a barrage (supported by big money) that drowns out what the other side has to say? With the rise of social media, even the most preposterous claims can gain circulation and distract voters. (In 2016, the Internet rumor that Hillary Clinton was involved in a child sex ring centered at a Washington, DC, pizza parlor led one credulous North Carolina man to show up with an assault rifle.)

During the election campaigns and the presidency of Barack Obama—the first truly viable African American candidate for the office—prominent "birthers" including Donald Trump falsely charged that Obama was "a Muslim," a "foreigner," "born in Kenya." A fair number of Americans believed it. The 2016 presidential election campaign was widely viewed as purveying more false, misleading, vile, and outrageous material than any other election in recent years (e.g., calling Obama "the founder of ISIS" or claiming that Senator Ted Cruz's father "was with Lee Harvey Oswald" prior to John F. Kennedy's assassination).

Negative campaigning has been with us for a long while. In 2004, decorated Vietnam War veteran John Kerry was "Swift Boated" with charges of cowardice. President Lyndon B. Johnson's 1964 "daisy girl" commercial (which showed an innocent young girl plucking flower petals while an ominous voice counted down to a nuclear blast) implied that his opponent, Senator Barry Goldwater, would be trigger-happy with nukes. Back in the nineteenth century, Grover Cleveland was charged with fathering an illegitimate child.

Negativity is not bad, of course, if it accurately depicts relevant character flaws or unpopular policy stands.[26] But in the United States, campaign ads and organized rumor campaigns—fueled with millions of dollars of private money—often go far beyond the truth, misleading voters or purveying absolute falsehoods.

Large amounts of money and professionally designed public relations campaigns can also puff up the personal image of a political candidate so that a novice seems knowledgeable; a cold fish seems warm; or a mediocre governor looks like a competent chief executive. A brashly confident personal style and a loud media megaphone can make terrible ideas (deporting ten or twelve million undocumented immigrants; "democratizing" a foreign country by military invasion) seem almost reasonable.

The U.S. mass media play a part in spreading false or misleading "facts" and arguments. In some cases, ideologically driven media owners tilt news coverage to fit their own prejudices, sometimes to the extent of publicizing rants from people who should not be taken seriously. But we should not blame the media for all our ills. More often, we believe, the media reflect available *sources* of news and opinion, including leading politicians, pundits, and anointed "experts." Often, too, the audience imperative—the need to attract purchasers, viewers, and advertisers to make money—creates pressures to focus on dramatic, personal, episodic stories rather than on providing accurate, sustained information relevant to public policy.[27]

We do not believe that citizens are helpless pawns blown this way and that by whatever nonsense is shouted at them. With a little help from their friends, most Americans can sift through the alternative claims and propositions they encounter. And most are resistant to persuasion by specious arguments, if alternative ideas get at least some voice.[28]

But under some conditions citizens are vulnerable to misinformation, particularly when it comes from high government officials or from an entire major political party—or, worse, from *both* parties—or when misinformation is broadcast through a powerful, big-money sound system (e.g., Fox News and its allies) that drowns out the opposition. Citizens need some protection against *systematically* false, biased, or one-sided information.

We believe that the problem of misinformation in elections could be somewhat reduced by general reforms to limit the political power of private money, such as strictly limiting spending on behalf of a party or candidate—or at least diluting the impact of private money by means of public financing. That would reduce the amount and/or impact of one kind of misleading information. Also, without infringing on rights of free political speech, it should be possible at least to regulate it so as to prevent *deliberately false* assertions. Demonstrably false and malicious language, even when aimed at public figures, should not be immune from the laws against libel and slander. Additionally, more could be done to ensure that diverse voices are empowered to get out the facts.

How Much Political Influence Do Citizens Actually Have?

As we've seen, many barriers obstruct democratic responsiveness in the United States: the unrepresentativeness of who votes; pervasive misinformation in elections; restricted choices of candidates for office; the outsize impact of campaign donors, organized interest groups, and party activists; institutional arrangements that cause gridlock and prevent policy change; and more.

So what is the total effect of all these factors? How much, if at all, do average citizens actually influence government policy making?

It has been surprisingly hard for social scientists to figure this out. Past research established that there tends to be a substantial *association* between the degree of policy support or opposition among the public and the likelihood that policy would change in accord with pubic preferences.[29] But this research did not really tell us much about how much *influence* citizens have. It generally considered only two factors—public opinion and actual policy—and asked how often they moved together. It mostly ignored other factors—such as the preferences of affluent or wealthy citizens, or the stands of organized interest groups—that might be exerting most of the real influence.[30] Researchers may have mistakenly concluded that citizens have impact even though they do not, if average Americans happen to favor some of the same policies as elites who really make things happen.

The conclusion that average Americans have significant influence does, in fact, turn out to be a mistake. Our own research indicates that business corporations and the wealthy significantly affect the making of U.S. government policy, but the average American citizen has *little or no* independent influence.

To assess the influence of these three sets of actors, extensive information was gathered on 1,779 cases of proposed changes in U.S. federal government policy—changes related to defense and foreign policy; economic regulation; social welfare policy (help with jobs, wages, education, health care, pensions, and the like); cultural and moral issues (women's rights, abortion, civil liberties, civil rights for minorities, gay rights); and just about every other important kind of policy change that was proposed between 1981 and 2002.[31]

For each proposed policy change, data from national surveys was used to calculate the percentage of "average citizens" (those in the middle of the income distribution) who favored that change. A similar calculation was made for the percentage of affluent citizens (those in the top 20 percent or so of income earners). Finally, an index of "interest group alignments" was constructed for each case, based on the extent to which major interest groups tilted for or against each proposed policy change.

Then a team of research assistants pored through documents and records to find out, for each case, whether or not the proposed policy change was actually adopted by the federal government. They allowed up to four years for policy makers to react, from the time when citizens' preferences and interest groups' alignments were measured.

After these data were assembled, we used a statistical technique to assess *how much independent effect* on change (or nonchange) in policy was exerted by each of the potential influencers: average citizens, affluent citizens, and organized interest groups.[32]

The Ignored Citizenry

The most important result of this research is rather alarming. After interest groups and affluent citizens are taken into account, it becomes clear that average citizens exert *little or no influence* on federal government policy.

This finding is illustrated in figure 3.1. Taking into account the preferences of the affluent and the alignments of interest groups, it shows what percentage of the time policy actually changes when different percentages of middle-income Americans favor policy change. The line in the graph is almost perfectly flat. That means that *it makes virtually no difference* whether an overwhelming majority or only a small minority of average citizens favors policy change. Taking into account the stands of interest groups and the affluent, even if a hefty 80 percent of average citizens favor a policy change, the change happens only about one-third of the time. And if only a feeble 20 percent of average Americans favor a proposed change (that is, if fully 80 percent oppose it), the change happens about one-third of the time anyhow!

One commentator who saw this graph called it "the most terrifying" graph concerning democracy in the United States."[33] It

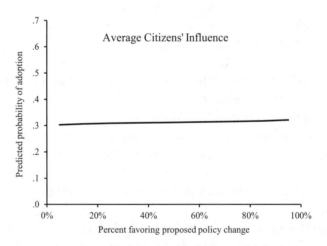

FIGURE 3.1 Average citizens have little or no influence on policy.

Predicted probabilities of policy change controlling for the preferences of affluent Americans and interest groups, based on 1,791 proposed policy changes between 1981 and 2002. See Gilens and Page 2014 for details.

certainly is likely to disturb anyone who holds high hopes for democracy in today's America. The barriers to democratic responsiveness that we have identified apparently have devastating effects. Ordinary citizens simply do not have a significant voice in policy making. They are drowned out by the affluent and by organized interest groups—especially by business groups and corporations.

Democracy by Coincidence?

Critics have pointed out—and we agree—that this does *not* mean that ordinary citizens never get what they want from their government. If the citizenry always lost out, there would probably be riots in the streets. As the past research indicates, however, public opinion and policy do mostly tend to move together. Policy is more likely to change when majorities of citizens favor a change than when majorities oppose it. Average citizens fairly often get what they want.

This could be called "democracy by coincidence." It occurs even though ordinary citizens have little or no influence of their own, because those citizens fairly often agree with the policies that are also favored (and won) by their affluent fellow citizens who *do* have a lot of clout.

So should we—as some political scientists have suggested—just not worry much about the lack of influence by ordinary citizens? If majorities of Americans agree with affluent citizens most of the time, and if the affluent generally get their way, what's the problem? Shouldn't we rejoice that the government is tending to do what the people want?[34]

We do not think so, for three main reasons.

First, "democracy by coincidence" is a feeble, precarious sort of democracy, if it can be called democracy at all. No doubt Americans are fortunate that they do not always disagree with their wealthier compatriots. Things could be worse. (In much of the world, they *are* worse.) But we believe that the essence of democracy is not just having reasonably satisfactory policies; the essence of democracy is popular *control* of government, with each citizen having an equal voice. Without such control, happy coincidences can turn into very unhappy tyranny on short notice.

Second, on many important issues, affluent and wealthy Americans seriously disagree with average citizens. Most Americans want the wealthy to pay more taxes, but the wealthy do not. Most Americans want tighter regulation of big corporations and financial institutions, but the wealthy disagree. Wealthy Americans also tend to oppose government help with jobs, wages, health care, education, retirement pensions, and other matters of great concern to average Americans.[35] So the political clout of affluent and wealthy Americans does *not* automatically translate into popular policies. Happy coincidences are far from universal.

Third, "democracy by coincidence" bumps up against a fundamental problem of the U.S. political system: our policy making process is *biased against change*. We have multiple veto points that can be used by a few opponents of the popular will to block policy changes. Even when most of the affluent agree with ordinary citizens, institutional conflicts and gridlock often obstruct action that they want. "Democracy by coincidence" works pretty well at *preventing* unpopular new policies from being enacted, but very poorly at *bringing about* policy changes favored by most Americans. Even overwhelming majorities of Americans usually lose out when they want policy to change.

The limits to "democracy by coincidence" are made clear in figure 3.2. This figure ignores the question of influence; it pays no attention to the fact that affluent individuals and organized interest groups are having big effects on policy. Instead, the figure simply presents descriptive facts about how actual policy outcomes relate to what majorities of Americans want. For various proportions of citizens who favor policy changes—moving from small minorities seeking change (on the left) to overwhelming majorities (on the right)—the graph indicates how often proposed policy changes actually occur.

Clearly Americans do enjoy some democracy by coincidence. When more Americans favor a proposed policy change, that change is more likely to occur. In particular, when large majorities *oppose* a policy change (that is, when very few people favor it), that change is unlikely to be adopted. When only 20 percent, 30 percent, or 40 percent of Americans favor a particular policy proposal, it tends

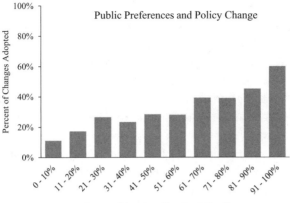

FIGURE 3.2 Even highly popular policies often fail.

Observed probabilities of policy change, based on 1,791 proposed policy changes between 1981 and 2002. See Gilens and Page 2014 for details.

to be adopted only about one-quarter of the time. Unpopular policy changes do not happen often.

But figure 3.2 also shows the strong bias of the U.S. political system toward *inaction*. Change is no more likely when a 55 percent majority wants it than when only a 25 percent minority does—in either case, a policy change occurs about one-quarter of the time. Even more strikingly, when large majorities of Americans favor policy changes—when 70 or 80 percent want change—they get it less than half the time.

This is a remarkable finding. It is worth pondering. In the "world's greatest democracy," as we like to call the United States, very large majorities of citizens are thwarted—do not get policy changes they favor—more than half the time.

WHAT DIFFERENCE IT MAKES. This finding means that the American people are deprived of many important public policies that could improve their lives and advance the welfare of the nation as a whole. In a rapidly changing world, it means that we are subject to dangerous policy "drift." Government policies do not adapt to new realities.[36]

In the following two sections of this chapter, we discuss some specific policy areas in which the will of the people has repeatedly been thwarted: cases in which majorities of Americans have favored policy changes, but those changes have been blocked.

These cases can be divided into two groups: policies that would provide "public goods" and policies that deal with equity or fairness. *Public goods* are things that would benefit most or all citizens but that private markets fail to provide efficiently. *Equity* policies provide safety nets and other benefits targeted at middle- and lower-income rather than upper-income citizens, or tax the affluent at higher rates than others. Large majorities of Americans want their government to provide many kinds of public goods and many equity policies. But both types of policy are often obstructed by gridlock or blocked by wealthy individuals and organized interest groups—especially business groups.

Failing to Provide Public Goods

Most economists agree that free markets and private enterprise cannot solve all problems. Certain kinds of *market failure* inevitably occur, including failures to provide enough *public goods*—things like clean air and clean water, national parks, law enforcement, national defense, good highways, and mass transit—which millions of people want to enjoy but which no private firm can produce and sell in an efficient manner.

Adam Smith, the great economic theorist and advocate of free markets, knew this. He advocated government provision of several things we would call *public goods*, including national defense, a system of justice, public works, and education of the young.[37]

Markets do not work well when there are "neighborhood effects" or "externalities": when people not involved in economic transactions get benefits (beautiful scenery, defense from attack, light from a lighthouse) without having to pay for them, or when they suffer harms (polluted rivers, random gunfire, disease epidemics) that the perpetrators do not have to pay for inflicting.[38] When goods or relief from harms can be enjoyed by large numbers of people with little or no extra cost per extra person—and when it is hard to make people pay for that enjoyment (how could you charge for clean air?)—there is little economic incentive for private businesses to provide them. Such public goods are likely to be under-produced and underconsumed. Free markets fail. Society suffers.[39]

Most people conclude that governments should do something about this, such as produce public goods themselves, or contract out for them, or subsidize their production—and then offer them free to everyone.

There are few, if any, pure cases of public goods. But many things that millions of people value—national defense, scenic national parks, clean air, safety from gun violence, uncongested roads and highways, public schools, and much more—share the fundamental characteristic that government action is required to provide them adequately and efficiently.[40]

Most Americans understand this. Again and again, surveys show that large majorities of Americans favor the kinds of taxes, regulations, and government spending programs that are called for by the theory of public goods.

Again and again, however, the U.S. political system has failed to provide sufficient public goods that majorities of Americans want and need. Examples include environmental protection; up-to-date trains, highways, mass transit, and other transportation infrastructure; immigration reform; protection against gun violence; high-quality, affordable schools and colleges; and regulation of the economy, especially the financial sector.

THE ENVIRONMENT AND CLIMATE CHANGE. Clean water, clean air, and a pristine natural environment are classic public goods. The Clean Air and Clean Water Acts have helped. As the horrific case of Flint, Michigan, illustrated in 2015, however, many Americans still cannot be sure that their tap water is free of lead poison.[41] On the national level, Congress in recent years has failed to deal with what may be the greatest single challenge of our time: climate change, which threatens to cause destructive storms, floods, droughts, and inundation of entire coastal cities (think New Orleans, Miami, even New York City.)

For years, majorities of Americans have said that climate change, or global warming, is an important problem that we need to address. As the earth's surface has registered record-high temperatures,[42] as polar ice has melted, and as unusually severe storms have hit populous areas, more and more members of the public have come to favor taking action. In one recent survey, 55 percent of Americans said the U.S. government should do "a great deal" or "a lot" about climate change. Only 25 percent said "little" or "nothing." An overwhelming majority (81 percent) attributed climate change at least in part to human activity, and two-thirds said they were less likely to vote for a candidate who called global warming a "hoax and fraud."[43]

Yet Congress keeps refusing to act. Fossil fuel companies resist. Republicans who used to sponsor environmental legislation have dropped out.

Between 2006 and 2012, surveys showed that large majorities of Americans favored the idea that government should encourage the reduction of greenhouse gases that businesses are allowed to emit. At the very moment in 2009 when the Clean Energy and Security Act (designed to make industries pay for their carbon dioxide emissions) was dying in the Senate,[44] roughly 75 percent of Americans supported government intervention in the reduction of greenhouse gases emitted by businesses, and many expressed a willingness to pay for it through tax incentives. These findings run counter to the excuse often made by elected officials opposing climate change legislation—that there is supposedly not enough public support or willingness to pay for it.[45] In 2016, Donald Trump (who had called climate change a "hoax" perpetrated by China) nominated Oklahoma Attorney General Scott Pruitt, a close ally of the fossil fuel industry, to head the Environmental Protection Agency (EPA)—an agency Pruitt had sued thirteen times—yet despite widespread opposition, Pruitt was confirmed in February 2017.[46]

TRANSPORTATION INFRASTRUCTURE. Americans who travel abroad are often amazed by the high-speed rail systems of Europe, Japan, and China. Trains leaving every hour cover the nearly one thousand miles between Shanghai and Beijing in just three or four hours. Nothing like that can be found in the United States.

What has happened to the great American railways, once a marvel of the world and a powerful engine of our economic development? What has happened to our interstate highway system, the proud, bipartisan creation of Republican President Dwight D. Eisenhower and a Democratic Congress? The concrete pavement on many major highways is crumbling. Critical bridges have fallen into rivers. Mass transit in our cities, which is supposed to provide speedy, efficient travel while minimizing pollution and road congestion, is chronically underfunded and is stuck with ancient equipment.

There is a sharp contrast between what Congress is (not) doing and what most Americans want. In a 2013 poll, three-quarters (77 percent) of the public supported federal government programs that would put people to work on urgent infrastructure repairs. That figure included a solid majority of Republicans as well as an overwhelming majority of Democrats.[47] A 2015 poll indicated that the vast majority (89 percent) of Americans thought that improving the country's roads, bridges, and public transportation system was important.[48]

IMMIGRATION REFORM. Historically, the United States has been a nation of immigrants from every part of the globe. But enthusiasm for new, culturally diverse, energetic, hardworking citizens has always been mixed with anxiety over whether new immigrants will compete for jobs with native-born workers and whether immigrants' foreign habits, looks, and languages will upset the established American way of life. Recent immigrants from Mexico and Central America have aroused just such anxieties. Fears of terrorism contribute to wariness about accepting refugees from Syria—or even visitors from predominantly Muslim countries.

Americans have been divided about whether to emphasize "secure borders" and low levels of immigration or to welcome new immigrants and help those who are here attain citizenship. But it is clear that *something* needs to be done about the eleven million or so undocumented immigrants in the United States, who live a shadowy and fearful existence.[49] Mass deportation would be both inhumane and extremely costly.

Surveys indicate that substantial majorities of Americans support a reform package that would include strict border enforcement as a high priority but also a pathway to citizenship for the undocumented people who are already here—a pathway insisting on law-abiding behavior, payment of taxes, competence in English, and the like. A 2014 Fox News poll indicated that nearly two-thirds (63 percent) of Americans supported a pathway to citizenship. That level of support had largely remained the same since 2011.[50] Americans' concern over controlling and reducing illegal immigration, and the belief that large numbers of immigrants and refugees to the U.S. are a "critical threat" to the country, have declined dramatically since the mid-1990s. They are currently at or near their all-time lows.[51]

Here, too, however, Congress has failed to act. Bipartisan cooperation has disappeared. In 2016, Republican presidential candidate and U.S. Senator Marco Rubio was derided for his past willingness to compromise on immigration. The eventual nominee, Donald Trump, advocated building a "Wall" on the Mexican border and deporting all undocumented immigrants. President Obama's executive action to provide temporary legal status—and protection from deportation—for millions of immigrants was held up by lawsuits and was vulnerable to change by incoming President Trump.[52]

STOPPING GUN VIOLENCE. Gun violence in the United States is unique among advanced countries of the world. Including homicides, suicides, and accidents, nearly *one hundred* Americans die *every day* from gunshot wounds.[53] Many of the dead are innocent victims of accidents or aggressive behavior. News outlets regularly report spectacular mass shootings in schools, malls, or movie theaters.

To be sure, millions of Americans cherish the right to use firearms for hunting and target shooting. Many also imagine that guns are useful for protecting oneself and one's home. There is little support for altogether *banning* the use of ordinary rifles or pistols—which, in any case, the Supreme Court has declared would violate the Second Amendment.[54]

Gun deaths could be greatly reduced, perhaps cut in half, by treating them like automobile fatalities—as a *public health* problem. Simple, unobtrusive regulations could make a big difference: careful background checks to keep guns away from the mentally ill; tighter regulation of gun dealers; safe-storage requirements; and "smart gun" technology (weapons that fire only with a personal identification number or fingerprint; microstamping to trace guns and bullet casings used in crimes).[55]

Overwhelming majorities of Americans, including majorities of gun owners, favor sensible safety measures of this sort. In a 2013 poll, 81 percent favored making background checks a requirement for people purchasing guns through private sales and at gun shows. Nearly three-quarters (73 percent) wanted Congress to pass a background-check bill that failed in the Senate.[56]

For years, however, Congress has failed to act. The assault weapons ban of 1994 was quietly allowed to expire in 2004.[57] Even after the horrible 2012 mass shooting of twenty-six adults and children at Sandy Hook Elementary School, efforts at gun safety regulations failed.[58] Members of Congress seemed terrified of electoral reprisal from a relatively small number of ideological gun activists, mobilized by the misleading "gun confiscation" alarms from the National Rifle Association.

GOOD, AFFORDABLE SCHOOLS. Educational opportunity is central to Americans' dreams for themselves and their children. Education is also a public good: it contributes—beyond what individuals would be able or willing to pay—to good citizenship and to the training of a skilled workforce.

Surveys regularly show that access to good education is a top priority for Americans and that they are concerned about the financial straits of public schools. Large majorities want government to spend the money needed to provide universal, affordable access to high-quality preschools, elementary and secondary schools, college, and beyond.[59] But here, too, something has gone wrong.

The United States pioneered the idea of free public schooling for everyone. Yet preschooling is now less accessible in the United States than in most advanced countries. Many U.S. elementary and secondary schools—especially in urban areas—suffer from limited resources, underpaid and demoralized teachers, and a heavy burden of trying to cope with millions of poor children suffering from malnutrition, challenging home environments, and random violence. The result is often weak test scores, poor attendance, and low graduation rates.

The Elementary and Secondary Education Act of 1965 passed Congress with bipartisan support. But Congress seems to have abandoned its tradition of broad bipartisan support for public education—squeezing appropriations, failing to find innovative solutions, and largely giving up on the very idea that every young American should have the opportunity to advance as far in school as he or she is capable of going.

U.S. colleges and universities have been the envy of the world. In contrast to much of the rest of the world, however—where college attendance is generally free of charge and admission is based purely on qualifications—U.S. colleges have become extremely expensive. Millions of young people from lower-income families are priced out. Most who go to college have to take out loans and pile up burdensome debts.

Nearly two-thirds (64 percent) of Americans say that the federal government is doing too little to make higher education available and affordable. Nearly as many (61 percent) favor capping student loan repayments at one-tenth of people's income, even if that would mean additional government spending. Nevertheless, recent attempts to address the issues of crippling student loan debt—such as Senator Elizabeth Warren's "Keep Student Loans Affordable Act" of 2013—have failed in Congress.[60]

REGULATING THE ECONOMY. All mainstream economists agree that governments need to provide the underpinnings for a market economy, including a sound currency, enforcement of contracts, and protection of private property. Most also agree that certain types of market failures need to be dealt with, particularly those involving externalities and lack of accurate information for consumers.

Most ordinary Americans, too, favor various kinds of economic regulations. Since the financial crisis and Great Recession of 2007–2009, large majorities have sought stronger regulation of the big banks, mortgage lenders, and investment houses whose high-risk behavior and questionable sales practices helped create the housing bubble and subsequent economic crash. A 2013 survey indicated that regulating such financial services was "important" or "very important" to an overwhelming 90 percent of likely voters, including 96 percent of Democrats and 89 percent of Republicans. A hefty 83 percent favored stricter rules for Wall Street financial companies. With such overwhelming bipartisan support from the public, one might think that Congress would respond.[61]

Yet policy lags behind what most Americans want. During and after the Great Recession, demands to nationalize or break up the biggest ("too big to fail") banks were rejected. The chief action to prevent a repeat of the financial crisis was the Dodd-Frank Act, a cautious compromise. Yet its implementation has been hindered by powerful pushback from banks. Many officials seemed to ignore the lessons of history, embracing the hopeful argument that financial and other markets will correct themselves, so long as they are free from government "interference."[62]

Later chapters will make clear how wealthy Americans, organized interest groups, extreme party activists, polarized parties, and institutional gridlock have caused these and other failures of government to provide adequate public goods.

Little Help for Economically Stressed Americans

Often, large majorities of Americans have also been thwarted in their desire for new *equity*, or fairness, policies.

Most Americans—and most people around the world—assume that one of the chief duties of governments is to pursue equity: to enhance equal opportunity, help the unfortunate, and soften the blows of an unpredictable world. This means helping average and lower-income citizens by ensuring that people can get good jobs at good wages, and by providing "safety net" benefits for those who fall on hard times due to unemployment, sickness, disability, old age, or just plain bad luck. One way to do so is to impose higher taxes on the wealthiest citizens (who can most easily afford to pay) and use the revenue to help others.[63] Most of today's advanced countries pursue equity through "redistributive" policies—not to completely equalize incomes but to provide a minimum standard of living for the people who are worst off and to soften the sharp edges of inequality that unfettered private markets tend to produce.[64]

True, there has always existed a contrary view. Some say that government activity in general—and redistributive policies in particular—should be held to a minimum to keep taxes low, to avoid bureaucracy and red tape, and to maximize individual freedom, particularly freedom to accumulate and enjoy private property.[65] It is striking, however, that even Milton Friedman—one of the most famous advocates of free markets—did not argue that markets, if left to themselves, would invariably provide fair or just wages. In fact, Friedman devoted much of one chapter of his book *Capitalism and Freedom* to advocating a "negative income tax" designed to subsidize the wages of low-income workers while providing incentives for them to work as hard as possible.[66] We would go further than Friedman and argue that it makes sense for governments to use a *number* of carefully designed, efficient redistributive policies to soften extreme inequalities of wealth and income.

HELP WITH JOBS AND WAGES. Plentiful jobs at good wages are crucial if Americans are to achieve self-fulfillment, decent incomes, and good standards of living. But market economies—left to themselves (or, often, misdirected by policies unfriendly to workers)—cannot always produce good jobs for all able-bodied citizens who want to work. This is clear from the low, stagnant wages and the high rates of joblessness that have plagued the United States since the late twentieth century.

Several types of worker-friendly government policies could help. Macroeconomic "stimulus" policies to avoid steep recessions and joblessness; policies that encourage strong labor unions or "codetermination" of wages by workers and management; extensive job training and apprenticeship programs; inexpensive or free day care, so parents can work outside the home; income supplements such as "family allowances" or tax credits; and, as a last resort, unemploy-

ment insurance—or, perhaps better, government-provided jobs—
for those who cannot find work in the private sector.

Big majorities of Americans favor many policies of those sorts.
On a general level, national polls and surveys regularly show large
majorities saying that the government in Washington should "see
to it" that "everyone who wants to work can find a job." More specifically, recent polls have shown majorities saying that government
should *provide* jobs for those who cannot find employment in the
private sector. Opinion tilts strongly toward expanding the Earned
Income Tax Credit (which subsidizes low-income wages) and making it available to workers without children. Large majorities favor
using tax dollars for retraining people whose jobs have been eliminated. Most Americans support job creation through infrastructure
spending. A strong majority (69 percent) has said that the U.S.
government is not spending enough effort on creating jobs.[67]

Public support for minimum wage laws is particularly strong.
A 2014 survey indicated that 62 percent of Americans supported
an increase in the federal minimum wage from $7.25 to $10.10 an
hour. The following year, a survey showed that fully three-quarters
of Americans would like to see the minimum wage increased to
$12.50 an hour by 2020, with nearly half of the public strongly
favoring this action.[68]

Yet politicians have allowed the purchasing power of the minimum wage to erode.[69] The federal minimum wage is worth less
now than it was in the 1960s, despite the dramatic overall growth
of the American economy since then. In 2014, Republican senators
again blocked a bill that would have increased the minimum wage
from $7.25 to $10.10 an hour.[70]

Contrary to the wishes of most Americans, U.S. policy makers have curtailed funding for many jobs programs and have completely rejected others. As a result, the United States lags behind
many other rich countries in providing good jobs and good wages
for its citizens. American workers have been battered for decades
by job losses and stagnant wages due to economic globalization
and automation, without the kinds of help that is provided by governments elsewhere.

Government *fiscal policy* (involving budget surpluses or deficits between amounts spent and tax revenue raised) and *monetary policy* (concerning how much money is printed, and how high or low interest rates are set) have regularly tilted toward the prevention of inflation (a bugaboo for investment banks and bondholders) rather than economic stimulus and job creation.[71] The federal minimum wage has eroded. The Earned Income Tax Credit has lost much of its support from Republicans in Congress and has never been extended to give full benefits to childless workers.[72] Labor unions have been severely weakened by unfriendly public policies that reinforce the negative pressures of technology and globalization rather than counteracting them. Only token efforts are made at job retraining for displaced workers. Good day care is available only to those who can afford to pay for it. Unemployment insurance benefits are meager.

Consider the case of day care. Flexible work hours and help with caregiving for children or aging parents are crucial to the well-being of the forty-two million women in America who are on the brink of poverty (women still supply the vast majority of care for children and aging parents). Not showing up for work because a child has an ear infection—or because schools close for a snow day, or an elderly parent has to go to the doctor—can put their jobs at risk. Yet their going to work in those circumstances jeopardizes their twenty-eight million children and others who depend on them. Our lack of affordable child care (nearly unique among advanced countries)—together with a "toxic work world" of stressful overwork for rigid hours at faraway workplaces—takes a toll on nearly all women and men with jobs and dependents. Yet Congress has done little or nothing about it.[73]

Congress's rejection of government-provided employment as a last resort for the jobless is also striking. Government-provided jobs are widely used in other countries. They have a solid pedigree in U.S. history—as exemplified by such programs as the Depression-era Civilian Conservation Corps (planting foliage and improving trails in national parks, as is fondly remembered today even in conservative Idaho[74]) and the Works Progress Administration (building roads, bridges, tunnels, and the like). When asked, most Americans have said they favor the idea of the government "providing" jobs for those who cannot get private employment. Since the demise of the Humphrey-Hawkins bill in the early 1980s, however, such programs have always been rejected or severely constricted by Congress, even in the 2009 depths of the Great Recession.

AFFORDABLE MEDICAL CARE. For more than half a century, the United States has compared poorly with nearly all other advanced countries in its much higher-cost medical care (spending roughly twice as much per person); its failure to provide access to all citizens; and its disappointing health outcomes. Despite all the money spent on cutting-edge medical technology and expensive new drugs, the United States has had higher infant mortality, shorter life expectancies, more suffering from preventable diseases, and more hospital admissions for chronic conditions than other advanced countries, including Australia, Canada, France, and the United Kingdom.[75]

For years, polls and surveys have made clear that large majorities of Americans want universal, affordable medical insurance and that most are receptive to government provision of it through something like a "single-payer" system. In one survey, fully 73 percent of Americans said that "it is the responsibility of the federal government to make sure all Americans have health care coverage," and 64 percent favored "national health insurance, which would be financed by tax money, paying for most forms of health care."[76] As of 2015, 72 percent of Americans also held the view that the cost of prescription drugs was unreasonable, and 83 percent favored allowing the federal government to negotiate with drug companies to get a lower price on medications for people on Medicare.[77]

Yet proposals for universal health insurance were dropped from the New Deal legislation of the 1930s; abandoned again when floated in 1948; set aside in the 1960s in favor of more limited Medicare for the elderly and Medicaid for the poor; and rejected once again (not even coming to a congressional vote) in 1993.[78] Finally in 2009, the Affordable Care Act (ACA, or "Obamacare") overcame fierce political opposition and scraped through Congress— without a single Republican vote in the House or the Senate. By the time President Obama left office, the ACA had brought insurance coverage to millions more people, substantial financial help for those with lower incomes, and improvements in the inefficient U.S. "fee for service" system, while (at least for a time) moderating annual increases in health-care costs.

Surveys have shown the Affordable Care Act as a whole to be rather *un*popular—but not because of most of its specific provisions. A survey for the Kaiser Family Foundation late in 2016 indicated that majorities of Americans supported all but one major provision of the bill. Fully 85 percent favored its requirement that insurance companies allow young adults (up to age twenty-six) to stay on their parents' insurance plans. Nearly as many (83 percent) supported its elimination of out-of-pocket costs for many preventive services. Eighty percent favored its provision of financial help to low- and moderate-income Americans for purchasing coverage. Eighty percent of Americans also supported the Obamacare option for states to expand their Medicaid coverage for low-income, uninsured adults. A solid majority (69 percent) supported the prohibition against health insurance companies denying coverage because of a person's medical history. In fact, the *only* major ACA provision opposed by a majority of Americans was the "individual mandate" that all Americans must have health insurance or pay a fine.[79]

Part of the substantial opposition to the ACA as a whole may have arisen from mischaracterizations of the act (e.g., as creating "death panels") by partisan opponents. But a good part of the opposition came because the ACA was seen as doing *too little* rather than too much: it did not offer a simple, tax-supported system for covering everyone's medical care but instead forced most people to pay insurance premiums themselves, often to the same private insurance companies that had been burying them in paperwork, capping reimbursements, and denying coverage on the flimsiest excuses.[80]

The 2016 Kaiser survey found that nearly one-third of Americans (30 percent) wanted to *expand* what the ACA did. Only about one-quarter (26 percent) actually favored repealing the entire law. Another 17 percent wanted to scale back what the law did, so that fewer than half of Americans in total (just 43 percent) favored cutbacks or a total repeal.

But politicians did not appear to listen. Repeatedly over the years after the narrow passage of the ACA, the House of Representatives voted for the total repeal—rather than improvement or amendment—of the act. Donald Trump advocated "repeal and replacement" in his 2016 campaign for president, and the first steps toward repeal—which provoked a fierce counterreaction—were taken by Senate and House Republican majorities early in 2017.

SOCIAL SECURITY. A startling example of failure to respond to the will of the American people involves the highly popular Social Security program. Social Security is the biggest, most popular, and probably most successful domestic program of the U.S. federal government. It was initiated in 1935 as the centerpiece of Democratic President Franklin D. Roosevelt's New Deal. Subsequently it was expanded under presidents of both parties, notably including Republicans Dwight Eisenhower and Richard Nixon.[81]

Social Security takes up roughly *one-third* of all federal government spending. It is highly efficient; administrative costs are only about 2 percent.[82] It provides a modest retirement income, up to a maximum of about $2,700 per month or $32,000 per year (a bit above the poverty line for a family of two) for a worker who retires at full retirement age and has made maximum payroll tax contributions for a number of years. Others get less. About thirty-eight million Americans are currently receiving retirement benefits. Social Security also provides badly needed money for disabled people who cannot work and help for widows, widowers, and children who have lost their family's chief wage earner. Social Security as a whole has raised millions of Americans out of poverty. Economists have found that Social Security has been "crucial" in reducing poverty among the elderly.[83]

The finances of the program are fundamentally sound. Talk of "financial crisis" or "bankruptcy" is nonsense.[84] For the foreseeable future, the costs of paying guaranteed benefits to large numbers of future retirees can easily be met by rather minor changes in the program. For example, gradually eliminating the payroll tax "cap"— which exempts all earnings above about $120,000 from paying any Social Security payroll taxes at all—would produce enough

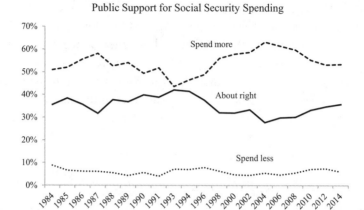

Public Support for Social Security Spending

FIGURE 3.3 Americans want higher spending on Social Security.

Source: General Social Surveys, 1984–2014.

money to cover roughly two-thirds of the anticipated Social Security revenue shortfall over the next seventy-five years. Strangely, this measure—favored by large majorities of Americans—has rarely even been discussed in the Capitol.[85]

Year after year, opinion surveys and scholarly studies have shown that far more Americans say they want to "spend more" on Social Security than say "spend less" (see figure 3.3.) Most Americans want Social Security benefits to be bigger, not smaller.[86] A 2013 survey for the National Academy of Social Insurance found that 84 percent of Americans thought the current Social Security program did not provide enough income for retirees. Sixty-five percent thought there should be an increase in future Social Security benefits to provide more secure retirement for Americans leaving the workforce. Most thought these changes critical even if it meant increasing Social Security taxes paid by currently working Americans, particularly wealthy Americans.[87]

Just about any proposal to *cut* Social Security benefits—by reducing cost-of-living allowances (COLAs), raising retirement ages, or otherwise tinkering with the program—almost always provokes opposition from large majorities of Americans. (Such proposals receive substantial support from the wealthy, however, as we discuss in chapter 4.)[88]

Yet in recent years Congress has shown no inclination at all to increase the rather slim benefits of Social Security. Remarkably, Congress—and presidents from both parties—have actually flirted with the idea (promoted through an intense, well-funded campaign by wealthy individuals and businesses) of *cutting* guaranteed retirement benefits and replacing them with a partly or wholly "privatized" system.[89] In a privatized system, retirement savings would be subject to high administrative costs and would fluctuate in value as the stock market goes up and down, hurting those who have to retire at the "wrong" time.[90]

So far this privatization disaster—which would appall most Americans if it occurred—has been narrowly averted. But it has come alarmingly close to enactment, as part of party leaders' secret negotiations toward a "grand bargain" allegedly designed to deal with unrelated budget deficits.[91] Such close calls clearly contravene the public's wishes. Moreover, the benefit *increases* favored by most Americans have been completely thwarted.

PROGRESSIVE TAXES. A promising way to soften the sharp edges of economic inequality is to levy "progressive" taxes—taxes that take a higher proportion of income from the wealthiest citizens. The revenue can then be used to help lower-income citizens with their jobs, wages, medical care, retirement pensions, and the like, narrowing the gap between rich and poor.

Ever since the big rise of inequality toward the end of the nineteenth century, many American political and economic thinkers have advocated progressive taxes. And since the 1913 ratification of the Sixteenth Amendment to the Constitution, the federal government has in fact imposed progressive income taxes. High tax rates on the highest incomes (a 90 percent marginal rate in the Eisenhower years, for example) played a significant part in the relatively equal "golden age" of the 1950s and 1960s.

Most Americans agree with the principle of progressive taxation, saying that people with higher incomes should pay a "larger" or a "much larger" share of their incomes in taxes than those with low incomes.[92] In a 2015 poll, 63 percent said that money and wealth in the United States should be more evenly distributed among a larger percentage of the people. A small majority (52 percent) even said the government should "redistribute" wealth (not a popular word, in the abstract) by taxing the rich. Nearly two-thirds of Americans say that corporations and the wealthy are not paying their fair share of federal taxes.[93]

This does not mean that Americans favor confiscatory taxation. They do not. But they definitely oppose loopholes for the wealthy, such as the "carried interest" provision that taxes hedge fund and private equity managers at only 15 percent. In a 2013 survey, strong majorities approved of closing tax loopholes and favored a minimum income tax of 30 percent for millionaires, to make sure that the wealthy do not pay a lower tax rate than the middle class.[94] When another survey asked how high estate taxes should be on estates worth $100 million or more, the average American said it should be about 25 percent. Fewer than one-sixth said the tax rate should be zero.[95] There is strong public support for the corporate income tax, a progressive tax that mainly falls on wealthy owners of capital. In one survey, six out of ten Americans singled out the corporate income tax as a tax that government should use "a lot" for getting revenue to fund government programs.[96]

Most Americans also favor making payroll taxes more progressive by raising the "cap" that entirely exempts from taxes all income over about $120,000. (Current U.S. payroll taxes for Social Security are extremely *regressive*: most wage earners pay a flat rate of about 13 percent on all their income, but billionaires pay the same percentage on only a tiny fraction of their income, so that their overall rate is far lower.)

Actual tax policy, however, has diverged markedly from what most Americans want. The progressivity of the income tax has been steadily undermined: the top rate has been reduced from 90 percent in the Eisenhower years to just over 39 percent today.[97] As a source of revenue, the progressive income tax has declined markedly while the payroll tax has increased—and has been kept highly regressive. The corporate income tax has been cut back so far that it has nearly disappeared as a source of federal revenue. The estate tax— contrary to propaganda about beleaguered family farms and small businesses—is now limited to the very largest estates (just 2 out of every 1,000 of them): estates worth at least $10.86 million (for couples), as of 2016. Rates have been reduced to an average of just 16.6 percent.[98] Yet in Congress, proposals to abolish the "death tax" get much more attention than proposals to increase it.[99]

All in all, the failure of the U.S. government to enact equity policies that majorities of Americans favor has added up to a failure to deal seriously with sharply rising economic inequality.[100]

In the following chapters that make up the rest of part 2, we will say more about exactly *why* these failures in democratic responsiveness have occurred. Chapter 4 deals with the political clout of affluent and wealthy Americans. Chapter 5 considers the power of organized interest groups, particularly large corporations and business-oriented groups. Chapter 6 turns to the problem of congressional gridlock and the obstructive role of our highly polarized political parties, fueled by extremist party activists.

FOUR

The Political Clout of Wealthy Americans

Chapter 3 showed that average Americans have little or no influence over the making of U.S. government policy. As we will see in this chapter, however, wealthy Americans wield a lot of influence. By investing money in politics, they can turn economic power into political power. Thus the United States suffers from what can be called "unequal democracy."[1]

The wealthy have won a number of important things from government: high-end tax cuts; minimal government spending; free-trade agreements; business subsidies and bank bailouts; "deregulation" of the economy. But ordinary citizens have not gotten much—especially citizens who feel pressured by economic globalization and low, stagnant incomes.

Our growing economic gap—with the fortunes of multimillionaires and billionaires soaring while most American families have been struggling to get by—has led to a widening *political* gap. The wealthy now have more to spend on politics. They have used their resources to lower their own taxes and to prevent any serious spending or regulatory efforts to ameliorate economic inequality. Thus economic inequality and political inequality mutually reinforce and increase each other. This mutual reinforcement threatens to cause a downward spiral that might continue indefinitely unless we make determined efforts to stop it.[2]

How Much Political Influence Do the Affluent Have?

Historians and journalists have always known that money plays a big part in influencing election outcomes and public policy in the United States. Examples are plentiful. Until very recently, however, no one has been able to use systematic data to figure out exactly *how much* influence the affluent have over a wide range of public policies.

Now, thanks to the unique data described in chapter 3—data covering 1,779 cases of federal government policy making over a twenty-year period—we have been able to estimate how much independent influence "affluent" Americans (the top 20 percent of income earners) have, while statistically taking into account the preferences of average Americans (those in the middle of the income distribution) and the alignments of major interest groups.[3]

As figure 4.1 indicates, we have found that the affluent have substantial influence, far more than middle-income citizens do.[4] In sharp contrast to the flat line of (non)influence by average citizens in the previous chapter, here the graph slopes rather steeply upward to the right. Taking into account the wishes of average citizens and interest groups, when a larger proportion of affluent Americans want a policy change, that change is much more likely to happen.

But even the affluent often fail to get the policies they want from government. As the figure shows, when large majorities of the affluent want to *prevent* a policy change, they can almost always do so. (Policies with very low affluent support, toward the left side of figure 4.1, are rarely adopted.) But our political system has a strong, built-in bias against policy change, exacerbated in recent decades by partisan polarization and gridlock. So even policies with overwhelming support among the affluent (toward the right side of figure 4.1) have only about a fifty-fifty chance of being adopted.

Despite the difficulty that even affluent Americans face in getting the policies they want adopted, their preferences do significantly affect policy outcomes—in sharp contrast to the preferences of average citizens.

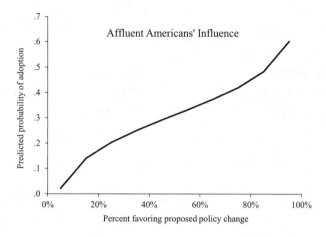

FIGURE 4.1 Affluent Americans have substantial influence on policy.

Predicted probabilities of policy change, controlling for the preferences of average citizens and interest groups, based on 1,791 proposed policy changes between 1981 and 2002. See Gilens and Page 2014 for details.

Our analysis shows that the affluent have influence over government policy making. But we cannot be sure exactly *who* among affluent citizens is exerting how much of that influence. Most of the "affluents" in our data are upper middle class, not really "rich." (Their median annual income of $160,000 [in 2016 dollars] may sound high to many readers, but it falls far short of the $500,000 or so needed to qualify for the top 1 percent of Americans.) We suspect that a lot of political inequality exists even among the affluent, just as it does in the general population. In fact, we suspect that much of the influence that we have detected is being wielded by a tiny group within the affluent: the "truly wealthy"— that is, multimillionaires and billionaires who can afford to donate thousands, even millions, of dollars to candidates and to superpowerful political action committees (PACs), or super PACs, that can accept unlimited donations.[5]

Although the *affluent* as a group frequently tend to agree with average Americans about public policy, we will see that the *truly wealthy* often disagree markedly. And the wealthy frequently get their way, especially in preventing policy changes that majorities of Americans favor. Money counts in politics. It makes sense that big money counts most.[6]

The Flood of Money in U.S. Elections

One of the chief ways for wealthy individuals to influence political outcomes is to contribute money to election campaigns. Contributions can enable wealthy-friendly candidates to run. Withholding money can discourage candidates who are seen as threatening to the wealthy from running. Money can also grab candidates' attention and shape their priorities. It can help wealthy-friendly candidates win office and can shape their behavior once they get there.

U.S. elections are awash in money from affluent contributors. A striking state-level example comes from Wisconsin.

RESHAPING WISCONSIN POLITICS. Throughout the twentieth century, Wisconsin had a strong tradition of Populist, Progressive politics, including strong support for public education, workers' rights, and progressive taxation. Along with its upper-midwestern neighbor Minnesota, Wisconsin was long seen as one of the bedrocks of progressive populism in the United States.[7] While this tradition is still alive in Minnesota, a stark reversal recently occurred in Wisconsin—a reversal that coincided with the governorship of Republican Scott Walker and an influx of cash from wealthy Wisconsinite and out-of-state conservative donors.

In 2010, America was mired in recession and Republicans were making gains in Washington and throughout the country. Walker was elected governor of Wisconsin along with a Republican majority in the state legislature. Once in office, he gained national notoriety for his proposed cuts to education spending and state aid to local governments, and especially for his swift and aggressive attacks on public employee unions. Protests erupted. Walker's opponents collected a million signatures (in a state with about four million eligible voters) to force a recall election.[8]

National conservative donors saw the 2012 recall election as a referendum on antiunion politics. They rose to the challenge, contributing enormous sums to Walker's campaign. *Reportable* contributions included $500,000 from Texas home builder Bob Perry and $250,000 each from Amway executive Richard DeVos of Michigan and casino magnate Sheldon Adelson of Nevada.[9] It is important to point out that reportable contributions exclude anonymous "dark money" contributions (unreported sums from unidentified donors). During a legal investigation into whether the Wisconsin Club for Growth (a free-market advocacy organization that spent millions on Walker's behalf) illegally coordinated with the Walker campaign, journalists uncovered $1,500,000 in dark money contributions from billionaire John Menard Jr. It is impossible to know how many other dark money contributions were made or in what amounts, but the size of Menard's donations, and the extensive national coverage that the recall campaign received, suggest that other big contributions may still be hidden.[10]

All told, about $60 million was raised to help keep Walker in office—almost three times as much as the backers of the recall were able to muster.[11] Sixty percent of the pro-Walker money came from out-of-state donors. After a nasty campaign filled with deceptive ads, Walker prevailed, retaining his governorship with 53 percent of the vote.

In the following years, Walker successfully pursued a series of policies that were largely at odds with the wishes of most Wisconsin citizens. In addition to legislation that essentially banned collective bargaining for public employees, he signed a "right to work" law hampering both private- and public-sector unions and a "voter ID" law that members of the Republican state party have admitted to using for their partisan political advantage.[12] He pushed for dramatic spending cuts, including the slashing of education funding, and he rejected federal funds to expand Medicaid as part of the Affordable Care Act.[13] Despite its unpopularity in Wisconsin, conservative donors see Walker's antiunion legislation as a model that they hope to pass in other states and even nationally.[14]

Similar changes have been pursued in Illinois,[15] Michigan, Ohio, Kansas, North Carolina, and elsewhere, often with striking successes for wealthy donors.

THE NATIONAL DELUGE OF CASH. Since the 1980s, political campaigns have become vastly more expensive. The costs of media advertising have skyrocketed. Professional pollsters and consultants charge high fees. Many of the campaign volunteers previously supplied by unions, churches, and other civic organizations have been replaced by paid campaign workers.

As a result, running for office now depends less than it used to on the support of large numbers of citizens and more on large numbers of dollars. Successful candidates for national office must first be successful fund-raisers.

At the national level, during the 2012 election cycle a total of $6.3 billion—that is more than *six thousand* million dollars—was spent by political parties, candidates, and supposedly "independent" groups to try to win elections. This amount easily set an all-time record for political spending in the United States—a record broken in 2016, in which early estimates placed total spending at just over $6.9 billion.[16] After adjusting for inflation, three times as much money was spent on congressional elections in 2012 as in 1980.[17] (See figure 4.2.) U.S. spending on elections is unmatched in the rest of the world. No other country comes close.

More important, perhaps, than the high cost of running for office is where the money comes from. In the United States, these vast sums of money come from *private* contributions rather than from the government, as is common in other countries.[18] This means that

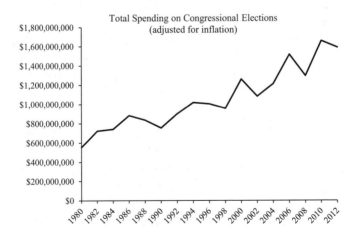

FIGURE 4.2 Congressional election spending has increased.

Spending for U.S. House and Senate races in constant 2016 dollars.
Source: Ornstein et al. 2017.

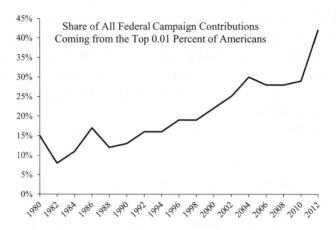

FIGURE 4.3 More campaign dollars come from the biggest donors.

Source: Bonica et al. 2013.

U.S. politicians are more dependent on private donors—especially the wealthy.

As figure 4.3 shows, large donations from a tiny, extremely wealthy fraction of the American population have provided a larger and larger part of the money spent in national campaigns. In the 1980s, about 10 percent of all campaign spending came from one-tenth of one-tenth of 1 percent (0.01 percent) of the voting age population. By 2012, more than 40 percent of spending came from this tiny sliver of wealthy Americans.[19] Observers often fret that only six out of ten eligible voters turn out for presidential elections, and only four out of ten for off-year elections. But when it comes to money, an increasingly large proportion comes from a minuscule stratum of superrich contributors.

The Internet has revolutionized small-donor fund-raising by political candidates, leading some people to hope that the dominance of big-money donors may be coming to an end. Bernie Sanders is the most recent high-profile candidate to build a campaign based largely on small donations from millions of individual donors. In his 2016 primary race, more than 60 percent of Sanders's money came from donors giving less than $200 each (compared with only about 20 percent of the money for his Democratic primary opponent, Hillary Clinton).[20] Relying on small contributions, Sanders

managed to nearly equal Clinton's direct campaign fund-raising total during the primaries. True, Clinton benefited from a $97 million
advantage over Sanders in super PAC and other *outside* spending,
giving her a substantial financial advantage overall.[21] Nevertheless,
Sanders showed that a viable presidential primary race could be run
based on the widespread popular support of small contributors.

As impressive as Sanders's (and, earlier, Barack Obama's) small-
donor fund-raising was, most of the money in federal elections still
comes from the "fat cats." In 2012, only 6 percent of all the money
spent trying to get Mitt Romney elected president came from campaign contributions of less than $200. The Obama campaign—
which liked to boast about the large *number* of small contributions
it received (but not about how much money that added up to)—
relied almost as heavily on big contributions. For team Obama, only
20 percent of spending came from campaign contributions of less
than $200—about three times as high a proportion as Romney's,
but still a small part of overall spending.[22] Indeed, in 2012 the combined contributions of the 3.7 million small donors to the Obama
and Romney campaigns amounted to less than the total contributions of the 159 largest individual super PAC contributors.[23]

In recent elections, the wealthiest Americans—unleashed by
court decisions that have overthrown limits on contributions to organizations that claim to be "independent" of particular campaigns
(even if they openly promote candidates)[24]—have opened their wal-
lets. Wealthy contributors have poured large sums of money into
super PACs and so-called social welfare organizations that are not
required to disclose their contributors.

Most of the political money from wealthy Americans goes to
Republicans (although Democrats have their billionaire donors
too, as we discuss subsequently). Billionaire Sheldon Adelson—
whose fortune comes mostly from gambling casinos in Las Vegas,
Macao, and elsewhere—spent tens of millions of dollars on Newt
Gingrich, a candidate for the 2012 Republican Party nomination
for president who shared Adelson's hawkishly pro-Israel foreign
policy views and his enthusiasm for minimal government at home.
Adelson's money kept Gingrich's campaign alive long after Gingrich had sunk from sight in the polls, affecting political discourse

and probably harming Romney's chances in the general election. (In 2016, Adelson became a major funder of Donald Trump.) Similarly, billionaire Foster Friess in 2012 gave over $2 million to the Republican primary campaign of extreme social conservative Rick Santorum, apparently keeping Santorum loudly campaigning and promoting his favorite issues long after polls indicated that Santorum had little appeal to most voters.[25] Our campaign financing system seems to be out of kilter when a few individuals such as Adelson and Friess can exert so much influence over our electoral process.

THE "KOCH NETWORK." The champion funders in recent U.S. elections, however—and the biggest individual players in American politics—have been the billionaire brothers Charles and David Koch (pronounced "Coke"), who have put together an extensive network of wealthy conservative donors. The Kochs amassed much of their wealth in the not-always-clean oil-refining business: they were hit with several court cases and fines over oil spills, mercury contamination, a deadly butane explosion from corroded pipes, theft of oil from Native American lands (subject of a U.S. Senate investigation), and the release of some 91 metric tons of cancer-causing benzene into the atmosphere. These tangles with government regulators apparently reinforced their antiregulatory, antitax, antigovernment libertarianism. The Kochs particularly object to environmental, safety, or climate-change regulations that could impose costs on the oil industry.[26]

In the late 1970s the Kochs became major funders and directors of various libertarian organizations and publications, including the Cato Institute.[27] In 1980, David Koch almost single-handedly funded the Libertarian Party's national election campaign and ran as its candidate for vice president, on a platform that opposed all income or corporate taxes and called for the abolition of Social Security, Medicare, Medicaid, the Securities and Exchange Commission (SEC), the Environmental Protection Agency (EPA), and even the Federal Bureau of Investigation (FBI) and Central Intelligence Agency (CIA).[28] After the Libertarians won only 1 percent of the vote, however, the Kochs realigned their strategy in a more pragmatic direction, creating a Washington presence and making major donations to Republicans—including Robert Dole's 1996 presidential campaign.

Later, as researchers have documented in detail, the Kochs built an extensive network of conservative donors and multiple inter-related organizations—centered around the political advocacy group Americans for Prosperity—to promote conservative ideas; to reach out to unlikely groups such as Latinos and millennials by offering beer, social events, and issue advocacy; and, most notably, to fund the primary and general election campaigns of conservative Republican candidates. In several cases the Kochs have opposed and defeated popular Republican officeholders they did not con-sider to be conservative enough. In other cases they have identified and groomed new political stars on the right, including Senator Joni Ernst. The Kochs' many state-level organizations, headed by paid professional directors, reach far down into state and local pol-itics: especially into elections for state legislatures, which deal with important issues but are barely visible to most Americans.[29]

Enormous amounts of money are involved. During the 2012 election cycle, the Koch network gave about $400 million to con-servative Republican candidates, almost certainly affecting who got nominated and who got elected.[30] For the 2014 "off-year" (non-presidential) elections, the Kochs again set spending records: a total of about $300 million.[31]

As the election contests of 2015–2016 unfolded, the Kochs re-portedly planned to spend about $900 million—almost one bil-lion dollars.[32] They did some rethinking when Donald Trump—definitely not a Koch-style libertarian—emerged as the presumptive Republican presidential nominee. The Kochs mostly abandoned the presidential contest and focused on other races, including a highly successful effort to help preserve Republican control of the U.S. Senate with a last-minute blitz of ad money.[33] But Trump's cab-inet appointments and early policy actions appeared to give the Koch brothers the last laugh on the presidential level, as well: they saved money while still getting a shot at many of the policies they wanted.[34]

Researchers have argued that the total budget of the Koch network is so vast, and its political reach so deep, that the network now actually rivals the national Republican Party organization itself. When the two have clashed, the Kochs have been known to win. A comparison: the Democracy Alliance, a roughly comparable but much less tightly organized group of wealthy Democrats, is far smaller.[35]

THE PUZZLES AND SURPRISES OF 2016. In the 2016 elections, several surprises shocked the political establishments of both parties. No doubt there were many factors that combined to make this a most unusual election. We will focus on money, which we believe played a critical role.

For starters, a puzzle: why did so many active candidates—at least sixteen of them—enter the messy, divisive race for the Republican nomination? Why did so many of them stay in the race so long? And why did Donald Trump, the brash outsider, emerge victorious over all the rest?

The sheer *number* of Republican candidates may not really be much of a puzzle. In 2016, as in 2012, each of the Republican candidates had at least one or two billionaire supporters who made it possible for them to run. Big contributions were sufficient to keep several of those candidates in the race even after they had lost badly in early primaries.

But why did Trump beat all the others, even though most of the big-money contributors—and most Republican think-tankers and officeholders—supported other candidates? Of course Trump benefited from a divided opposition, from his celebrity status, and from his ability to grab and hold the limelight. But we believe there is more to it than that.

One clue: of all the candidates, only the bombastic billionaire Trump had enough money of his own to be independent (at least initially) of large contributions from others. Only Trump, therefore, could defy Republican orthodoxy without fear that his funding would dry up. Contrary to the usual party line at the time, Trump declared that he would protect Social Security and Medicare benefits. That he would tax hedge fund managers and other financial "paper-pushers" at the same rates as everyone else.[36] That he would create many jobs through massive spending on infrastructure. That he would avoid costly foreign wars. Repeatedly and emphatically, Trump declared that he would act against high levels of immigration and would renegotiate trade agreements that had undercut Americans' wages.

Each of those stands was highly popular among rank-and-file Republicans, many of whom lived in places that had been hard-hit by competition from Chinese imports, and many of whom had come to resent immigrants—especially Mexican immigrants—for reasons both economic and social.[37] Yet Trump's positions were anathema to wealthy Republican donors, nearly all of whom wanted to cut Social Security spending; to avoid "wasteful" infrastructure boondoggles; to reduce taxes on high-income people; to facilitate immigration of low-cost workers; and to enjoy unregulated international trade and capital mobility. Trump's positions went directly contrary to the views of wealthy donors and wealthy Americans generally. They directly contradicted the Republican orthodoxy articulated by Washington think tanks and acted on by nearly all Republican officeholders.

The other Republican presidential hopefuls generally avoided even rhetorical nods to such positions. They stuck closely to the orthodoxy. All of them—from hard-line social conservative (and party-activist favorite) Ted Cruz, to the establishment-anointed Jeb Bush, Scott Walker, and Marco Rubio, to social conservatives Mike Huckabee and Rick Santorum, to libertarian Rand Paul, to the allegedly "moderate" John Kasich, to the "outsiders" Carly Fiorina and Ben Carson, to Newt Gingrich, Rick Perry, and Bobby Jindal—all of them, despite differences in personal images and ideological labels, adhered closely to the orthodox Republican positions. All favored free trade; tight limits on government spending; high-end tax cuts; economic deregulation; hawkish, neoconservative foreign policy (with one exception);[38] and (more quietly) "entitlement reform": that is, cuts in Social Security and Medicare.

It is hard to know exactly what was in the hearts, minds, or political calculations of these Republican candidates. But the most plausible explanation for why they all took so many stands that were unpopular with Republican voters was that major Republican donors insisted on it. Only Trump broke away from what was essentially a wealth-enforced orthodoxy. Trump, appealing directly and emotionally to the Republican voter "base," overwhelmed his opponents.

But that helps clear up only one of the puzzles of 2016. On the Democratic side, why did front-runner Hillary Clinton— tremendously knowledgeable, experienced and energetic, and potentially a history maker (the first woman to have a serious shot at the U.S. presidency)—not coast comfortably to win the Democratic nomination? Why did little-known, seventy-two-year-old, democratic socialist Senator Bernie Sanders win so many caucuses and primaries and come so close to beating Clinton? And why, even though Sanders and most of his supporters rallied to her side, did Clinton—to the utter shock of most Democrats—lose the general election to the inexperienced, fact-challenged, trash-talking Trump?

There were many reasons. They included Clinton's perceived lack of personal warmth, her various missteps and scandals, and meddling by "fake news" purveyors,[39] Russian hackers, and even the director of the FBI. Many observers believe that Clinton's loss of the electoral vote (she actually won the popular vote) owed much to the latter factors, as well as to the celebrity and communications savvy of Trump and his ability to inflame racial and ethnic resentments[40]—which tend to be linked to the economic resentments we have emphasized. But we believe that *private political money*—money from both Republican and *Democratic* wealthy donors—also played a critical part in the downfall of Clinton and the Democrats.

In the years leading up to 2016, Clinton and establishment Democrats—like most of Trump's establishment Republican opponents—were widely blamed for embracing free-trade agreements and immigration without doing much for those who were hurt economically. They were blamed especially by white, non-college-educated men (and quite a few women) and by many people living in the South, in small towns or rural areas, or in the midwestern rust belt, where many manufacturing jobs had been wiped out.[41]

Sanders's primary election successes provided an early warning to Clinton. Sanders sharply attacked the rise in economic inequality and emphasized the damage done to many Americans by free international trade. He advocated such ameliorative measures as more progressive taxes, a much higher minimum wage, subsidized day care, universal health insurance, and relief from student debt. These stands won Sanders a lot of support from Democratic primary voters. As abundant survey data show (recall chapter 3), such policies are also highly popular with the American public more generally, which holds much more "progressive" views on economic matters than many pundits seem to think it does.

By the time of the general election, Clinton had adopted some carefully calibrated (and—to some observers—lukewarm-sounding) versions of Sanders's egalitarian policy stands. (Her heart seemed to be more in the identity politics of women and minorities, which may have helped inflame a new identity politics of white men.[42]) She attempted to adjust her position on trade. But she could not escape her past enthusiastic support for free-trade agreements, including the North American Free Trade Agreement, or NAFTA (enacted when Bill Clinton was president) and the Trans Pacific Partnership, or TPP (which she helped negotiate as part of the Obama administration.) Nor could Clinton escape the perception that she had friendly ties with Wall Street and had for years been receiving lucrative speaking fees from big banks.[43]

Most 2016 Democratic candidates up and down the ticket were stuck with a similar record of backing free trade and relatively open immigration, while not seeming to do a great deal for angry sufferers in the U.S. heartland. Most Democratic candidates did poorly. With Trump in the lead, the Republicans maintained control of both the House and the Senate, while also capturing the presidency with a majority of electoral votes.

Why did so many Democratic political candidates and office-holders take certain positions that were unpopular, not only with most rank-and-file Democrats but also with majorities of Americans generally?

The answer, we believe, is that most Democratic candidates—just like most Republicans—have had to rely heavily on money from wealthy contributors. Wealthy Democratic contributors have tended to be liberal on such matters as the environment, women's issues, and gay rights, but rather conservative on key economic issues including free trade, spending programs, economic regulation of banks, and taxing the wealthy. Most Democratic candidates, like most Republicans, have had to take certain prowealthy stands on policy to get the money needed to run for office.

That created an opening for Donald Trump to break through unpopular policies espoused by the establishments of both parties and to win.

Our point is definitely not that money is everything in politics. The better-funded candidate sometimes loses, as Hillary Clinton herself did. But money is a *big* thing. It clearly does affect election outcomes, and the bigger the money advantage, the better the chances of success.[44] So the donors of big money have substantial power to affect what sorts of people run, what they stand for, and whether they are elected.

Nor are we saying that candidates will adopt whatever policy they think will bring them the largest campaign contributions. Many candidates have strong beliefs and long-standing commitments to particular policies and political outlooks. But the system of private financing of elections has the effect of boosting candidates whose positions appeal to the wealthy. And it leaves those candidates who oppose the preferences of the well-off strongly disadvantaged in the resources that they need to compete for office.

EARLY MONEY AND THE "158 FAMILIES." In politics, "early money" is crucial. It enables candidates to run. Candidates who cannot get early money generally drop out quickly or don't try in the first place.

In the early months of the 2016 election cycle (that is, in the first six months of 2015) nearly *half* of all the money backing a Republican or Democratic presidential candidate—$179 million of it—came from *just 158 families* and the companies they owned or controlled. Each of those families contributed $250,000 or more, mainly to super PACS with no limit on the size of contributions. The vast majority of this money went to Republicans, including the uncompromisingly conservative Ted Cruz and Rick Perry.[45]

To identify these 158 families, a team of investigative reporters had to sort through a mass of documents and penetrate a veil of privacy. (The donors refused to speak to reporters; many donations were made from post-office-box addresses or were passed through limited-liability corporations or trusts.) After the 158 families were identified, it became clear that they constituted "a class apart": white, wealthy, older, and living in exclusive neighborhoods isolated from any plebeian neighbors. Many enjoyed fortunes built up in finance (hedge funds, private equity, venture capital) or energy (oil wildcatting, fracking supplies). Most leaned rightward politically, contributing to candidates who pledged to cut back economic regulations; to cut taxes on high incomes, capital gains, and estates; and to shrink entitlement programs.

One observer commented that these donors represented a "countervailing force" to "the way the actual voters of the country are evolving and the policies they want."[46]

STEALTH POLITICS BY BILLIONAIRES. An overwhelming majority of billionaires make political donations, but only a few choose to share their political views with the public. A thorough web search has revealed that nearly three-quarters of America's one hundred wealthiest billionaires said nothing whatsoever, over a ten-year period, about the specifics of federal tax policy. Almost all were entirely silent about Social Security policy.[47]

It's hard to know what individuals think about politics when they do not openly express their views. But our surveys of multimillionaires (described later in this chapter) show that as a group, wealthy Americans tend to be far more conservative on economic policy than the average citizen is. It seems likely that America's billionaires share these multimillionaires' commitments to low taxes and little regulation and their opposition to strengthening Social Security. They would just prefer not to discuss their apparently self-interested preferences in public. Many of them go to great lengths to obscure the financial support they give to politicians and organizations that pursue their conservative economic policy preferences.

Our own collaborative research indicates that several billionaires who have been highly active in politics—including Adelson,

Friess, and the Koch brothers—have engaged in "stealth politics." They have given enormous sums of money to political causes, including donations to organizations with such highly specific policy objectives as abolishing the estate tax or privatizing Social Security. Yet they have said little or nothing in public about the specific policies they are trying to influence.

In this respect, Adelson and the Koch brothers have been fairly typical of the wealthiest U.S. billionaires. Over a ten-year period, David Koch made only one specific statement about tax policy (favoring lower taxes). He said nothing at all about Social Security. Charles Koch said nothing on either topic. The Koch brothers just spoke vaguely about the need for "economic freedom."

Similarly, Sheldon Adelson made only one statement about tax policy (in favor of lower taxes) and no specific statements at all about Social Security. Adelson tended to offer vague but ideologically charged remarks about public policy such as the following, from a *Forbes* interview:

> What scares me is the continuation of the socialist-style economy we've been experiencing for almost four years. That scares me because the redistribution of wealth is the path to more socialism, and to more of the government controlling people's lives. What scares me is the lack of accountability that people would prefer to experience, just let the government take care of everything and I'll go fish or I won't work, etc."[48]

The public silence of most billionaires contrasts markedly with the willingness of a small, unusual group of billionaires—including Michael Bloomberg, Warren Buffett, and Bill Gates—to speak out about specific public policies. It is striking that these three billionaires have taken positions on these economic issues that are relatively centrist or even liberal (and closer to what surveys show that most Americans think). All three have favored a substantial social safety net, progressive taxes, and moderate regulation of the economy. An ordinary American who tried to judge what U.S. billionaires think and do about politics by listening to Bloomberg, Buffett, or Gates would be badly misled.

The practice of "stealth politics" raises questions that go beyond the general issue of unequal, money-based political influence. Stealth politics also weaken *political accountability*. Stealthy billionaires can quietly use their money to promote ideas that are narrowly self-interested and in conflict with the views of most ordinary citizens. By remaining largely silent about their views and obscuring their financial contributions, billionaires can fly under the radar—promoting policies that most citizens reject but drawing little attention.

Of course we cannot and should not force billionaires—or anyone else—to publicly reveal their political preferences. But we can require that all major political *spending*—including dark money spending—be disclosed. Billionaires and others active in politics should not be allowed to obscure their spending through trusts, limited liability corporations, and nonreporting "social welfare" organizations.

THE DEMOCRATS' BILLIONAIRES. As we have mentioned, in most election cycles most of the political money from wealthy Americans goes to Republicans. In 2011–2012, for example, two-thirds of the wealthiest billionaires who made partisan contributions that were reported to the Federal Election Commission (FEC) contributed primarily or exclusively to Republicans.[49]

The outpouring of election money from wealthy individuals to the Republicans tends to push the outcomes of elections in a conservative direction—especially in low-salience, low-turnout elections such as party primaries and contests for state legislatures. The rise of the Tea Party faction of the Republican Party in Congress and state legislatures, for example, owes a great deal to the Koch brothers. The direction of the partisan tilt caused by money power is important, and such a tilt would be undemocratic and disturbing no matter which party it advantaged. But a different (and perhaps even larger) concern is that *both* parties are profoundly affected, in an undemocratic way, by reliance on donations of private money.

Billionaires' money is important to Democrats too. The Democrats get about one-third of the total amount given by extremely wealthy Americans. And they have their own key billionaire supporters. The Democrats' billionaires can generally be called "liberal" on certain issues. They are nearly always liberal on women's issues; lesbian, gay, bisexual, and transgender (LGBT) rights, and nondiscrimination against African Americans, for example— probably more so than most Americans. They are often liberal on environmental policy and fairly often on help for poor people.

But wealthy Democratic donors are much less liberal concerning certain other policies that would be important for ameliorating high-end economic inequality, such as high progressive taxes on the wealthy; strict economic regulations, especially of the financial sector; prioritizing government spending over deficit reduction; and compensating losers from international trade. Some big democratic donors just do not care much about such matters. Others actually embrace much the same conservative economic policies that nearly all wealthy Republican donors favor. This attitude has the effect of nudging some of the economic policy stands of Democratic politicians to the right of where surveys show that rank-and-file Democrats—and Americans as a whole—would like them to be.

George Soros, for example, a major funder for Democrats in a number of elections, is unusually liberal (for a billionaire) on a number of issues. But his core concerns focus on foreign policy: opposing what he sees as reckless U.S. uses of force abroad and upholding civil liberties, the rule of law, and education in ex-communist and developing countries. Soros is by no means a champion of economic equality. He understandably feels that the U.S. economic system has been good to him, and he does not want to overhaul it.

Eric Schmidt of Google, known for his ubiquity in Democratic Party gatherings during the Obama administration, has been a leading voice for "innovation," for the unleashing of smart and creative people to do their stuff. No harm to that; an exciting idea. But the innovation perspective, which has been warmly embraced—along with Silicon Valley campaign contributions—by many Democratic politicians, tends to favor unfettered markets over economic regulation. And it tends to celebrate inequality (wonderful that creative people get such rich rewards!) rather than worry about it. It pushes the Democrats toward highly educated professional supporters, away from their former working-class base.[50]

Haim Saban, known as "Team Clinton's favorite billionaire," was a major contributor (of more than $20 million) and fundraiser in Hillary Clinton's 2016 campaign; he enjoyed friendly, unobstructed e-mail access to Clinton's top aides. Saban has called himself a "one-issue guy" (referring to Israel), which meshes well with Clinton's hawkishly pro-Israel approach to the Middle East. As chair of Univision, Saban is also attuned to the social and cultural (though not so much the economic) concerns of Latinos. But his $3.6 billion private equity fortune has not led him to become a crusader against economic inequality or for higher taxes on the wealthy.[51]

Hedge fund billionaire Tom Steyer, a crucial Democratic donor, appears to be an exception. In the past he focused heavily on environmental issues (he founded NextGen Climate, a political advocacy group working for environmental protection), but recently Steyer has also begun initiatives, including the "Fair Shake" commission, to address economic inequality.[52] Steyer, who made a $1.6 billion fortune in hedge funds, was the largest single contributor—excluding unreported dark money—to federal races in 2016. All of his $67 million in contributions went to Democrats.

The broader pattern, however, is that a number of rather economically conservative, wealthy individuals have continued to support the Democrats despite the general "right turn" of American business since the 1970s.[53] These supporters include heavyweights from capital-intensive, internationally oriented businesses including New York investment banking, Silicon Valley high-tech firms, and New York and Los Angeles entertainment and communications businesses. The "Goldman Sachs" investment-banker wing of the Democratic Party has supplied several recent secretaries of the treasury for Democratic administrations, including Robert Rubin, Lawrence Summers, and their associate Timothy Geithner. (Another treasury secretary, Jacob Lew, had been chief operating officer of Citigroup.) These officials, with close ties to the finance industry, have tended to shape economic policy in ways contrary to the wishes of liberal Democrats—nixing Bill Clinton's idea of a middle-class tax cut, for example, and downsizing Barack Obama's 2009 economic stimulus plan.[54]

People in the top 1 percent of wealth holders (that is, people who have about $10 million or more in net worth), like the top billionaires, tilt their contributions toward the Republicans by about two to one. But these multimillionaire 1-percenters are an important source of cash for the Democrats too. Individually, their political contributions come nowhere close to what billionaires can give, but there are many more 1-percenters than there are billionaires. The money adds up.[55]

Perhaps equally important to the Democratic Party have been hundreds of thousands of still smaller financial contributions from upper-middle-class professional people, including college teachers, lawyers, doctors, high-tech engineers, and computer experts. These professionals tend to be quite liberal on sociocultural issues such as civil rights for minorities, women's rights, gay rights, and civil liberties, but less so on equality-related economic issues such as progressive taxation.

In recent years, as substantial numbers of socially conservative working-class Americans have defected to the Republican Party, higher-income professional people have become a major part of the "base" of the Democratic Party. In 2012, for example, 55 percent of Americans with postgraduate degrees voted Democratic, while a majority of college graduates voted for the Republican presidential candidate.[56] In 2016, the Democratic share of highly educated (mostly high-income) people was even higher, while most whites without college degrees abandoned the Democratic Party.[57]

Some Democratic officials and party activists have seemed quite happy to raise money from a few multimillionaires and billionaires plus a large cadre of upper-middle-class professionals. They rejoiced that doing so made it possible to stay more or less financially competitive with the Republicans in several recent elections. Some, therefore, seemed to be complacent about our system of private financing of election campaigns. But such a view ignored serious problems for their party that came crashing down on them in 2016.

First, taken as a whole, the outpouring of private money in elections is a sure loser for the Democrats. Millionaires and billionaires tilt heavily Republican. Second, most of the wealthy or affluent Americans who *have* tended to support the Democrats have viewpoints that do not align with the labor unions and working-class

Americans who once formed the core of Franklin Roosevelt's New Deal coalition. This difference in perspective has affected what the party stands for, in ways that have turned off many traditionally Democratic voters. As a result, many working-class people (especially less-educated white males) have been moving more and more Republican.[58]

We see these big problems of the Democrats—and much of the current turmoil and infighting within the Republican Party as well—as traceable to a tension between the need for big-money contributions and the need to appeal to ordinary voters. At the time we are writing, both parties are struggling to figure out what to do about this conflict. We have no crystal ball to predict what they will do. But it seems clear that private political money is a major problem for democracy in the United States.

The Corruption of American Politics

We believe that *both* major parties tend to be corrupted—and pushed away from satisfying the needs and wishes of ordinary Americans—by their reliance on wealthy contributors. We see this reliance as one of the major reasons for today's feeble state of democratic responsiveness. It is one of the main reasons that so many Americans are so angry at politicians. No wonder most Americans tell pollsters that public officials "don't care much what people like me think."[59]

When we say that both parties are "corrupted" by political money, we do not mean that public officials are regularly *bribed*, in quid pro quo ("this for that") exchanges of money for policy. Such bribery is a criminal offense. Spectacular examples do occur. Representative Randy Cunningham was caught taking lavish gifts in return for government contracts. About $90,000 in cash—given in return for promoting high-tech business abroad—was found in Representative William Jefferson's freezer. But outright bribery of federal government officials is probably very uncommon.[60]

Much more pervasive is a broad pattern of undue influence that amounts to *systemic* corruption. According to legal scholar Lawrence Lessig, an institution such as Congress is corrupted when

key individuals within it are subject to an "improper or conflicting *dependency*."[61] U.S. officials are clearly *dependent* on private
money. Members of Congress spend an enormous amount of time
raising campaign funds, in order to fend off opponents and get
reelected. (In his wry preretirement "Confessions," Representative
Steve Israel estimated that he had spent roughly 4,200 hours in
"call time," whispering sweet nothings to potential donors; that
he had attended about 1,600 fund-raisers for his own campaigns;
and that he had raised nearly $20 million per election cycle.[62]) This
means that officials are pulled away from doing the public's business by the need to spend time and energy soliciting money and
pleasing major donors—especially since those donors tend to steer
the conversation toward topics far from the concerns of most citizens, such as hedge fund managers' cherished "carried interest" tax
break. As Lessig gently puts it, officials may develop "the wrong
sensibilities."[63]

We would add that the flood of private money corrupts the U.S.
policy-making process in another sense as well: it *affects what sorts
of officials are elected* in the first place.[64] It gives us public officials
whose values, experiences, economic interests, and policy preferences often diverge from those of the citizens they are supposed to
represent. Research has shown that—despite the availability of numerous well-qualified Americans with blue-collar backgrounds—
hardly any U.S. officials have had working-class experience. Nearly
all are "white collar"—that is, fairly affluent, mostly professionals
or businesspeople. They tend to think and vote quite differently
from the few officials who do have working-class backgrounds.
One example: a majority of members of Congress now have a net
worth of more than a million dollars.[65]

The Founders of the United States held strict views about corruption. For example, the "gifts rule" in the U.S. Constitution flatly
prohibits any official from receiving any gift from a foreign government without the approval of Congress. The golden, diamond-
encrusted snuffbox that Benjamin Franklin received from King
Louis at the end of his ambassadorship to France stirred up an
enormous fuss. No one thought Franklin had been bribed. But
they worried that the "intimate obligations" arising from such gifts

might cloud his judgment about French actions. Would Franklin (perhaps unconsciously) hesitate to say critical things about King Louis after accepting what one historian has called the "most precious treasure" in Franklin's entire estate?[66]

Through the first two hundred years of U.S. history, our people, our leaders, and our courts of law insisted on a broad concept of corruption. They feared the many subtle ways in which politicians might be led to serve private interests at the public's expense. They adopted preventive rules—including limits on the amount of money that could be contributed to political campaigns—that were designed to avoid even any *appearance* of corruption, and designed to change politicians' incentives and behavior by avoiding *temptations* or unconscious *tendencies* to serve private interests rather than the public good.

Unfortunately, however, beginning with the U.S. Supreme Court's *Buckley v. Valeo* decision of 1976, the court has shifted toward an extremely narrow concept of corruption, a concept confined to quid pro quo bribery. And it has severely limited the ways in which Congress is permitted to regulate political money. This shift has undermined the key democratic principle of political equality ("one person, one vote"). It has moved us toward a principle of *one dollar*, one vote.

In the *Citizens United* case of 2010, the Supreme Court went so far as to strike down all limits on *corporate* political expenditures, on the grounds that (1) the expenditure of money for political advertising is a form of "speech" protected by the First Amendment to the Constitution; (2) corporations are just "associations" of people, with the same free speech rights that individuals have; (3) corruption (not political equality) is the only public interest that might justify regulating such speech; and (4) as a matter of federal constitutional law, *corruption* now means only quid pro quo corruption. Justice Anthony Kennedy, writing for the court, declared, "The fact that speakers may have influence over or access to elected officials does not mean that these officials are corrupt: Favoritism and influence are not . . . avoidable in representative politics. . . . [A] substantial and legitimate reason . . . to make a contribution to one candidate over another is that the candidate will respond by producing those political outcomes the supporter favors. Democracy is premised on responsiveness."[67]

In short, in the recent view of a majority of justices on the U.S. Supreme Court, democratic responsiveness need not mean responding to all citizens equally. It can mean responding unequally, giving special weight to people or corporations that spend large amounts of money.

In a later chapter we will have more to say about this constitutional doctrine—which we view as mistaken and destructive of democracy—and how it might be overturned.

But what effect does all this have on public policy? What do wealthy Americans want from government? And *what do they get* in return for the money they invest in politics?

What Wealthy Americans Want from Government

As best we can tell from their contributions to political candidates and issue-oriented groups, most American billionaires tend to be conservative on economic issues. Most of them favor limited social spending, relatively low taxes on upper-income people, and only modest (if any) government regulation of the economy.[68]

We actually have better information, however, about *multimillionaires*: people in the top 1 or 2 percent of U.S. wealth holders, who have a net worth around $10 million or more. This information comes from a small but statistically representative, Chicago-area study known as SESA—the Survey of Economically Successful Americans. SESA allows us to compare multimillionaires' political opinions and actions to those of ordinary Americans.[69]

At the time of the SESA survey in 2011, the United States was still struggling to recover from the financial crash and Great Recession of 2007–2009. We were still suffering from severe wage losses and high levels of unemployment. At that time, most Americans thought that the "biggest problem facing the country" was a lack of *jobs* and good wages. But to a large plurality of the SESA multimillionaires, the biggest problem was *budget deficits* or excessive government spending.[70] This was a peculiar choice, given that inflation—the main danger thought to arise from deficits—was nowhere on the horizon; the economy was too slack to produce any upward pressure on prices. Perhaps it reflected not so much a worry about deficits in themselves but rather a general dislike of government spending and distaste for paying the taxes needed to fund government programs. Either way, the multimillionaires did not share the job worries of most Americans.

Some striking contrasts between the policy preferences of the SESA multimillionaires and the preferences of average Americans are shown in table 4.1. For example, 68 percent of a national sample of Americans, but only 43 percent of the multimillionaires, said that government must see that no one is without "food, clothing and shelter."

Several of the biggest differences in opinion concern policies to help with jobs and wages, a crucial matter for many Americans. At the time of the SESA study, fully two thirds of Americans were saying that the federal government ought to "see to it that everyone [who wants to work] can find a job," but only one-fifth of the wealthy agreed. More than three-quarters of Americans said the minimum wage should be set high enough so that no family with a full-time worker falls below the official poverty line, but fewer than half of the SESA multimillionaires said the same.[71] Half of Americans, but fewer than one-quarter of the multimillionaires, wanted to provide "a decent standard of living" for the unemployed. Remarkably, a majority of the general public said that the federal government should "*provide* [emphasis added] jobs for the unemployed," specifically for everyone able and willing to work who cannot find a job in private employment, while only a tiny 8 percent of the multimillionaires agreed (see table 4.1).

When it came to medical care, a substantial 61 percent majority of the American public favored "national health insurance be financed by tax money," paying for most forms of health care. But only a minority—32 percent—of the wealthy SESA respondents agreed. A solid majority of Americans expressed willingness to "pay more taxes for health coverage for all," but fewer than half of the multimillionaires expressed such willingness (see table 4.1).

There are particularly big disagreements between the wealthy and average Americans about Social Security, our largest and most

TABLE 4.1 Policy preferences of multimillionaires vs. average citizens

	Percent in favor		
	All citizens	Multimillionaires	Difference
Jobs and incomes			
Government should see to food, clothing and shelter	68	43	−25
Minimum wage should be above the poverty line	78	40	−38
Increase the earned income tax credit	49	13	−36
Government should see to it that everyone can find a job	68	19	−49
Government should provide jobs for the unemployed	53	8	−45
Provide a decent standard of living for the unemployed	50	23	−27
Health care			
National health insurance financed by tax money	61	32	−29
Willing to pay more taxes for health coverage for all	59	41	−18
Retirement pensions			
Expand Social Security	55	3	−52
Social Security should ensure minimum standard of living	68	55	−13
Raise the cap on income subject to Soc. Sec. payroll tax	60	47	−13
Education			
Spend whatever is necessary for really good public schools	87	35	−52
Government should make sure everyone can go to college	78	28	−50
More government investment in worker retraining	57	30	−27
Economic regulation (% answering "more" minus % answering "less")			
More federal government regulation needed of:			
Wall Street firms	(+45)	(+18)	−27
Oil industry	(+50)	(+5)	−45
Health insurance industry	(+26)	(+4)	−22
Big corporations	(+33)	(−20)	−53
Taxes			
Rely a lot on corporate income taxes	62	38	−24
Government reduce differences between high and low incomes	46	17	−29
Reduce inequality by heavy taxes on the rich	52	17	−35

Sources: Survey of Economically Successful Americans (SESA) Chicago-area study of multimillionaires; various national opinion surveys of the general public. See Page, Bartels, and Seawright 2013.

popular domestic program: 55 percent of all Americans, but only a bare 3 percent of multimillionaires, favored expanding the program. A remarkable contrast. A solid majority of Americans (60 percent) also favored raising the cap on income subject to Social Security payroll taxes. (At the time, no income over $107,000 was taxed. Raising or eliminating the cap would be a promising way to improve Social Security's finances while reducing income inequality.) But fewer than half of the multimillionaires (47 percent) agreed with raising the cap (see table 4.1).

On education, wealthy and average Americans agreed that we have a problem and that something needs to be done about it. But wealthy Americans are much more reluctant than other Americans to spend tax money for public schools or for defraying college costs—both of which seem crucial to advancing equal opportunity and the American Dream. A whopping 87 percent of a national sample of Americans said that the federal government should spend "whatever is necessary" to ensure that all children have "really good public schools" they can go to. But—tellingly—only 35 percent of the SESA multimillionaires said the same. (Many wealthy people, including President Trump's secretary of education, Betsy DeVos, favor privatization of public schools. Many went to private schools themselves.) Fully 78 percent of the public said that the federal government "should make sure everyone can go to college" who wants to do so, but only 28 percent of the wealthy agreed. The multimillionaires were also much less favorable than other Americans toward devoting resources to worker retraining or early childhood education (see table 4.1).

On economic regulation, the wealthy SESA respondents were less supportive than average Americans of tightening the regulation of Wall Street firms or the health insurance industry, and much less supportive of tighter regulation of the oil industry or "big corporations" generally (see table 4.1.)

On tax policy, the SESA multimillionaires were much less eager to say that government should rely a lot on *corporate* income taxes, and (not surprisingly) less enthusiastic about government "redistribut[ing] wealth by heavy taxes on the rich." Not shown in table 4.1: when multimillionaires were asked exactly what tax rates they favored on top-bracket incomes, on capital gains, and on large estates, their average responses resembled the low actual rates that prevailed at the time of the survey. But most Americans favored closing loopholes, raising federal income taxes on people who make more than $200,000 per year, and imposing higher taxes on large estates than the wealthy SESA respondents favored.

These are big disagreements.

We cannot be certain that the Chicago-area multimillionaires held exactly the same opinions as multimillionaires in the nation as a whole. But we suspect that they probably did not differ dramatically from the national average, which would include wealthy people from Seattle and Silicon Valley (possibly more liberal than the Chicagoans) as well as from Dallas and Atlanta (perhaps more conservative). Only a national survey will enable us to tell for sure.

Meanwhile, our data on the opinions of the merely "affluent" top 20 percent of U.S. income earners, from hundreds of representative national surveys, are suggestive. The affluent differ less sharply from the general public than the truly wealthy do, but the *patterns* of differences are similar. On a number of important economic issues involving jobs, wages, income redistribution, taxes, and economic regulation, affluent Americans hold significantly more conservative opinions than the average American does.[72]

Since affluent and wealthy Americans have more political influence than other Americans, these preference gaps between the wealthy and everyone else indicate that U.S. public policy is systematically shifted away from what most Americans want on important issues of public policy, especially economic and social welfare policy. What wealthy Americans want—and what they get—from government is often quite different from the relatively progressive economic policies that most Americans want.[73]

Techniques of Influence by the Wealthy

We have emphasized money's role in elections. Campaign contributions make a big difference: they help recruit politicians with wealthy-friendly policy agendas to run for office, enable them to campaign, and help them win. Big election money also catches the attention of candidates and tends to tilt their priorities.

But money matters *between* elections as well. Wealthy Americans can exert political influence in many ways. These include *contacting and persuading* officials who hold office (especially those the wealthy helped elect) to pursue policies that wealthy contributors want and defeat policies they oppose; *shaping opinion* among elites and the general public, so that others in society help push for—or at least go along with—government policies that the wealthy want; and *mobilizing outside pressure* on officials through real or artificial "grassroots" campaigns.

GIVING MONEY TO PARTIES AND CANDIDATES. For wealthy individuals, the most important influence technique is probably making financial contributions to election campaigns. As we have noted, most of the one hundred wealthiest U.S. billionaires are extremely active at giving money to political parties and candidates.

Millionaires obviously have less money to invest in politics than billionaires do, but they too are very active. Two-thirds of the SESA multimillionaires said they had given money to a party or candidate or other political cause in the last three or four years. On average they reported giving $4,633, a substantial amount that would be way beyond the reach of the average American. Many (about one-fifth) also solicited or "bundled" contributions from others.[74]

How, exactly, might financial contributions affect public policy? Research has indicated that members of Congress do not generally cast roll call votes contrary to their party loyalties or their ideological stands in response to heavy PAC contributions.[75] Money can "buy time" from legislators—win their attention and get them to step up their activity[76]—but it seldom pushes them into switching sides. Instead, the big effects of money giving mostly involve *getting friendly officials elected* and *getting access* to officials once they are in office.

It is well established that money has important effects on election outcomes. Little-known challengers, for example, have little hope of defeating incumbent officials unless they can spend a lot of money to get name recognition and make contact with voters.

The effect of campaign money on the kinds of public officials we get is probably strongest in primary elections that choose the candidates who will come before the voters in November. In low-visibility, low-turnout primaries, early money is crucial for hiring staff, getting favorable media attention, making contact with voters, and getting supporters to the polls. Within *both* parties, Republican and Democratic, donors can strongly influence what kinds of choices (or nonchoices) the voters will get in the general election. Within both parties, candidates who are friendly to millionaires and billionaires—or at least broadly acceptable to them—have the best chance of making it through to the general election.

To be sure, Bernie Sanders's reliance on small donors in 2016 suggests that success in the "money primary" may not always be crucial—at least not for the right candidate at the right time. It is more likely to be true, however, in high-profile presidential races than in comparatively obscure primaries for the U.S. Congress or for state legislatures.

A more subtle point is that the potential candidates who can even *think* seriously about running for office are limited to those who can raise large sums of money. It generally makes sense to run only if a potential candidate is acceptable to people who can give large amounts of money—if he or she is not too keen on taxing the rich, for example. This point applies to both parties, Democrats as well as Republicans. The need to raise money acts as a sort of *filter* that tends to screen out potential candidates who are unacceptable to wealthy Americans. That is why we compared wealthy campaign funders to Iran's Guardian Council: they have considerable control over election outcomes by controlling what sorts of candidates can mount viable campaigns.

ACCESS TO OFFICIALS. Obtaining *access* to public officials—talking or writing to them and getting favorable attention—is another way in which money giving affects public policy. Access is much easier for big donors.[77] What politician wants to offend those who help him or her win elections? Wealthy people often seek access to important officials regardless of those officials' ideological stands or party affiliations. For that reason, the wealthy often give money to incumbent officials (and likely winners) of various ideological stripes and both political parties—especially to party leaders and the chairs of key committees.

For years, studies of Congress and the executive branch have made clear that gaining access to officials is an important means for trying to influence public policy. If the official already shares a donor's worldview, access can turn into active collaboration about what policies to support and what the details of rules or legislation might be. Excellent access can even lead officials to introduce bills drafted by donors or occasionally to take still stronger personal actions. For example, a filibuster-empowered senator might promise a donor to kill any effort to take away a favorite subsidy or tax break by threatening to talk it to death. This practice has been described as billionaires' "get a senator" strategy.[78]

Even if a donor and an official have serious partisan or ideological disagreements, campaign money can help defuse opposition. So can friendly socializing—giving the official a couple of bottles of whiskey for the holidays (big gifts are now outlawed), sharing a meal, sponsoring an "information-gathering tour" or vacation abroad, inviting (and paying) the official to give a speech, and the like. Friendly contacts can lead to small favors such as a promise to support—or at least not oppose—a bit of low-visibility special legislation that is worth a lot of money to its beneficiaries. And even on highly visible, ideologically charged issues, friendly contacts can help persuade an official to be "moderate" and not go all out for the other side.

It is hard to obtain systematic evidence about political contacts by billionaires. Often no public record exists to tell the tale when a billionaire lunches with a senator or enjoys a quiet White House chat. (Some White House visitors are deliberately omitted from the official public log of daily events.) It is still harder to find out exactly what billionaires say to politicians when they do contact them. But we know from media reports that certain billionaires have regularly gone golfing with presidents or have enjoyed "Renaissance Weekends" with them. It defies credulity to suppose that politically potent people never talk politics between holes on a golf course. Common sense also tells us that if Bill Gates or Warren Buffett calls the White House, someone important—perhaps the president—is likely to answer.[79]

Thanks to the SESA study, we know more details about political contacts by *multimillionaires*. Fully half of the SESA interviewees reported that they had recently initiated one or more contacts with various types of federal government officials: with their own senator, their own House representative, a senator or representative from another district or state, a White House official, an executive department official, or a regulatory agency official. Close to half said they had made two or more contacts with such officials or their staffs within just the previous six months.[80]

Most of the SESA multimillionaires told interviewers the title or position of the official with whom they had had their most important recent contact. Several revealed the officials' names, sometimes indicating that they were on a first-name basis with "Rahm" (Emanuel, then White House Chief of Staff) or "David" (Axelrod, then President Obama's top political adviser.) Such marked closeness to the White House may not be typical; these particular multimillionaires happened to share Chicago as a hometown with several Obama administration officials. But we see no particular reason to think that wealthy Chicagoans would have more contact with members of Congress or regulatory officials than wealthy people in other parts of the country do. Several of the SESA interviewees mentioned that a senator or representative was a "friend" and that they had had lunch or dinner together.[81]

When the SESA multimillionaires were asked an open-ended question about the main purpose of their most important recent contact, most of them reported a specific topic. Many provided a fair amount of detail. Many of them had discussed such broad topics as deficit spending or health care, on which (as we have seen) most wealthy Americans hold different views than average citizens do.

In addition, close to half of the SESA multimillionaires mentioned that they discussed matters that the researchers judged to involve narrow economic self-interest. Their main purpose was "to try to get the Treasury to honor their commitment to extend TARP [Troubled Asset Relief Program] funds to a particular bank in Chicago," or "to better understand the new regulations of the Dodd-Frank Act and how it will affect my business [banking/finance]," or "I own stock in several banks. I was concerned about legislation he was drafting that I think could be harmful for the banks." Some of these wealthy interviewees were undoubtedly pursuing special policy favors that would have been opposed by average Americans.

SHAPING THE CLIMATE OF OPINION. Still another important technique that wealthy Americans can use to influence public policy involves effort to shape the opinions of ordinary citizens, pundits, and policy makers.

In any one case, it is hard to be sure exactly how effective or ineffective such an effort is. But it is clear that efforts at opinion shaping take up a great deal of money and effort from a lot of savvy people—money and effort that they would be unlikely to spend if it were known to be totally wasted. Cumulatively, opinion-shaping efforts have probably had substantial, wealthy-friendly impacts on what Americans think about politics and what policies are adopted.

Relentless efforts to undermine trust and confidence in government, for example, may have helped convinced many citizens that there is no point in even trying to enact policies they want: "Nothing works, anyhow." Lack of trust or confidence in government has proven to be a potent influence on a wide range of political opinions and actions.[82] It has probably contributed to—as well as being partly caused by—the disjunction between actual policy making and the wishes of most Americans.

Political scientists Jacob Hacker and Paul Pierson have examined the history of how the U.S. government (and bipartisan cooperation) played a central role in generating post–World War II prosperity and building a thriving American middle class. This positive role has been forgotten, they argue, as corporate America and the wealthy have turned increasingly against government. Or not exactly forgotten: perhaps expunged from memory by increasingly extreme condemnations of government and glorification of radical individualism and the "free market."[83]

In analyzing opinion-shaping efforts by wealthy corporate elites, it is useful to distinguish between what sociologist G. William Domhoff calls a wealthy-influenced "policy-planning network," which formulates policy alternatives and persuades elites to back them, and an "opinion-shaping network," which targets public opinion.[84]

The policy-planning network brings together philanthropic foundations, universities, think tanks, policy discussion groups, and "blue ribbon" commissions and task forces—all of which tend to feature wealthy individuals and corporate elites among their funders and leaders. Key think tanks and policy discussion groups get about two-thirds of their funding from corporations and wealthy individuals and about one-third from foundations—whose board members tend to be wealthy. These institutions work together to formulate policy ideas, issue reports, and present testimony to Congress.[85]

Historically, these institutions have sometimes represented a relatively liberal bipartisan consensus on such issues as civil rights, the environment, and family planning. Important roles have been played by more or less centrist major foundations including Ford, Gates, Buffett, Hewlett Packard, Rockefeller, and Robert Wood Johnson; and by prominent centrist think tanks such as the Brookings Institution, the Urban Institute, the National Bureau of Economic Research, the RAND Corporation, the Atlantic Institute, and the Center for Strategic and International Studies.[86]

But now the major players in opinion shaping include highly active "ultraconservative" think tanks such as the American Enterprise Institute, the Heritage Foundation, and the Cato Institute, which are mostly funded by corporations and by ultraconservative wealthy individuals.[87] These organizations propagate more ideologically conservative, wealthy-friendly, and often partisan (pro-Republican) views of economic and social welfare policies.

In her eye-opening book about dark money, journalist Jane Mayer has told in detail how a series of multimillionaires and billionaires—Richard Mellon Scaife, John M. Olin, Harry Bradley, Charles and David Koch—founded and funded organizations that played central parts in promoting right-wing ideas that have (especially since 1980 or so) gained great prominence in U.S. political discourse.[88]

Scaife was a pioneer; over the course of fifty years he spent upwards of $1 billion from his family fortune (mostly derived from banking, Gulf oil, and aluminum) on philanthropy. Some $620 million of this was aimed at influencing public affairs.[89] Back in 1964, Scaife founded the Carthage Foundation to fight against what he saw as the country's "liberal drift." By 1973 he had reoriented the Sarah Scaife Foundation toward politics. Scaife became the biggest donor to the conservative American Enterprise Institute, and then the largest backer of the new, ultraconservative Heritage Foundation. By 1980, Heritage had become extremely influential (its bulky *Mandate for Leadership* book was adopted wholesale by the Ronald Reagan administration). Scaife was also an early backer of the libertarian Manhattan Institute, which launched the careers of highly influential welfare critic Charles Murray (*Losing Ground*) and supply-sider George Gilder. A loud message from all these think tanks was that government was "the problem, not the solution"—an idea that took root among many Americans.

Olin too was a pioneer. Way back in 1953, with family money from weapons and chemical manufacturing, he set up the John M. Olin Foundation, aiming to reorient American higher education to the right.[90] He focused on top Ivy League colleges, where Olin grants funded conservative scholars including Allan Bloom, Harvey Mansfield, and Samuel Huntington, and helped mold a whole new generation of conservative thinkers—creating the foundation for opinion shaping to come. At least fifty-six of the eighty-eight Olin fellows at Harvard went on to teach at highly prestigious universities themselves. (One notable faculty fellow was John Yoo, who later wrote the George W. Bush administration's famous Iraq war "torture memo.")

Olin's biggest beachhead was in U.S. law schools, where—during the late 1980s—the Olin Foundation underwrote a remarkable *83 percent* of all the costs of business-friendly "law and economics" programs. Those programs, together with the Federalist Society (which Olin helped start up), have had an enormous conservatizing impact on American lawyers, judges, and courts, including the Supreme Court.[91]

Bradley was a relative latecomer. In the mid-1980s, a lucrative corporate merger (defense contractor Rockwell International bought the Allen-Bradley electronics firm) turned the Lynde and Harry Bradley Foundation into a nonprofit juggernaut. Over the next fifteen years it gave away about $280 million to its favorite conservative causes, including some six hundred fellowships and extensive support for right-wing think tanks and journals. The Bradley Foundation drove the early "school choice" movement, attacking teachers' unions and traditional public schools. It stuck with Charles Murray even after his *Bell Curve* book on blacks' low IQ scores was thoroughly debunked. Generous ($250,000) "Bradley prizes" went to conservative heroes George Will, Bill Kristol, Harvey Mansfield, Roger Ailes, and Ed Meese. Despite Rockwell's heavy dependence on government contracts, the Bradley Foundation financed a movement that ascribed poverty to "dependency" on government handouts—rather than to the paucity of U.S. policies to help victims of forces beyond their control.[92]

We earlier discussed the Koch brothers' outsize role in U.S. elections. But they have also placed high importance on shaping Americans' *ideas*. Back in the mid-1970s, Charles Koch set up the libertarian Cato Institute. Soon the Kochs began establishing conservative beachheads in academia, particularly George Mason University's antitax, antiunion Institute for Humane Studies and its Mercatus Center—which specialized in attacking regulation of the environment or energy. (Mercatus's Wendy Gramm and her senator-husband Phil Gramm played key parts in the deregulation of energy-based and other financial derivatives that later contributed to the 2007–8 financial meltdown.) In 1993, Citizens for a Sound Economy (an organization heavily funded by the Kochs) was instrumental in killing President Clinton's proposed carbon-emissions-reducing energy tax. By 2015, the Charles Koch Foundation had branched out to subsidize probusiness, antiregulatory, and antitax programs at some 307 institutions of higher education.[93]

The most recent manifestation of the Kochs' development and promotion of ideas is a large set of tightly controlled *in-house* organizations linked to the tax-exempt Americans for Prosperity Foundation and the Americans for Prosperity (AFP) advocacy organization. In 2009, AFP and other Koch-funded organizations played a big part in attacking President Obama's economic stimulus program (promoting misleading "studies" that called it a political slush fund) and his health care proposals. Together with Dick Armey's noisier FreedomWorks, AFP quietly promoted the Tea Party rebellion against Obama and mainstream Republicans. As Jane Mayer recounts, AFP was also instrumental in flacking climate-change denial. Koch money joined the DeVos clan's ten-year struggle for the "money is speech," campaign-finance deregulation idea that fed into the 2010 *Citizens United* Supreme Court decision. Similar efforts continue.[94]

THE CURIOUS CASE OF SOCIAL SECURITY. Social Security is the biggest, most popular, and arguably most effective of all federal government programs. As we've seen, the majority of Americans (55 percent) want to expand Social Security, not cut it back, but only a scant 3 percent of the wealthy SESA respondents agree (table 4.1).

We believe that this massive opinion gap is related to a relentless, decades-long campaign to cut or privatize Social Security, waged by certain wealthy individuals and their organizational allies. Their efforts to shape opinion about Social Security have probably succeeded in convincing many affluent Americans, pundits, and politicians. They have also come very close to success at reshaping government policy. At minimum, this campaign has helped prevent the *increases* in Social Security benefits that most Americans want.

How is this possible?

The campaign's leader has been Wall Street billionaire Peter G. Peterson, with wealthy corporate allies who oppose government spending in general, plus bankers and stockbrokers who would love to get lucrative fees for managing private retirement accounts. Peterson and his allies—including the Cato Institute and the Heritage Foundation—have been abetted by amenable academics, pundits, and politicians, and by acquiescent media.[95]

Peterson—who before the rise of the Koch brothers was arguably "the most influential billionaire in U.S. politics"[96]—made his fortune as CEO of Bell & Howell and Lehman Brothers, and from the Blackstone private equity firm. By 2008, *Forbes* magazine calculated Peterson's net worth at $2.8 billion. Along the way Peterson served as secretary of commerce for Republican President Richard Nixon; as chair of the Council on Foreign Relations; and as a member of Democratic President Bill Clinton's Commission on Entitlement and Tax Reform.[97]

Most U.S. billionaires pursue quiet, even stealthy, political strat-

egies. Not Peterson. Beginning in the early 1980s, he wrote a series
of books and articles with such titles as "Social Security: The Coming Crash," arguing that without major benefit cuts Social Security
would run huge deficits that would be a disaster for the elderly and
would push the country into economic stagnation and social conflict. He funded nonprofit organizations—including the Committee
for a Responsible Federal Budget and the Concord Coalition—that
worked to convince politicians and the media that the federal deficit must be tamed by cutting "entitlements."

In 2008, Peterson used $1 billion (more than one-third of his for-
tune) to create the Peter G. Peterson Foundation, the goal of which
was to "increase public awareness" of fiscal challenges. The Peterson Foundation funded the anti–Social Security movie "I.O.U.S.A."
(screened in four hundred theaters and broadcast on CNN). It gave
$3.1 million to the new organization Comeback America (headed
by a former CEO of the Peterson Foundation), which pursued the
same agenda. Peterson's son Michael served on the board of Fix the
Debt, which mobilized corporate CEOs (themselves enjoying comfortable private pensions that could pay an average of $66,000 per
month) to work to reduce federal deficits—not by giving up their
own corporate tax breaks but by cutting Social Security and other
benefits. (Fix the Debt and its associated youth group, the Can
Kicks Back, ran into trouble when they were caught writing op-eds
for college students about "generational theft," placing identical
op-eds in campus papers around the country.)[98]

In his anti–Social Security efforts, Peter Peterson peddled arguments that were highly misleading or simply false, arguments
that have been thoroughly discredited by policy experts. It is *not*
true, for example—and never was true—that Social Security faces
"bankruptcy." The temporary funding shortfall of the early 1980s
(brought on by reduced revenues during an economic recession)
was fixed by modest 1983 amendments to the program. Future
strains on the program resulting from our growing population of
old people can easily be dealt with by minor adjustments, such as
subjecting more of the income of America's millionaires to the payroll tax—from which the bulk of their income is currently exempt.

There is no "crisis." No "generational theft." We can easily guarantee Social Security benefits to our children and all future retirees, just as those benefits have been guaranteed in the past. Indeed, there is a good argument for *expanding* rather than cutting Social Security's current rather meager benefits, as large pluralities of Americans have repeatedly indicated that they want to do.[99]

Still, Peterson and his allies won a great deal of attention. As a prize-winning journalist has shown, the mass media mostly got fooled.[100] They produced headlines and TV assertions about "a big ticking time bomb that will eat us up," "both Medicare and Social Security are going broke," and the like. Polls showed that ordinary Americans continued to stand by Social Security but were worried that the benefits might not be there for them. Many politicians knuckled under. Two Democratic presidents, Clinton and Obama, each appointed a "bipartisan commission" (a favorite device to provide cover for inaction or to foist unpopular policy changes on the public) concerning deficits and "entitlement reform." Each commission was stacked with members hostile to Social Security.[101] If news accounts are to be believed, both presidents came very close to approving a "grand bargain" between Republican and Democratic officials that would have harmed Social Security beneficiaries.

So far, Peterson's crusade has been much less successful than those of Scaife, Olin, Bradley, or the Kochs. So far, Social Security has dodged the big bullet. But the "entitlement reform" campaigners have not given up. As of early 2017, leading congressional Republicans were still rooting for billionaire Peterson's agenda of cuts and privatization (a pet project of budgeteer Paul Ryan), as were some key members of the Trump administration—though it was not certain that President Trump himself would go along.

One clear success of Peterson's campaign: while it was using up public-discourse oxygen pushing for cuts, proposals to *expand* Social Security—as favored by large majorities of Americans—were completely thwarted.

GREED AND SHORTSIGHTEDNESS? Based on the evidence we have considered, it is hard to avoid the impression that the political views and actions of many wealthy Americans have been greedy and shortsighted. In this era of economic globalization and technological innovation, the wealthy have accumulated vast fortunes. Productivity increases and gains from trade have been enormous—sufficient, if widely shared, to significantly better the lives of all Americans. Yet most U.S. multimillionaires and billionaires have shown little interest in sharing their riches. Far from it: they have worked for government policies designed to augment their own fortunes, not to help others.

This selfishness seems shortsighted. It may bring long-term harm to those who are pursuing it. By the second decade of the twenty-first century, millions of ordinary people who had lost out to globalization seemed to be seething with anger and resentment. In the United States and much of Europe, right-wing populists began winning elections. Britain voted to exit the European Union. Nationalist and protectionist tides seemed to threaten the entire project of international trade and global integration.

In January 2017, just before Donald Trump was inaugurated as president of the United States, the world's economic elite—heads of state, billionaire hedge fund managers, technology CEOs—congregated in Davos, Switzerland, for the annual meeting of the World Economic Forum. The mood was glum. There was much talk about how the middle class needed to gain more from globalization. The solution? They should try harder to emulate the winners. Working people should train for the jobs of the future. Enthusiasm for making money should be unleashed by stripping away government regulations. There was little mention of tax policies or how to broaden access to education or health care, let alone how to strengthen the collective bargaining rights of workers or to redistribute wealth from the top to the bottom. Little or no talk of sacrifice or sharing by the economic elite itself.[102]

A more equal, more just, and more democratic society is not beyond our reach. But it will likely take a lot of effort by large numbers of Americans to persuade—or pressure—the wealthy to accept more democracy and more economic equality. We address how this might be accomplished in chapter 9.

FIVE

Corporations and Interest Groups

James Madison and other "pluralists" have argued that diverse groups of Americans with widely varying interests tend to offset each other politically. No one group, therefore, should be able to tyrannize over the others. If all goes well, everyone's interests will get at least some recognition.[1]

In recent times, however, this vision of pluralist democracy has run up against some unpleasant realities. "Groups" that in Alexis de Tocqueville's day generally amounted to clubs, church congregations, or associations of small farmers have given way to multibillion-dollar corporations and large, professionally staffed organizations. The system does not represent all interests. Most organized groups represent business owners and managers or upper-middle-class professionals such as doctors and lawyers. Such organizations spend many millions of dollars lobbying in Washington and contributing money to political campaigns. And they—unlike ordinary citizens—have a great deal of influence over public policy. (We use the term *lobbying*, which originally referred to hobnobbing with officials in the lobbies of legislative chambers, to denote any type of communicating or interacting with public officials that is designed to influence public policy.)

The "Unheavenly Chorus" of Organized Interest Groups

Political scientist E. E. Schattschneider famously declared that "the flaw in the pluralist heaven is that the heavenly chorus sings with a strong upper-class accent."[2] Contemporary researchers have shown that the universe of registered Washington lobbyists is indeed unheavenly.[3]

The system of interest group representation is heavily biased toward business and the professions, with average working people and the poor having much weaker voices. In 2006, for example, more than half of all the registered lobbying organizations represented corporations or business associations, while a bare 1 percent each represented labor unions and poor people.[4]

Each of those corporations and business associations tends to devote much more resources to influencing politics than do groups representing average Americans. In 2000–2001, the average business association active in politics spent about $625,000 on lobbying. The average occupational association (mostly of upper-middle-class professionals—such as the American Medical Association and the American Bar Association) spent nearly as much, and so did the average corporation. But "public interest" groups, identity groups, and propoor groups were far outspent. The average social welfare or propoor group spent only $116,000 on lobbying. Working people were heavily outweighed. The average trade union spent $555,000, a figure comparable to that of a single business group, but unions were vastly outnumbered by businesses–by a factor of fifty or sixty to one.[5]

The sheer number of lobbying organizations has surged, roughly doubling—from 6,681 to 13,777—between 1981 and 2006. An avalanche of money goes into lobbying. One expert calculates that in 2012, politically active organizations reported a remarkable total of $3.31 *billion* dollars in direct lobbying expenses, almost seven times as much as in 1983. More than three-quarters of that money has consistently gone to represent corporate America. In 2012, about four hundred companies reported spending $1 million or more. And all these figures probably *understate* the total corporate investment in politics because many activities are not covered by legally required disclosures.[6] (Later in this chapter we discuss the kinds of activities in which lobbyists engage.)

Part of the story of increased corporate influence in Washington involves the decline of traditional *mass-membership* organizations. At one time, politicians in Washington heard regularly from many organizations with hundreds of thousands, or millions, of members: veterans; farmers; industrial workers; women; people identifying with a particular race, ethnicity, or religion. Those organizations helped make it possible to believe that we enjoyed a pluralist democracy.

But recent researchers have documented—and lamented—a steady drop in the membership of such organizations. For example, four major voluntary organizations peaked in the early twentieth century and then declined precipitously. Membership data from the second half of the twentieth century show sharp drops in the proportions of Americans enrolled in major fraternal organizations such as the Masons, Eagles, Elks, and Shriners. Membership in the formerly very influential American Legion (a major force for enacting the post–World War II GI Bill) dropped by 41 percent between 1955 and 1995.[7]

Especially important has been the decline of organized labor, which used to look out effectively for workers' interests over a wide range of public policies, including the enactment of Medicare and Medicaid and the expansion of Social Security. The strength of organized labor was a pillar of the pluralist idea of "countervailing power": that business corporations could not run roughshod over the political interests of workers because vigorous unions would stand in the way.[8] But U.S. unions—always plagued by racial and ethnic divisions and never as powerful as in most other advanced countries—have steadily declined in membership, from about 33 percent of American workers in 1955 down to just 11 percent in 2015.[9] Once-powerful unions including the United Auto Workers and the Steelworkers shrank to a fraction of their size as manufacturing jobs were automated or moved overseas.

The decline of American unions partly reflects three devastating forces: the postwar shift of U.S. industry to the antiunion South; automation and mechanization that cut jobs; and the upsurge in global wage competition that has undermined the bargaining power of workers in all advanced countries. But labor's decline has been exacerbated by fierce employer offensives and by deliberately antiunion public policies. Business leaders have fired union organizers and obstructed votes to unionize. The Taft-Hartley Act, the

Landrum-Griffin Act, and antiunion appointments to and decisions by the National Labor Relations Board have all made it harder for workers to win union representation.[10]

The central importance of *political choices* in undermining American unions is made clear by comparison to Canada. In the mid-1960s, unionization rates in Canada and the U.S. were nearly identical. But the global economic forces that impacted both countries led to disparate outcomes: Canadian unionization rates are actually higher now than a half-century ago, while union membership in the U.S. has plummeted. The most important reason? Canadian labor laws are much more union-friendly than their American counterparts.[11]

All industrial countries have faced the challenges of globalization and automation. But among the twenty-one wealthy countries with comparable data, the United States ranks dead last in the percentage of workers covered by union collective bargaining agreements.[12]

What public policies have done, however, other policies could undo. If our officials are pressed to do so, they can enact policies that will help revitalize labor unions and create a more level political playing field with business.[13]

Interest Groups' Influence on Public Policy

Political scientists have not had an easy time figuring out precisely how much impact organized interest groups have on public policy. Many case studies describe particular victories by particular groups, but no one can be sure from these cases what the general patterns are.

Several broader studies have illuminated certain aspects of groups' influence, demonstrating, for example, that—in a sample of cases in which interest groups actively lobbied—the amount of group resources arrayed on one side or the other did not seem to have a great deal of effect on the results.[14] To assess the overall extent to which groups actually influence policy outcomes, however, it is necessary to take into account also cases where specific interest group activity is not apparent. Groups that seem to be "inactive" may influence policy through quiet actions (perhaps a single phone call from the CEO of Microsoft or Google to a key committee chair) or through even quieter "anticipated reactions" by officials who know what important groups want and preemptively act to avoid electoral retribution from them. And to estimate the *independent* impact of interest groups, it is important to take into account the influence of other actors, such as the general public or wealthy individuals.

The same data on 1,779 cases of federal government policy making that we used to investigate the influence of average citizens in chapter 3 and affluent citizens in chapter 4 make it possible, in this chapter, to present the best estimates to date of how much influence interest groups have.

These estimates are not perfect. Our measure of "interest group alignment" is rather crude: it is based on the policy stands taken by just forty-three particularly prominent interest groups and industries, out of the thousands that seek to influence policy (see the appendix at the back of the book for a list of the groups included).[15] To construct our measure, we tallied up the number of these groups that favored each proposed policy change in our dataset and subtracted the number of groups that opposed that change. But despite its imperfections, this measure works surprisingly well to assess the influence of organized interest groups. Since the sort of measurement error it suffers from generally leads to *underestimates* of effects[16]—and yet we find evidence of substantial group influence anyhow—there is reason to suspect that the actual political influence by thousands of interest groups is probably even greater.[17]

When we include interest group alignments in our analysis of who affects changes in federal government policies, it turns out that interest groups have substantial impact. Figure 5.1 shows that (taking into account the views of average citizens and the affluent) the more the interest group lineup tilts toward favoring a particular policy change, the more likely it is that that policy change will occur. The impact of interest groups does not appear to be quite as big as the clout of affluent individuals, but it is far greater than the meager or nonexistent influence of average citizens. (As in our earlier analyses, we use middle-income Americans—those at

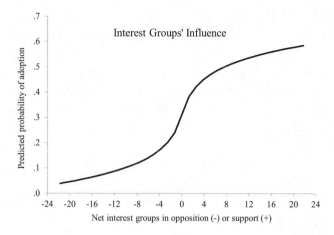

FIGURE 5.1 Interest groups have substantial influence on policy.

Predicted probabilities of policy change, controlling for the preferences of average citizens and affluent Americans, based on 1,791 proposed policy changes between 1981 and 2002. See Gilens and Page 2014 for details.

the fiftieth income percentile—to assess the influence of "average citizens.")

When confronted with these findings, a true believer in interest group pluralism might say, "Fine: we all know that interest groups affect public policy. But perhaps ordinary citizens—even if they have no *direct* influence on policy—may affect policy *through* organized groups that faithfully represent their interests."

Alas, no. Across our 1,779 cases, the policies supported by interest groups do *not* tend to correspond with what most Americans want. There is no significant relationship at all between interest group alignments and the preferences of average citizens. The interest group system as a whole is simply not translating average citizens' preferences into policy.[18]

But what about those mass-membership groups that are (or were) supposedly the bulwark of pluralist democracy? Not much comfort there, either. The current array of membership groups as a whole does little or nothing to represent the average citizen. True, a few groups with big memberships and broad policy aims—most notably the AARP, and the four unions we examined: the AFL-CIO, the American Federation of State, County, and Municipal Employees, the Teamsters, and the United Auto Workers—*do* rather strongly tend to favor the same policies that most citizens favor. But other mass-based interest groups mostly pursue relatively narrow concerns. Their stands tend to be only weakly (in some cases *negatively*) related to what most Americans want (for example, the National Rifle Association, or NRA, on gun sale background checks; or the American Israel Public Affairs Committee on U.S. government aid to Israel).[19]

When we examined all our mass-membership organizations combined, it became clear that as a collectivity they do a very disappointing job of representing most Americans. There is a significant but quite small relationship between their policy alignment and the preferences of most citizens. They are not effectively working for pluralist democracy.[20]

Moreover, when we did the same analysis as in figure 5.1 but separated mass-membership groups from business-oriented groups, it turned out that the business groups have nearly *twice as much influence* as the mass-membership groups.[21] The stands of those business groups, all taken together, have only a slightly negative relationship with the policy preferences of average citizens. But several powerful business groups—including oil companies, defense contractors, the National Association of Manufacturers, and the U.S. Chamber of Commerce—regularly tend to take stands *opposed* to what most Americans want.[22]

A determined pluralist might offer one final defense of the idea of interest group–led democracy: OK, so average citizens have no direct impact on policy; organized groups are powerful; and existing groups are biased against the average citizen; but perhaps *potential groups* may save the day. If ordinary citizens' wishes were being callously ignored, perhaps those citizens would rise up, form new groups, and punish the politicians. If such a reaction looked likely, policy makers might *anticipate* the formation of such groups and act on behalf of the unrepresented.[23]

Once again, no luck. Our analyses show that "potential groups" do not in fact have such an effect on policy making in the contemporary United States. If they did, when we took account of the stands of existing groups, the preferences of ordinary citizens should be seen to have a clear impact on policy making, via those hoped-for "anticipated reactions." But they do not. As chapter 3 made clear, when one takes account of what policies affluent individuals and organized interest groups want, ordinary citizens have little or no detectable influence upon policy making at all.

To be sure, specific interest groups have at times been instrumental in pushing policies beneficial to, and supported by, the majority of ordinary Americans. Over the decades, unions have played a central role in advancing workers' rights and workplace safety, in raising the minimum wage, and in pushing back against trade policies that harm American workers. Religious institutions have promoted "faith-based" social services that channel government resources through private religious organizations. Advocacy groups have helped defend and expand Social Security and Medicare and helped achieve important policy victories for women, racial and ethnic minorities, environmental protection, gay rights, and many other important causes.

But taken as a whole, the organized interest group system as it exists today does not—on balance—help American democracy. It undermines democracy.

How Corporations Get Their Way

One might imagine that the wealthy individuals we considered in chapter 4 and the corporate and business interest groups we are focusing on here amount to pretty much the same thing. After all, aren't many wealthy Americans owners or managers of business firms? And aren't most CEOs and major owners of businesses quite wealthy? Yes, they certainly are. But it turns out that the *issues* that most businesses care about, the *stands* they take, and many of the *political techniques* that they use to get their way differ from those of most wealthy individuals.

Across our set of 1,779 policy decisions, in fact, the net alignments of business-oriented groups are almost *entirely unrelated*, statistically, to the policy preferences of affluent Americans.[24]

If this seems hard to believe, think about why business firms and wealthy individuals might want different things from politics.

Businesses are mostly driven by the profit motive. They enter politics chiefly to cut their costs (to get lower taxes, less-expensive labor, or lighter regulation, for example); or to increase their revenue (perhaps by winning lucrative government subsidies or procurement contracts). They mostly seek narrow, self-interested benefits, sometimes designed to help a single industry or even just a single firm.[25]

Wealthy individuals, on the other hand, often have broad *ideological* goals unrelated to—or in conflict with—the narrow material interests of businesses. Some wealthy Americans believe strongly in protecting the environment, a cause that is vehemently opposed by many companies in heavily polluting industries such as oil, coal, chemicals, and paper. Other wealthy Americans are dedicated *libertarians* who oppose almost any government activity, even the "corporate welfare" that some corporations avidly seek. Many— probably most—wealthy Americans are rather liberal on cultural or moral issues involving race, sexual orientation, women's rights, and the like. All in all, U.S. corporations and wealthy individuals often seek unrelated things from politics. Thus, they have disparate effects on public policy.

Business firms and wealthy individuals do use some similar techniques for influencing politics, but their tactics and strategies also tend to differ in significant ways. In particular, large corporations (but few wealthy individuals) regularly *lobby* in Washington, DC, through big, active, year-round *professional staffs* of attorneys and consultants as well as officially registered lobbyists. Some of these lobbyists work for general business associations (for example, the Chamber of Commerce, National Association of Manufacturers) or for sector-specific associations (for example, the American Petroleum Institute or the associations of Home Builders, Beer Wholesalers, Restaurants, Broadcasters, Bankers, Hospitals, Health Insurers, and the like). But many lobbyists are hired, either as "in-house" employees or as outside contractors, to represent individual corporations.

That is where most of the big corporate money goes. Of the total of $2.5 *billion* worth of business lobbying expenditures in 2007, for example, $20.3 million was spent by General Electric, $19.1 million by Altria (tobacco), $17.2 million by AT&T, $16.9 million by ExxonMobil, $16.3 million by Amgen (pharmaceuticals), $14.7 million by Southern Co. (electric and gas energy), $14.3 million by General Motors, $13.8 by Pfizer (pharmaceuticals), $12.7 million by Verizon (telephones), $11.4 million by AIG (insurance), about $10 to $11 million each by Northrop-Grumman and Boeing (defense contractors)—and on down a long list of big corporations. By 2012, Google had leapt up near the top of this list, spending $18.2 million.[26]

But what, exactly, do all those business lobbyists do?

LOW-VISIBILITY LOBBYING. One of the keys to understanding lobbying is that most of it proceeds out of the public eye, in *low-visibility* settings where no public awareness or opposition is likely to arise.[27] Narrow interest groups tend to get their way when the political *scope of conflict* is constricted, limited to just a few participants. When policy is made "in the dark"—when no one else is watching, and neither government officials nor anyone else has much information with which to challenge interest groups—it is easy for business firms to win special subsidies, tax breaks, fat contracts, or other favors that large majorities of the American people would oppose if they knew about them.[28]

The prevalence of low-visibility lobbying concerning narrow issues is apparent in a 2009 study of ninety-eight issues that lobbyists themselves identified as the most recent ones on which they had spent time. Those issues touched on some rather broad, important matters affecting many people (a "patients' bill of rights"; repealing the estate tax; banning late-term abortions.) But they included many more "small" (but multimillion-dollar) issues of interest only to a few corporations: patent extension for pipeline drugs; increasing funding for the CH-47 Chinook helicopter; easing credit union membership; requiring that airline ticket fees be used only for aviation; supporting Securities and Exchange Commission (SEC) regulation of over-the-counter derivatives; and so forth. Even though the sample was designed to emphasize issues mentioned by several lobbyists, most lobbyists named relatively small matters that could be dealt with in low-visibility settings.[29]

It would be unrealistic to expect ordinary citizens to weigh in on the thousands of narrow and obscure issues that government deals with. That is precisely why we need political leaders who will put the needs of average Americans above those of the industries and corporations that lobby for their own narrow interests.[30]

CONGRESSIONAL COMMITTEES. A favorite setting for low-visibility corporate lobbying is the *standing committees* of the House of Representatives, where the House does most of its business—usually quietly, out of the limelight. Formal congressional hearings are generally "public" (though little-attended), and corporations certainly do testify at hearings. A more important part of day-to-day lobbying, however, involves informally cultivating warm relationships with committee chairs and key committee members, through campaign contributions, friendly social contacts, revolving-door employment, and the like. Corporate lobbyists then use those close personal ties to advocate legislation that the corporations care about. This advocacy can include providing memos, talking points, or research reports about the pros and cons of a given issue. Lobbyists also provide drafts of speeches for members of Congress to make; legal language to go into bills; and even drafts of amendments and entire bills for members to introduce.

Members of Congress, short on resources or expertise of their own, are generally happy to get such help from friendly lobbyists. The problem is that the arguments or information that is provided may be incorrect or biased, with no one around to correct it.

Some crucial lobbying contacts probably amount to a simple e-mail or phone call to a key legislator: "I have checked with management, and my company cannot live with that provision." With luck, the committee may kill the provision so that it never makes it to the floor of Congress for a vote.

The tax-writing House Ways and Means Committee has long been known as a source of "Christmas tree" tax bills full of goodies for many companies, with the goodies sometimes added to a bill late at night just as the legislative year is ending. Then the bill is usually reported to the House floor under a "closed rule"[31] that forbids any amendments. Often, no time is allowed for careful reading or debate. The "peoples' representatives" have to take it or leave it. They almost always take it.

NEW WAYS FOR CORPORATIONS TO WIN. Low-visibility lobbying has always been bad. But several recent changes have made things worse. Polarized parties and divided government in Washington have led to a frequent practice of passing enormous, last-minute "omnibus" spending and tax bills. Instead of following "regular order"—that is, scrutinizing each federal agency's budget for months in specialized committees, and then debating, amending, and passing each budget separately on the floor of the House—a whole year's worth of taxing and spending by the entire federal government now often gets decided by just two huge, complex, quickly passed laws. This increased size, complexity, and haste in legislating greatly increases the ability of lobbyists to insert special provisions into the law.[32]

A striking example is the omnibus tax and spending legislation that was passed in December 2015. Members of Congress and their staffs were given only three days to review a 2,009-page spending plan and a 233-page list of tax breaks. Then they had to vote on it. It later turned out that the omnibus bills included thousands of special add-ons. These included such standard pork barrel items as Coast Guard cutters and Navy destroyers sought by particular senators but not by the armed forces. They also included continuation of a lucrative ($1-billion-plus) tax loophole for Real Estate Investment Trusts that was designed to benefit Caesar's Palace and Energy Future Holdings (formerly called TXU). This "Caesar's-TXU carve-out," backed by the top Senate leaders of both parties, was a last-minute reaction to a December 7 proposal to close the loophole. A coalition of lobbyists, including big contributors to both parties, quickly agreed on a simple postponement of the loophole closing and wrote the key language that eventually made it into the bill.[33]

LOBBYING REGULATORY AGENCIES. Much the same logic that works for congressional committees also applies to obscure *regulatory proceedings*, in which affected companies may be the only parties who show up before an administrative agency. They often get their way.

Interviews with professional lobbyists have helped illuminate how they go about their work. For example, in-house corporate lobbyist Christina Mulvihill (director of Sony Electronics' DC office) declared that "the bulk of the work is off the Hill now." Mulvihill estimated that contacting people on Capitol Hill is now only 15 to 20 percent of a lobbyist's job. She calculated that *twenty* federal agencies play a part in regulating the sale of TV sets to consumers: the Internal Revenue Service, or IRS (tax treatment), the Department of Commerce, the National Institute of Standards in Technology, the Consumer Product Safety Commission, the Department of Transportation, and a dozen more. Each of these regulators issues rules that matter to Sony and other firms. Each regulator is besieged by corporate lobbyists.[34]

Mulvihill noted that a crucial time to lobby regulators is during the public "notice and comment period," after an agency indicates that it plans to issue a rule on some topic but before it actually does so. Each agency works in its own way, so savvy corporations often contract this work out to a lobbying firm that has special expertise on—and perhaps a special "in" with—the particular agency concerned. "Comments" can go well beyond a simple typed letter. Those who care enough and can afford the cost (mainly large corporations) often submit a big package, including an economic impact study, industry statistics, and public relations materials. It sometimes takes a corporation, its attorneys, and its contracted lobbying firm a month to put together such a package. Ordinary consumers and their few organized advocates can seldom compete.[35]

An especially important case of lobbying regulators involves the Federal Reserve Board. The "Fed" has amassed broad powers to affect the American economy through opaque, little-publicized decisions that are heavily influenced by the bankers and investment houses that the Fed is supposed to regulate. Researchers have found, for example, that in its response to the 2007–2009 financial crisis, the Fed closely consulted with Wall Street financial firms and pursued a "consistent pattern of favoritism" toward them, launching a host of obscure programs that granted long-term, low-interest loans and accepted as "security" dubious (or worthless) mortgage-based derivatives. Alternative policies could have helped homeowners and workers more and saved the taxpayers a lot of money.[36]

THE MONEY CONNECTION. Interest group lobbying often goes hand in hand with financial support: campaign contributions, hosting fund-raisers, donating to a representative's private foundation. The vast majority (86 percent) of political action committee (PAC) contributions come from groups that also employ lobbyists.[37] Directly buying votes is illegal and probably rare. But politicians need money to run their campaigns, and interest groups need politicians to advance their interests, which leads to long-term, mutually beneficial relationships.

Long-term investments in politicians help ensure that sympathetic representatives get elected, remain in Congress, and remain sympathetic. Such investments may or may not shift an individual member of Congress's roll-call votes (studies on this are inconsistent), but contributions clearly facilitate access to officials and encourage them to prioritize their donors' concerns in allocating their scarce time and attention.[38]

Most of the decision making that affects policy takes place before legislation ever reaches the voting stage, in formulating new policies, moving them through the committee system, dealing with amendments, and corralling support from other members of Congress. This process typically requires a substantive understanding of the issue and the interests involved—which lobbyists are happy to help with—and a great deal of time and effort.[39]

When scholars have dug into this mostly hidden aspect of policy making, they have found clear associations between interest group contributions and efforts made by members of Congress. Two researchers who collected extensive data on behind-the-scenes behavior by members of Congress and their campaign contributions concluded that "the more money a supporter received . . . the more likely he or she was to allocate time and effort on the industry's behalf (e.g., work behind the scenes, speak on the group's behalf, attach amendments to the committee vehicle, as well as show up and vote at committee markups)."[40]

Interest groups' long-term investments in elected representatives can have huge payoffs. One striking example is the role of Senator Joseph Lieberman (I-CT) in killing the "public option" in the lead-up to the 2010 Affordable Care Act. The public option was designed to compete with private insurance and thereby guarantee competition and affordability in places where few private insurers were operating. Surveys showed that most Americans liked the idea of a government alternative to private insurance, and studies showed that it would help drive down the cost of health care.[41]

But Lieberman's state of Connecticut was headquarters to seventy-two insurance companies, and Senator Lieberman had received more than half a million dollars from the insurance industry leading up to his election in 2006.[42] The House of Representatives passed a version of the health care reform bill that included a public option, but the Democrats needed sixty votes in the Senate to advance the legislation. Lieberman, an Independent who caucused with the Democrats, was their only option for hitting the magic number of sixty. But Lieberman broke with the Democrats and announced that he would not vote to move forward with the bill, thereby single-handedly killing the public option.

After the public option died, an optional buy-in to Medicare for those aged fifty-five through sixty-four was added to the bill as a consolation prize for incensed progressives. This approach was even more popular among ordinary Americans, 70 to 80 percent of whom supported the idea.[43] Yet it too was dropped after Lieberman changed his mind and opposed it at the last minute. By killing this alternative, Lieberman made it clear that he opposed any new program that might compete with his insurance-industry backers.

It is impossible to say with certainty that Senator Lieberman's stance toward health care reform would have been different without the financial support of the insurance industry. But clearly the industry's PACs and lobbying organizations felt that the time and money they lavished on Senator Lieberman (and many other senators and representatives) was a good investment. The public option was killed. Health insurers avoided having to compete with a lower-priced government healthcare option. And the American public is, quite literally, paying the price.

GRASS ROOTS AND "ASTROTURF" LOBBYING. Most lobbying occurs quietly in offices or meeting rooms in Washington, DC, and in various state capitals. But some lobbying is much noisier. Interest groups sometimes pursue an "outside strategy," in which citizens at the grass roots bombard public officials with communications designed to influence them—petitions, phone calls, e-mails, Tweets; sometimes rallies or demonstrations. Outside strategies can be designed to send a signal to policy makers that they had better go along with group demands because the group has the capacity to affect their reelection chances.[44]

Genuine grassroots campaigns are important to democracy. They give ordinary citizens a way—as the First Amendment to the Constitution puts it—to "petition the government for a redress of grievances." When large, mass-membership organizations such as AARP and trade unions mobilize their members to urge the enactment of policies that large majorities of Americans favor, they are clearly contributing to democracy. So, we believe, are the activities of groups that *lead* public opinion. History shows that truly grassroots campaigns that start out small, representing minority voices, can grow in size, activity, and organizational prowess to become major forces in American politics. Some grassroots movements have articulated important new demands—such as equal rights for African Americans, for women, and for gays and lesbians—that have gradually won support from majorities of Americans and have led to major changes in public policy.

But there is a dark side. Some outside campaigns that appear to reflect the grass roots do not really do so. These are nicknamed "Astroturf" (after a brand of artificial grass) campaigns, because they are bought and paid for by corporations or other interest groups. There are professional firms that specialize in flooding officials' offices with apparently spontaneous e-mail and snail mail—which may fool the recipients, at least some of the time. Special interests create front organizations with fine-sounding names (for oil companies, for example, perhaps "Americans for Effective Energy Policy") and produce ads, op-eds, and reports—both to persuade citizens to favor policies friendly to the interest behind them (in this case, oil-friendly policies) and to convince politicians and officials that there is strong grassroots support for such policies.

Sometimes elements of grassroots and Astroturf are combined in a single sustained campaign. The Sagebrush Rebellion of the 1970s and the more recent Wise Use movement, for example, were partly energized by small-time ranchers in the West who chafed at environmental and other regulations on federally owned land that they leased or coveted. Such were the armed men led by rancher Ammon Bundy, who took over the Malheur National Wildlife Refuge in Oregon at the beginning of 2016.

But it turns out that the ideology of Wise Use (set forth in a book by a timber-industry adviser named Ron Arnold) was in fact largely developed and propagated by a coalition of big economic interests—large cattle ranchers and big oil, logging, and mining companies—that could increase their profits if federal regulations were reduced or eliminated. In 1988, Arnold held a conference that brought together Exxon, the National Cattlemen's Association, and other interests to seed the West with so-called grassroots groups that would wrest control of federal lands away from the government. Arnold sent organizers into economically distressed rural communities to set up front groups with environmentally friendly-sounding names and whip up hostility against the government. As a researcher explained, the result was a "coalition of natural-resource companies, property developers, and conservative activists working with a network of community organizations." This coalition succeeded in introducing or passing legislation in nearly thirty states, purportedly giving local governments and citizens expanded powers to lay claim to federal land. Its ideas also helped inspire far-out antigovernment militia movements and Bundy's armed occupation of the Malheur Refuge.[45]

INVESTING IN IDEAS. In chapter 4 we described efforts by wealthy individuals to shape the way that policy makers and ordinary Americans think about various issues: the Koch brothers' heavy investment in libertarian ideas opposed to government taxation, spending, or regulation, for example; and Pete Peterson's crusade against Social Security. With the "right turn" of corporate America that started in the late 1970s,[46] many *corporations*, too, increasingly sought to turn Americans' thinking and discourse against a wide range of government activity.

Historians have documented how tobacco and oil companies, with help from a handful of renegade scientists, have obscured the truth and peddled deceitful "science" touting the harmlessness of tobacco smoke and denying the reality of climate change. The Tobacco Industry Research Committee during the 1950s persuaded media to "even-handedly" report baseless doubts about the link between tobacco and cancer. It also funded ideological think tanks and developed close ties with many doctors, medical school faculty, and public health authorities. In recent times, ExxonMobil channeled millions of dollars to about forty organizations that challenged the scientific evidence of global warming.[47]

More broadly, as we noted in chapter 4, a "policy-planning network" and an "opinion-shaping network" transmit influence by corporate elites through philanthropic foundations, universities, think tanks, policy discussion groups, blue-ribbon task forces and commissions, the mass media, and other institutions.[48] Especially important in recent years has been the rise of libertarian and conservative, corporate-funded think tanks such as the Cato Institute, the Heritage Foundation, and the American Enterprise Institute, which produce reports, memos, and op-eds that get a great deal of media attention and play a big part in discourse about public policy.

The right turn of business, along with the rightward shift of the Republican Party, has also meant that the usual narrow-issue corporate lobbying has more and more been supplemented by broad corporate coalitions aimed at cutting corporate and personal income taxes, slashing government spending (especially on the big "entitlement" programs, most notably Social Security and Medicare), and reducing or eliminating regulation of financial institutions, workplace health and safety, the environment, and other matters.

The Results of Corporate Lobbying

One result of corporate lobbying is that U.S. laws and regulations are full of special provisions designed to favor just a few corporations—highly specific tax breaks, subsidies, and exemptions from regulation. Any one of these may seem trivial. Taken as a whole, however, they constitute a wasteful and counterproductive drag on the country.

As the old Washington saying goes, "a billion dollars here, a billion there, and pretty soon it adds up to real money." Every billion-dollar favor that goes to ExxonMobil or General Electric is a billion dollars that could have been spent on programs that majorities of Americans favor (such as child nutrition, mass transit, or public schools), or to lower working-class Americans' tax bills, or to reduce the budget deficit. A lot of good could be done with the scores or hundreds of billions of dollars that are given away to corporations every year.

Corporate lobbying also tends to tilt the outcomes of bigger, more visible political struggles—hard-fought conflicts over broad tax cuts for business and wealthy Americans, for example—away from what most Americans want. With unions weakened, "countervailing power" against business is at a low ebb. The corporations tend to get their way.

Equally important, interest group lobbying also has the effect of *stopping* important and popular legislation from being passed, often before it even gets started. The same warm personal relations with key policy makers that enable firms to get special favors can be used to get those policy makers to use the "veto points" they occupy (House and Senate leaders' control of the legislative agenda; committee chairs' power to bury bills) to prevent legislation the corporations oppose from ever coming up. As we have seen, inaction has thwarted progress on dealing with a number of pressing problems that large majorities of Americans want solved: climate change, immigration reform, infrastructure repair, gun violence, decaying public schools, help with jobs and wages. Many decisions not to act occur quietly, as a result of corporate lobbying, without ever coming to a vote by Congress.

The ability of interest groups to stymie legislation they oppose reflects not only the power of lobbyists in Washington but also the unique challenges of changing public policy in our political system. In the next chapter, we examine the gridlock that afflicts our national politics.

SIX

Polarized Parties and Gridlock

Many failures of democratic responsiveness in the United States involve government *inaction* when majorities of Americans want new policies.

In recent years the federal government has often seemed paralyzed, not acting on the policies that citizens want even when there is strong popular demand for action. As we saw in chapter 3, even when an overwhelming majority of the public favors a policy change, it happens only about half the time.

This failure to do what the public wants is often a result of obstruction by wealthy individuals, corporations, and organized interest groups. But such obstruction is made easy by our political rules and institutions, which deserve some of the blame as well. Our American "separation of powers" means that any one of several political institutions—the president or officials acting on the president's behalf (executive branch), the House of Representatives or the Senate (legislative branch), or the Supreme Court (judicial branch)—can generally prevent a new law from being adopted or implemented. Even *within* the House and Senate, there are a number of veto points that can stop legislation from happening—veto points controlled by party leaders, committee chairs, or just a single senator determined to engage in a filibuster. (We will discuss the specifics of veto points later in this chapter.) When a few defenders of the status quo control even one veto point, they can prevent policy changes that large majorities of Americans want.

Our political system has always made it easier to stop new policies than to enact them. But recently, as our political parties have

become more polarized (that is, as the parties have come to disagree with each other more and more sharply about policy), and
as divided government has become more common (with different
parties controlling different parts of government), the parties have
more and more often refused to compromise with each other and
have systematically prevented action. The result is *gridlock*.

Gridlock has prevented the United States from dealing with
such urgent problems as climate change, gun violence, decaying
infrastructure, and wage stagnation. It has even interfered with the
basic, day-to-day operation of government. In 1995 and again in
2013, budget deadlocks forced most of the federal government to
shut down. These shutdowns caused not only inconvenience (tour-
ists were shocked to find parks and museums closed) but also serious economic uncertainty.[1] Routine adjustments to U.S. debt limits
have also been obstructed, which has threatened to prevent the
government from making legally required payments such as send-
ing Social Security checks. In 2011 and 2013, it led credit agencies
to take the unprecedented step of lowering the credit rating of the
United States.[2]

Certain impediments to government action could easily be reformed. But others are deeply embedded in our laws or in the
Constitution itself. Moreover, the *order* in which reforms were
enacted would make a difference. Removing obstacles to policy
adoption could actually have *anti*democratic effects, if the party
in power were pursuing goals that most Americans reject. Further,
facilitating policy change when the same party controls all the
institutions of government could lead to wild swings in policy—
even if the preferences of the voters changed not at all. (Later
we discuss just this situation in connection with the House of
Representatives.)

Logically, then, reforms to reduce partisan extremism—such as
efforts to reduce the power of the parties' campaign donors and
extreme activists—should precede most reforms aimed at facilitating policy making through institutional rule changes. Moreover,
institutional support for minority rights is essential. Eliminating
all checks on majority rule would be a mistake. But we believe that
the balance has tipped too far—many broadly popular policies that

would do little or no harm to anyone are now being stymied by obstructive minorities.

Deadlock by Design?

James Madison and other Founders of the United States deliberately designed a political system in which there would be restraints on taking action, a system full of checks and balances.[3] The Constitution provided for federalism, with much power reserved to the individual states. Within the national government, decision making was fragmented among the House, the Senate, the presidency, and the Supreme Court. Any one of the four can prevent important kinds of government action by saying no—or, in some cases, simply by doing nothing.[4]

This does not mean that the Founders favored gridlock. Far from it. The main point of the new Constitution, after all, was to overcome the paralysis and ineffectiveness of the Articles of Confederation. Most of the Founders, including Alexander Hamilton and James Madison, wanted to institute a vigorous national government that could act in the common interest.

Our constitutional design does mean, however, that the Founders wanted to avoid hasty or intemperate action that might trample on individuals' rights. As political theorist Jane Mansbridge points out, many of the Founders were motivated by a "resistance theory." The resistance tradition holds that government actions—whether initiated by King George of England when he ruled the American colonies, or by some selfish faction of Americans, or even by a majority of American citizens moved by an ill-conceived "passion"—can constitute major threats to the liberty of individuals. Such threats must be resisted. In the *Federalist Papers*, Madison argued that federalism in an extensive republic, together with separated, counterbalancing national institutions and severe limits on democratic control of each institution (at first only the House was directly elected) would protect individual Americans against government "tyranny"—tyranny pursued by anyone, even a popular majority.[5]

A healthy wariness about possible government tyranny has persisted throughout American history. But we believe the system has gotten out of balance, so that it now has too strong a bias toward inaction. As our society and economy have grown much larger and more complex, and as the world keeps changing, new needs for government action have arisen. Climate change, economic pressures from globalization, social tensions over immigration, extreme inequalities of income and wealth—all seem to cry out for government action. Yet action is often stymied. We suffer from "policy drift": our needs change, but government policy does not keep up and we are left worse off.[6]

It is time, Mansbridge urges, to think less about resisting government and think more about how to get things done. We agree.[7]

Over the course of the past few decades, sharpened conflict between the two major political parties, together with close elections and divided party government, have increasingly interacted with our system of multiple veto points to make stalemate and gridlock more and more common. The legislative productivity of Congress has been in a general declining pattern since about 1960, and particularly in the twenty-first century (see figure 6.1). Fewer and fewer laws have been enacted. During much of the Obama administration, the Democratic President seemed to be constantly at war

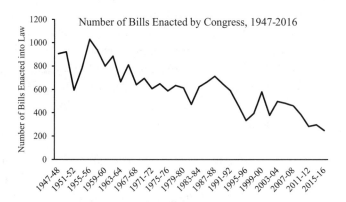

FIGURE 6.1 Congressional productivity has declined since the mid-twentieth century.

Includes only public bills.

Sources: 1947–2012 Brookings, Vital Statistics on Congress Table 6-4; Résumé of Congressional Activity, 2013–16, www.senate.gov/reference/Resumes.htm.

with Republicans, especially the uncompromising Tea Party faction in the House of Representatives.[8]

Why Gridlock

To figure out how to overcome gridlock, it is important to be clear about precisely what the causes are. There are several.

MULTIPLE VETO POINTS. One fundamental cause of gridlock is the existence of multiple veto points in American politics. But veto points come in two distinct forms. One involves barriers *within* political institutions, such as the filibuster in the Senate or the practices that facilitate one-party rule in the House. Most such barriers could quickly and easily be demolished—if officials were persuaded to do so—by a simple majority vote of legislators to change the rules. But not all such reforms by themselves would necessarily enhance democratic responsiveness, unless other reforms ensured that majorities of legislators within each chamber of Congress faithfully represented majorities of Americans.[9]

Other veto points arise from a more fundamental, harder-to-change source: our basic constitutional arrangement of separate political institutions sharing power and checking one another. When disparate political parties control disparate national institutions, partisan disagreement can seriously impede government functioning. But we believe that the problem lies more with the polarization of the parties and with undemocratic features of U.S. elections than it does with the separation of powers itself—which has a number of virtues, including multiple forums for deliberation and a check on overly hasty action.

DIVIDED PARTY RULE. In recent years, it has become common for one political party to control the presidency while the other party controls the House of Representatives and/or the Senate.[10] Divided government, permitted by the separation of powers and facilitated by staggered elections and varying electorates, creates a *possibility* for gridlock if the parties that control different institutions disagree with each other.

But divided government, like the separation of powers itself, does not *necessarily* produce gridlock. It only does so if there is *disharmony* between the parties: that is, if they disagree sharply about policy. Back in the 1980s, when the parties were relatively moderate and amenable to bipartisan compromise, it was hard to detect any harm at all from divided party rule. Major legislation got passed; nominees to office got confirmed; legislative oversight mostly proceeded in a sensible fashion.[11]

DISHARMONY AMONG INSTITUTIONS. We believe that the most important cause of gridlock that can be fixed without causing unintended damage is *disharmony* among political institutions that leads them to conflict with one another. The simplest and best way to avoid disharmony is to make sure that all our government institutions faithfully represent all Americans, so that all of our institutions pursue similar policies—policies that majorities of Americans favor.

Separate institutions generally engage in conflict and obstruction only if they disagree about what sorts of policies to pursue. Such disagreements, in turn, generally reflect polarization of the parties, differences in the methods or the timing by which the members of the particular institutions are chosen, or both. For example, the people who vote in party primaries and in "off-year" elections for the House and Senate tend to be quite different—and less representative of Americans as a whole—than the larger numbers who vote in "on-year" elections for the president and legislators. This difference contributes to disagreement among institutions. (Senators elected in unrepresentative "off-years," for example, generally stay around for full six-year terms, even after an "on-year" election may have transformed the House and the presidency.) Members of both the House and the Senate are chosen from districts with boundaries that distort democratic representation, but their districts are undemocratic in different ways—producing disagreements between the two chambers. When the parties are sharply polarized, any difference in the timing or the working of elections that leads to different parties controlling different institutions is also likely to result in conflict.

Polarization is the heart of the matter. The biggest single cause of gridlock in recent years has been sharp, uncompromising conflict between the Republican and Democratic parties, during periods when different parties controlled different institutions of the federal government. It is partisan warfare—during the Obama administration, for example—that has led to periodic crises, threats of government shutdown, and inaction on a great deal of major legislation.

The separation of powers is likely to be with us for a long time, and there are reasons to expect that government institutions may be divided between parties fairly often in the future. If we want to overcome the gridlock problem, therefore, it is essential to understand the causes of polarization and the ways in which we might reduce it.

Why the Parties Are So Polarized

Republican and Democratic officials now disagree more deeply about public policy than they have at any time since the 1890s, more than a century ago. Researchers have shown that party polarization within both the House and the Senate has increased greatly over the last few decades.[12] In terms of the liberal–conservative continuum that encompasses most of what goes on in Congress, the parties have become so deeply divided that there seems to be a chasm between them. There is no longer a large, bipartisan group of moderates. Nearly all the Republicans cluster together as conservatives, and nearly all the Democrats are liberals. In recent years there has been little or no overlap at all: the most liberal Republican in the House of Representatives has been more conservative than the most conservative Democrat (see figure 6.2).

This increasingly sharp party division has contributed to conflict, anger, incivility, and a breakdown in cooperation between the parties. Not long ago, Republican and Democratic members of Congress used to get together for meals and drinks, travel together, work out together in the gym, and share housing in Washington, DC. Socializing across party lines helped smooth the way for working together on legislation. It encouraged compromising to get things done.[13]

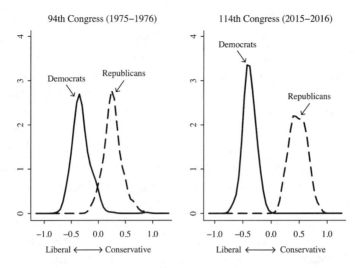

FIGURE 6.2 The parties in Congress now show little to no overlap.

Source: Adapted from Poole 2017.

No longer. Hostility has mostly replaced cross-party friendship. *Compromise* and *bipartisanship* have become dirty words[14]—in fact, they have become dangerous. A member of Congress who looks like a compromiser may face a primary election challenge from true believers among activists in his or her own party. Primaries are typically low-turnout elections, where small groups of strong partisans can shift the results in favor of an ideologically extreme candidate.[15]

The decline of bipartisanship is especially striking in the Senate. In the early 1960s, a leading political scientist wrote about how the norms, or "folkways," of the Senate, including bipartisan friendships and willingness to compromise, softened personal conflict and discouraged senators from using their awesome powers to obstruct action. Without these folkways, he said, the Senate "could hardly operate." Presciently, he worried that new, inexperienced members, with political ambitions beyond the Senate, playing to the mass media, and facing sharp political competition, were likely to deviate from the old norms of Senate behavior.[16]

Evidence suggests that new members of Congress do in fact tend to ignore previous norms of behavior. Many older members have been replaced by younger, often inexperienced hyperpartisans.[17] One researcher describes "old guard" legislators as possessing the qualities of "friendship, respect, and comity," while "new school" members exhibit "personal ambition, finger-pointing, and in-your-face attitude" while practicing "search and destroy tactics."[18]

Not long ago, Mitch McConnell, the minority (and later majority) leader of the U.S. Senate, declared that his major objective was to make Barack Obama a one-term president. McConnell devoted a great deal of effort to preventing the president from claiming any legislative achievements, blocking the president's proposals and undermining bipartisan compromise. John Boehner, the Speaker of the House, was rebuked by his own Republican Party members for attempting to negotiate with the Democratic president. Boehner changed course and engaged in scorched-earth confrontation. The Congresses of 2011–2014 turned out to be the least productive in decades, passing very little major legislation.[19] But even Boehner proved too moderate for the extremely conservative Tea Party faction of Republicans; in 2015 he was replaced as Speaker by the more reliably conservative Paul Ryan.

WHAT CAUSES DIFFERENCES BETWEEN THE PARTIES? If issue-oriented voters determined the outcome of elections, we might expect that both parties would compete for votes by taking positions that are as popular as possible—positions right in the middle of the voters. So both parties might take stands that are nearly identical.

As even the most casual observer of American politics knows, however, this is not how the political world works. Republican and Democratic officials regularly disagree about policies. They have done so ever since the Republicans and Democrats emerged as the two major U.S. parties around 1860. Even Republican and Democratic senators from the same state, facing the same set of voters, generally favor highly contrasting policies.

How can this be? The short answer is that U.S. elections are more complicated than the simple idea of issue-oriented "electoral competition."[20] First, many voters lack a strong policy basis for choosing one candidate over the other, either because they are closer to the Democrats on some issues and closer to the Republicans on others, or because they lack strongly held policy views altogether. Such voters often base their votes on current economic conditions and either reward or punish the incumbent party accordingly. This kind of "retrospective voting" gives officeholders incentives to boost the economy (especially around election time) but maybe not to hew to the policy preferences of the typical voter.[21]

In addition, campaigns often provide voters with only the vaguest sense of candidates' issue positions, while playing up candidates' personal qualities as "patriotic" or "caring" or "a real fighter for the district." Most important, voters can only choose among the candidates on their ballots, and those candidates must appeal to the often extreme views of party activists and donors to get on the ballot in the first place.[22]

A major cause of party differences about policy, then, is *party donors and party activists with distinctive policy preferences.*

EXTREME PARTY ACTIVISTS AND DONORS. Because money and campaign work are essential for winning elections, each of the parties must energize a distinctive set of contributors and party activists associated with that party. Republican and Democratic activists tend to be distinct from each other—and sometimes extreme—in their policy views. The need to satisfy their own activists and financial donors tends to push the parties' policy stands apart from each other.[23]

Extremist activists and donors are a big problem mainly because they have so much influence on the selection of their parties' candidates—particularly for state legislatures and the U.S. House of Representatives—in obscure, low-turnout, one-party primary elections. When very few citizens vote (often fewer than one-fifth of those eligible), extreme activists in the party's "base" can turn out a few like-minded voters and win nominations for extreme candidates. In overwhelmingly one-party districts, these nominees can usually win the November election, even if they poorly represent their constituents' views. When they take office, they tend to distort or obstruct the decisions of their legislatures. The activists also influence other officials in their party, including senators and presidents, by threatening to mount primary challenges and replace anyone who seems "too moderate" or dares to compromise with the other party.

In recent years a number of sitting senators—some of them quite distinguished, such as foreign policy expert Richard Lugar of Indiana—have been thrown out of office in their own party's primaries because they worked with the other party or were not seen as ideologically pure. Such behavior punishes bipartisanship and intimidates other incumbent officials.

A dramatic illustration of the power of a small number of party activists in primary elections was the 2014 defeat of Eric Cantor, the Republican House majority leader (and an important liaison to the business community), by David Brat, a little-known favorite of the Tea Party. Brat ran ads showing Cantor standing near President Obama at the State of the Union address and implying that Cantor was a compromiser, insufficiently conservative on immigration, the budget, "crony capitalism," and other issues. (This was news to Washington Democrats, who considered Cantor an implacable foe.)

After Cantor's startling upset loss, some observers claimed that he had fallen culturally and politically "out of touch" with his Virginia district. Yet Cantor had won seven consecutive general elections by large margins, including a 17-percentage-point win in 2012. Essential to Brat's victory was extremely low turnout that is typical in congressional primaries: only about 14 percent of the eligible voters in the district. A few Tea Party activists from Richmond— spurred on by radio talk-show host Laura Ingraham—were able to mobilize 36,110 voters for Brat, a tiny fraction of citizens in the district but just enough to achieve a surprise victory in the primary.[24]

THE PROBLEM OF ONE-PARTY DISTRICTS. The power of extremist party activists depends heavily on our system of nominating candidates in low-turnout primary elections, and the fact that the vast majority of electoral districts for the House of Representatives and state legislatures (and, for senators, quite a few whole states) are "safe" one-party districts in which the majority party nominee— even one who poorly reflects the views of his or her constituents— can usually win the general election. In recent years, "marginal" (closely contested) districts have mostly vanished. About three-quarters of all incumbent members of the House have been winning reelection with 60 percent or more of the vote.[25] Only a tidal-wave election can dislodge them.

Part of this problem arises from deliberate partisan "gerrymandering" of district boundaries, which are sometimes drawn in bizarre shapes so that many districts have a comfortable winning margin for the favored party, while opposition voters are crammed into a few much more concentrated districts. Some evidence suggests that gerrymandering has accounted for as much as one-third of the reduction in competitive congressional districts since the early 1980s.[26]

But gerrymandering is only part of the problem, perhaps a relatively small part.[27] Most noncompetitive, one-party-districts actually result from drawing more or less "natural" (compact and contiguous) district boundaries because residential segregation often means that politically distinctive population groups are clustered together in high concentrations.[28] This is true of heavily rural districts that include no urban dwellers. It is also true of many central-city districts that are heavily African American or Latino. One effect of this "natural" districting is to ensure that some legislators are elected who (in race, ethnicity, and personal backgrounds) closely resemble these distinctive populations. But another effect is to contribute to the problem of noncompetitiveness. Since extreme party activists play a key role in nominations, "natural" one-party district boundaries often lead to the election of legislators with relatively extreme views—more extreme than those of the average constituent in the district.

The high concentration of certain groups of citizens in one-party districts also has the effect of cutting down their overall voting power, which would be greater if they were spread among more districts and had to be taken into account by many more legislators. Some African American members of the House win 90 to 95 percent of the votes in their districts. Their constituents are not well served by this system. If substantial numbers of those constituents were spread around to other districts, they could affect the results of many more congressional elections and have considerably more total influence on Congress.

Since highly concentrated districts of African Americans and Latinos tend to vote heavily Democratic, the Democratic Party regularly wins fewer House seats than its total share of the votes would suggest. In 2012, for example, House Democratic candidates received 1.2 million more votes nationwide than their Republican counterparts, but Republicans won 54 percent of the House seats and kept control of the House of Representatives. Observers of congressional elections have written of the continuing "Republican advantage" in House districts, and "why the Democrats can't win."[29]

Such a built-in advantage for either party seems undemocratic. But our main point is that "natural" one-party districts, even more than gerrymandered districts, contribute to noncompetitiveness and party polarization. Gerrymandering should be easy to fix, by entrusting the drawing of district boundaries to independent commissions rather than partisan state legislatures—as several states have begun doing. As we will see in chapter 8, however, the problem of "natural" one-party districts is much knottier and harder to solve.

CAUSES OF INCREASED POLARIZATION. Scholars disagree about exactly why party polarization has increased so much in recent years. But the causes certainly include the partisan realignment of the South that was accelerated by the Democrat-sponsored Civil Rights Acts of 1964 and 1965. At one time the Democratic Party had an overwhelming majority of the representatives from the "solid South." But white southerners gradually deserted the Democrats, electing more and more Republican representatives and senators—all of them conservative. The Democrats were left with only a few representatives from the South, nearly all of them liberal African Americans from predominately African American congressional districts.[30]

At the same time that the Republican Party was gaining southern conservatives, it was losing most of its liberal northern members. Each of the parties became more ideologically pure. Policy disagreements between the parties sharpened.[31]

Increased polarization between the parties probably also reflects certain fundamental economic and social changes in recent years, including increased economic inequality, globalization, and shifts in the racial and ethnic makeup of the U.S. population.

ECONOMIC CHANGES. The dramatic rise of economic inequality since the 1970s may have led the Republican Party to adopt more conservative economic policies, consistent with the interests of its higher-earning constituents.[32] For the Democrats, reliance on wealthy campaign donors has dampened any liberal drift on economic policy. The result is an asymmetric polarization over the period from 1975 to 2015, with the Republican party moving sharply to the right and the Democratic party just a bit to the left (figure 6.3).

Economic globalization over the course of several decades has had important consequences for American workers, American corporations, and American politics. American workers must now compete in a global labor market that has forced their wages downward, while American businesses, threatened by lower-cost foreign competition, try to reduce production costs within the United States—whether from wages, benefits, taxes, or government regulations.[33]

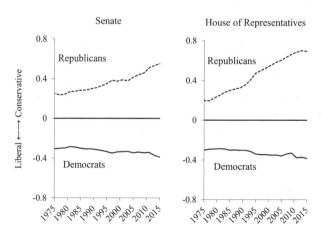

FIGURE 6.3 Congress has become increasingly polarized.

Source: Adapted from Poole 2017.

American workers have suffered from years of wage stagnation, job losses, and increasing health care costs. But most U.S. business firms and wealthy Americans have turned away from the government social programs that would help cushion these blows, even seeking cuts in Social Security and Medicare. Most want lower taxes on themselves. Many favor less government regulation of workplace health and safety (which raises costs) and less regulation of air and water pollution (which increases costs for coal, oil, and gas companies and for the producers of paper and chemicals) without making any commitments that they will preserve jobs if these changes are made.[34]

As U.S. businesses turned to the right, most of them—even many that had once provided the Democrats with campaign funds and leadership—joined with the Republican Party. They pushed the Republicans rightward on economic, regulatory, and trade issues and thereby increased conflict and disagreement with the Democrats.[35]

Economic pressures from globalization may also have contributed to alienating some lower-income Americans from mainstream U.S. culture and politics, moving them rightward on *social* issues: toward fundamentalist religious beliefs, aggressive individualism, adherence to gun rights, and resentment of "foreign" influences.[36]

SOCIAL AND DEMOGRAPHIC CHANGES. Rapid social and demographic changes—including immigration from Mexico and changes in people's thinking about race, gender, and sexual orientation—have produced a great deal of cultural unease. To a substantial number of Americans, especially older white males in rural areas, the traditional social order seems turned upside down: Women can no longer be relied on to accept a subordinate place at home. Gays openly declare their sexual orientation and demand legal rights. African Americans claim an equal place in society and rejoice at the election of an African American president. Social resentment by some whites was clearly a factor in the 2016 elections.

In recent decades the Republican Party has moved to the right on social issues, at the same time that the Democrats—with support from newly empowered women, gays, Latinos, and African Americans—have moved to the left and taken more liberal social stands. Thus conflict between the parties has increased on social as well as economic issues, which has opened a wide ideological gulf between Republican and Democratic officials in Washington.

As the political parties have become more distinct, the American *public* has become increasingly polarized in terms of party and ideology as well. Individuals may not have become more extreme in their policy views, but Americans are better "sorted" into distinctive partisan identities, with fewer liberal Republicans or conservative Democrats.[37] Partisan sorting of the public can increase or reinforce polarization among politicians in Washington. Increasingly well-sorted electoral constituencies may tend to disdain compromise and favor intransigence. Elected officials may react by taking positions strictly along party lines in efforts to win reelection. Party sorting among the public likely encourages elected officials to use harsh partisan rhetoric and take sharply partisan issue positions to secure reelection.[38]

In our view, political elites—especially donors and party activists—are probably most responsible for increased polarization in Washington. Members of the public tend to take their cues from activists and officials. Angry, energetic social and economic conservatism has produced a new breed of conservative political activists in the Republican Party. These activists play a powerful part in nominating candidates in low-turnout, obscure primary elections.[39] The result is that many members of Congress hold more extreme views than the vast majority of their constituents—indeed, they often hold more extreme views than the voters of their same party who live in their state or congressional district.[40]

To the extent that extreme financial contributors and party activists are responsible for these developments, polarization could be reduced by curbing the influence of money and activists in both primaries and general elections. We will discuss ways to do so in chapter 8. It is clear that party polarization is a major cause of disagreement, conflict, and deadlock.[41]

The Clogged-Up Senate

The United States Senate is unique among the world's legislative bodies in its tolerance for obstruction. Each individual senator has the power to block action by withholding consent from doing routine business; by offering numerous dilatory amendments; by putting "holds" on nominations; or by conducting—or merely threatening to conduct—a filibuster (talking endlessly until a proposal is abandoned).

Major legislation favored by strong majorities of Americans has often been turned aside, due to either small-state overrepresentation in the Senate or partisan obstruction. After the horrific mass shooting in 2012 at Sandy Hook Elementary School in Newtown, Connecticut, where twenty children ages six or seven and six staff members were killed, Senators Joe Manchin and Pat Toomey introduced mild, bipartisan legislation to require universal background checks on commercial gun sales—a policy favored by between 65 and 90 percent of the public.[42] Senator Manchin commented, "If we muster just one ounce of the courage these families [of victims of the Newtown shooting] have shown, then we, as a legislative body, can truly make a difference."[43] But even that mild legislation failed to pass. In subsequent years, neither the usual daily gun carnage nor new spectacular mass shootings—including the 2016 killing of forty-nine people at an Orlando nightclub—pushed the Senate into serious action.

It has been true for years that a single, highly ideological—or just plain cranky—senator can gum up the works in the Senate. But intensified disagreement and conflict between the parties has discouraged compromise and led to routine use of the filibuster and other tools for delay and obstruction as weapons of partisan warfare.

It's a vicious circle. Increasingly polarized parties resort to procedural tricks to obstruct their opponents' proposals. Perceived procedural abuses inflame the other party. Polarization and conflict increase still more.

PREVENTING ACTION BY FILIBUSTER. A substantial minority of senators (forty-one of the one hundred) can permanently prevent most legislative actions simply by supporting a filibuster. Sixty votes are required to cut off debate and force a vote on most proposed measures. Thus a unified, moderately large minority party can stop just about anything the majority party wants to do.

President Obama learned this to his sorrow when he took office in 2009 with what appeared to be a solid majority of fellow partisans (fifty-eight of them) in the one hundred-member Senate, as well as a substantial majority in the House. His Senate majority was illusory, however, because the Senate does not operate by majority rule. Most major Obama proposals were blocked. Even an economic stimulus bill designed to speed recovery from the Great Recession was held up, cut back, and made less effective by the need to scrape together three votes from the opposition party to attain the necessary sixty-vote supermajority.[44]

President Trump faced the same problem in 2017: the large minority of forty-eight Senate Democrats, when united in strong opposition, could stop legislative proposals.

As a result of the filibuster and other tactics of delay and obstruction, the Senate has become an impediment to policy change. Even senators recognize that the Senate does not work. Senator Tom Udall declared, "[The] Senate is a graveyard for good ideas. And the shovel is unprecedented abuse of filibusters—of delay and obstruction."[45]

The filibuster is fairly well known outside the Beltway, if only because of Jimmy Stewart's heroic efforts to talk sense into the Senate in the movie *Mr. Smith Goes to Washington*. That is the ideal: "extended debate" in which a Senate minority—even a single senator—employs eloquent rhetoric and powerful argumentation to convince the "world's greatest deliberative body" to change its collective mind.

In practice, however, the classic filibuster—which was never used much—has virtually disappeared. Most filibusterers have abandoned serious debate and instead have engaged in lengthy readings of irrelevant material like children's stories and telephone books.[46] Most filibusterers no longer aim to convince anyone. Instead, they seek to display "intensity" and force the majority to accommodate an intense minority by dropping or drastically modifying a proposal.

These days, moreover, most "filibusters" are not filibusters at all—they are just *threats* to engage in irrelevant, time-consuming talk. Often the majority leadership caves in to the threat and modifies or gives up its proposals, so that no one has to actually filibuster.

In principle it may not be unreasonable to allow displays of intense feelings, sometimes even to defer to them. We can imagine scenarios in which a minority should be able to resist "tyranny of the majority." But the minority views that have actually been served by the filibuster have seldom been so noble. For years, white southern senators used the filibuster to block civil rights for African Americans, as in Strom Thurmond's record-breaking twenty-four-hour filibuster in 1957.[47] In recent times filibusters have blocked a great deal of important and popular legislation.

The heart of the problem is that the balance of power has shifted in favor of filibusterers. Senate majorities used to employ an "attrition strategy" of wearing down filibusters by forcing them to keep talking until they were exhausted. But a huge increase in the amount of business that government has to do has made it hard to employ the attrition strategy without costly loss of time for working on legislation.[48] This change has strengthened the hand of potential filibusterers, especially during a year-end rush to adjournment. They can credibly threaten to bring all action to a halt and inflict great harm unless they get their way.

Shutting down a filibuster requires that sixty senators vote for *cloture* (forcing an end to the debate).[49] But the cloture rule is hard to use, and it is no help at all against a unified, forty-one-senator minority. With sharply polarized parties, the filibuster has been used much more often.[50] Figure 6.4 shows one indicator of the increased use of the filibuster: the increase in cloture votes (rarely successful) to try to overcome filibusters, which spiked markedly in the twenty-first century.

Minority-party threats to filibuster have become so routine that there is little point in even proposing a policy change unless it can command the sixty votes required to shut off a filibuster. With the exception of issues that can be treated as part of the budget process,[51] we now have a "sixty-vote Senate." This is very different from a majority-rule (fifty-one-vote), democratic institution. On debt ceilings and other matters that absolutely have to be acted upon, the threat or use of filibusters has contributed to frequent fiscal crises and has occasionally led to government shutdowns.

The crucial long-term remedy is to reduce party polarization—to

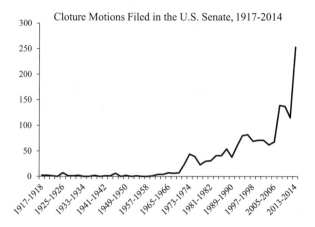

FIGURE 6.4 The filibuster has become more common in the twenty-first century.

Source: Adapted from U.S. Senate 2017.

move the parties closer together in their policy stands. (We will discuss how this can be done in chapter 8.) Once the parties are less sharply divided, the minority party in the Senate (or a Senate majority party controlling just one part of government) will have less reason to obstruct. It will be easier to compromise and produce legislation.

We believe that the filibuster is fundamentally undemocratic and should be sharply curtailed. The Democrats took a big step in this direction in 2013 when they abolished the use of the filibuster for executive branch nominees and judicial nominees other than the Supreme Court. But curtailing the filibuster, by itself, will not guarantee democratic outcomes unless party polarization is reduced as well, by making both parties more representative of the American citizenry as a whole. Otherwise, the filibuster might conceivably be a useful means to restrain actions that are opposed by most Americans but are being pushed on behalf of donors or activists. Similar logic applies to reforming the Senate "hold," another tool for obstructing Senate action.

THE SENATE "HOLD." Together with the filibuster, the "hold"—little known outside Washington—has become a devastating barrier against staffing top-level positions in the federal government.

During much of the twentieth century, the Senate confirmed nominees for district and appellate courts more than 80 percent of the time. The Reagan years brought tumultuous judicial battles, especially over the closely divided Supreme Court. Residual bitterness plus increased party polarization led to a downward spiral. In recent years the norm has fallen to roughly a 60 percent nominee success rate.[52]

Under informal but long-established Senate practice, a single senator can put a "hold" on—that is, unilaterally stop—the confirmation of any nominee for an executive or judicial position who comes from that senator's state. Holds need not be based on reasons related to the nomination, or on any stated reasons at all. They can be exercised in secret. They can stay in place indefinitely, until the senator is satisfied by some sort of concession or the nomination is withdrawn.[53]

Sometimes holds are designed to extort a concession on an unrelated matter, such as a pet project affecting a senator's state or a grievance about foreign or domestic policy. On other occasions holds are used as tactics in a concerted minority-party strategy designed to win major policy concessions or to permanently block nominations by a president of the opposite party. In either case, if the executive branch considers the price too high, the nomination is withdrawn. The position then stays unfilled—often leaving an important agency rudderless—until another nominee can be nominated and confirmed.

The hold has roots in old-style, state-level politics. It was apparently designed, as a matter of "senatorial courtesy," to allow a senator to withhold government positions from political rivals or foes from the senator's state. But the costs of this practice now far exceed the benefits. It should be an easy matter for a simple majority of senators to change the rules and abolish or severely limit the use of holds—with the caveat, again, that polarized and undemocratic parties are the bigger and the logically prior problem.

THE GERRYMANDERED SENATE. Just as the Senate is unique among the world's legislative bodies in its tolerance for obstruction, so it also stands out as for its defiance of democratic principles in the way legislators are chosen.[54] In Europe, the "upper houses" of parliament no longer provide the landed gentry with a veto on policy making. European upper houses have been democratized or shorn of most of their power. But our Senate still reflects its peculiar, eighteenth-century origins.

As a result of the 1787 "Connecticut compromise"—which was necessary to win support from the smallest states—the Constitution was written to provide that the U.S. Senate "shall be composed of *two senators from each State,* for six years; and *each senator shall have one vote.*"[55] Today, this means that the rather sparse population of Wyoming gets just as many votes in the Senate as the far more numerous (about 66 times as big) population of California. So one resident of Wyoming gets about sixty-six times as much Senate clout as one California resident, which clearly violates the principles of equal democratic representation and majority rule. To some constitutional scholars, it makes the Senate "illegitimate."[56]

As America's cities and suburbs have grown, the malapportionment of the Senate has become more and more extreme. As of 2010, the twelve smallest states, with only about 4 percent of the total U.S. population, had a total of twenty-four senators—nearly one-quarter of the entire Senate.[57] If nothing is done, the imbalance is likely to keep getting worse.

This flouting of basic democratic values has real consequences. The smallest, mostly rural states keep getting big, expensive (and sometimes bizarre) government projects (for example, the famous "Bridge to Nowhere" in Alaska), while funding for urban areas—whether for storm relief in New Orleans or mass transit in New York—is squeezed. Studies show that small states receive far more than their proportional share of federal benefits.[58] This pattern does not result from greater needs, such as having higher proportions of poor people than big states: often they do not. (New York has higher poverty rates than all but one other state, for example). Homeland security needs would certainly seem to be greater in New York than in Wyoming or Alaska, yet those states have received five or six times as much money per capita for homeland security.

The Senate bias toward small, rural states means that rural areas get a lot of what they want, such as subsidies for farming and mining, while urban states get less—less gun control, mass transit money, antipoverty funds, or social welfare benefits. As our point about "disharmony among institutions" implies, the unrepresentativeness of the Senate also increases the likelihood of gridlock with other, more democratically elected branches of government, particularly the presidency.

The Unrepresentative House

Under our original constitutional scheme, the House of Representatives was supposed to be the most democratic part of the federal government, the institution most directly responsive to the will of ordinary citizens. Sadly for democracy, however, the "people's House" has now become a rather *un*democratic institution. It is often out of touch with the majority of Americans. Its sometimes-extreme stands have become a major contributor to gridlock.

Instead of steadily, year-in and year-out reflecting the wishes of the average American, the House now tends to lurch from one partisan agenda to a contrasting one when an election changes which party holds a majority of House seats. Such changes in party control can be triggered by a razor-thin margin of votes. The lurch results from two factors: sharp *polarization* between the parties, and rules that permit *one-party domination* of the House. When a polarized (and sometimes extreme) party takes control of the House, the rules permit that party to impose its will on a large minority opposition party—and on some of its own members, who together with the opposition party would constitute a majority—in a way that is not possible in, say, the U.S. Senate.

The polarization of party officials has been asymmetric: that is, congressional Republicans have moved far to the right of most Americans on many issues, without as big a leftward move by Democrats.[59] So the House's contribution to gridlock with other institutions is greatest in years when Republicans control the House but Democrats have the Senate and/or the presidency—as during the Obama administration.

An example of House extremism: in 2013, lawmakers were discussing a proposal to raise the minimum wage to $10.10 per hour.

(The minimum wage had never been indexed to inflation, and the then-current rate of $7.25 per hour was worth about 25 percent less than it had been forty-five years earlier.) Surveys at the time showed that 72 percent of Americans favored the proposal (including the majority of Republicans and almost 90 percent of Democrats). President Obama strongly supported the increase, and a majority of senators came out in favor as well. But Republicans in the House were united in opposition, and the proposed raise went down to defeat.[60]

THE ONE-PARTY HOUSE AND MINORITY RULE. Undemocratic decisions and gridlock result from sharply alternating—and sometimes extremist—House majorities partly because of a crucial feature of the House as an institution: *one-party dominance*. House rules and practices now allow the majority party to do just about anything it wants, entirely disempowering the minority party. In recent years the majority party has regularly followed the "Hastert Rule"[61] (just a practice, not really a rule) and prevented action on any proposal that a "majority of the majority" opposes. This majority of the majority can actually be a *minority* of all House members: as few as 26 percent of them![62] (See figure 6.5 for an illustration of how small a majority of the majority can be.) Under one-party dominance, this minority can obstruct any action it opposes, even if as many as 74 percent of all members of the House (all of the opposition party and nearly half of the majority party) want action. When a minority of House members insists on extreme policy stands and rejects popular policy decisions that the other branches favor, gridlock tends to result.

If the House were a majority-rule institution—that is, if decisions consistently reflected the preferences of the majority of House members—alterations of party control in which only a few seats change hands should make little difference. Majority-rule decisions by all House members would settle on policies that have the most support from all members of both parties taken together. That should result in moderate legislation that reflects the wishes of the "median member" of Congress, who stands at the center of all members on the liberal–conservative continuum.[63] Close elections

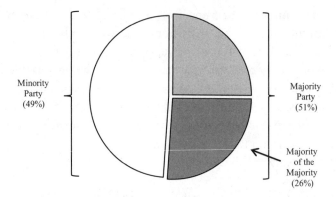

Minority
Party
(49%)

Majority
Party
(51%)

Majority
of the
Majority
(26%)

FIGURE 6.5 How the majority of the majority can be a minority.

that switch the party majority in the House might shift the precise location of the median member a bit—perhaps from a relatively conservative Democrat to a relatively liberal Republican—
and might produce small shifts in legislation, but nothing like the
extreme lurches in policy that now result from changes in party
control. If the House were a majority-rule institution, the moderate
legislation that it would produce would be much easier to meld into
compromises with the Senate and the president, producing substantial legislative achievements.

But in fact, the House is *not* now a majority-rule institution. The
Founders' idea of a "people's House" has been badly distorted.
Unequal voices from big money, organized interests, and ideological party activists push members away from democratic responsiveness. And special rules and procedures permit one-party dominance, at a time when representatives from the two parties radically
disagree with each other.

"CLOSED" RULES. The rules and procedures that permit one-party
dominance are not well understood outside Washington, DC. One
critical element is the "closed" rule, which can be imposed on proposed bills by the Committee on Rules. The rules committee is the
"traffic cop" of the House, which decides—usually at the direction of majority party leaders—which proposed legislation will be
considered by the House, and under what conditions. A "closed"

rule provides that no amendments at all can be offered to a particular proposal: a vote up or down, that's it. The majority party leadership can use closed rules to control the agenda, insisting that only proposals favored by a majority of the majority party's members will be considered, without any amendments allowed.[64] Even if a large majority of House members (that is, a majority of all the representatives from both parties taken together) would prefer something else, they can be forced to take what the majority party leaders offer or get nothing at all.

The House's system of *standing committees*, to which all proposed legislation is referred for hearings (and on each of which the majority party always has a solid majority of members), provides further opportunities for majority party leaders to exert agenda control and contribute to gridlock. It is virtually impossible for the House to consider legislation that is not reported out of a relevant committee. So it is easy for leaders to bury proposals in committee. The bills are just never reported out. "Discharge petitions" supposedly allow a majority of representatives to pry bills out of committee and consider them on the floor of the House, but such petitions are rarely successful—they prevailed only 37 times out of 597 attempts between 1931 and 2006.[65]

Quiet death by committee inaction is the fate of most legislative proposals, including bills passed by the Senate and favored by the president but opposed by a majority of the majority party in the House—which can be a minority of House members as a whole.

Even before we fix the complex problem of party polarization, it should be easy to remedy some of its most destructive effects by restoring the House to being a democratic, majority-rule institution. This restoration can be accomplished by simple changes in House rules and practices. Eliminating or severely restricting the use of closed rules and easing the discharge of bills from obstructive committees would effectively abolish the "Hastert Rule" and end one-party dominance of the House.

Moving the House toward majority rule by its members, even without reforming parties and elections, would increase democratic responsiveness under most scenarios. But if the party controlling other institutions were severely out of touch with the majority of

Americans, while a more majority-heeding party controlled the House, one-party dominance might actually help block undemocratic policy proposals. Procedural reforms in Congress—whether aimed at the clogged-up Senate or the one-party House—can be certain to have fully democratic effects only if democratic electoral reforms ensure that the members of Congress faithfully represent the American citizenry as a whole. The sequencing and packaging of reforms matter.

The Wayward Supreme Court

During the Gilded Age in the late nineteenth century—and for quite a while afterward—a probusiness Supreme Court systematically constrained workers' rights to organize, tolerated violent suppression of strikes, and obstructed state and federal policies designed to cope with the pains and problems of rapid industrialization. The court struck down state and federal measures to limit working hours, to improve working conditions, to regulate child labor, and to break the monopoly power of railroads and huge "trusts" that stifled competition and forced consumers to pay excessive prices. Only in the late 1930s—under strong political pressure from President Franklin D. Roosevelt's "court-packing" plan—did the Supreme Court reluctantly go along with most major New Deal programs.[66]

Today's Supreme Court has not gone nearly so far to obstruct the popular will. But it has derailed a fair amount of important legislation—legislation banning guns near schools, requiring states to expand Medicaid for the poor and elderly, core protections of the Voting Rights Act, and regulation of campaign money, for example. It has even interfered directly in the political process, halting Florida's efforts to work out a fair way to count its citizens' votes in the 2000 presidential election and effectively deciding the election in favor of George W. Bush.[67]

In short, the current Supreme Court, working under a doctrine of *judicial supremacy* (the doctrine first enunciated in the 1803 case of *Marbury v. Madison*: that the Supreme Court has final power to interpret what the Constitution means), sometimes contributes to gridlock and seriously obstructs the democratic policy-making process.

Most Americans tend to take judicial supremacy for granted as an entrenched and probably desirable feature of the U.S. political system. But it should not simply be accepted without question. The full-fledged doctrine of judicial supremacy is a rather recent invention. Neither the Founders nor (despite *Marbury*) many generations of Americans contemplated anything like it. Instead, the prevailing view—a view that may still have something to recommend it— was that "the people themselves," who instituted a Constitution based on popular sovereignty, are the proper interpreters of that Constitution. One legal scholar urges us to reclaim the legacy of the Constitution as (in Franklin D. Roosevelt's words) "a layman's instrument of government," not a lawyer's contract to be interpreted by a legal elite.[68]

This does not imply that we should undo judicial independence or lifetime tenure for judges; they are important to the protection of liberties and the rule of law. But it does mean that we may want to think differently about the role of the court in overturning popular and important legislation. It suggests that some moderate reforms, and some tools of majority-rule pressure on the court that have been used in the past, should be considered seriously when the Supreme Court defies the will of the people.

For a full picture of the causes of gridlock resulting from *disharmony* among our political institutions, it is important to bear in mind that the unelected justices of the Supreme Court sometimes take stands—based on questionable and contested constitutional theories—that are out of harmony with the majority of Americans and that stymie government action. In chapter 8 we discuss whether and how we might deal with the entrenched undemocratic features of the Supreme Court, along with undemocratic and gridlock-producing features of the Senate and other institutions.

PART THREE

What Can Be Done

SEVEN

Equal Voice for All Citizens

An essential step toward increasing democratic responsiveness is to ensure that all citizens have an equal voice in what the government does. Unequal power wielded by those who control money, corporations, or organized interest groups—who sway elections, lobby officials, and exert special influence within political parties—needs to be curbed. Ordinary citizens need to be empowered.

This chapter explains how certain reforms could greatly reduce the political power of money and organized interests. Other reforms could empower citizens, ensuring that those who vote in elections represent all Americans. Reforms of electoral rules and institutions could make each citizen's vote count equally in choosing government officials and affecting policy decisions.

Americans Are Fed Up

Americans are fed up with a political system that is not responding to their needs. Large majorities say that government officials do not "pay attention to people like me"; that government programs are full of waste; and that government is run by "a few big interests."[1] The research reported in this book tends to confirm what most Americans have known or suspected for a long time.

Unfortunately—though all too naturally—realistic skepticism about the current state of American government tends to turn people off from politics. If the political system is fundamentally corrupt, or if neither party has the interests and desires of ordinary citizens at heart, why bother to vote? Why take part in election campaigns? If no one is listening, why take the trouble to contact public officials? Instead of working within the system (which is apparently useless), or trying to fix it (a daunting prospect), many people give up and drop out.[2]

The problem is that fatalism can become a self-fulfilling prophecy. If everyone thinks it is impossible to clean up our political mess, no one will do anything about it. The mess will not get cleaned up. Fatalism tends to be paralyzing. (Some who benefit from the status quo may actually encourage others to hate government and give up any idea of fixing it.) But we believe that such fatalism is not warranted.

Many state and local efforts are under way to reform our dysfunctional political system and give ordinary citizens a bigger voice in politics. A number of states and localities have adopted publicly financed "clean election" systems to reduce the power of campaign donors and special interests. Others have adopted automatic registration to make voting easier and enhance the representation of marginalized groups. Still others are experimenting with new voting systems designed to reduce polarization and empower candidates who appeal to the widest possible number of voters. We detail these efforts, and assess their promises and pitfalls, in this and the following chapter.

Progress Is Possible

In 2011, Connecticut became the first U.S. state to guarantee its workers paid sick leave. How it did so says a lot about the power of organized interests but also about the ability of political reforms to empower citizens and bring public policy more in line with the needs and preferences of the majority.

In almost every other affluent country, citizens are guaranteed paid sick days as a matter of national policy. But not in the United States. The overwhelming majority of Americans think companies should be required to provide paid sick days, but business interests often oppose such measures. Most high-income workers already have them. But only a handful of American cities or states guarantee all workers paid sick days.[3]

For years, Connecticut activists and sympathetic officeholders had fought for a paid sick days law. But the Connecticut Business and Industry Association (CBIA) and key Democratic and Republican leaders (who took campaign donations from the CBIA) were opposed. Then in 2008, Connecticut's new Clean Election law went into effect. Participating candidates must rely on public funds for the bulk of their campaign spending, augmented by small donations from private contributors—but none from interest groups or political action committees (PACs).[4]

In the next gubernatorial election, the Democratic primary race pitted self-financed millionaire businessman Ned Lamont, who opposed paid sick days legislation, against publicly funded Dannel Malloy, who supported it. Relying on grants from Connecticut's' Clean Election program and small donations allowed under the Clean Election law, Malloy prevailed. He then went on, relying again on public funding, to defeat his Republican opponent in the general election.

With three-quarters of the winning Connecticut legislators (and all five winners of statewide offices) participating in the Clean Elections program, the political dynamics in the state shifted. By the end of Malloy's first year in office, the paid sick leave bill had been signed. Connecticut's publicly financed election system has also been credited with helping to pass an increase in the minimum wage, an expansion of the state's Earned Income Tax Credit for low-income households, and a long-sought change in the state's bottle deposit law that secured $24 million a year for the state treasury (money that had previously been kept by beer and soda distributors).[5]

Connecticut's paid sick leave policy is hardly perfect. It applies only to companies with fifty or more employees, for example, leaving many workers uncovered. But it is a step in the right direction, a policy that can make a real difference in people's lives. By reforming Connecticut's campaign finance system and giving ordinary citizens a greater voice in shaping state policy, political power was shifted in a modest but consequential way.

Connecticut's Clean Elections program is only one example of state and local efforts to give ordinary citizens a bigger voice in determining what their governments do. Arizona and Maine have also enacted statewide clean elections programs aimed at reducing the role of big money in elections. Those states' experiences show both the potential and the challenges that such programs face. Later in this chapter we discuss alternative campaign finance reforms that have been proposed or adopted in various places. For now we simply note that reducing the power of moneyed interests *is possible*, and that doing so can make government more responsive to the needs of ordinary citizens.

Right now states and cities are leading the way in adopting progressive political reforms. But change is possible at the national level as well, as our history—including recent history—makes clear. In November 2013, for example, after months in which the confirmation of appointees to federal judgeships and executive branch positions were blocked or delayed by a minority of U.S. senators—leaving important jobs unfilled and agencies without direction—the Senate decided by simple majority vote to make it easier to shut off obstructive filibusters on nominations. This action did not completely solve the problem—many nominations continued to be delayed in other ways[6]—but it did make clear that some significant reforms can rather easily be achieved.

Certain other, more far-reaching reforms—especially those that would require amending the U.S. Constitution—would be much harder to accomplish. Several times in the past, however, we have in fact amended the Constitution to achieve major, prodemocratic political reforms. Constitutional amendments have helped lead to more or less direct election of the president (rather than by a cumbersome and undemocratic scheme involving state delegations in the House of Representatives); established the right of all citizens to vote, regardless of race, color, or previous condition of servitude; provided for popular election of U.S. senators (rather than appointment by state legislatures); given women the right to vote; given residents of the District of Columbia the right to vote for president; abolished poll taxes that discouraged lower-income citizens from voting; and allowed eighteen- to twenty-year-olds to vote.[7]

As we will see in chapter 9, some of these important advances in democracy occurred only because of sustained efforts by broad-based social movements. We will explore whether and how such a movement for Democracy might be mobilized now to accomplish major reforms. But some important changes may be possible right away, especially in more progressively minded states and localities, if large majorities of citizens apply sufficient political pressure.

In this chapter we outline a number of specific reforms that could help give all citizens a more equal voice—and a loud voice—in American politics. First we consider reforms to reduce the power of money and organized interests that drown out what ordinary citizens are saying. Then we turn to reforms in the way elections are conducted that will help empower citizens and make sure that *all* citizens are represented.

No one reform—indeed, no conceivable combination of them—will completely level the playing field. But we believe that the reforms we outline in this and the following chapter can have a positive impact on the American political system, and—as a result—a positive impact on the quality of Americans' lives.

Curbing the Political Power of Money

In our judgment, the top priority among political reforms is to reduce or eliminate the power of private money in American politics.

Money profoundly corrupts U.S. politics. Our point is not that all politicians are "on the take" for personal gain. Today—as contrasted with the late nineteenth century—outright bribery of federal government officials is probably rare.[8] (Of course indirect perks for politicians are legion, and we cannot be sure how much direct bribery actually occurs—since successful cases are likely to be kept secret.) But even perfectly legal money corrupts the most fundamental principle of democracy, the principle of political equality.

In democratic politics each citizen is supposed to get one and only one vote, and to gain equal responsiveness from elected officials.[9] In the United States today, however, individuals and organized groups are able to amplify their political influence well beyond one person, one vote by spending money on politics. Those who spend the most—especially wealthy individuals, multibillion-dollar corporations, and corporate owners and managers—get, in effect, many extra votes to decide which public policies will be enacted and which rejected.

As we have noted, political money affects which candidates—standing for what sorts of policies—get elected, and who is able to run in the first place. Of course other factors matter too, and the candidate with the most money is not always victorious (ask Hillary Clinton or Jeb Bush). Nevertheless, money is a critical resource for political success. Money affects whom officials listen to. Money shapes how candidates spend their time (much of it begging for money), and what they think about; for example, they are frequently pressured to support tax breaks for hedge fund managers and other wealthy individuals. Money affects which policy ideas gain traction in think tanks, the media, and public opinion, and which ideas are ignored.

All in all, political money makes a mockery of the idea of one person, one vote.

The most important reforms of all, therefore, are those that will reduce the role of money in politics. Money, like water, flows easily through any available channel, and high-priced lawyers can be hired to invent clever ways to evade new regulations. But if reforms are carefully designed and frequently revisited to close loopholes, they can make a great deal of difference.

DILUTING OR ELIMINATING PRIVATE MONEY IN ELECTIONS. The experience of other countries makes clear that a tidal wave of corrupting political money is not an inevitable feature of modern elections. Several other democracies, for example, place strict limits on campaign spending or contributions, or they allow for a mixture of public and private funds that can dilute and decrease large-donor contributions.[10]

Efforts to constrain the role of money in American elections date back to the early decades of the twentieth century. Various contribution and expenditure limits, as well as disclosure requirements, were adopted for federal elections. But no enforcement mechanism was provided, and the regulations proved predictably ineffective.

The first serious efforts at federal campaign finance regulation were the 1971 Federal Election Campaign Act that mandated disclosure of campaign contributions and the 1974 amendments to that act that placed restrictions on contributions and spending and established the Federal Election Commission (FEC) to enforce them. But the Supreme Court struck down the spending limits, citing (incorrectly, we believe) First Amendment protection of free speech. Since the 1970s, federal campaign finance law has seen a series of legislated reforms that have been struck down, in whole or in part, by the Supreme Court.

RETHINKING CONSTITUTIONAL LAW. The biggest single barrier against reducing the power of money, therefore, is a legal barrier created by our judiciary. A series of Supreme Court decisions have moved things in the wrong direction. Beginning with *Buckley v. Valeo* in 1976, the court has taken what we consider to be a mistaken view of what the Constitution has to say about money and politics. In *Buckley* the court wrongly rejected the principle of political equality (an "equal playing field" for all citizens)—which is enshrined in the Declaration of Independence and the Fifth and Fourteenth Amendments and is clearly implied by the Founders' "republican principle"[11]—as a basis for authorizing congressional action to limit campaign contributions. In the *Citizens United* case of 2010, the Supreme Court declared that corporations—which state laws say can be treated as fictitious "persons" for the purpose of entering into business contracts—have the same constitutional liberties as real people do, and it ruled that the spending of money on politics amounts to "speech" that is protected by the First Amendment. The 2010 *Speech Now* case, which followed *Citizens United*, ruled that supposedly "independent" expenditures to help a political candidate cannot be regulated at all.

A top priority for reform, therefore, is to reverse these decisions and reestablish a clear constitutional doctrine that Congress has the power to regulate political money. To do so may require a change in Supreme Court personnel. Or it may require a difficult-to-enact constitutional amendment. (We will have more to say about the constitutional amendment strategy in chapters 8 and 9.) But an essential first step toward reversing the Supreme Court's decisions is to develop and publicize compelling legal arguments that make clear the court has erred.

A number of lawyers and legal scholars are crafting and circulating such arguments. Several prominent scholars argue, for example, that corruption (the only allowable justification for restricting spending, according to current Supreme Court rulings) goes beyond quid pro quo exchange and has historically been understood to include the corrupting dependence of legislators on moneyed interests.[12] If the Supreme Court's conception of corruption is broadened beyond the quid pro quo exchange of money for favors, some restrictions will become permissible, including restrictions on private political money spent by outside groups such as super PACs.

More fundamentally, many constitutional scholars argue that combating corruption is only one of the constitutionally legitimate objectives that might justify restricting political speech. *Political equality* has long been recognized as a core constitutional value. The Supreme Court recognized this value in its one person, one vote cases concerning the apportionment of legislative districts. It has also recognized, in its rulings on poll taxes and property requirements, that political quality cannot be denied due to lack of financial resources.[13]

Legal scholars are developing the foundations for a new jurisprudence of campaign finance that is more consistent with the needs of ordinary citizens and more supportive of genuine democracy. At the same time, advocacy organizations such as Dēmos in Washington, DC, and the Brennan Center at New York University are working to bring these alternative understandings to the attention of policy makers and the public.

By design, the Supreme Court enjoys a degree of insulation from public pressure, but scholars of the court agree that public opinion does influence the court—which, lacking any institutional means of enforcing its rulings, is perpetually concerned with upholding its popular legitimacy.[14] A future Supreme Court, faced with increasing public pressure to revise its constitutional jurisprudence on campaign finance, might well come to a different understanding. After all, the five-to-four vote that decided *Citizens United* meant that four Supreme Court justices already held a dissenting view of what our Constitution requires and permits.

One indication of growing pressure for fundamental change in the way money is regulated (or not regulated) in politics is the call for a constitutional amendment to overturn *Citizens United* and related rulings. As of 2016, sixteen states and almost seven hundred municipalities had come out in support of an amendment to overturn *Citizens United*. A majority of the U.S. Senate voted in September 2014 in support of such an amendment, and in a 2015 survey of the American public, 78 percent of respondents said that *Citizens United* should be overturned.[15]

A shift in the Supreme Court's thinking or a constitutional amendment could usher in a new era in American democracy. Strict legal limits could be put on political spending by campaigns or by outside individuals or organizations, and the size of individuals' contributions could be capped. Campaign contributions by corporations could be banned altogether. These moves would greatly reduce the power of money in politics.

To approach the ideal of equal voice for all citizens, however, and to further reduce or even eliminate the unequal political clout of the affluent, it would also be necessary to completely eliminate private money from elections. Since campaigns are expensive, the only way to do this is to *substitute* public money for private. Only such a shift would provide a "clean" way to fund election expenses and to give candidates of all sorts—including those who appeal to ordinary citizens but not to donors—a fair chance to compete.

We believe that changing constitutional doctrine concerning money in politics should be one of the highest priorities for democratic reform. But public financing of election expenses should be another top priority. Through public financing, much can be done right away—even under the Supreme Court's current interpretation of constitutional law.

USING PUBLIC MONEY TO FUND ELECTIONS. Under current Supreme Court rulings, *voluntary* systems of publicly financed elections can include constraints on donating or spending as conditions for candidates to receive public money (that is, money supplied by the government from the taxes it collects). In Connecticut's Clean Election system, for example, candidates who opt into the system must rely only on public funding and forgo private fund-raising (beyond the specified number of small contributions required to qualify for participation in the program).[16] If public funding is set at sufficiently high levels, this is an excellent way to greatly reduce the corrupting effect of private money.

For this system to work well, however, the level of public funding must be high enough to persuade all candidates to participate, or at least high enough so that candidates who participate have a reasonable chance to compete strongly with those who do not. When public funding is set too low—as it was with the moribund tax checkoff system for presidential campaigns—the candidates will simply ignore it and go for big private money.

EMPOWERING SMALL DONORS. If we cannot achieve legal or voluntary restrictions on the quantity of private money that is spent in politics, the best we will be able to do with public money is to at least *dilute* private money's effects.[17] One possible way is through *matching*: augmenting small contributions with public funds. If parties and candidates received large amounts of money from small contributors—who may be more representative of average citizens than billionaires are—then parties and candidates would be less dependent on big donors and, one hopes, more likely to respond to the citizenry as a whole. If the bulk of political money—ideally, *all* political money—came from donors who were fully representative of the citizenry as a whole, then ordinary citizens would be empowered and the voices of the wealthy would be muted.

In New York City, for example, small contributions from city residents (up to $175) are matched with public funds on a six-to-one basis, so that a contribution of $20 is worth $120 to the candidate receiving it, and a contribution of $175 is worth $1,050. To qualify for the matching money, candidates must first get a minimum number of small contributions from voters in their district (e.g., one hundred contributors for candidates for borough president). The program has been effective at broadening participation in campaign funding and increasing the proportion of campaign money coming from less affluent areas of the city.[18]

A bill has been introduced to Congress to apply the matching idea to federal elections. The Government by the People Act, proposed by Representative John Sarbanes, would finance the matching of contributions of up to $150 and provide a refundable tax credit for small contributions.[19] As compared with the present system, this legislation would bring significant progress. Congress should be urged to consider it seriously. Similar arrangements could be applied to major political races in all states and localities.

A serious problem with contribution-matching reform proposals, however (including those that work through tax deductions or tax credits[20]), is that they give a special advantage to relatively affluent citizens, who can easily donate $50 or $100 and get the matching money or tax credits. Hard-pressed lower-income people have a much harder time coming up with such sums. Thus, these proposals would leave the influence of campaign money tilted somewhat toward the middle to upper middle classes—and, in some cases, toward highly motivated people with extreme political views.

BETTER: DEMOCRACY VOUCHERS. By contrast, reforms that would give each citizen *equal* power over how public money is allocated— especially if supplementary contributions were banned—would push our system toward real political equality. Every citizen could allocate exactly the same number of dollars to politics. Unequal economic resources could not be so easily translated into unequal political influence.

As an alternative to matching programs, "Democracy Vouchers," along the lines advocated by Lawrence Lessig, are particularly appealing. Lessig would give each citizen a voucher (or stored-value card) from the U.S. Treasury worth $50, which could be allocated to any candidate or candidates the citizen specifies. In our version, each candidate could receive such money only if the candidate agrees that it is the *only* money he or she will accept.[21] This system would be entirely voluntary. Yet—if the vouchers were big enough so that all candidates would accept them—it could ultimately lead to totally ending the role of private money in elections.[22]

Democracy Vouchers are doable. Seattle recently adopted a voucher system for its municipal elections. Starting in 2017, every registered voter receives four $25 vouchers that he or she can donate to candidates for mayor, city council, or city attorney. South Dakota recently voted in the first voucher system for statewide offices. The big advantage of Democracy Vouchers is that they could potentially *equalize* the money-based influence of every citizen, rather than just magnify the clout of small to medium-sized donors.

The same idea could be applied to federal elections for Congress and the presidency.[23] In fact, Democracy Vouchers could be made to apply to any candidate, for any state, local, or national office, and at any stage of the electoral process—including the worst sore spot of our present system: primary elections.

THE PUBLIC OPINION PROBLEM. A potential political obstacle to the public funding of political campaigns is that many Americans dislike the idea of giving tax money to politicians.[24] This sentiment is understandable, but it misses the point. We need to do a better job of explaining that a modest investment of tax money would bring big benefits in the form of a more democratic political system. We also need to make clear that the leading proposals for public funding all rely on free choices by citizens of which candidates to support, and free choices by candidates on whether or not to accept the public money and the restrictions that go with it. Democracy Vouchers, when fully explained and well publicized, may prove to be very appealing.

In places where publicly financed clean election laws have been adopted, they have in fact proven popular with voters. For example, 79 percent of respondents to a 2010 Connecticut poll expressed support for their state's publicly financed elections program. When the state legislature tried to reduce the program's funding to help balance the state's budget in 2015, they were forced to back off after a public outcry.[25] Overwhelming majorities of Maine's voters similarly support their state's clean election program. In 2015 they passed an initiative to strengthen the program and increase its funding.[26]

REQUIRE FULL DISCLOSURE OF MAJOR POLITICAL SPENDING. In addition to public funding, another simple but crucial step can be taken even while constitutional doctrine remains hostile to legal limits on private campaign money. We can require *full disclosure* of political spending. "Stealth politics" by means of secret spending enhances the power of private money by making it hard to identify the donors or to work against them. Full legal disclosure of how much money is spent, by whom, for which causes or candidates, would help create accountability. It would make it possible, for example, to expose publicly the name of a person who paid for a particularly egregious, false, or misleading TV advertisement. Such publicity might mitigate the impact of the ad, or at least discourage others from doing the same kind of thing.

Direct contributions of $200 or more to candidates for federal office and to PACs must already be reported to the Federal Election Commission, which makes public the amounts contributed and the names of donors and recipients. Any citizen can access the FEC data (which, however, are hard to use), and watchdog groups such as the Center for Responsive Politics analyze those data to add up the total contributions from people who are affiliated with a particular type of business or profession. The center's OpenSecrets website, for example, shows which politicians get money from oil companies, defense contractors, teachers unions, and so on. This is very helpful.

But not all organizations are required to report the identity of their donors. A growing amount of money in American elections comes from so-called social welfare organizations that can accept contributions of unlimited size and need not report their source. In the 2012 elections, more than $300 million was spent by groups that did not disclose their donors.[27]

One easy (though only partial) fix would be to require all companies that do business with the federal government to fully disclose their political contributions. In 2015, more than one million signatures were collected on a petition that unsuccessfully urged President Obama to issue an executive order that would do so. Because so many of America's largest companies have contracts with the federal government, this small step would have a wide effect.[28]

A more complete solution would be to apply the same disclosure laws to corporations that already exist for unions. At present, corporations are required to report only expenditures that explicitly support or oppose a candidate for federal office (or otherwise meet the definition of "electioneering"). Unions, on the other hand, must disclose "all direct or indirect disbursements to all entities associated with political spending at the federal, state, or local level for either a candidate or ballot issue." In addition, unions must refund to their members the portion of union dues spent on political advocacy if a member so desires. Shareholders do not even have a right to know what the corporation they "own" has spent on politics.[29]

DEAL WITH UNRESTRICTED "OUTSIDE SPENDING." Even the most carefully considered campaign finance reforms—whether matching funds, vouchers, or publicly financed clean elections—can be undermined by so-called independent expenditures made by super PACs and dark money "social welfare" organizations. In 2010 the Supreme Court let stand a lower court's ruling (in *Speech Now v. Federal Election Commission*) that spending by organizations that are not formally coordinating with a candidate or political party cannot be restricted, even if those organizations expressly advocate for or against a candidate or ballot issue. This ruling gave birth to super PACs and an explosion in outside spending. As the chart in figure 7.1 shows, spending by these formally "unaffiliated" groups reached almost $2 billion in the 2016 presidential election.[30]

The unrestricted money collected by super PACs and other unaffiliated groups comes overwhelmingly from the superrich. In 2012, 93 percent of super PAC money came from only 3,318 people, and more than half of all super PAC money came from just 159 individuals.[31]

If we cannot find a way to tame these enormous expenditures by America's richest citizens, then campaign finance reforms that seek to give ordinary citizens a stronger voice will be in danger. Even if all candidates voluntarily opt into a state's clean election system, for example, outside groups can spend unlimited sums to promote their preferred candidate—or, more often, to attack his or her opponent.

We are starting to see exactly this kind of threat emerge in close elections where clean election laws limit participating candidates' own fund-raising and spending. In the 2014 Connecticut governor's race, for example, outside groups spent $18 million while the public grants from Connecticut's Clean Election program totaled

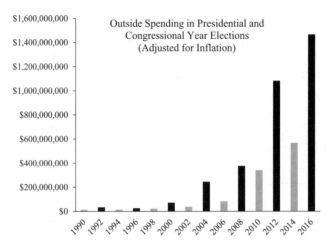

FIGURE 7.1 Outside spending has skyrocketed.

Spending by unrestricted political action groups (super PACs) and other unaffiliated groups calculated in constant 2016 dollars.

Source: Center for Responsive Politics 2017e.

only $13 million. Maine's clean election program has faced similar obstacles, although the 2015 changes were to increase funding to candidates, which will help them compete with outside groups.

In the long run—after we establish the constitutional principle that spending unlimited amounts to influence political campaigns does not constitute protected "speech" under the First Amendment—we can impose legal limits on the amount of money that individuals and organizations can spend. In the meantime, voluntary publicly funded election systems can help even the playing field. Even with the threat of outside spending, public funding has been shown to increase the competiveness of elections and give otherwise poorly funded candidates a chance to compete.

Controlling Lobbying and Organized Interests

As chapter 5 showed, organized interest groups and corporations have a great deal of influence over government policy making, and they tend to use that influence in ways that obstruct or work against the policies that average Americans want. Part of their political influence is exerted through lobbying. To deal fully with the power of organized interests, therefore, we need to deal with lobbying.

We should not go too far. James Madison was right: it would not be wise or consistent with our traditions of free speech to try to silence organized interests altogether.[32] We should not try to forbid interest groups or business firms from assessing the impacts of alternative policies, communicating their concerns to officials, drafting proposed laws and rules, testifying at congressional hearings, and the like. Lobbying can provide useful information to policy makers.

But providing useful information is far from the whole story of what happens now. The "information" that lobbyists provide is often biased or misleading. Amounts of information are lopsided: business firms have very loud voices, but average citizens are badly underrepresented. In any case, lobbyists do not just provide ideas; often their main value to the groups that hire them is their personal connections with elected officials. (One study of lobbying behavior found that lobbyists tend to switch issues when the politicians they are connected to through campaign donations switch committee assignments.[33] As the study's title put it, when it comes to lobbying it's not *what* you know, but *whom* you know that matters.) Perhaps most important, politicians may pay more attention to the *campaign money* that lobbyists' employers wield, or to the potential for lucrative job opportunities at lobbying firms when those politicians leave government, than to the merits of the ideas that lobbyists put forth.

Several types of reforms would help deal with these problems.

DIVORCE CAMPAIGN MONEY FROM LOBBYING. The most important step is to dilute or eliminate big-money contributions to political campaigns, in the ways we have just discussed. When interest group money is no longer crucial to the electoral survival of public officials, officials will be less tempted to flout the wishes of average citizens by responding to business corporations instead. Changes in campaign finance will be particularly effective if recent Supreme Court decisions including *Citizens United* are reversed and corporate political spending is completely prohibited. Whatever liberties our Constitution may guarantee to individual human beings, there is no persuasive reason to give fictitious corporate "persons" a constitutionally protected right to make campaign contributions or to spend money on political advertising.

How much further should we go, and how?

As in the case of campaign finance reform, several promising moves involve *full disclosure* of lobbying activities; *dilution* of the impact of today's heaviest hitters (mostly corporations and professional groups) by building up the capacities of others; and working toward a system of lobbying and information providing to government that is much *more representative* of the needs and wishes of ordinary citizens.

REQUIRE FULL DISCLOSURE OF LOBBYING ACTIVITIES. One helpful measure would be to require full disclosure of all expenditures aimed at influencing government officials. Current federal legislation requires registration—and some reporting—by people who officially call themselves lobbyists. But that legislation is full of loopholes. We also need to require full disclosure of lobbying activity by law firms, consultants, advocacy groups, and "public affairs" units of corporations. Perhaps we do not need to keep track of every citizen who sends an e-mail or drops by a member of Congress's office, but the public deserves to know about everyone who is paid to influence legislation or who systematically engages in contacts designed to influence legislation.

More broadly, it would be helpful to regulate lobbyists through a "lobbying procedure act." Such a law could specify exactly what sorts of lobbying activities must be disclosed, and it could specify what types of contact with which officials are or are not permitted. Moreover, it could (as one expert puts it) further a "genuine public conversation," by requiring the immediate electronic posting on a central website of brief summaries of every advocacy meeting with an official, plus copies of all white papers, draft legislation, and written policy recommendations. If properly organized, such a website could permit citizens and government watchdog groups to locate all the important arguments for or against a given policy with a few clicks. And it could alert everyone to undue influence.[34]

STOP FAVOR GIVING AND "REVOLVING DOORS." In harmony with the trend away from the grossest sorts of bribery, recent rules have made it difficult to give a federal government official anything of substantial value—whether a case of liquor, a Hawaiian vacation, or even an expensive meal.[35] (State governments need to catch up.) But there are loopholes that allow for "consulting fees"; book royalties from guaranteed sales to members of an interest group; speaker fees for expense-paid trips to conventions in exotic locales; and other types of compensation for services allegedly rendered. We should consider prohibiting any compensation beyond an official's salary for any speech, travel, or other political action. Short of that, we should certainly disclose such compensation fully and publicly, hoping that public pressure will minimize abuses.

Certain types of favor giving, such as secret advice about surefire investments based on private information, are extremely difficult to detect. But scholars have documented suspicious, abnormally high investment returns to U.S. senators.[36] Favor giving by way of investment tips needs to be made clearly illegal, beyond the already illegal cases of certain insider disclosures and quid pro quo bribery. Suspicious circumstances such as abnormally high stock market profits—or a member of Congress's purchase of stock in a constituent's company just before highly positive information is publicly disclosed—need to be vigorously investigated, publicized, and prosecuted.

One notable kind of favor giving involves the "revolving door," in which officials retire from government and take jobs with companies that formerly lobbied them (or with the lobbying organizations that represent those companies in Washington).[37] The revolving door can affect officials' behavior while in office, if they are promised—or even just hope for—such a future job. After retirement, revolving-door employment can give unfair clout to organized interests that can afford to hire the retired official to influence his or her former government colleagues. Lobbying is the top career choice for former members of Congress.[38] And many who do not officially register as lobbyists engage is similar work but skirt the rules against lobbying and call themselves "consultants" or "advisers" instead.[39]

Existing revolving-door regulations are rather feeble: retired members of Congress and high-level staff are prevented from directly lobbying their former colleagues for a year or two.[40] But they can supervise others who lobby Congress on their behalf, and they retain lifetime access to congressional cloakrooms, the congressional gym, and even the floor of Congress. Incoming administrations of both parties typically promise to crack down on lobbying abuses, but the main result thus far has simply been to encourage lobbyists to "deregister" and continue their work of shaping government policy under another job title.[41]

BUILD UP GOVERNMENT CAPACITY. The political power of organized interests can also be countered by building up the analytical capacities of government agencies. The Congressional Budget Office and the Congressional Research Service already contribute respected, nonpartisan information to members of Congress. But these are small institutions with limited mandates, and since the early twenty-first century, their resources have been shrunk, even as the demand for their services from Congress has grown.[42] We need to reverse this trend and also build up the staffs of congressional committees and regulatory agencies so that their independent expertise can have a better chance of standing up against lobbyists' arguments. Creative ideas include a "congressional clerkship" program for law students (law school deans are enthusiastic); "policy research consultants" for congressional offices; and better pay and working conditions for congressional staffers.[43]

CONSIDER CREATING "PEOPLE'S LOBBIES." Business corporations are doing fine, but certain types of interests—including those of millions of consumers, taxpayers, and working people—are not well represented in the interest group system. Political scientist Lee Drutman notes that a "Madisonian solution" to this problem would not involve limits on lobbying, but the opposite: *expansion* of the interests that are effectively represented.[44] Madison, after all, based his argument for the control of "factions" on the idea that *diverse* factions, representing just about everyone's interests, could check and control one another. So why not boost lobbying that reflects the interests of people who are currently ignored?

A possible approach would be to encourage the formation of

"people's lobbies" by providing subsidies, tax breaks, expertise, and special official access to groups that represent widely held points of view that would otherwise be left out of the lobbying process. The federal government might set up an Office of Public Lobbying and maintain a team of public lobbyists who would represent various public interest clients.[45]

The details would have to be worked out carefully. Only truly *substantial* interests held by many Americans should be helped out in this way. They should be selected through an objective, independent process that is based on concrete evidence (from opinion surveys, the U.S. Census, rosters of existing interest groups, and the like) concerning needs and preferences shared by large numbers of Americans that are poorly represented by organized groups.

A related idea is that "citizen panels" could be given special standing as advisers to public officials.[46] The idea would be to constitute (and regularly refresh) panels with fully representative samples of ordinary Americans, who would embody the diverse values and interests of the U.S. population as a whole. They would devote the time and effort needed to acquire expertise in a given policy area, deliberate about alternative proposals, and offer an informed-citizen view of which public policies would be best. At the state level, Voice of the People is already working to implement "citizen cabinets" of this sort to advise state governors and legislatures.[47] The same idea could be applied to regulatory agencies, to executive branch bureaus and departments, and to individual congressional committees. If citizen panels regularly watched over and testified before congressional and regulatory hearings, they might well transform deliberations that are now often held in obscurity and dominated by organized special interests.

INCREASE DIVERSITY AMONG ORGANIZED GROUPS. James Madison's benign view of "factions" or interest groups depended on the assumption that there would be a great deal of diversity among factions in an extended republic like the United States, so that they would represent pretty much everyone.[48] Today, however, the interest group system is tilted steeply toward business and the professions, leaving many Americans represented poorly or not at all.

People's lobbies and citizen panels could help remedy the situation, particularly with respect to needs and preferences that are widely shared in the whole population.

But we might also consider ways to encourage more specialized organizations that could amplify the voices of specific population groups that are currently underrepresented in the interest group system. Poor Americans, for example, currently have some vigorous advocates such as the Children's Defense Fund, but such groups are vastly outnumbered and outgunned by thousands of corporate lobbyists. New advocacy groups might be designed (and subsidized through tax credits) to represent the beneficiaries of various social welfare programs. Doing so would bring unique experiences and viewpoints into policy deliberations that currently tend to be dominated by academic experts, service providers, and (especially) antitax groups.

A key factor in the unrepresentative tilt of U.S. interest groups has been the weakness of organized labor. Compared with nearly all other advanced countries, we have lower levels of union membership, less centralized bargaining over wages (a crucial factor that affects income inequality),[49] and less political influence by unions— even though unions are more supportive than most other groups of the policies that average Americans favor (see chapter 5).

Historically, American labor unions played an important role in shaping U.S. social policies, including Medicare, civil rights, family leave, and the minimum wage.[50] But private sector union membership has declined dramatically in the United States, from 35 percent in the mid-1950s to less than 7 percent today.[51] Even so, some unions (such as the Service Employees International Union) have been central in organizing for policies that benefit less-advantaged Americans, such as raising the minimum wage and improving family leave policy in states and cities across the nation. The decline in union membership has not been an accident or an inevitable response to changing economic conditions. The political power of corporations and the wealthy has produced a decades-long decline in political support for union rights at both the federal and state levels.[52]

Long-term thinking about reform of our interest group system should consider measures to encourage rather than discourage unions. Democratic responsiveness could be greatly improved, and economic inequality reduced, if we could reverse the trend toward deunionization of American workers.[53]

Reforming Elections to Empower Ordinary Citizens

"People's lobbies," citizen panels, and citizen cabinets can help bring the voices of ordinary citizens into the policy-making process, especially when the noise from wealthy individuals, corporations, and organized interest groups has been muted. But we also need to make sure that the wishes of average citizens are heard through elections. Only elections can regularly hold officials to account and throw them out of office if they blatantly defy the will of the citizenry.

Among advanced democratic countries, the United States is unique in its low levels of voter turnout. As we saw in chapter 3, barely more than half of eligible Americans vote in presidential elections, only about 40 percent in off-year congressional elections, and seldom more than 20 percent in obscure but important primaries and local elections. Moreover, in contrast to most of the rest of the world, the Americans who do vote tend to be unrepresentative of American citizens as a whole. The affluent are much more likely to vote than the poor, the old more likely than the young, and whites more likely than members of racial or ethnic minorities.[54] Thus the voice of the people in U.S. elections is both *weak* (easily outshouted by partisan activists and campaign donors, especially in low-visibility primary elections) and *biased*. To the extent that the people's voice is heard at all, it is off-key—it does not sound the notes that the average American wants officials to hear.

Weakness and bias in the public's voice are two different problems. The reforms needed to deal with them overlap but are not identical. We will discuss the two problems separately, arguing that pronounced biases in citizens' electoral voice, including the large bias based on socioeconomic class, ultimately do the more fundamental harm. If we want government to respond to average citizens, we need to ensure that elections accurately reflect the will of those citizens.

THE VALUE OF CITIZEN PARTICIPATION IN POLITICS. Most Americans believe that it would be good for individuals—and for the country as a whole—if more people voted and actively participated in politics. Several theorists of "participatory democracy" have elaborated on the reasons. Fuller participation exposes people to more information, better analyses, and a better understanding of politics, which contributes to sounder collective decisions. Individuals who pay attention to the wants and needs of others and take part in political decision making become better citizens and better human beings, with a stronger sense of community.[55]

BARRIERS TO VOTING. Oddly, however, our political system—in sharp contrast to that of most other advanced countries—seems designed to discourage rather than encourage political participation, especially the fundamental act of voting. We have put many unnecessary barriers in the way. Instead of making the government responsible for compiling a list of eligible voters, as most countries do, we impose a requirement of "personal registration." Anyone who wants to vote must take the initiative and go through a separate step of registering. This often requires a special trip to some office that may be inconvenient to get to—especially for people who live in rural areas and poor people without a car or easy access to public transportation. Often the trip must be made well before the election itself, at a time when politics is not much on people's minds. And in many states, whole categories of people—such as ex-felons who have already paid their debt to society—are forbidden to register or vote.[56] The net result is that, on average, only about 66 percent of Americans are registered to vote in congressional elections and 70 percent in presidential elections.[57] This may be the biggest single barrier preventing higher turnout in presidential elections.

Even for those who manage to get registered, we impose other obstacles to voting. In many states people must show up personally at a polling place, which may be inconveniently located. Often they must do so during a limited number of hours on a particular day— generally a working day (traditionally a Tuesday), not a holiday, so that working people must either get time off or brave long lines of would-be voters during evening or early morning hours. Recently, deliberate partisan efforts have been made in some states to restrict the number of polling places, voting machines, and hours they are available, particularly in lower-income neighborhoods.[58] And new "voter identification" laws have the effect (in some cases the intended effect) of discouraging those who lack a handy photo ID such as a driver's license—particularly lower-income urban dwellers who do not drive cars.[59]

In short, instead of encouraging electoral participation, we impose significant *costs* on voting. Participation costs are even higher for obscure, off-year elections of state or local officials and for low-visibility primary elections—when many citizens may not even be aware that Election Day is at hand, let alone have access to reliable information about the candidates. Furthermore, in many cases the potential *benefits* of voting can reasonably be seen as slight. In our many one-party districts and one-party states, general election outcomes tend to be preordained. And in some primaries where extreme party ideologues and campaign donors pick the candidates, all the choices may look unattractive.

We should also note that our *two-party system* itself may discourage participation. Many voters find neither of our two major parties much to their liking.[60] For example, Americans with libertarian views (economically conservative but socially liberal) or populist views (economically liberal but socially conservative) may feel left out when the Republican and Democratic parties lump everything together as either "conservative" or "liberal." The United States strongly discourages third-party candidacies by means of various legal obstacles (such as burdensome petition-signature requirements) and by our single-member-per-district system—which makes it difficult for minor parties to gain representation in the legislature. Turnout rates tend to be higher in proportional representation systems in which votes for small parties can win them legislative seats. When multiple parties are encouraged, more citizens can find an attractive party to vote for.[61]

Even within a primarily two-party system, it could be helpful to remove measures that deny access to a place on the ballot (such as prohibiting "fusion" tickets, in which a candidate may appear on more than one party's ballot line) that unnecessarily discourage third parties. Going further, ranked choice voting—in which voters can rank their first, second, and third choices, and front-runners who lack a majority have to go through an "instant runoff"— could boost the candidacies of third-party candidates. In such a system, voters can express their support for a minor party candidate without worrying that they are "throwing away" their votes (or throwing the election to their least-preferred candidate).[62] This system would avoid such problems as Ralph Nader voters in 2000 handing the presidency to their disliked rival candidate George W. Bush, or 1992 Ross Perot voters inadvertently helping Bill Clinton.

In chapter 8 we will have more to say about institutional and structural changes that could make our parties, our elections, and our whole political system more responsive to the citizenry. Here we focus on more modest—and more immediately feasible—reform measures that could help empower citizens within the electoral and governing institutions that we now have.

REFORMS TO FACILITATE VOTING. It is easy to come up with reforms that would lower individuals' costs of voting and thereby increase voter turnout. The best single reform would be universal, government-administered registration, about which we will have more to say in a moment. Short of universal registration, we could at least allow same-day registration at polling places when people show up to vote.[63] Online registration and registration updating were shown in the 2012 California election to increase the number of voters, especially among young people.[64]

After more (preferably all) Americans are registered, we could make it much easier to vote by holding elections on a holiday rather than a working day; by allowing for early voting or universal absentee voting;[65] or by holding all-mail elections. Longer in-person voting hours, more polling places and voting machines, and perhaps Election Day voting centers in high-density population areas would help as well.

MAKING THE ELECTORATE REPRESENTATIVE OF ALL CITIZENS. All of the aforementioned reforms would tend to increase the number and proportion of Americans who vote. When it comes to our central objective, however—making government policy more responsive to average citizens—the *number* of Americans participating in politics is actually less important than the *representativeness* of those who participate. Since universal participation is probably not feasible, we want government officials to listen to a fully *representative* set of citizens. As a statistician might put it, we want elections to be decided by an "unbiased sample" of Americans, not by a sample that is biased toward the affluent or any other particular group.

This point is easy to understand if we think about an imaginary "reform" effort that focused on registering customers at high-end jewelry stores and luxury automobile dealerships. This might well increase registration and turnout a bit, but it would make the current class bias in voting worse. Most of the new voters would be affluent. Affluent Americans are already overrepresented in the electorate. Why work to increase their overrepresentation?

Unfortunately, something similar is true of several reform proposals for increasing election turnout: they may increase participation, but they do not do much to decrease—and in some cases they would actually increase—biases in participation.

Research indicates, for example, that the "motor voter" law (the National Voter Registration Act of 1993, or NVRA), which made it easy to register at the Department of Motor Vehicles and other public offices, may well have increased overall registration, but it has only modestly reduced the bias of the voting population toward higher education, income, and age groups.[66] By contrast, it would probably reduce participation biases substantially to fully enforce provisions of the NVRA as applied to the Affordable Care Act, by offering voter registration through federally facilitated Health Benefit Exchanges.[67]

Election Day registration, which clearly has a positive impact on overall turnout, appears to reduce biases in turnout between individuals with the lowest and highest incomes, at least in those states that previously had large income-based gaps in turnout.[68] Online registration mobilizes more young people, but it does not have much effect on other electoral biases.[69]

Again, all-mail elections tend to increase overall turnout modestly, but mainly by making it easier for people who resemble current voters to participate, not by mobilizing chronic nonvoters into the electorate. All-mail elections do not make the electorate more representative of the voting-age population.[70]

Even more disappointing so far have been the results of *early* voting, both in person and absentee. This popular reform, now common in many states, is most likely to help individuals who are already registered and more likely to vote in the first place. Early voting can actually decrease turnout and the likelihood of voting, if not paired with reforms such as Election Day registration.[71] Moreover, political campaigns appear to react to early voting systems in ways that tend to undermine the reforms. Even more money is required to run an effective campaign, and there have been many postelection court cases questioning the validity of ballots cast early, especially those cast via absentee ballot.[72] Unless same-day registration is already in place, early in-person voting can exacerbate existing gaps between the resource-advantaged (wealthy or highly educated people) and the resource-disadvantaged, particularly when campaigns spend more money to strategically target the most-likely early voters.[73]

One extremely disadvantaged group consists of people who were once convicted of a felony and have served prison time. Many states either flatly bar ex-felons from voting or impose difficult requirements before they can regain the franchise. This means that millions of Americans—about 5.8 million, including roughly one in every thirteen African Americans—are unable to vote because of a felony conviction. This slows the reintegration of ex-prisoners into society and has negative effects on whole communities. Since the United States has many more prisoners in proportion to its population than any other advanced country does, felon disenfranchisement leaves a large set of our citizens unprotected, with no way to hold politicians accountable for their welfare. These laws need to be changed.[74]

UNIVERSAL VOTER REGISTRATION. It is clear from the mixed record of the reforms tried so far that we need to be very careful about the details of future reforms. The biggest lesson seems to be that if we really want a representative electorate, we should make voter registration automatic and *universal*. Federal, state, and local governments should be made responsible for maintaining accurate and complete lists of people who are eligible to vote. Universal voter registration would demolish one of the biggest barriers to participating in elections: the burden on individuals to register themselves. It would open the way for further steps to reduce biases in who actually casts ballots. If properly administered, universal registration could also reduce errors in voter rolls and minimize concerns about voter fraud.[75]

To be sure, the idea of universal voter registration has some strong political opponents, who raise much the same arguments as those that were once made to prevent voting by lower-income people, religious minorities, African Americans, and women. They say that the masses do not know enough about politics to vote correctly; they do not have a "stake in the system"; they are too easily swayed by demagogues. As one conservative columnist put it, "some people just shouldn't be voting."[76] The same organizations that have worked to make registration and voting harder rather than easier—including the American Legislative Exchange Council (ALEC)—would undoubtedly fight against universal registration.[77]

We do not find the opponents' arguments at all convincing. Participation in politics helps people become better informed and encourages them to be better citizens.[78] Fears by our Founders and others of runaway popular "passions" have proved to be unwarranted. Studies show that gaps in individuals' political knowledge are largely offset in the public as a whole: Americans, as a collectivity, hold policy preferences that are generally real, stable, consistent, coherent, and reflective of the available information.[79] Most important, whatever the cognitive and other limitations of ordinary citizens may be, those citizens are almost certainly better at defending their own interests and promoting the common good than any elites that one might ask to rule on their behalf, whether kings, aristocrats, theocrats, oligarchs, or property holders—or simply fellow citizens with higher levels of education or political knowledge.

True, formal education generally leads to better knowledge about many aspects of politics (though not always about ordinary people's day-to-day needs). But formal education is generally associated with affluence, and with distinctive values and material interests. When the values or interests of highly educated people diverge from those of other citizens, there is no guarantee that the well-educated will work for the good of others—or, indeed, that they will correctly judge what the common good entails. We believe that democracy must rest on the will of average citizens. The best way to enforce that will is through full, unbiased political participation.

FOLLOWING UP TO ENSURE REPRESENTATIVE VOTING. After the barrier imposed by the onerous requirement of personal registration has been removed, other reforms that we have discussed can help increase the number of people who actually vote. And they can make voters more representative of the citizenry as a whole. Holding elections on a holiday and providing more convenient polling places that are open for longer hours and have more voting machines (that leave written records) would help.

We need to make special efforts to be sure that we bring into the electorate those who are presently most disadvantaged and underrepresented. Nongovernmental organizations—including civil rights groups for racial and ethnic minorities, the Rock the Vote organization for young people, and community health care providers for lower-income people—can help supplement legal reforms by making sure that the disadvantaged are actually able to cast ballots.

We also need to be sure that the *benefits* of voting are maximized and made clear to everyone. This means minimizing the number of one-party districts, where general election outcomes are preordained and voting has no discernable impact. It also means lowering the obstacles to third-party listings on the ballot, so that voters who are disenchanted with the two major parties can send a clear signal that the major parties need to change to win their support.

Some institutional changes of these sorts will be addressed in the following chapter, when we turn to reforms designed to overcome gridlock, party polarization, and other institutional problems. In chapter 9 we will have more to say about the political strategies and tactics by which such major reforms as universal voter registration can actually be attained.

EIGHT

Overcoming Gridlock and Democratizing Institutions

Governmental gridlock, paralysis, and inaction—which obstruct democratic responsiveness and thwart efforts to solve pressing national problems—can be partly overcome by the equal voice reforms discussed in chapter 7. When ordinary citizens are empowered; when the political power of money, organized interests, and party activists is reduced; and when the electorates that choose our officials are made more representative, several sources of gridlock will be diminished. As both political parties and all institutions of government pay more attention to ordinary citizens, government institutions will all tend to make more similar—more democratic—policy decisions. With more similar agendas, they will be less prone to conflict with one another.

But even if all the equal voice reforms are enacted, several sources of gridlock will remain. They will require changes in our institutions—some of them relatively easy to accomplish, others very difficult.

Remaining sources of inaction and gridlock include certain artificial barriers to action *within* government institutions, such as the U.S. Senate filibuster and "hold," and rules and practices that create undemocratic, one-party rule in the House of Representatives. These barriers can be lowered or removed by legislators themselves through simple majority-vote rule changes. But the sequence of reforms matters. Abolishing or severely curtailing the Senate filibuster, for example, should probably come only after equal voice measures (and perhaps other reforms as well) so that it is a *more democratic* Senate that is enabled to act. On the other hand, it probably makes sense to end one-party rule in the House as soon as possible.

The most fundamental, hardest-to-reform sources of gridlock involve disharmonies *among* institutions that result from various undemocratic arrangements concerning how our elections are organized, our political parties are constituted, and our institutions relate to the citizenry as a whole.

Since the separation of powers and staggered elections are conducive to divided party government, *sharply polarized parties* that control different chambers or branches of government are one prime source of gridlock. The *highly undemocratic apportionment of senators*—by state instead of by population—creates a prorural bias in nearly everything the federal government does; it also creates conflicts and gridlock with the very differently apportioned House of Representatives. Undemocratic *distortions in choosing presidents* can add to disharmony among institutions. Our *independent and unelected Supreme Court* sometimes imposes undemocratic decisions that conflict with other branches of government.

In each of these cases, we believe that the best remedy involves more democracy. More democracy is desirable in itself. It also has the virtue of tending to harmonize our institutions, so that all of them are aiming for the same thing—public policies that reflect the will of all Americans. There is less reason for them to conflict with one another.

Some of the reforms needed to address these problems would involve extensive institutional changes that are likely to be strongly resisted by those who are happy with the status quo. Some might be achievable only by amending the U.S. Constitution, which is very hard to do. Still, a measure of optimism about feasibility seems warranted. Major prodemocratic amendments to the Constitution have been enacted in the past—to grant voting rights to African Americans, women, and young people, for example. And pressure from a constitutional convention might accomplish a great deal without requiring any actual amendments.

We begin this chapter by discussing reforms that would be relatively easy to accomplish. Some barriers to government action just result from rules or informal practices that have been created by legislators themselves and could be easily modified or abolished. We then proceed with the more difficult ones.[1] In chapter 9 we turn to the question of exactly how major democratic reforms might be brought about.

Unclogging the Senate

Abolishing the hold. The "hold"—by which a single senator (usually from the party opposing the president) can unilaterally and silently stymie an executive or judicial appointment of anyone from his or her home state—is one significant cause of gridlock over appointments. It often narrows the pool from which appointees can be drawn. Sometimes it prevents vacancies in important government positions from being filled, or it holds up unrelated legislation in order to extort idiosyncratic and unpopular policy concessions from the executive branch.

Various senators have proposed sensible but incomplete reforms of the hold: limiting its duration; curtailing "unanimous consent" requirements; and—most obvious of all—ending secrecy and insisting that senators own up to their actions.[2]

Fine. But we do not believe that such reforms would go far enough. We know of no coherent argument in favor of the hold itself. It should simply be abolished. No law gives individual senators such arbitrary power. Nor does any rule of the Senate. It is just a traditional practice, a practice that could be overturned by Senate majority leaders and chairs of the committees that vet appointments.

The problem is that significant reforms of the hold have been blocked so far by senators who cherish the perk or want it available as a weapon in partisan warfare. But there are no *procedural* obstacles to abolishing the hold. It can be done easily, if senators face sufficient pressure from an outraged public. To make sure that this actually happens, the Senate should probably adopt a new rule, by majority vote, explicitly repudiating and disallowing the practice of the hold.

LIMITING THE FILIBUSTER. More important to unclogging the Senate is dealing with the *filibuster*, which has become a routine tool by which any opposition party with forty-one senators (41 percent of the Senate membership) can prevent action—generally just by *threatening* a filibuster rather than actually carrying one out. As discussed in chapter 6, the "sixty-vote Senate" has become a major cause of gridlock and a major impediment to democratic responsiveness.

Any changes in the Senate's traditions of "extended debate" and deliberation should be made with caution, however. When the Founders designed the Senate, they aimed to encourage careful discussion and avoid hasty, imprudent action. Public deliberation by senators can serve to educate the broader public and force senators to offer plausible rationales for their stands. We should be careful not to prevent senators from deliberating.

Under some circumstances, even lengthy, obstructive talk can be useful in a democracy, if it signals intense feelings that deserve to be taken into account—feelings about protecting minorities, for example, or preventing an out-of-touch majority party from railroading through a measure contrary to the wants and needs of most Americans.

But there are simple reforms that would help unclog the Senate without undercutting serious debate or disarming intense minorities. One is to insist that filibusterers actually engage in debate, not just threaten it, so that they have to pay a price: standing for several hours on their feet talking. That would reduce frivolous or excessive use of the filibuster. Another simple, sensible reform is to insist that all debate be *germane*—that is, relevant to the issue at hand. That would end the spectacle of obstructionist senators reading telephone books or nursery rhymes to their colleagues, but it would preserve the right of a Jimmy Stewart–type "Mr. Smith" or a Robert La Follette[3] to make an all-out effort to convince the Senate.

It seems prudent keep open the possibility of forcing majorities to accommodate minorities when those minorities are intense enough to carry out a genuine extended debate. But by insisting on real, relevant debate, we could get rid of time-wasting trivia, and we could discourage filibusters by making them harder to use.

It would also help if senators vigorously enforced such existing rules as the requirement that a filibusterer must stand at his or her desk (not sit or walk around) and the rule that the filibusterer may not "yield" time to anyone else until he or she is finished.[4] (Yielding to let a friendly senator ask long-winded questions can give filibusterers time to eat snacks, chat with staff, or rest.)

These measures would help discourage filibusters because they would increase the *costs* of filibustering. In effect, they would tilt the balance of power away from potential filibusterers and back toward majorities of senators, which in turn would permit a return to what can be called an "attrition" strategy by Senate leaders: force filibusterers to talk, and wait them out.[5]

If the costs of filibustering were substantially increased, *cloture* (shutting off debate) might be necessary only in a few extreme circumstances. On the other hand, if it turned out that filibusters continued routinely despite these mild reforms, we could consider pressuring the Senate to take such further measures as restricting the substantive scope of filibusters and/or easing the number of votes required for cloture, perhaps doing so in stages as debate continues on a given bill. History shows that significant congressional reforms *can* occur.[6] In 2013, faced with frequent filibusters of President Barack Obama's nominees, the majority Senate Democrats voted to eliminate the filibuster for all judicial and executive branch nominees except for the Supreme Court. Despite pressure from reform groups, the use of the filibuster to block Senate legislation was left intact. (This preserved a weapon that some Senate Democrats were glad to have after the 2016 elections, when the Republicans won control of the House, the Senate, and the presidency.)

A more fundamental but also more difficult strategy for reducing routine *partisan* filibustering—the most prevalent and destructive kind of filibustering—is to reduce the extreme party polarization that motivates such obstruction. We will discuss how to depolarize the parties later in this chapter.

Democratizing the House of Representatives

Undemocratic features of the U.S. House of Representatives contribute to gridlock by producing policy outcomes that do not reflect the will of majorities of Americans—or even majorities of

House members—which leads to clashes with more democratic stands taken by other institutions. By making the House more democratic—that is, by returning it to the Founders' vision of being "the people's House"—we could reduce gridlock while improving democratic responsiveness more generally.

Equal voice reforms would somewhat moderate the undemocratic aspects of the House by empowering a more representative set of voters to elect more representative members of Congress. To go further, the most profound reforms would require difficult measures to reduce party polarization, including alterations in the American electoral system. But one set of clearly desirable reforms should be relatively easy: demolishing the rules that artificially permit *one-party dominance* of House policy-making decisions.

ELIMINATING ONE-PARTY MINORITY RULE IN THE HOUSE. Rules and practices that permit the House majority party to ignore the opposition party—and even to ignore its own minority—are a recipe for *minority rule* in the House. The "Hastert rule" of deferring to a "majority of the majority" may sound fine, superficially, but that majority of the majority can actually constitute a rather small minority of all members of the House: as few as barely more than one-quarter of them. (Look back at figure 6.5 in chapter 6 for an illustration.)

An essential step is to *reverse the "Hastert rule,"* which is not even a real rule but just a practice. To make this happen by something more durable than a (possibly temporary) change of heart by a Speaker of the House,[7] it will be necessary to change some of the rules that make it possible for leaders of the majority party to enforce the "Hastert rule." One is the use of *closed or semiclosed procedural rules* by the Rules Committee, which limit or prevent any amendments to a bill. Use of these rules can force a majority of House members to either take what a minority of members (a majority of the majority) want or get nothing at all.

Closed rules are sometimes justified as facilitating action and preventing members from offering attractive "killer" amendments that could unravel supportive coalitions. (Before the Civil Rights Act of 1964, for example, economic conservatives sometimes disingenuously added civil rights amendments to social spending legislation to prod southern Democrats into opposing the whole package.) Our view is that closed rules are too easily abused. They too often result in *inaction*. If open rules occasionally result in killer amendments, then representatives should step up, vote those amendments down, and explain to their constituents why they voted as they did.

Since both parties have used closed rules—sometimes backsliding on promises not to do so—it may not be politically easy to accomplish this reform. But House rules could be changed by simple majority vote. As with obstructive Senate rules, sufficient popular pressure from reform groups and a social movement for Democracy might induce the legislators to act.

Another key to minority rule in the House is the *burial of proposed bills in committee*. If a committee chair won't schedule a vote, or if majority-party members of a committee oppose a bill, the bill will generally not be "reported out," so the House as a whole will never get a chance to vote on it. Burial in committee is another way by which a minority (a majority of the majority party) can impose its will on the majority of House members and prevent action.

A simple rule change, made by majority vote, could greatly reduce that type of obstruction: make *discharge petitions much easier*. The present requirement that a majority of all members (218 of the 435) sign a petition is too burdensome because it is too easy for party leaders to threaten or intimidate members out of signing. Why not permit (say) 35 percent or 40 percent of the representatives to demand that a bill be given a vote on the floor of the House? There is little reason to fear frivolous use of easier discharge petitions because they will still raise the ire of party leaders and committee chairs. Most rank-and-file representatives will sign discharge petitions only when there is strong reason to do so.

These simple changes in rules and practices could help a lot. They would largely prevent minority congressional factions within the majority party from ignoring House majorities consisting of members of both parties. They would lead to more centrist, bipartisan legislation and less gridlock with other branches.

But serious problems are likely to remain when party polarization leads an actual *majority* of House members to take extreme views that conflict with the wishes of average Americans and with the actions of other branches. We discuss party polarization next.

Depolarizing Our Political Parties

Sharp polarization between the two major political parties is an important contributor to gridlock and nonresponsiveness in Congress. Reforms that help bring the two parties closer together would do a lot to overcome gridlock and could also help give an equal political voice to all citizens.

Because money and on-the-ground campaign activity are essential for winning elections, each of the parties must energize a set of donors and party activists. Republican and Democratic donors and activists tend to be distinct from each other—and often extreme—in their policy views. The need to satisfy their own activists and donors, therefore, tends to push the parties' candidates and policy stands far apart from each other, particularly in low-visibility, low-turnout primary elections in which the donors and activists have a lot of clout.[8]

We have suggested that the current, exceptionally deep disagreements between Republican and Democratic activists and donors may have roots in regional realignments (the disappearance of white southern Democrats); in economic globalization (which has created sharply divergent interests between American workers and the owners of U.S. businesses); in job-displacing technology (ditto); and in social and demographic changes that have sparked conflicting views about immigrants, minorities, women, gays, and young people. No political reforms are likely to eliminate the impacts of these factors on people's interests or opinions. But certain reforms can profoundly alter their *political effects* by decreasing the power of activists and private-money donors generally. Ultimately, these reforms should also alter the sorts of people who choose to become donors and activists.

EMPOWER ORDINARY CITIZENS. One way to reduce the power of donors and activists is to increase the power of ordinary citizens. The equal voice reforms discussed in chapter 7—applied to both primary and general elections—would help tilt power away from contributors and ideologically extreme activists.

Such measures as universal voter registration; Election Day holidays; more voting machines and more convenient polling places; an end to burdensome voter identification laws; enfranchisement of ex-felons—all would help a representative set of ordinary voters wield more influence in our elections. All would reduce the relative power of extremist activists and donors to nominate and elect the extreme candidates who drive our parties apart.

DEFANG PRIVATE MONEY IN ELECTIONS. Perhaps even more important, equal voice reforms aimed at reducing the power of large private campaign donations can also help reduce party polarization. Individuals who make political contributions are generally more extreme partisans than other voters, and larger donors may tend to be more extreme than smaller donors.[9] Campaign finance reforms that empower smaller donors, such as New York City's matching program or John Sarbanes's Government by the People Act, could help spread political influence over a wider range of less ideologically polarized citizens. But even small donors are more polarized than voters in general, so increasing their influence will not eliminate party polarization.

A better solution would be what we introduced in chapter 7 as "Democracy Vouchers." Voucher systems like the one recently adopted by the city of Seattle allow voters to financially support candidates even if they are unable or unwilling to use their own money. This approach has the potential to mobilize an even greater segment of the public, empowering candidates who appeal to a wide and diverse set of citizens.

Changing constitutional doctrine and strictly regulating campaign money (including outside spending) would be transformative. Even within the current Supreme Court's current rulings, however, reforms like these could dilute the impact of extremist campaign donors and spread money power more equally among all citizens.

Reforming our campaign finance system is critical to making government more responsive to ordinary citizens. But reforms must be evaluated carefully, since they can have multiple and not easily predictable consequences. For example, public financing systems that shift power from business groups to individuals might exacerbate rather than reduce polarization. While activist groups and advocacy organizations are often extreme, many businesses and business associations have narrow, concrete policy objectives. Such associations often favor moderate candidates. They may even support candidates from both political parties who are willing to advance their particular interests. Thus reforms that shift the source of campaign money from business groups to individuals—especially affluent individuals—risk exacerbating partisan polarization even as they reduce the influence of organized interests. (Whether this has in fact happened in states that have reduced interest group influence through "clean election" laws is debated by scholars.[10])

We see this as another argument in favor of Democracy Vouchers, which shift money power to *all* citizens equally, rather than to small private-money donors—who tend to hold more extreme views than voters overall (even if less so than big donors).

ENCOURAGE MODERATE CANDIDATES TO RUN. No matter how we fund our electoral campaigns, voters can only choose among the candidates who appear on their ballots. Candidates running for the U.S. Congress and for many state legislatures have recently become more extreme, but not because voters prefer extremist candidates. On the contrary, it is clear that—given the opportunity—voters prefer centrist candidates. Studies show that when moderates are on the ballot, they are more likely to win, they win by wider margins, and they are less likely to be voted out of office in the future.[11]

But moderates all too rarely appear on the ballot. As the power of activists and ideological interest groups has increased over time, their influence over who runs for office has increased as well. Republican primary candidates depend on support from business groups, religious conservatives, gun rights organizations, and so on. Democratic candidates also depend on business support (helping to account for the bipartisan shift toward deregulation and free trade over the past decades), as well as unions, environmentalists, and racial, ethnic, sexual orientation, and gender identity activists and groups. These groups serve as recruiters and gatekeepers in primary elections, boosting potential candidates who favor their agendas and undermining those who don't.[12] Through their influence on the nomination process, interest groups and activist organizations limit the ability of voters to support the more centrist candidates they would otherwise choose.

NOMINATE AND ELECT CANDIDATES IN *COMPETITIVE* DISTRICTS. Lack of competition between the parties for the votes of ordinary citizens is an important cause of candidate extremism. When one party in a particular district can be confident of winning the general election almost regardless of what sort of candidate it nominates, that party's activists and donors are free to nominate the ideologically extreme candidates that they prefer, even if those candidates are significantly out of tune with their district.

A major source of noncompetitiveness in elections for members of Congress and state legislatures is *safely one-party districts*. Reducing the number of one-party districts, therefore, would increase competitiveness between the parties and reduce polarization. It would have the side benefit of making more equal the political influence of groups that are heavily clustered within districts (urban minorities, for example) and that currently have fewer representatives than their numbers would dictate.

The relatively easy part of this task is to *eliminate partisan gerrymanders*. States should take away decisions about district boundaries from partisan legislatures and give them to truly independent commissions that follow objective criteria. This is doable. A number of states—including Alaska, Arizona, California, Idaho, Montana, and Washington—are already doing it.[13] Studies show that electoral competition is increased when states use independent commissions to draw district boundaries.[14] If too few additional states act on their own, it may be desirable to work for federal legislation mandating that all states arrange for independent districting.[15]

The harder part of creating more competitive districts concerns "naturally" one-party districts where distinctive social groups are clustered geographically. Such districts are probably an even bigger impediment to competition than gerrymandering is.[16] What to do?

In one sense, the answer is straightforward: make *promoting two-party competition* a chief criterion (more important than compactness or contiguity) for independent commissions to follow in drawing district boundaries. In other words, if necessary in order to increase party competition, cross traditional neighborhood boundaries and create districts with somewhat irregular shapes. The experience of Illinois suggests that this can be done without bad side effects such as eliminating members of Congress from racial or ethnic minorities.[17]

But there is a serious problem. In a state with, for example, 60 percent Democratic and 40 percent Republican voters in the state as a whole, if every district were designed to have the same maximum level of competition, by copying the state's partisan proportions in each district—that is, if every district were made 60 percent Democratic and 40 percent Republican—it might turn out that every single representative elected was a Democrat. Not a very democratic (small *d*) result. Yet if only *some* districts were designed to be highly competitive, it would be difficult to decide exactly how many, and which, districts those should be. The more heavily the population of a given state leans toward one party, the more inherently limited will be any effort to increase two-party competitiveness within most districts.

RANKINGS AND INSTANT RUNOFFS. Along with minimizing the number of one-party districts, a clever way to reduce some of the party-polarizing effects would be to open up primary elections to all citizens of *either* (or neither) political party; to put on the ballot all candidates from any party who can gather a reasonable number of signatures; and to let voters *rank* the candidates. Voters' rankings would then be used to conduct an "instant runoff" among the top vote getters, picking the two candidates (from whatever party) who are most preferred to go onto the general election ballot.[18]

By adopting a single primary open to all voters, the aim would be to ensure that candidates are picked who appeal to the *whole* district, not just to unrepresentative voters from each party's base. No U.S. state currently uses ranked voting in open primaries. But studies show that just allowing all voters to participate in any party's primary does modestly reduce the extremism of elected candidates in competitive districts (while having no effect on extremism in noncompetitive, one-party districts).[19]

INFORM VOTERS. Getting more moderate candidates on the ballot and opening up primary elections to any voter can help. But to choose more moderate candidates, voters need to know who those candidates are. California recently adopted a "top two" open primary system (which lacks ranked voting but does allow every voter to choose any candidate from any party, with the top two vote getters advancing to the general election). The first election under this new system failed to produce the more moderate legislature that reformers had hoped for. A central reason, it turned out, was that few voters could identify which of the candidates on their ballot were more moderate and which were more extreme.[20]

Other studies show that when voters do have this information, they put it to use and elect more moderate candidates. For example, in places where local media provide voters with more information about their congressional candidates, voters choose more moderate candidates in both primary and general elections.[21] Voters are often derided for being uninformed, but these studies show that some of the blame must be placed on the information-poor environments in which many voters find themselves.

In our view, the basic logic of the open primary with an instant runoff is highly promising. What it alone does *not* address, however, is a central problem of our primary system itself: that primary elections tend to be very low-visibility affairs, with little information, and with very low and biased turnout. No matter how you count the votes of a poorly informed and unrepresentative electorate,[22] you are not likely to end up with representative results.

ABOLISH PRIMARIES? What can be done about the problem of low-visibility, low-turnout, biased primary elections?

Equal voice reforms—including universal, automatic voter registration for all citizens and Election Day holidays—should help. But the big problem is that most primaries are held on obscure dates—usually well before the general election—when few citizens are paying attention to politics. If people do catch word that a nonpresidential primary is coming up, the stakes may seem low. And the candidate choices are usually obscure or nonexistent. Few people are likely to have heard of same-party challengers to incumbents. Often there are no such challengers at all. So hardly anyone except dedicated partisans bothers to vote.

We can imagine efforts to raise the visibility of primary elections through massive public information campaigns and the like. They might help. But we fear that the reality of relatively low stakes and obscure or nonexistent choices may put severe limits on what can be accomplished. Turnout is likely to remain low and biased.

So it may be time to declare this progressive experiment a failure and abolish primary elections as a means of nominating nonpresidential candidates.[23] Primaries were designed to replace nominations by "party bosses" with choices by "the people." But the American people as a whole have not in fact been at all well represented in primary elections.

SUBSTITUTE INSTANT RUNOFFS IN *GENERAL* ELECTIONS. If primaries were abolished, we would not want to return to the old system in which party nominees were chosen by party officials, officeholders, and activists. A more attractive alternative is to apply the open candidacy and instant runoff ideas to *general* elections. Then a far more representative electorate (especially after equal voice reforms are adopted) would have charge of both nominations and elections at the same time. If party officials and activists want to get together and promote a particular candidate, fine. (We expect that they would continue to do so.) But that candidate would potentially have to face serious competition from others, both within and outside his or her own party. So party officials and activists would have strong incentives to pick candidates who appeal to all citizens in their districts, not just to the party base.

Arend Lijphart, a scholar who has studied electoral systems around the world, points out that the U.S. primary system is unique among democratic countries. It is clearly not necessary—in fact, for the reasons we have given, it is almost certainly harmful—to democracy. Besides endorsing various equal voice reforms, Lijphart recommends abolishing primaries and using an instant runoff system.[24]

If one wanted, the instant runoff could be used to improve primary elections. But we believe it would work best to abolish primaries and use instant runoffs in general elections. Candidates from any party (or no party) could get on the ballot by collecting a substantial—but not excessively burdensome—number of citizens' signatures. Voters would rank all candidates. The candidate with the fewest first-choice votes would be dropped, and then the top remaining choices on each ballot would be counted again. In each subsequent round of the instant runoff, the candidate with the lowest vote total among those who are left would be dropped, each time redistributing his or her votes to the remaining candidates most preferred by each of the dropped candidate's voters.[25] The result should be a winner highly representative of the electoral district as a whole—usually a moderate, centrist winner. Party polarization would be much reduced, and democratic responsiveness would be much increased.[26]

PROPORTIONAL REPRESENTATION? For his American audience, Lijphart barely alluded to the elephant in the room: the fact that most democracies around the world use an electoral system quite different from ours, some variant of *proportional representation* (PR).[27] In pure PR systems, multiple parties compete for general election votes, voters choose among parties rather than candidates, and each party gets the number of parliamentary representatives to which its share of the total votes entitles it. When members of parliament take office, they form a coalition with other parties (if necessary) to reach a majority, and they put together a set of cabinet members, including a prime minister.

Proportional representation systems are not perfect. For one thing, coalition formation can be indeterminate and can work in odd ways. But PR systems do well at ensuring that minorities as well as majorities are represented. And (in countries with similar populations and similar levels of economic development) PR systems tend to be associated with various elements of flourishing democracy: voice and accountability; electoral pluralism; high levels of participation and turnout; civil liberties; and women serving in government.[28] PR systems also generally avoid a problem typical of winner-take-all systems like ours, where the top vote-getting party often gets a disproportionate number of seats in the legislature relative to its share of the popular vote.[29]

But the U.S. electoral system has a deeply entrenched anti-PR character, which follows partly from two features of state laws. First, most states provide that all state and federal legislative elections are held in *single-member* ("winner-take-all") districts that pick just one legislator per district. Second, nearly all decide the winners by "plurality voting," in which the candidate with the most votes wins even if he or she falls far short of a majority. Together, these arrangements strongly encourage a two-party system.[30] (In any given election, only the top two candidates—usually major-party candidates—have a serious chance, so there is little point in "wasting" votes on other parties.) With that initial advantage, our major parties have built up additional legal barriers against third parties.

Also important in preventing proportional representation are certain features of our hard-to-amend Constitution, including the election of one president in a single nationwide "district." And the Constitution appears to rule out the development of the usual sort of parliamentary PR system—in which members of parliament constitute the leaders of the executive branch—by declaring that "no Person holding any Office under the United States, shall be a Member of either House" while in office.[31]

It would be very difficult to overturn the whole U.S. electoral system and move to pure proportional representation. Fortunately, doing so may not be necessary to enhance democracy. Some of the advantages of PR could be obtained by abolishing primaries and using open ballot access and instant runoffs in all elections for both chambers of Congress and state legislatures (and, for that matter, for president.) Still more advantages would come from an "American-style" variant of proportional representation, based on *multimember districts*.

PROPORTIONAL REPRESENTATION, AMERICAN STYLE. An American version of proportional representation for Congress and state legislatures could be achieved within individual states without a

Constitutional amendment. The trick would be to require by federal law[32] that each state select all its legislators together, in a single, statewide "district" (or, for the biggest states, in several "megadistricts"),[33] through ranked voting and instant runoffs in the general election. All candidates who qualified—perhaps by submitting a moderate number of signatures on nominating petitions—would be listed on the general election ballot. Voters would rank as many of them as they wished. The instant runoff feature would be used to eliminate surplus candidates, working upward from the lowestranked ones and redistributing ranking votes among the remaining candidates until the right number of candidates remain to fill all the offices being contested.

This highly competitive statewide procedure would skirt around the knotty (perhaps insoluble) problem of how to increase competitiveness within each legislative district in predominantly oneparty states. With American-style PR, a state with 60 percent of voters favoring one party could quite possibly elect 40 percent of its representatives from the minority party (or from multiple minority parties)—a highly unlikely outcome under our current arrangements.

THE ADVANTAGES OF MULTIMEMBER DISTRICTS. Making elections more competitive is a crucial step for decreasing party polarization and increasing democratic responsiveness. No other reforms are likely to be effective without it. American-style PR would also remedy another significant defect of multiple districts that pick just one winner in each: it would more often produce officials who represent—in proportion to their size in the population—small ideological or demographic groups that constitute minorities in most or all districts. Such groups might not be able to muster a majority and win a representative in any one district, but they could win their fair shares under state-wide (or megadistrict) proportional representation. So American-style PR would be very helpful to minority voices. It could also open up some space for the development of third or fourth parties, if many Americans were unhappy with the two major parties. The mere threat that this might happen would put more pressure on the major parties to respond to the citizenry as a whole.

American-style PR, without primary elections and with multiple representatives chosen from each district, would give more voters a voice in their legislature, reduce the ability of party activists and donors to push through candidates who are out of step with their district, enhance the prospects of minor party candidates, provide a mechanism by which new ideas can gain traction, and eliminate the scourge of obscure, low-information, biased-turnout primaries.

One downside—but a relatively small one, we believe—involves the possible loss of direct geographical connections between particular legislators and particular neighborhoods—unless some candidates chose to focus on, learn about, and communicate with people in particular geographical areas, which might be a feasible strategy. The broader answer: voters themselves would decide exactly what kinds of representation they wanted: ideological, demographic, or neighborhood-based.

Another possible downside of American-style PR concerns feasibility. This idea might upset Republican and Democratic party officials even more than the prospect of rankings and instant runoffs within geographically defined districts because it would threaten the two parties' control. And it would create more uncertainty about who would be elected. Which incumbents (or party-favored challengers) would make it to the top of statewide (or megadistrict) rankings? Which would slip off at the bottom? Such uncertainty might be anathema to party officials trying to plot electoral strategies and to incumbents seeking stable careers. But it would be all to the good for maximizing democratic control.

Harmonizing Our Government Institutions

Given the multiple veto points in the U.S. political system, government action is stymied whenever those who control any one veto point strongly and persistently disagree with a policy change favored by other political actors—even if the policy change is desired by a large majority of Americans. It is *disharmony* among institutions—especially disharmony among the president, the House, the Senate, and the Supreme Court—that produces the deepest and most intractable kind of gridlock. When any one institution is determined to block a policy change, it generally can do so, no matter how urgently a problem needs to be solved or how large a majority of citizens favors the change. The bigger the policy disagreements, the more gridlock.

Serious reforms to overcome gridlock, therefore, must reduce disharmony among our governmental institutions. This need not mean a wholesale overturning of our constitutional order, such as abolishing federalism or doing away with the separation of powers, which are firmly rooted in the Constitution and in American political thought and embody useful principles.

The equal voice and depolarization reforms that we have already discussed can go a long way toward both democratizing and harmonizing institutions by increasing the extent to which all of them respond to average citizens rather than to campaign donors, organized interests, or ideological party activists.

But even if all these reforms are enacted, certain critical sources of institutional disharmony will remain: most notably, the strange and extremely unrepresentative way in which the Senate relates to our citizenry as a whole. Lesser but still significant problems are undemocratic distortions in the way our presidents are chosen and the occasional misuse by our unelected Supreme Court of its power to block policy making by declaring legislation or executive action unconstitutional.

Can We Make the Senate More Democratic?

Equal voice reforms will encourage each senator to respond more democratically to the citizens of his or her state, and procedural reforms can permit majorities of senators to overcome gridlock and act. But there remains a serious problem: the Senate as a whole poorly represents the whole people of the United States. The fact that Wyoming and Nevada, with their tiny populations, each have just as many senators (two) as big-population states like California, New York, and Florida means that the Senate does far better at representing sparsely populated rural areas than our great urban and suburban metropolitan centers.

This disparity becomes obvious after horrific mass shootings, when the Senate goes along with the National Rifle Association and rejects even mild gun safety regulations. (Heavily rural states are much more progun than states with big cities.) But it also pervades day-to-day aspects of policy: where the federal money goes, what projects are built, whose needs are met and whose are not.

Over the years, as our population has concentrated more and more heavily in metropolitan areas, the small-rural-state bias of the Senate has become a more and more serious problem. Equal state representation in the Senate, a relic from political compromises made two and a half centuries ago, has now become the most undemocratic single feature of our Constitution.[34]

Can we do anything about it?

Yes, by Constitutional amendment. But that will not be easy. The Founders were very protective of equal state representation. The Constitution clearly prescribes that there shall be two senators from each state, each having one vote.[35] Then, in discussing the amendment process, the Constitution tries to dig in: it specifies that no state shall be deprived (without its consent) of equal suffrage in the Senate.[36] This "no amendment" provision is probably not really legally binding, because it itself surely can be amended. But it is bound to be invoked with great passion by those opposing reform.

Substantively, a constitutional amendment could provide that each senator will cast a number of votes more nearly proportional to the population of his or her state, adjusting that number after each U.S. Census. For example, each of California's two senators might cast as many as sixty-six votes (though we might want to make it fewer than that, stopping short of pure population-based representation), while each of Wyoming's senators would cast just one vote.[37] Imagine the difference in the Senate!

If this multiple-votes scheme seemed awkward, an alternative would be to increase the number of senators from big states—with American-style PR in one or more multimember districts within each state—but not all the way up to full representation of their populations. (To do that would produce a huge, unwieldy legislative body.) Or the two methods could be mixed. Either way, if we wished, we could still preserve a special position for small states in Senate deliberations, debates, and leadership by giving them more senators or more Senate votes per capita than big states.

In thinking about such a change, it is worth remembering that for much of our country's history the U.S. House of Representatives and many state legislatures had the same sort of extreme bias in favor of sparsely populated areas that the U.S. Senate still exhibits now. But in the 1960s, the Supreme Court declared this imbalance a violation of equal protection of the law and required that all states redraw their electoral districts in accord with a one person, one vote rule. The results were dramatic: state policies and spending decisions that had been excessively tilted in favor of over-represented rural residents were abandoned. Urban and suburban residents gained greater political influence. State money was distributed among citizens more equally, or on the basis of need, not to reflect artificially enhanced rural voting power.[38]

By design, constitutional amendments are extremely difficult to propose and ratify. It requires supermajorities in both the House and the Senate—or a supermajority of state legislatures applying to Congress for a constitutional convention—to propose an amendment. Then a supermajority of state legislatures or state conventions must ratify it before it goes into force.[39]

A CONSTITUTIONAL CONVENTION. As Lawrence Lessig and other legal scholars and historians have pointed out, however, the *prospect* of a constitutional convention could be a powerful tool to push Congress and the states into action. If a popular mass movement were to urge state after state to apply for a constitutional convention and consider a broad package of "Democracy Amendments," the House and Senate and state legislatures might well go along with some constitutional amendments in order to fend off even broader changes.[40] That is more or less how the Seventeenth Amendment to the Constitution—taking the selection of U.S. senators away from corrupt state legislatures and establishing direct popular elections for the Senate—was proposed and ratified in a big hurry during the 1911–13 period, after decades of bitter resistance.[41]

If a constitutional convention were actually called, all the better. (The extreme difficulty of ratifying amendments makes fears of a "runaway" convention seem overblown.) It could be authorized to consider a broad range of prodemocratic constitutional reforms: for example, clearly authorizing Congress to regulate political money; prohibiting partisan gerrymandering of legislative districts; abolishing the electoral college and moving to a direct popular vote for president; and restricting the Supreme Court's power to obstruct democratic policy making. It might also more clearly emphasize the central role of political equality in the Bill of Rights.

To be sure, a constitutional amendment seeking to democratize the Senate would face formidable political obstacles. The very same pro-small-state bias that the amendment would seek to correct would infect the constitutional amendment process. Simple arithmetic makes clear that the thirty-eight states required for ratification of an amendment to democratize the Senate—or even the thirty-four states needed to apply for a constitutional convention—would have to include many states that would thereby lose much of their own power in the Senate. Only a selfless, far-seeing view of the importance of democracy—aided, perhaps, by pressure from an energetic, multistate social movement—might persuade the necessary number of state legislatures to act.

As Lessig points out, however, the very process of working toward a constitutional convention could itself have great benefits. It would create a golden opportunity to organize and coordinate grassroots reform movements within the states. It could provoke a serious, sustained conversation about democratic reform and about what sorts of constitutional amendments may be needed to fully empower American citizens and overcome gridlock. Thus the constitutional convention strategy might produce important gains even if it fell short of its most ambitious aims.[42]

Undemocratic Distortions in Choosing Presidents

Elections for president are the most democratic elections in the United States, at least in the sense that popular participation is more widespread and less biased than in any other type of U.S. election. If equal voice reforms are enacted to defuse the power of private money and organized interests and to empower a broader and more representative body of citizens, then presidential elections will become even more democratic. But there will remain two problems, one with the formula by which votes for president are counted and the other with the way presidential candidates are nominated.

THE UNDEMOCRATIC "ELECTORAL COLLEGE."[43] The constitutional provision for choosing presidential "electors" by state, together with state laws that have mostly adopted "winner-take-all" systems that give all the electoral votes to the candidate who wins a plurality of the popular vote in that state, have set up the possibility of awkward, embarrassing, and clearly undemocratic conflicts between the electoral college winner and the winner of the popular vote. In two recent elections—those of 2000 and 2016—the president who took office had won fewer of the people's votes than his opponent did (in 2016, nearly *three million* fewer votes). Given the current extreme polarization of our political parties, the selection of a vote-losing "winner" can make a huge difference in the shape of government policy.

Surveys have regularly shown that large majorities of Americans favor moving to a strictly popular vote system.[44] Hardly anyone seriously believes that the electoral college—an artifact of eighteenth-century thinking about states' rights and wise, well-born, independent electors—is a good thing now.

A promising way to effectively abolish the electoral college without needing a constitutional amendment is for individual states to agree to award all their electoral votes to the winner of the national popular vote, contingent on enough other states doing the same so that together they can determine the winner. So far, eleven states, with more than half the needed electoral votes, have agreed to do so.[45]

PARTY CONTROL OF NOMINATIONS. Our system of usually giving voters only two viable general election choices for president, with the two major parties controlling who those candidates are, invites trouble. Small, biased primary electorates can leave general election voters with two unappealing candidates. Then citizens are stuck with just three unpleasant options: (1) give up and forget about voting at all; (2) waste a vote in protest on a third-party candidate who can't win; or (3) grudgingly vote for whichever candidate seems to be the lesser evil.

Under the current system, in which many citizens are disenfranchised and in which donors, party activists, and interest groups heavily influence the parties' decisions, it is not uncommon for the parties to nominate candidates other than those that most Americans would prefer.

Here, too, reforms for equal voice and for the depolarization of the parties will help a great deal. But there may remain some temptations for party leaders—including *superdelegates*[46] at party nominating conventions—to flout the will of ordinary Americans. In the end, the restriction of serious candidates to just two nominees selected by the parties severely limits citizens' freedom of choice. It helps open the way to unpopular policy making by implicit collusion between the Republican and Democratic Parties, as occurred for decades when both parties embraced free international trade but offered little help to those who were harmed by it.

The ideal solution for presidential elections would be the same as for legislative elections: a general election instant runoff, decided by voters' rankings among a list of candidates from any party (or no party) who had received a substantial number of signatures on nominating petitions.

This system would not necessarily eliminate the key roles of the major parties; they would very likely go ahead and nominate their favorite candidates, by whatever procedures they choose (quite possibly the same procedures that they use now). And one of the two majority-party nominees might very well win most of the time. But the instant runoff system would make it much harder for the major parties to abuse their nominating power by nominating unpopular candidates. To do so, would likely lead to a loss. There would be a meaningful safety valve for third- or fourth-party candidates to win, if more Americans favored them than either of the major-party nominees. The ranking system would allow citizens to express their real first choices without fear of wasting their vote. Democracy would be advanced.

Perhaps a constitutional amendment would be required to upend the whole, messy current system of nominating and electing presidents. If so, the usual difficult decisions would have to be made about whether, and how strongly, to push this idea—perhaps as part of a package of Democracy amendments at a constitutional convention. But conceivably an instant runoff system might be implemented *without* a constitutional amendment, by keeping electors but changing how they are chosen. Federal legislation (under Congress's power to regulate the "manner" of elections) might require each state to list all qualifying presidential candidates on their general election ballots; to permit voters to rank them; to count the votes so as to determine the extent of support for each candidate; and to appoint the appropriate numbers of electors pledged to each viable candidate. Voila! A state-based instant runoff that would broaden choices, pressure the major parties to nominate the strongest possible candidates, and eliminate the winner-take-all distortions of the electoral college. It would be an important advance for democracy.

What about the Supreme Court?

Fortunately, the contemporary Supreme Court has not gone as far as the rigidly probusiness court that blocked a great deal of progressive legislation during the late nineteenth and early twentieth centuries.[47]

But today's Supreme Court has derailed a fair number of important laws that majorities of Americans favor—laws banning guns near schools, requiring states to expand Medicaid for the poor and elderly, protecting civil rights under the Voting Rights Act, and—perhaps most important—laws limiting the power of money in politics.[48] To a significant extent, then, the court's use of the power of *judicial review*—to declare federal government legislation unconstitutional—has worked against democracy and has created gridlock with the other branches. So what, if anything, should we do about it?

The Constitution and our history leave room for many political actions in response to an overly assertive Supreme Court. In extreme cases, justices can be impeached. The court's budget can be slashed. The president can ignore its mandates. Congress can strip the court of jurisdiction over specific matters; shrink or expand its size; pack it with new members; give it burdensome new responsibilities; or revise its procedures. All of these actions have been taken, on one occasion or another, by Thomas Jefferson, Andrew Jackson, Abraham Lincoln, the Reconstruction Congress, and Franklin Roosevelt—a list that includes some of our most admired leaders.[49]

We believe that judicial independence can be useful for preserving the rule of law and protecting the rights of minorities. So actions that would interfere with the Supreme Court's independence should be reserved for extreme cases in which the court blatantly defies majority rule without clear constitutional justification. But if we hold open the *threat* of such actions as perfectly legitimate, the court is likely to hesitate before making drastically undemocratic decisions.

In the normal course of events, the Supreme Court tends to adjust over time and defer to federal lawmaking majorities, particularly as new presidents appoint new Justices.[50] (This process will occur even more smoothly and democratically if we can further democratize presidential elections.) So major changes in the court's role may not be necessary.

But a constitutional amendment may be needed to accomplish one crucial reform: the regulation of money in politics. If the Supreme Court does not soon change its doctrine that money (even corporate money) is "speech" and cannot be effectively regulated, a constitutional amendment is clearly called for. Too much damage is being done to democracy by the flood of private money in our politics. An amendment permitting—perhaps mandating—the strict regulation of private political money could be included in a whole package of Democracy amendments to be considered by a new constitutional convention. Such a convention—or just the threat of calling it—could play an important part in revitalizing democracy in America.

But powerful forces that benefit from the status quo can be expected to resist major prodemocracy reforms. The next chapter discusses what it may take to overcome such resistance.

PART FOUR

How to Do It

NINE

A Social Movement for Democracy

Major reforms to make American politics more democratic will be hard to bring about. Those who benefit from the undemocratic status quo—especially big corporations and the wealthy—have many resources for blocking changes that would reduce their political clout. The outsize role of money in our political system means that America's growing economic inequality tends to perpetuate and reinforce political inequality in a vicious circle that will not be easy to break. The distorted, money-driven political system that we want to reform is the same political system that will have to be used to get reform proposals adopted.

But American history shows that power and wealth do not inevitably concentrate ever more narrowly in the hands of the already advantaged. There is a powerful egalitarian current in American political life that has periodically triumphed over entrenched interests to produce progressive political and economic change.[1] The Jacksonian period, the Progressive Era, the New Deal, and the social and political upheavals of the 1960s, for example, all brought important advances in democracy.

It Will Take a Social Movement

We believe that our ultimate goal—a major increase in government's responsiveness to average citizens while reducing the political power of wealthy individuals and corporate interest groups—can only be attained through a broad, energetic, and persistent *social movement*: a coalition of millions of people joined together to bring about democratic reforms over the long term.

American history offers many examples of social movements. Some have emerged from the grievances and aspirations of particular subgroups of the population—groups defined in terms of race (the civil rights movement for African Americans); ethnicity (Latinos, nineteenth-century immigrants); gender (women's rights movements); sexual orientation (the gay, lesbian, bisexual, and transgender [LGBT] movement); religious faith (Christian conservatives, the right-to-life [antiabortion] movement); economic position (the labor movement); or age (young war protestors, the Townsend movement for old-age pensions). Other movements have had more diverse social bases, together with broad moral or ideological foci: the abolitionist, Populist, Progressive, environmental, consumer rights, and antinuclear movements, for example.

Historians and sociologists who have studied past social movements have learned a great deal about what sorts of objective grievances, group resources, political opportunities, and specific strategies and tactics tend to lead to movements' success—and what leads to failure. Past successes and failures can provide useful lessons for us today, as we think about how to build a social movement for democratic reform.

The Populists and the Progressives

During the Gilded Age around the end of the nineteenth century, America faced many challenges similar to those we face today: enormous economic inequality; an unresponsive political system beholden to moneyed interests; a strongly probusiness Supreme Court. Spurred by these challenges and by social disruptions due to mass immigration and rapid economic transformations, first the People's Party and the Populist social movement surrounding it and then the Progressive movement proposed—and eventually achieved—significant political and economic reforms. Their struggles, victories, and defeats hold important lessons for us now.

Over the course of the nineteenth century—as trade and commerce expanded, canals and railroads were built, the West was settled, urban areas grew, and the United States enjoyed rapid economic growth with larger and larger industrial corporations— our politics changed as well. The relatively high degree of equality among white males (though not women or slaves) that had characterized the mostly agrarian Jacksonian period that Alexis de Tocqueville observed gave way to the Gilded Age of extreme economic inequality. Impoverished small farmers and industrial workers lagged far behind extremely wealthy titans of industry.[2] Economic inequality was accompanied by a great deal of political inequality.

The economic successes of capitalism brought painful side effects: in factories, long, arduous working hours at low pay; tough urban conditions for women and children; for farmers, increasing dependence on an unforgiving global market and a tightening web of mortgages. Yet the political system seemed unresponsive to citizens' concerns. The U.S. Senate, filled with senators chosen by state legislatures rather than the voters, was notoriously corrupt: many senators of both parties were paid by major corporations or had close ties with them.[3] State legislation to regulate monopolistic railroads, limit working hours for women and children, and enact other reforms of benefit to individual citizens was thwarted by a business-oriented Supreme Court.[4] Both major parties placed business interests above the needs of ordinary Americans.[5]

Our politics today are not so blatantly corrupt as they were in the late nineteenth century. But more than one observer has argued that we are living in a "new Gilded Age," in which high levels of economic inequality have once again led to political inequality.[6] Once again wealthy Americans and business interests have a great deal of political power. Once again the Senate is filled with multimillionaires; the Supreme Court is overturning popular legislation; and both major parties appear to be swayed by the wishes of the business and financial communities. It is helpful to think about how Americans of an earlier generation dealt with similar problems.

THE PEOPLE'S PARTY AND THE POPULISTS. Frustrated with the Republicans and Democrats, members of the Farmers' Alliance (mostly small farmers in the South and West) decided to form a third political party, the People's Party.[7] They hoped to ally with labor unions and the urban working class and build a broader, stronger social movement that could challenge the political establishment. (Most people refer to the People's Party and their social movement as *Populists*. We will do the same, but they should not be confused with today's right-wing populists in the United States or Europe—who are very different.)

The 1892 People's Party platform opened with an angry recital of grievances—some of them particular to that historical moment (currency deflation was forcing farmer-debtors to repay expensive seed loans with the proceeds from undervalued crops; monopolistic railroads were extorting high shipping prices from isolated western towns)—but many of which resonate with similar, though less drastic, ills in twenty-first-century America. The platform first complained about politics: "Corruption dominates the ballot-box, the Legislatures, the Congress, and touches even the ermine of the bench." It asserted that there were efforts to intimidate or bribe voters. Newspapers were largely subsidized or muzzled. Public opinion was silenced. The People's Party sought to "restore the government of the Republic to the hands of 'the plain people.'"[8]

Foreshadowing today's concerns about economic deprivation and inequality, the People's Party platform asserted that homes were covered with mortgages; labor was impoverished; urban workmen were denied the right to organize for self-protection; imported pauperized labor was beating down their wages; "the fruits of the toil of millions are boldly stolen to build up colossal fortunes for a few." We were, the platform said, breeding "two great classes—tramps and millionaires."[9] Both major parties were ignoring these issues.

The People's Party platform went on to advocate a series of economic reforms, including nationalization of railroads, telegraph, and telephone companies; a "safe, sound, and flexible" (i.e., not deflationary) national currency based on coinage of silver as well as gold; a graduated income tax; and some mild regulations of work hours.[10] To spread political power more broadly, the Populists favored a variety of democratic reforms: a free ballot and a fair count in all elections through the secret ("Australian") ballot system;[11] legislation through initiative and referendum; limitation of the president and vice president to a single term; and election of senators by direct vote of the people.

The Populists' economic and political ideas endured. Indeed, a leading scholar of the period has argued that the "periphery agrarians" were "the principal instigators of progressive reform."[12] Many of their ideas were later enacted by the Progressives, under Presidents Theodore Roosevelt (Republican) and Woodrow Wilson (Democrat).

But the People's Party itself crashed and burned in 1896, when its "fusionists" prevailed over "midroader" third-party enthusiasts and joined with—some would say were co-opted by—the Democrats. With the charismatic agrarian William Jennings Bryan as their candidate, running on a single-issue "free silver" platform (which was cheered by silver miners and small farmers but mocked by sound-money advocates and disliked by urban consumers who feared price rises), the 1896 election turned into a referendum on industrial progress versus reactionary agrarianism. The Populists/ Democrats utterly failed to appeal to urban workers, losing heavily in the East and Midwest. William McKinley and the business-oriented Republicans triumphed.[13]

Both the successes and the failures of the Populists suggest important lessons. The Populists' melding of political and economic reforms; their grassroots energy, based on cooperative institutions that united farmers; their efforts to reach out across regions, economic sectors, races, and genders; and their dramatic incursion into electoral politics all offer promise for a similar movement facing today's somewhat similar kinds of economic and political problems.

On the other hand, the Populists' premature abandonment of their reform platform for the sake of electoral fusion with the Democrats contributed to a decade-or-so loss of momentum for some of their key ideas. Their bet on Bryan and "free silver" unnecessarily wrecked the prospect of an alliance between working people in the two Americas, agricultural and industrial. And given the political power of affluent Americans, the Populists' failure to build a cross-class alliance (instead pursuing a coalition of disaffected, mostly lower-income people) almost certainly limited their chances

for success.[14] They heaped scorn on the same small-town and urban bankers, professionals, and owners of medium-sized businesses
who later contributed to the Progressive movement.

THE PROGRESSIVES. In the later 1890s and on into the early twentieth century, Progressivism rose from the ashes of the Populist
movement, embracing many of its ideas (moderating some of them
and adding urban-oriented twists) but building on a contrasting
social base among the middle and upper middle classes nationwide.
Historians describe how onrushing industrialization, the consolida-
tion of big corporations into giant "trusts," and the accumulation
and conspicuous display of huge fortunes by a few industrialists and
bankers ("the plutocracy") alienated many austere, hardworking,
but not enormously wealthy civic leaders who felt they were losing status.[15] Professional people—including lawyers, the Protestant
clergy, and professors in the newly emerging modern universities—
provided crucial Progressive leadership. People in small businesses,
well-to-do farmers, and even some wealthy individuals with strong
social consciences (for example, Rudolph Spreckels, E. A. Filene,
and inheritors Tom Johnson and Joseph Fels) joined in.[16]

Progressive leaders rejected the prevailing laissez-faire attitude
toward citizens' well-being. They took up the problems of urban
laborers (though most Progressives remained suspicious of foreign
immigrants and hostile toward African Americans). They combined
concerns about public health, workforce education, child poverty,
and the like with businessmen's focus on regulating finance and big
corporations; with prosperous farmers' desires to ship their crops
at fair prices; and with many citizens' dislike of political "bosses"
and desire for good, honest government in cities and the nation.
This wide reach enabled the Progressives to organize a broad movement that eventually won the day.

Many members of the "new middle class" (or, more precisely,
upper middle class) of rapidly professionalizing doctors, lawyers,
teachers, journalists, social workers, and university professors
formed a variety of organizations—occupational associations,
women's clubs, Chautauquas, Hull House–type settlement houses,
municipal reform leagues—that worked together to address various parts of the Progressive agenda. These spilled over into political

reform organizations such as the National Civic Federation and the National American Woman Suffrage Association.[17]

"Muckraking" journalists including Ida Tarbell, Upton Sinclair, Lincoln Steffens, and David Graham Phillips—writing in new, mass-circulation magazines such as *McClure's*—exposed economic and political evils, including the Standard Oil monopoly, adulterated food, and corrupt ties between business and politicians. These exposés heightened demands for change.[18]

Ultimately, with leadership—or in some cases reluctant acquiescence—from Republican President Theodore Roosevelt[19] and Democrat Woodrow Wilson,[20] a number of Progressive economic and political reforms were enacted.

Some of these measures actually had *un*democratic consequences. As historians have shown, several electoral reforms such as literacy tests, toughening of residency-length or citizenship requirements, restricting municipal elections to property owners or taxpayers, and burdensome registration procedures—while ostensibly designed to eliminate corruption or produce a more competent electorate—effectively disenfranchised many immigrants, members of ethnic minorities, and low-income citizens. The nonpartisan ballot adopted for many municipal elections, designed to release the public from the grip of party machines and partisan politics, actually depressed voter turnout.[21] Other political reforms, including "direct democracy" through the initiative, referendum, and recall, do often empower ordinary citizens but can be hijacked to benefit well-funded interest groups with self-serving agendas.[22]

The Progressives were particularly weak on dealing with race. They generally ignored the plight of African Americans altogether and in some cases made it much worse, as with the segregation of the federal government under Wilson.[23]

But the Progressives achieved some historic reforms that reduced economic inequality and spread political power more broadly. The first federal income and estate taxes were adopted (both targeted the wealthy). Corporate regulation and antitrust legislation was passed by Congress. Many states adopted child labor laws, workmen's compensation programs, primary elections to reduce the power of party machines, and various forms of direct democracy.

Two prodemocratic political reforms of the Progressive era were especially important: the Seventeenth Amendment to the Constitution (1913), providing for the direct election of U.S. senators; and the Nineteenth Amendment (1920), establishing women's right to vote.[24]

There were subsequent setbacks, but progress on economic and political reforms resumed in the 1930s, amid a new set of social movements.

The New Deal of the 1930s

The 1929 stock market crash and the Great Depression had devastating effects on millions of Americans. Industrial production dropped to half its former level. One-quarter to one-third of the labor force was out of work. Bread lines formed in cities. The federal government—paralyzed by an ideology of limited government and balanced budgets—initially refused to help.

But social unrest—strikes, demonstrations, land seizures, resistance to home evictions, and the like—grew. A disparate set of social movements emerged. In 1929, about twenty thousand World War I veterans, insisting on immediate payment of their bonus certificates, formed a "Bonus Army" and camped across the Potomac from Washington, DC. (They were put down by force.) Spontaneous strikes by longshoremen, teamsters, and textile workers in 1934 fed into a broader labor movement, particularly after the formation of the militant Committee for Industrial Organization (later the Congress of Industrial Organizations). Workers in rubber and auto plants and packinghouses organized sit-down strikes, including major strikes at Firestone, Fisher Body, and Republic Steel in 1936 and 1937.[25]

In 1933, Francis Townsend publicized his Townsend Plan for old-age pensions and used techniques he had learned as a real estate salesperson to create a social movement with organizers in almost every state. In 1934, Charles Edward "Father" Coughlin founded the National Union for Social Justice, calling for economic reforms and protection of the rights of labor; it grew into a movement with millions of members. Huey Long in Louisiana and Upton Sinclair in California, among others, led large movements focused on poverty and unemployment.

There can be little doubt that these social movements helped spur the Franklin D. Roosevelt administration to undertake several major reforms, including the 1935 Social Security Act, the 1938 minimum wage and child labor act, regulation of business, and more progressive taxes. Especially significant for our purposes was the passage of the Wagner Act of 1935, which made it much easier for trade unions to represent American workers.[26] This important change was largely a result of an active labor movement, involving both spontaneous action by workers and systematic organizing by unions. The rapid growth of unions, in turn, produced major *political* effects, including the growth of a "countervailing power" against business groups.

The empowerment of labor unions and the expanded role of the government in promoting ordinary citizens' economic well-being also helped reduce economic inequality. Together with the economic stimulus and geopolitical effects of World War II,[27] the political alignments and public policies that emerged from the Progressive and New Deal eras contributed to the postwar golden age of widely shared economic growth. During those postwar years, a relatively bipartisan federal government pursued broadly popular policies that helped millions of ordinary citizens. Newly adopted or expanded programs provided support for higher education, public health, transportation, housing, scientific research, and an expanded safety net for the elderly.[28]

Poverty was not eradicated in postwar America. Leftist political figures were repressed, especially in the late 1940s and early 1950s. And many social groups—including women, gays, and members of racial and ethnic minorities—faced continued discrimination or repression. But economic inequality dropped sharply from its height in the late 1920s, and economic prosperity was greater and more widely shared during the postwar boom years than in any previous era. With unions counterbalancing business, politics tended to be moderate, bipartisan, and reasonably democratic.

The Civil Rights Movement

Despite the improved economy of the postwar period, African Americans remained far worse off than whites. The black/white income ratio barely budged between 1950 and the mid-1960s,[29] and African Americans continued to face violence, segregation, discrimination, and denial of their voting rights—especially, but not only, in the South.

The struggle for racial equality in the United States has been long and uneven, and it is far from finished. But the civil rights movement of the 1950s and 1960s brought about some of the most important advances toward equal rights for African Americans, including the demise of Jim Crow segregation; ending legal discrimination in public accommodations, housing and employment; and—the crucial *political* reform—securing black voting rights. By establishing federal control over voting registration in large areas of the South, the Voting Rights Act of 1965 redeemed the broken promise made after the American Civil War: that the right of citizens to vote "shall not be abridged . . . on account of race, color, or previous condition of servitude."[30]

None of these achievements are complete—African Americans still face discrimination in housing and employment, and blacks' voting rights have been undermined by a weakening of the Voting Rights Act, the adoption of voter identification requirements, and felon disenfranchisement laws. But the advances of the modern civil rights movement were of enormous significance.

How could African Americans, a politically and economically disadvantaged minority, overcome those disadvantages and force changes in racial policy and race relations? A few key factors stand out.

First, the race-related political advances of the 1960s were the products of decades of organizing, litigation, protest, and partisan engagement. The 1964 Civil Rights Act (outlawing discrimination in employment, voting, and public accommodations), the 1965 Voting Rights Act (providing federal oversight of voting rights and banning literacy tests and other discriminatory barriers), and the 1968 Fair Housing Act (outlawing discrimination in housing) resulted from the efforts of the civil rights leaders and organizations of the 1950s and 1960s. But the groundwork was laid over many decades by thousands of activists, working through a wide variety of organizations at the state and local, as well as the national, level.

In the 1930s and 1940s, state and local organizations to pro-

mote African American voting rights, such as the League of Ne-
gro Voters, were established in South Carolina, Alabama, Georgia,
Virginia, and elsewhere. By 1920, the National Association for the
Advancement of Colored People (NAACP) had more than three
hundred local branches. Black churches played a central role in
organizing, inspiring, and supporting black resistance to white oppression. These and other groups used a variety of approaches to
combat segregation, to secure black voting rights, to promote antilynching laws, to fight racism within labor unions, and to bring the
plight of African Americans to public consciousness.[31]

Over the following decades, these organizations grew in size,
shifted in tactics and focus, and were joined by other organizations,
including the Congress on Racial Equality (founded in 1942), the
Reverend Dr. Martin Luther King Jr.'s Southern Christian Leadership Conference (1957), and the young and militant Student Nonviolent Coordinating Committee (1960). Although the "modern
civil rights movement" is sometimes viewed as beginning with the
important and highly publicized bus boycotts, sit-ins, and marches
of the mid-1950s and early 1960s (such as the Selma march, led by
Dr. King, that spurred the passage of the Voting Rights Act), its
major victories were the result of persistent efforts by a wide variety
of actors on multiple fronts over many decades.

As a disadvantaged minority, African Americans found that
their struggle for equal rights depended strongly on the allies they
could secure among other groups. Critical in this regard was the
alliance between the civil rights movement, on the one hand, and
the labor movement (chiefly the Congress of Industrial Organizations, or CIO) and the northern faction of the Democratic Party,
on the other.

In the mid-1930s, the CIO split off from the American Federation of Labor (AFL). Unlike the AFL, the CIO embraced the
struggle for racial equality. With its focus on industrial and mine
workers, the CIO had strategic reasons to embrace black workers
(who were more numerous in these occupations than in the AFL's
craft-based unions).[32] But this strategic logic was reinforced by a
genuine commitment to racial equality.

The CIO played a central role in expanding the liberal, class-based coalition of the Democratic Party to include African American voters and a programmatic commitment to civil rights. Although many of the core New Deal programs were racially discriminatory (in part, at least, in order to secure southern Democratic support),[33] Roosevelt's programs brought significant benefits to northern blacks, large numbers of whom were employed by the Works Progress Administration (WPA) and Civilian Conservation Corps (CCC) or received federal relief payments.[34]

Roosevelt's New Deal helped erode the historic ties between African Americans and the Republican Party that were rooted in the Civil War and Reconstruction. But the Democratic Party's halting embrace of civil rights varied dramatically from place to place. Southern Democrats as a whole remained staunchly racist (and antiunion), and many national Democratic Party leaders tried to avoid the civil rights issue to maintain their precarious North–South coalition. But individual members of Congress, mayors, and state and local party leaders, with their independent local power bases, could be swayed by civil rights activists and their union allies. As one analyst observed, "African American activists, often joined by CIO unions, Jewish groups, and other urban liberals were gradually . . . transforming the Democratic program from within," reshaping state party platforms and winning over Democratic state legislators.[35]

Gaining the support of unionists, Jews, economic liberals, and northern Democratic party leaders depended not only on strategic alliances but also on civil rights leaders' cultivation of, and appeals to, Americans' shared values. Advocates for racial equality have drawn on and expanded our received moral understandings about justice and equality. Abolitionists made religious as well as secular moral arguments to denounce slavery. During the early years of the Cold War, civil rights leaders tied racial justice in the United States to American foreign policy, as the United States and the Soviet Union fought for the allegiance of third-world countries in Africa and elsewhere.[36]

The powerful moral resonance of Dr. King's appeals for equal rights, and the moral repugnance of most Americans at southern violence against peaceful civil rights protestors, reflected a broadened understanding of American values of justice and equality. The civil rights movement succeeded in winning new rights for a small and disempowered minority of the population by making clear that those rights followed logically from our founding principles and from widely embraced moral and religious values.[37]

Lessons from the Past

Every social movement is different. Every era has its unique characteristics. But there are some common threads in the history of American social movements that can help inform today's efforts to democratize our politics.[38]

FOCUS ON SERIOUS GRIEVANCES THAT VIOLATE SHARED VALUES. One lesson from past social movements is the importance of serious grievances, shared values, and clear goals. The driving force in social movements is a collective sense that many people have suffered serious wrongs. Those wrongs may involve economic deprivation; economic and social discrimination based on race, ethnicity, gender, sexual orientation, or some other personal characteristic; exclusion from participation in political life; or violation of some strong moral principle. For a social movement to arise and persist, the grievances must be widespread; they must reflect real experiences in daily life; and they must relate to basic values or concepts of fairness that will win widespread sympathy. With the increasing role of the Internet and social media, framing and communicating grievances to millions of people has gotten easier.[39]

Successful social movements start with real grievances and then make arguments that can win widespread support by evoking strong, widely shared American values: the equal worth of every human being; the need to allow everyone a fair opportunity to achieve self-fulfillment and economic success; the right of everyone to participate equally in the political process.

Suffragist leader Susan B. Anthony expressed such shared values at the close of her centennial speech on July 4, 1876: "We ask of our rulers, at this hour, no special favors, no special privileges, no special legislation. We ask justice, we ask equality, we ask that all the civil and political rights that belong to citizens of the United States, be guaranteed to us and our daughters forever."[40] Anthony's words have echoed through decades of the women's movement. Similar language has helped mobilize hundreds of thousands of people to demonstrate for various causes throughout American history.

For a democratic reform movement, the underlying value of *political equality*—embraced in one form or other by most Americans—holds promise as a foundation for persuasive arguments. Most ordinary Americans already believe that their government pays too little heed to the concerns of people like them. Most already believe that our political system needs fundamental change. And most already believe that big money and corporate lobbyists play far too large a role in our country's political life.

LINK REFORMS TO DAY-TO-DAY REALITIES. Still, political reforms of campaign finance, congressional districting, or even voting rights may initially seem too abstract—not worth fighting for—unless they are explicitly connected to specific harms caused by money-driven, undemocratic politics. To form the basis of a social movement, the damaging results of our dysfunctional, money-dominated political system need to be better understood by more people. They need to be clearly linked to economic and social harms in people's daily lives.

The consequences of political dysfunction are no secret, but they are often obscured or overlooked. The precise links need to be made plain. The high cost of prescription drugs, for example, is linked to the pharmaceutical lobby. The decline of middle-class manufacturing jobs is linked to trade agreements promoted by American business and opposed by American unions. The shamefully low federal minimum wage and the lack of paid family leave for most American workers are linked to the power of business interests in Washington. These and many other specific failures of government can be explained as resulting from a political system that is awash in money, that relies on industry lobbyists for advice, and that offers a revolving door to lucrative corporate lobbying for those leaving government.

Many successful social movements have been focused on a single unifying goal—abolishing slavery, winning women's suffrage, establishing marriage equality for gays and lesbians—and/or were able to draw on a deeply-felt shared identity (female, LGBT, African American).[41] A social movement for Democracy does not have these advantages: its concrete goals are necessarily diverse, and its "membership" is united by a shared commitment to democratic reforms rather than a preexisting social group identity. Consequently, it is even more important to tie citizens' grievances over lack of affordable day care, declining job opportunities, the government's failure to address climate change or global warming, and other specific issues to the broader agenda of democratic reform.

In short, generating widespread pressure for political reforms will require connecting them in Americans' minds with the real, concrete, day-to-day grievances that only a more democratic political system is likely to address. This can be done. Just as the Progressives and the civil rights movement fought simultaneously for economic and political reforms, a contemporary social movement for Democracy could meld substantive concerns about medical costs, middle-class jobs, the environment, and other issues to the political reforms necessary to make progress on them.

DEVELOP AND PUBLICIZE CONCRETE REFORM IDEAS. We have put forward our own reform ideas in previous chapters, but many other people and organizations are devising new reforms and testing their effectiveness. Several major philanthropic foundations—including Ford, Carnegie, MacArthur, Open Society, Hewlett (with a large-scale "Madison project"), and Rockefeller Brothers, along with the smaller Russell Sage, Joyce, Omidyar, Mott, WT Grant, Spencer, Roosevelt Institute, and New America, among others—have funded important research and advocacy work on how to enhance democracy.

These foundations have supported individual researchers and many small, nonprofit organizations that carry out practical research on the effects of specific reform provisions—and that, in many cases, energetically advocate the reforms they consider most promising. These organizations include some mentioned in earlier chapters, such as Dēmos, the Brennan Center for Justice, the League of Women Voters, FairVote, Election Protection, the California Civic Engagement Project, Nonprofit VOTE, and Rock the Vote—and many others as well. Such organizations could constitute a key part of a social movement for Democracy.

It is particularly important to help all Americans understand what can be accomplished by political reforms because public support for some reforms has been uneven in the past.[42] Educational efforts will be crucial.

Another lesson from the past is that a successful social movement requires both broad support among ordinary citizens and alliances that bring sympathetic groups and organizations into the cause.

ACTIVE VOLUNTEERS ARE ESSENTIAL. Large numbers of actively engaged, committed volunteers are the heart of any social movement. Thousands of African Americans and others who "sat in," marched, and protested racial segregation in the South energized the civil rights movement of the 1950s and 1960s.[43] The thousands of college students who demonstrated in the 1960s and 1970s against the Vietnam War increased the costs of waging that war and helped speed its end.[44] Protests and marches by thousands of suffragists in the early twentieth century raised the country's consciousness and eventually helped win women the right to vote.[45] Even Progressivism, a middle-class movement that was wary of the masses of urban workers and new immigrants at the turn of the twentieth century, benefited from years of grassroots organizing at the state and local level by nineteenth-century Populists and Socialists.

Often volunteers can be enlisted from among the membership rolls of preexisting organizations that can be brought into a social movement alliance.

FORM ALLIANCES WITH DIVERSE ORGANIZATIONS. When abstract democratic reforms concerning such matter as congressional districting or campaign finance are linked with concrete grievances, they can be used to create alliances among groups with a wide range of substantive concerns. For example, the Sierra Club has explained its commitment to democratic political reforms on its website: "Corrupting corporate money pouring into our government. Assaults on the right to vote. Gridlock and obstruction in Washington. There's no question—our democracy is in trouble. To protect our environment, we must protect our democracy."[46]

A Democracy reform movement can find allies among churches, temples, and mosques concerned with social justice; environmental organizations frustrated by policy gridlock; labor unions whose members feel battered economically and neglected by politicians; business organizations troubled by political waste, inefficiency, and gridlock; racial and ethnic minority organizations whose members feel politically left out. Even scientific associations alarmed by politicians' efforts to undermine scientific knowledge with misinformation.

The dysfunctional political system is failing many ordinary Americans by preventing progress on a wide range of policy issues. By combining their efforts, groups with disparate interests can forge a formidable collective movement.

RECRUIT AFFLUENT AMERICANS. Social movements to help the disadvantaged can gain a great deal of strength by recruiting allies from among the advantaged. Allies who have extensive social and economic resources can play important leadership roles and can provide money and political influence.

The "middle class" that led the Progressive movement, for example, did not come from the middle of the U.S. income distribution but almost entirely from the top 20 percent. Central figures such as Jane Addams were born to families of substantial wealth.[47] Successful businesspeople played an important role in economic and "clean government" reforms (though few were enthusiastic about extending democracy to the urban masses, and some worked to restrict it).[48] The civil rights movement of the 1950s and 1960s leveraged grassroots organizing in black communities throughout the South with outside support from white liberals, federal courts, and the mass media.[49]

Social movements often rely on "weapons of the weak" wielded by unpaid, volunteer labor. But money matters, too. Full-time activists—even if they are not paid salaries—have to be fed, sheltered, and transported. Money is especially important these days, when politicians depend so heavily on campaign funds and when TV ads are extremely expensive. Wealthy, socially conscious "angels," as well as a multitude of small contributions, can be significant sources of movement strength.[50]

The effort to reduce the dominance of money in our politics will—ironically—require a great deal of money to succeed. Some of that money can come from millions of small contributions from ordinary citizens to candidates and organizations committed to democratic political reforms. But the moneyed interests that benefit from the current system will be devoting big resources to preserving the status quo. Fortunately, there are some wealthy sympathizers who recognize that our political system is broken. By combining big money and small money, reformers have more of a chance.

In 2014, for example, Lawrence Lessig's Mayday PAC (dubbed "the Super PAC to end all Super PACs") raised more than $10 million to help congressional candidates who were committed to campaign finance reform. Supporters included almost seventy thousand small donors along with twenty-four wealthy individuals, each of whom contributed at least $100,000.[51]

There are dangers, of course, for a democratic reform movement that relies too heavily on wealthy "angels" who may try to alter its agenda.[52] Pressures to lose focus, or to make bad compromises, need to be resisted. But the practical fact is that money is probably needed to fight political money. Some help from well-to-do people is likely to be critical to a successful democratic reform movement today, just as it was in the Progressive Era.[53]

ADOPT DIVERSE STRATEGIES AND TACTICS. Successful social movements have flexibly pursued their goals through diverse strategies, operating in a variety of settings with a variety of targets. For example, the civil rights movement pursued legal avenues in the courts, policy change through legislation, and public education and advocacy through mass demonstrations, sit-ins, boycotts, and other forms of peaceful resistance. In the end, nonviolent protests such as the Selma march that provoked violent reactions by southern sheriffs proved crucial to winning national sympathy and support.[54]

Contemporary advocates for democratic reforms, too, have adopted a wide variety of strategies. Mayday.US, Issue One, and Every Voice advocate for publicly financed "clean elections" and contribute to candidates who commit to clean election reforms. Public Citizen lobbies Congress and represents public interests before the Supreme Court. Democracy Matters mentors activists and supports public education about money and politics at colleges and universities. Black Lives Matter engages local communities through social media to protest oppressive policing and to advocate for racial justice. And the Occupy movement used mass demonstrations to bring attention to the gross inequalities that permeate our economy and our politics. Leafleting, protest marches, town hall meetings; many tactics may be appropriate under various circumstances.

PURSUE STATE AND LOCAL REFORMS. Social movement success can be enhanced by working simultaneously or sequentially at both local and national levels. The Townsend movement, for example, made significant progress on old-age pensions in the 1940s (when Congress was unreceptive) by targeting state governments. The women's suffrage movement, too, initially focused on the states. By the time women gained the right to vote nationally through the Nineteenth Amendment, the majority of states already allowed women to vote in some elections, and in fifteen of the forty-eight states, women had the same voting rights as men.[55]

The civil rights movement—when largely thwarted in the South—built a power base within the northern Democratic Party and went after national policy, winning a federal antilynching bill in the 1930s, a series of antisegregation court decisions (culminating in the Supreme Court's *Brown v. Board of Education* decision in 1954), and, a decade later, the Civil Rights and Voting Rights Acts of 1964 and 1965.[56]

Working at the state and local level can have advantages. Since there is wide variation in political conditions across the United States, opportunities for change are bound to be greater in some locales than others, and greater in some cities and states than they are at the national level. Advocates can take advantage of propitious opportunities to achieve local success. Each local success can serve as a model for efforts elsewhere. Each can show that change is possible and that the fight is worth the effort. In addition, multiple local efforts can serve as laboratories for trying various organizational techniques and creative new policy solutions. If particular results are disappointing—such as the ineffectiveness of vote-by-mail reforms at expanding the electorate—then other approaches can be tried elsewhere.

Important democratic reforms such as clean election laws have been won in states and cities (recall chapter 7.) With time, these reforms can spread. And as more citizens come to believe that our politics can be improved, the pressure for change at the national level will increase.

MOBILIZE MASS-MEMBERSHIP ORGANIZATIONS. Small, community-based reform groups and large, mass-membership organizations are both needed to wield real political clout. Several large or mass-membership organizations are already actively pursuing reform. Common Cause, with 400,000 members and a long track record of working to regulate lobbying and campaign finance, has broadened its reach to include further democratic reforms. The League of Women Voters, about 150,000 members strong, has a similar history of working for clean, democratic politics. More recently the environmentally focused, 2.4 million-member Sierra Club has instituted a Democracy Program. Civil Rights organizations such as the 300,000-member NAACP work to attain full political participation for minorities. Several large labor unions, such as the Service Employee International Union, United Auto Workers, and Communications Workers of America, are working to increase voting turnout among working-class people, who are underrepresented in the voting electorate.

In the age of near-universal communication by Internet and smartphone, not all organizations need geographically concentrated memberships that meet face-to-face. Potentially, anyone can be a virtual neighbor and fellow group member with anyone else.

The Internet-based group MoveOn (a liberal organization chiefly focused on issues of war and peace and economic inequality) also has a broad interest in furthering democratic politics. The eight million–plus members of MoveOn represent an enormous potential army of political reformers who could be mobilized by e-mail and through social media to join in on petitions, demonstrations, or other actions.

A smaller but more directly democracy-oriented netroots group is RootStrikers (now a part of Demand Progress) that was created to fight political corruption in the United States and reduce the role of special-interest money in elections. The idea is not to hack at the *branches* of the problem but rather to focus on its *root*, a corrupt campaign finance system. Interested (and careful) readers can locate many other national, state, and local organizations that work primarily through the Internet and social media.

COORDINATE ACTION. A particularly important aspect of social movement strategy is *coordination*. Not everyone working for democratic reforms has to do the same thing or even pursue exactly the same goals. But sharing a core strategy in common can help bring massive force to bear on a well-defined objective and can avoid wasteful duplication or working at cross-purposes. A grand coalition among reform organizations can help reformers reach agreement about exactly which reforms to emphasize first, where to work (in states, in localities, nationally, or some combination of these), and what techniques of influence to pursue. The Democracy Initiative—an umbrella organization led by the NAACP, Sierra Club, AFL-CIO, Communication Workers of America, and Greenpeace, and embracing dozens of other organizations—may be one possible nucleus for coordinating a social movement for Democracy.

WORK WITH AND WITHIN POLITICAL PARTIES. Social movements typically bring pressure to bear from outside the formal political system. The Populists, New Deal–era movements, the civil rights movement, the anti-Vietnam War movement, and the women's movement all engaged effectively in the "unconventional" politics of mass demonstrations and protests. But lasting political and social change eventually requires policy action—legislation and court decisions. And that means that ultimately one or more political parties must probably play a central role.

On many important issues there are significant partisan differences, so a social movement may find one party to be much more receptive than the other. Social movement scholars point out that historically, social movement activists have often moved into and worked *through* a sympathetic political party. During and after the 1960s, for example, civil rights and other activists moved into, and fundamentally transformed, the Democratic Party.[57] Christian conservatives did the same within the Republican Party, particularly starting in the Reagan era.

Sometimes, when one party holds a commanding position in all branches of the federal government (as the Democrats did during the New Deal period), vigorous support from one party may be sufficient for success.

But often—as in the Progressive and civil rights periods— bipartisan support is essential. In a political system with multiple checks and balances, significant change usually requires at least some degree of support from both political parties. The landmark civil rights bills of the 1960s, for example, though pushed by Democratic President Lyndon Johnson, actually received more support from congressional Republicans than Democrats.[58]

Many of today's existing democratic reform groups are predominately liberal or oriented toward the Democratic Party, or both. But to be successful, a democratic reform movement must probably also include a number of conservatives and Republicans. Some important conservative values and principles fit well with measures that would enhance democracy. Most conservatives favor encouraging a sense of community; promoting efficiency and avoiding waste; insisting on honesty and transparency in government; encouraging civic involvement and a well-informed citizenry. The distortions of public policy that result from wealthy individuals and corporations purchasing wasteful subsidies, inefficient pork barrel projects, and unfair tax loopholes, for example, should help persuade principled conservatives to back reforms to reduce the political power of money.[59]

From Barry Goldwater to the Tea Party, American conservatives have stressed the need to return political power to ordinary citizens. In his 1960 classic *The Conscience of a Conservative*, Goldwater wrote, "In order to achieve the widest possible distribution of political power, financial contributions to political campaigns should be made by individuals and individuals alone. I see no reason for labor unions—or corporations—to participate in politics."[60]

But we have to face the fact that many Republicans are wary of small-*d* democratic reforms because they perceive some of them—probably correctly—as likely to help big-*d* Democratic candidates and policies. Principled beliefs in clean politics and political equality can clash with short-term political calculations. The most difficult single challenge for a social movement for Democracy, therefore, may be figuring out how to recruit supporters among conservatives and Republicans.

DON'T IGNORE ELECTIONS. Petitioning and persuading public officials can be very helpful. Ultimately, however, the most surefire way—sometimes the only way—to gain support from officials is to work to elect democratic reformers and throw out of office those who resist. That means locally as well as nationally. And it means officials of either party, including your own.

A THIRD PARTY? The big impact that the People's Party and Theodore Roosevelt's "Bull Moose" Progressive Party had in preparing the ground for Progressive reforms—together with today's widespread disillusionment over the state of the established Republican and Democratic Parties—suggests that democratic reformers might want to consider forming a new political party. This is a crucial decision that should be made after careful reflection by a clear-thinking and well-coordinated social movement. U.S. electoral laws are so heavily stacked against third parties, and there is so much danger (under winner-take-all voting rules) of throwing election victories to the least-preferred major-party candidate, that we urge great caution. A full-scale third-party effort might best be reserved as a weapon of last resort, if efforts to win over one or both of the major parties fail conclusively. On the other hand, carefully designed third-party candidacies might be helpful on occasion (for example, if two major-party candidates are equally unacceptable) to alarm the major parties and prod them into changing.

BE PATIENT AND PERSISTENT. Another lesson that comes though clearly from the history of social movements is the need for persistence. To get from popular demands to major accomplishments took the Populists and Progressives decades. The fight for women's suffrage spanned more than seventy years. The civil rights movement grew slowly over decades before bursting into national prominence in the 1960s.

Contemporary efforts to redress political and economic inequalities, too, will require sustained action. Some of the organizations at the forefront of these efforts have already been fighting for decades to give ordinary citizens greater voice in government. Several unions, including the AFL-CIO and the Service Workers International Union; civic groups, such as Common Cause; voting rights and good-government groups including the League of Women Voters; and foundations, such as Ford and Carnegie, have all been engaged for a long time in trying to make America a more democratic nation.

Major changes to our political system are not likely to come quickly. But there can be small victories along the way, each of which will make the next battle easier to win. States and cities have been taking the lead. Small reforms at the federal level (such as modest restrictions on the use of the Senate filibuster) have already been achieved. It may take some time before the Supreme Court reverses its campaign finance decisions, but court reversals of this magnitude have happened throughout our history, and there is no reason to believe they cannot happen again.

BE CAREFUL WHAT YOU WISH FOR. Finally, policy changes enacted with great hope and hoopla do not always achieve their desired ends. Past laws attempting to regulate campaign finance are classic examples of reforms that have been undermined, in unanticipated ways, by people who have found new methods for pursuing their old objectives.

In picking democratic reforms to support, it is important to be reasonably certain that they will actually have democratic effects. As noted in chapter 7, certain reforms can have the *opposite* of their intended effect. Early voting, for example, can actually decrease overall voter turnout, unless it is coupled with such other reforms as automatic registration.[61] It is crucial to think through carefully exactly what policy changes are worth working for, in what order. And what sorts of compromises are acceptable.

Success is certainly not guaranteed.[62] But if many of our readers and others join together in the fight for democratic reforms, they may find themselves members of a powerful social movement for Democracy. Such a movement could well transform American politics.

TEN

Signs of Progress

American democracy is ailing. In the preceding chapters we have laid out our diagnosis of the disease and our prescriptions for treatment. Unfortunately, there is no single pill, potion, or medical procedure that can bring a cure. Only a great deal of hard work—by many committed citizens, over a long period of time—can do it.

The challenge is not to restore some lost utopia of responsiveness and equality. Alexis de Tocqueville's America is not our America, and we would not want it to be. Our challenge, instead, is to turn our country onto a path of increasing democracy. This is a path we have strayed from more than once in our history, but a path to which we have frequently returned.

When the robber barons of the Gilded Age corrupted our government to serve their own wealth and power, Americans pushed back, made changes, and set the country on a more egalitarian path. Today we again find that the wealthy few are amassing power and distorting our political system for their own ends. And once again, Americans are pushing back.

Entrenched interests that benefit from the current system will not relinquish their advantages without a fight. For significant progress to occur, three conditions must be met. First, there must be widespread agreement that we have serious problems—that our society and economy are failing millions of citizens. Second, those failures must be understood, at least in part, as failures of government to respond to the wants and needs of ordinary Americans. And third, enough people must care enough about these problems to devote a lot of time and energy to bring about change.

We believe all three of these conditions are increasingly being met in today's America.

First, there is widespread recognition that our economic system is failing to meet the needs of average citizens while heaping rewards on the already advantaged. This failure is so widely recognized that it has become central to the appeals of politicians across the political spectrum. In the 2016 presidential elections, for example, both "outsider" and "establishment" candidates in both the Democratic and Republican parties stressed the unfairness of our economy and the struggles of ordinary citizens. It was not surprising to hear Bernie Sanders, the democratic socialist from Vermont, proclaim that "for the past 40 years, Wall Street and the billionaire class has rigged the rules to redistribute wealth and income to the wealthiest and most powerful people of this country." But similar sentiments were expressed by center-left Democrat Hillary Clinton ("The deck is stacked for those at the top"); by center-right Republican Jeb Bush ("If you're born poor today, you're more likely to stay poor"); and by hard-right conservative Ted Cruz ("We're facing a divided economy—the top one percent are doing great . . . but working men and women across this country . . . are finding it harder to make ends meet"). The ultimate victor, too—outsider Donald Trump—repeatedly charged that the system is "rigged" against ordinary Americans: "it's not just the political system that's rigged. It's the whole economy. It's rigged by big donors who want to keep down wages. It's rigged by big businesses who want to leave our country, fire our workers, and sell their products back into the U.S. with absolutely no consequences for them. . . . It's rigged against you, the American people."[1]

Our point is not that all of these politicians' policy proposals would help reduce inequality, or even that all of them genuinely wanted to do so. Our point is that the economic travails of the American middle class and the widespread sense that the economy and political system are strongly tilted to favor the privileged few are so widely understood and of such deep concern that politicians across the political spectrum have proclaimed their commitment to a fairer and more egalitarian economy.

Americans have also come to believe that government is implicated in our distorted and unfair economic system and that political reforms are urgently needed. Fervent opposition to the Supreme Court's *Citizens United* decision (which allows corporate money free rein in politics, and which four out of five Americans think should be overturned) is one indication of the public's belief that special interests and the wealthy dominate our politics.[2]

Another indication is the appeal of the two major "outsider" candidates in the 2016 presidential election. Bernie Sanders refused to accept any political action committee (PAC) money and relied mainly on small donations to fund his insurgent campaign. Billionaire Donald Trump asked voters to trust him because he was too rich to be bought, and he denounced his primary election opponents for their dependence on big donors. Referring to Jeb Bush, Trump said, "He raises $100 million, so what does $100 million mean? $100 million means he's doing favors for so many people, it means lobbyists, it means special interests, it means donors . . . Who knows it better than me? I give to everybody. They do whatever I want."[3]

Even "establishment" candidates who were themselves collecting millions of dollars for their campaigns and super PACs echoed the claim that moneyed interests have distorted democracy in America. Republican candidate Marco Rubio declared, "If you can afford to hire an army of lawyers, lobbyists, and others to help you navigate and sometimes influence the law, you'll benefit. And so that's why you see big banks, big companies, keep winning. And everybody else is stuck and being left behind."[4] Hillary Clinton proposed a thorough overhaul of federal campaign funding (including a Constitutional amendment to overturn *Citizens United*), and promised to reform "a political system that has been hijacked by billionaires and special interests who will spend whatever it takes to crowd out the voices of everyday Americans."[5]

Perceiving a problem and attributing it to the power of moneyed interests to shape government policy is important. But change also requires a belief that our political system can be improved and a commitment to make that happen. Americans are rightly cynical about politicians' promises to fix the system. Our history of largely failed campaign finance reform at the federal level gives them good reason to doubt how much impact future campaign finance reforms would be likely to have. Cynicism can spill over into despair and inaction.

But we also see signs of hopefulness and a willingness to push hard for desperately needed political and economic reforms. As we noted in earlier chapters, cities and states are often leading the way—perhaps blazing a trail for change in Washington.[6]

Since the turn of the twenty-first century, "clean election" laws have spread to more places, and stronger reforms are being tried. In some cases, hard-won improvements to the ways elections are run have been weakened by elected officials or court decisions. But citizens are fighting back.

In 1996, Maine voters passed the nation's first statewide clean elections law. But Supreme Court decisions and opposition from some of Maine's own elected officials threatened to undermine the system. In 2015, Maine's citizens, working with a coalition of reform groups, succeeded in passing an initiative to strengthen Maine's publicly funded elections and increase funding for their clean election program. Maine's commitment to clean elections is not rooted in left-leaning politics—Republicans currently control the state Senate and governorship and outnumber Democrats in Maine's congressional delegation.

Across the country from Maine, the city of Seattle (which *is* a liberal bastion) adopted the country's first campaign voucher system—the most far-reaching campaign reform yet. As described in chapter 7, as of 2017, every voter in Seattle gets $100 worth of vouchers that they can use to support any candidate for city office. Candidates who accept vouchers must abide by strict limits on spending and outside fund-raising. The voucher system allows every citizen to participate, even those for whom a small donation from their own pocket would be a hardship. If Seattle's experience turns out like that of the many other states and cities that have adopted clean election programs, candidates who opt into the system of public financing will be spending less time raising money from big donors and more time talking with ordinary citizens.[7]

In 2016, South Dakota followed Seattle's lead when voters approved a referendum adopting the first statewide campaign voucher system (along with a range of other electoral reforms that include lower contribution limits, greater disclosure, a new state ethics commission, and enhanced enforcement of campaign finance laws). But the reforms approved by the voters of South Dakota were immediately attacked by South Dakota's own legislators and governor. In a clear demonstration of the power of reforms to upset the status quo, the legislature declared a "state of emergency" allowing it to nullify the results of the referendum and legally preventing advocates from again putting the reforms up to a vote of the citizens.[8] This sorry spectacle underlines both the determination of entrenched interests to retain their power and the potential of reforms to remake the political order. Only time will tell whether the interests that benefit from current arrangements will prevail or whether the citizens of South Dakota, like those in Maine, will be able to force democratizing reforms on politicians who would prefer to leave arrangements as they are.

On voting rights, too, reform groups have had some success, first in fighting back against new restrictions such as voter identification laws and more recently in adopting automatic registration systems that promise to bring underrepresented groups more fully into the electoral process. Oregon passed an automatic voter registration program in 2015 and quadrupled its monthly new voter registration rates as a result.[9] In 2016, West Virginia and Vermont both passed groundbreaking automatic registration bills, with strong bipartisan support.[10]

As we have argued, political reforms on such matters as campaign finance and voting rights are critical to healing what ails American democracy. But substantive changes to improve the lives of ordinary citizens need not—indeed, *should* not—wait until the political reforms are secured. Citizens and reform organizations across the country have also been organizing and lobbying for immediate changes that can improve conditions for the less well-off. The campaign for a $15 an hour minimum wage was dismissed as unachievable when it began. But we have recently seen a $15 minimum wage adopted in the states of California and New York and in about a dozen cities around the country. These increases were not achieved without a struggle. But they *were* achieved, and they have helped change the nation's perceptions about what is possible. This and other reforms may ultimately be enacted at the federal level so that the whole nation is covered.

Paid family leave has been another focus of advocates for American workers. In 2015 and 2016, two additional states adopted such laws (joining Massachusetts and Connecticut and thereby doubling the number to a still tiny four out of fifty). One was California, where Democrats had strong control of all the state political institutions. But the other was New York, where the Republican-controlled Senate was convinced to go along.

Reforms designed to shift power and resources away from the wealthy and toward ordinary citizens never come easily. But our political institutions, for all their shortcomings, do provide avenues for citizen influence—so long as those citizens organize, mobilize broad support, and persist. When enough Americans demand change, major moves toward more democracy can be achieved.

ACKNOWLEDGMENTS

We are grateful to many institutions and individuals for contributing to this book. Northwestern University, Princeton University and its Center for the Study of Democratic Politics, and Stanford's Center for Advanced Study in the Behavioral Sciences provided outstanding working environments as well as important material support. Our data collection, data analysis, and writing benefited from generous support from the Russell Sage Foundation (under the leadership of Eric Wanner and then Sheldon Danziger) and the John D. and Catherine T. MacArthur Foundation (under Bob Gallucci and Julia Stasch), and from a hardworking NORC team headed by Cathy Haggerty (with brilliant assistance from Fritz Scheuren).

We benefited from comments and suggestions—by colleagues too numerous to list—at a number of professional conferences and talks, including (for Page) visits to Cornell, the University of Chicago, the University of Montreal, Dēmos, the University of Illinois–Chicago, the University of California–Santa Barbara, Lone Star College, the University of Michigan, Beijing Foreign Studies University, and Tsinghua University; and (for Gilens) visits to Michigan State, the Massachusetts Institute of Technology, Pennsylvania State, the Humphrey School at the University of Minnesota, St. Norbert College, Kalamazoo College, Wesley College, the University of Montreal, Plymouth State University, and Syracuse University.

Many ideas, suggestions, and criticisms—some of them rather hard-hitting—came from Larry Bartels, Ed Greenberg, Tom Ferguson, Dan Galvin, Ben R. Page, Mary Dietz, Mara Suttman-Lea, Matt Lacombe, Jacob Rothschild, Lee Drutman, Jane Mansbridge, Anna Galland, Elizabeth Sanders, Michele Epstein, Doug McAdam, Sidney Tarrow, and Dan Rodgers, among others. We also thank Adele Simmons for moving and shaking; Jeff Isaac and Jon Stewart for launching us; Ellen and George Galland for the title; Ine Jansen for promoting tranquility; Theda Skocpol and the Scholars Strategy Network for linking us with a remarkable group of scholars; two very thorough anonymous reviewers for the University of Chicago Press; and Lara Heimert and Sydelle Kramer—who gave us much-needed reality checks on whether and how the book might be written so as to make sense to general readers.

For crucial help in making the project actually happen, we are grateful to two outstanding editors at the University of Chicago Press: John Tryneski, who was present at the creation and full of ideas about how to shape the book; and Chuck Myers, who added fresh ideas, scrutinized the manuscript line by line, and kept our eyes on the ball. We also owe a great deal to many Press specialists on production, promotion, and marketing (special thanks to Lori Meek Schuldt and Levi Stahl), who dealt skillfully with the demands of a book intended to speak both to academic experts and to a broad general audience.

We are also indebted to colleagues who collaborated on some of the research that is reported here, most notably to Sandy Jencks, Larry Bartels, Jay Seawright, Fay Cook, Rachel Moskowitz, and Matt Lacombe.

We were blessed with the fruits of hard work by a number of very talented research assistants, including those who helped gather the original "affluence and influence" data for Gilens (Marty Cohen, Jason Conwell, Andrea Vanacore, Mark West, Oleg Bespalov, Daniel Cassino, Kevin Collins, Shana Gadarian, Raymond Hicks, and Lee Shaker) and those who analyzed the Survey of Economically Successful Americans (SESA) multimillionaires data (notably Rachel Moskowitz and Fiona Chin) or the billionaires web-scraping data (especially Matt Lacombe), as well as those who contributed directly to this book: Mara Suttman-Lea, Matt Lacombe, Jacob Rothschild, Pavielle Haines, Dan Edelman, and Sean Diament.

Their contributions went well beyond customary graduate student toil, to include creative ideas and extensive writing.

As always, our greatest debts are to our families, especially Mary and Janet, who put up with considerably more than the usual travails of professors' spouses (distracted stares, absences at critical moments, ponderous pronouncements, occasional rants). Over the all-too-many years of research and writing that fed into this book, they accepted all that and more. They offered a good many substantive ideas and, most importantly, their continual loving support. Thank you!

Ben Page and Marty Gilens
Evanston, Illinois, and Princeton, New Jersey
March 2017

APPENDIX

Interest Groups and Industries Included in the Index of Interest Group Alignment

1. AARP
2. AFL-CIO
3. Airlines
4. American Bankers Association
5. American Council of Life Insurance
6. American Farm Bureau Federation
7. American Federation of State, County, and Municipal Employees
8. American Hospital Association
9. American Israel Public Affairs Committee
10. American Legion
11. American Medical Association
12. Association of Trial Lawyers
13. Automobile companies
14. Christian Coalition
15. Computer software and hardware
16. Credit Union National Association
17. Defense contractors
18. Electric companies
19. Health Insurance Association
20. Independent Insurance Agents of America
21. International Brotherhood of Teamsters
22. Motion Picture Association of America
23. National Association of Broadcasters
24. National Association of Home Builders
25. National Association of Manufacturers
26. National Association of Realtors
27. National Beer Wholesalers Association
28. National Education Association
29. National Federation of Independent Business
30. National Governors Association
31. National Restaurant Association
32. National Rifle Association
33. National Right to Life Committee
34. Oil companies

35. Pharmaceutical Research and Manufacturers
36. Recording Industry Association
37. Securities and investment companies
38. Telephone companies
39. Tobacco companies
40. United Auto Workers
41. Universities
42. U.S. Chamber of Commerce
43. Veterans of Foreign Wars

NOTES

CHAPTER ONE

For comments and suggestions on this chapter we are especially grateful to Larry Bartels, who (we fear) may not be entirely happy with the results.

1. Among decision rules that aggregate individuals' preferences into a collective choice between two alternatives, *only* majority rule can guarantee all of the following: that there is always a decisive and unique result; that all individuals are treated equally; that no particular alternative has a special advantage; and that decisions respond positively if one individual changes his or her preferences (May 1952.)

   For more than two alternatives, the "possibility theorem" put forth by Arrow (1963) holds that neither majority rule nor any other decision rule for aggregating individual preferences that satisfies a set of apparently reasonable conditions can *guarantee* that a definite collective choice will always be made. Riker (1982) and others have argued that this means democracy is impossible, due to voting cycles and strategic manipulation. But Mackie (2003) replies that the Arrow conditions—especially the "independence of irrelevant alternatives," which rules out cardinal utilities and interpersonal comparisons—have "no descriptive or normative force" (156), and that there is a "nearly complete absence of cycles" in the real world (441).

2. See Dahl 1956, chap. 2. Reviewing the literature, Sabl (2015, 345, 349) asserts that normative political theorists "all but universally" reject majority-rule responsiveness.

3. Schumpeter (1950, chap. 22.

4. *Wikipedia*, s.v. "Iranian Presidential Election, 2013," February 7, 2017, http://en.wikipedia.org/wiki/Iranian_presidential_election,_2013;Aljazeera 2013.

5. Bonica et al. 2013.

6. Bowie and Lioz 2013.

7. Federalist papers no. 10, 49, 62, 63, 68, 71, in Hamilton, Madison, and Jay [1787–88] 1999); Lippmann (1922) 1965; Delli Carpini and Keeter 1996, 65–89.

8. Converse 1964.

9. Somin 2013, 192.

10. Achen and Bartels (2016) make good points about capricious and erroneous factors that often enter into "retrospective" voting decisions concerning past government performance (largely, we believe, because relevant information is not made

easily available to citizens; see Healy and Lenz 2014.) We see the feeble state of democracy in the United States as much more reflective of defects in the political system—money run wild, disenfranchised citizens, polarized parties, and unrepresentative institutions, for example—than reflective of defects in the citizenry.

11. See Downs 1957, chaps. 11, 12.

12. Converse (1964, 246) called groups of individuals with particular knowledge of and concern about specific issues "issue publics." He argued that ordinary citizens who belong to one or another issue public nearly match political elites in the nature and "quality" of their preferences on those specific issues.

13. See Page 1996; Page and Shapiro 1992, 15–27.

14. Page and Shapiro 1992.

15. Surowiecki 2004. See Landemore 2013. The "Condorcet jury theorem" provides one illustration.

16. But such leaders need not be numerous, so long as each citizen recognizes and attends to one of them. If everyone has at least one cue giver he or she can trust, the leaders on different sides need not be equal in number to guide everyone fairly. On competitive framing, see Zaller 1992; Chong and Druckman 2007.

17. Page and Shapiro 1992, esp. xi, 1, 17, 383–90; Gilens 2012, chap. 2.

18. Apparent contradictions sometimes vanish under scrutiny. Expressed desires for lower taxes but more spending, for example, may reflect a wish for lower taxes *on the interviewee* rather than lower rates overall; or a demand to cut government waste; or support for cuts in unmentioned programs; or a higher tolerance for deficits than the Beltway consensus would dictate.

19. George Bishop (2005) offers some devastating examples of misinterpreted data from poorly worded poll and survey questions. But even the data he cites can be used to discern coherent patterns of collective public opinion (see Page 2007).

20. Across 235 issues, the aggregate "fully informed preferences" simulated by Althaus (2003) differed from poll-measured collective opinion by an average of only 6.5 percentage points. Not a trivial amount, but not nearly enough to overturn large poll-measured majority support for policies like those that will be discussed subsequently in chapter 3. Similarly, aggregate opinion changes on 48 issues after four days of focused study and deliberation at James Fishkin's "National Issues Convention" averaged only 5 percentage points—barely more than the 3-point average in a control group (Gilens 2012, 30–32.) On "don't know" responses, see Berinsky 2004.

21. For discussions of elite manipulation of public opinion, see Page and Shapiro 1992, chap. 9; Gilens 2012, 24–29.

22. Mueller (2001) compares democracy to the Garrison Keillor creation "Ralph's Pretty Good Grocery Store." We see true majority-rule democracy as better than that.

23. Federalist paper 10, in Hamilton, Madison, and Jay (1777–78) 1999.

24. Here and elsewhere we occasionally capitalize the word *Democracy* for emphasis in reference to the social movement we are discussing. No suggestion related to the Democratic Party is intended.

CHAPTER TWO

1. Tocqueville (1835) 2000, vol. 1, introduction, 1.3, 2.7.

2. Keyssar 2009; Wilentz 2005, 2016.

3. Tocqueville (1835) 2000, vol. 1, 2.7. Tocqueville worried that America was *too* democratic; he considered "tyranny of the majority" to be a great peril.

4. Tocqueville devoted considerable space to the evils of slavery ([1835] 2000, vol. 1, 2.10).

   He said little about women. He asserted that they make the "mores" (norms, customs), thereby indirectly affecting politics, and he celebrated the independence of American girls. But he described—and apparently approved of—traditional patriarchal gender roles for adult women, calling them "the equal of men," but only in the sense of enjoying equal esteem and performing with equal excellence quite different functions: "domestic occupations," not conducting a business or entering into the political sphere ([1835] 2000, vol. 1, 2.9, p. 279; vol. 2, 3.9, 3.12).

   Early in his "three races" chapter, Tocqueville spoke of "tyranny" and "oppression" against both blacks and Native Americans, and he gave a moving account of how white settlers—abetted by government—seized the natives' land, scared away the wild game they lived on, drove them ever westward, forced them into poverty, and drastically reduced their numbers so that they were "condemned to perish" ([1835], 2000, vol. 1, 2.10, pp. 302–25).

5. Piketty 2014, 613n12.

6. With slaves included, the top 1 percent of wealth holders had about 25 percent of all the wealth, compared with more than 50 percent in Europe at that time (Piketty 2014, 348, 349). In the American South around 1800, the total economic value of slaves exceeded the total value of agricultural land and constituted nearly half of all capital (Piketty 2014, 161).

7. In colonial 1774, the top 1 percent of Americans got only about 8.5 percent of all the income, compared to 17.5 percent in England. We have no good data on Jacksonian times, but by the middle—and especially the late—nineteenth century, inequality began to rise. By 1910, the top 1 percent of Americans received fully 17.5 percent of all the income (Lindert and Williamson 2016, 38, 39, 115, 116, 154–55, 173.)

8. Keyssar 2009, 21.

9. Keyssar 2009, 23–24, 314.

10. Burnham 2007, esp. 522–37. After 1832, turnout levels continued to rise, reaching fully 80 percent in 1840 and staying about that high for nearly all of the nineteenth century, until the systematic disenfranchisement that followed the 1896 election. The definitive source is Burnham, Ferguson, and Ferleger 2010.

11. On the elections of 1800 and 1828, see Wilentz 2005, chap. 3 and 295–97, 301–5; Remini 1963. On 1832, see Wilentz 2005, 372–74.

12. Quoted in Wilentz (2005, 312–13).

13. This is not to say that money and organized interests played no part in American politics during the 1830s. In the bitter conflict over rechartering the Bank of the United States (BUS), for example, outsize influence was exerted by Philadelphia capitalists (pro) and New York and other state bankers (con); see T. Ferguson 1995, 56–57, 98–99. Wilentz (2005, 360–74) disputes the "impression" of a mere fight between rival bankers and businessmen but acknowledges the important roles of pro-BUS Southern plantation owners and of an anti-BUS "crony consortium" of bankers that wanted to take over the BUS's functions. Jackson's veto of the BUS—which he portrayed as a privately owned bastion of privilege and unaccountable power—appears to have been quite popular with the general electorate.

14. U.S. Bureau of the Census 1975, 8.
15. Gordon 2016, part 1, 27–318.
16. Tocqueville (1825) 2000, vol. 2, 20. We are indebted to Mary Dietz for drawing our attention to this chapter.
17. Bryce 1995, 2:1413. Bryce had little to say about a decline in democracy, except to note the corrupting presence in Congress of "The Lobby" (1:618–22). He considered public opinion still to be largely sovereign (2:916–928) but found little evidence of "tyranny of the majority" (2:986–93).
18. Piketty 2014, 348.
19. Piketty 2014, 300. According to Lindert and Williamson, using different data and methods, the share of income received by the top 1 percent was already higher than in colonial times in 1850 and 1860 (about 10 percent); it rose to 17.8 percent in 1910 and stayed around that level through 1929 (2016, 38, 115, 116, 173).
20. McGerr 2003, 4–6. Cornelia's costume ball was apparently too much to take even for the Gilded Age. Heavily criticized, the Martins decamped to Europe.
21. D. Phillips 1906.
22. Keyssar 2009, chap. 5; Burnham 1970, chap.4; T. Ferguson 1995, chap. 2; T. Ferguson and Chen 2005.
23. Burnham 2007, 559, see also 553–58; Burnham, Ferguson, and Ferleger 2010, 85–89.
24. A quick, engaging account of unionization is Geoghegan 2004, 40–50.
25. On the economically leveling effects of wars generally, see Scheidel 2017; Scheve, Stasavage, and Russell Sage Foundation 2016.
26. Piketty 2014, 348, 291. The *income* share of the top tenth dropped from its late-1920s peak of nearly 50 percent to about 33 percent in the 1950s.
27. Gordon 2016, part 2, 331–521.
28. One bit of collateral evidence is that Richard Nixon's issue stands in 1968 tended to be close to the center of public opinion. On eighty-two issues, he agreed with a plurality of the public 79 percent of the time (Page 1978, 40.)

   Our account of rising democratic responsiveness in the golden age is roughly consistent with the finding by Bartels, Clinton, and Geer (2016, 414–15) that the divergence between national opinion (as measured by presidential voting) and policy making (the roll-call position of the median House member) hit a low point between 1920 and 1980. As the authors note, however, those measures of opinion and policy rest on strong and questionable assumptions (411).
29. Figures from Mishel et al. 2012, 186, updated to 2015 dollars using the Bureau of Labor Statistics inflation calculator. For the methodology of wage measurement using CPS/ORG, see Mishel's Appendix B (2012, 465).
30. Mishel et al. 2012, 59. Between 1947 and 1979, the average family income of the middle quintile more than doubled, from $26,548 to $56,466 (in 2011 dollars). By 2010, it had only crept up to $62,268. According to the U.S. Congressional Budget Office (2016, 15), between 1979 and 2013 the "market income" of the middle three fifths of American households grew by only 18 percent, while the incomes of those in the top 1 percent rose by *188* percent. *After-tax-and-transfer* income growth was nearly as unequal: 41 percent and 192 percent rises, respectively (U.S. CBO 2016, 22, 23). That is, government taxes and transfers did little to reduce the growing inequality.
31. Mishel et al. 2012, 29, 236–37. As Gordon (2016) notes, U.S. productivity growth

has slowed markedly since Mishel's 2011 figures. But workers have not received much of anything from the huge total gains in productivity since 1973.

32. See A. Hochschild 2016; Cramer 2016; Khoury 2016. On political effects: Gest 2016; Lee 2016; MacGillis 2016.

33. Auten, Gee, and Turner 2013, Table 1.

34. Mishel et al. 2012, 150. Correlations between fathers' and sons' incomes from Lee and Solon's IGE estimate: $r = 0.49$; daughters' $r = 0.46$. See Chetty et al. 2014.

35. Mishel et al. 2012, 150–54. See also Corak 2013.

36. Corak 2013.

37. Piketty 2014, 291–96. Piketty's data, based on income tax returns, include capital gains. See also U.S. CBO 2016.

38. Piketty 2014, 290, 323, 349.

39. Piketty 2014, 298–303.

40. Mishel 2015. Data from Computstat's ExecuComp database. A striking report on CEO salaries in Illinois is Yerak 2015.

41. Lublin 2015. Data in this source from the Hay Group. The *Journal* did not publish a correlation coefficient or other measure of association, but its flat-line graph suggests that the correlation between pay and performance was near zero.

42. Popper and Silver-Greenberg 2015.

43. Some big private equity firms (e.g. Carlyle, Blackstone, KKR) have gone public, but most continue to be private partnerships. The same is true of hedge funds, including the largest, Bridgewater.

44. Taub 2016. For contrast, see also Taub 2015.

45. Polgreen 2015. Data from Pew Research Center tabulations of Survey of Consumer Finances (Kochhar and Fry 2014).

46. Hines 2014, Coy 2014.

47. *Wikipedia*, s.v. "List of Countries by GDP (PPP)," November 11, 2016, https://en.wikipedia.org/wiki/List_of_countries_by_GDP_(PPP). The 2016 estimates are from IMF.

48. "The Forbes 400" 2016, 128–36, 202.

49. "The Forbes 400" 2016.

50. Gladwell 2008, 50–68.

51. Regarding Donald Trump's help from his father, see Johnston 2016, esp. 15, 17); Kessler 2016; and Berzon and Rubin 2016. Donald Trump has claimed to have a fortune of $10 billion, but *Forbes* (2016, 160) estimated it at $3.7 billion.

52. Gladwell 2008, 50–55.

53. See the official website at http://www.givingpledge.org.

54. See Lamarche 2014. Far from accepting higher taxes, many or most of the wealthiest billionaires appear to favor abolishing the estate tax, and most oppose high tax rates on corporate or personal income (Page, Seawright, and Lacombe 2015). Even in the 1950s, when the top marginal income tax rate was 90 percent, wealthy people worked hard and the economy did fine.

55. On Stephen Schwartzman's over-the-top sixtieth birthday party, see Stewart 2008.

56. R. Frank 2015, drawing on data from NetJets and Wealth-X. On the cost of purchasing private jets, see the website Secret Entourage, http://www.secretentourage.com/lifestyle/cost-of-ownership-g5. Most of the rich rent, rather than buy, their planes. NetJets, a major provider, reports making many hundreds of flights each year to the Super Bowl (250 flights to Phoenix in 2015), the Masters Golf Tour-

nament in Augusta (250–300 flights), heavyweight boxing matches, the Cannes Film Festival, Art Basel, and Warren Buffet's Berkshire Hathaway shareholders' meeting—known as "Woodstock for Capitalists." On the newly wealthy of the first decade of the twenty-first century, see R. Frank 2007, including chap. 7 on yachts, mansions, and jets. Freeland 2012 analyzes sources as well as uses of wealth.

57. Keates 2015. See also S. Chen 2015 on the sale—as a second home—of a remarkable $30 million Los Angeles estate; Searcey 2015.

58. Thal 2016.

59. On the lives of EITC recipients, see Halpern-Meekin et al. (2015). On Food Stamp recipients, see Hoffman 2013.

60. See West 2014.

61. Ehrenreich 2001. Halpern-Meekin et al. (2015) make clear that the Earned Income Tax Credit provides important help to many of the working poor, but eligibility is limited and benefits are far from generous.

62. Khoury 2016. As Khoury foresaw, the political tides of the nation did indeed follow those of Ohio in the 2016 elections. For similar evidence from Wisconsin, see Cramer 2016; on Louisiana, A. Hochschild 2016.

63. Bankruptcy can discharge personal liability on home loans, but not the lenders' lien on the property. So people can lose their homes unless they keep paying. Even after the massive home foreclosures of the Great Recession, Congress refused to give bankruptcy judges "cram down" authority to force reductions in the amount owed.

64. A comprehensive discussion is Stiglitz 2012, esp. chaps. 2, 3. See also Teles 2015 on "regressive rents," legal barriers to entry, and other government-imposed market distortions that generate income inequality, which include licensing requirements for medical fields, limited direct sales from car manufacturers, subsidies for banks, and intellectual property regulations. Such state-imposed rents increase profits, reduce mobility, and drive up consumer costs. See also Kelly 2009; Hacker and Pierson 2010; Reich 2015; Baker 2016.

65. The percentage of total income that the top 1 percent of U.S. income earners actually paid was fully *one-third lower* in 2004 than in 1970 (Hacker and Pierson 2010, 48). See U.S. CBO 2016.

66. See Kelly forthcoming.

67. See T. Friedman 2007. Stiglitz (2012, 59–64) emphasizes the role of financial liberalization in producing economic inequality.

68. Average annual wages in China leapt up from a minuscule 445 Chinese "new" yuan (CNY) in 1952 to 21,001 CNY in 2006, 37,147 CNY in 2010, and 62,029 CNY in 2015 (Trading Economics 2017).

69. See Samuelson 1950. Gains from trade would permit a "Pareto improvement," in which no one came out worse off.

70. B. Davis and Hilsenrath 2016; Autor, Dorn, and Hanson 2016.

71. Bivens 2013.

72. Samuelson 1948, 1949. Transportation costs can modify the wage-equalizing pressure of trade, but those costs have steadily fallen. Samuelson was analyzing only the impact of international trade in goods; the high present-day mobility of investment capital and technological ideas adds further force and speed to the equalizing process. On the consequences, see Page 1997.

73. Gordon (2016) reports that both real GDP per capita (327) and standards of living

(22) doubled roughly each generation during the "special century" from 1870 to 1970. See also Chetty et al. 2016.

74. For a number of ideas and examples in this section, we are indebted to Edward Greenberg. See Ford 2015; Thompson 2015.

75. Ford 2015.

76. Greenberg et al. 2010.and personal communications from Greenberg.

77. See Reich 2015, chap. 22.

78. On AT&T and Google, see Thompson 2015. On YouTube, Facebook, and Instagram, see Ford 2015, 175.

79. See Bivens 2013; Temin 2016.

80. Mishel 2012.

81. On jobless future, see Ford 2015. On steady decline, see Thompson 2015.

82. R. Freeman 2014.

83. Borjas 2014.

84. Mishel 2012, 448. On "egalitarian capitalism" abroad, see Thelen 2014, chap. 1.

85. Mishel et al. 2012, 450. For international comparability and for correspondence to how people actually think about poverty, these poverty rates are defined in *relative* terms: as the proportion of households receiving less than half the median after-tax, after-transfer household income.

86. Mishel et al. 2012, 451.

87. In 1969, the Census Bureau declared that 12.1 percent of Americans were poor; in 2014, the official poverty rate was 14.5 percent (Jencks 2015a). On the effects of specific antipoverty programs, see Jencks 2015b; Bailey and Danziger 2015.

88. Jencks 2015a.

89. On active labor market policies, see Martin 2014. On unionization and collective bargaining, see OECD and Visser 2013. On family allowances, see Van Mechelen and Bradshaw 2013. On unemployment insurance, see Esser et al. 2013. On universal health care, see Reid 2010.

90. Atkinson 2015. See also Piketty 2014, chaps. 13–15; Piketty 2015.

91. Reich 2015, chap. 20. See also Baker 2016, chap. 8; Stiglitz 2012, chap. 10.

92. On reinventing corporations, and the "citizen's bequest," see Reich 2015, chaps. 21, 23.

93. McCall 2013; Page and Jacobs 2009; McClosky and Zaller 1984; J. Hochschild 1981.

94. Scheiber and Sussman 2015, reporting on a May 2015 *New York Times*/CBS survey. Minimum wage question from Public Religion Research Institute American Values Survey, September 2015 (Cooper et al. 2015).

95. Carnes (2013) documents that government officials come overwhelmingly from affluent backgrounds, despite the availability of many talented people from the working class.

96. On downward spiral, see Kelly forthcoming.

CHAPTER THREE

1. Political theorists have devised several "ideal models" of exactly how two-party elections might produce democratic outcomes. For reflections on their strengths and weaknesses, see Page 1978, chaps. 2, 7; Mansbridge 2003. On "responsible party government," see American Political Science Association 1950; Ranney 1962. On "electoral reward and punishment"—based on retrospective voting—see

Key 1961, 267–68, 472–80; Fiorina 1981; Achen and Bartels 2016. On "electoral competition," see Downs 1957; O. Davis, Hinich, and Ordeshook 1970.

In our view, any one of these models—if it worked perfectly—would in the long run produce nearly the same results: public policies preferred by most citizens. (Policy zig-zags by responsible parties alternating in power would just fluctuate around the center of evolving opinions. Because of collective deliberation, the underlying values and interests responded to in electoral reward and punishment models would closely resemble collective policy preferences.) The problem is that none of the models works anywhere near perfectly in the real world.

2. Schlozman, Verba, and Brady 2012; Leighley and Nagler 2013.
3. Anzia 2012; Suttmann-Lea forthcoming; Overton 2007; Wang 2012.
4. But many states forbid voting by people formerly convicted of a felony, including many African Americans convicted of minor drug offenses (Manza and Uggen 2006).
5. United States Election Project 2017.
6. Sides et al. 2015, 333–38. See also Pintor, Gratschew, and Sullivan 2002.
7. Sides et al. 2015, 336.
8. Schwarz 2014.
9. Holbrook and Weinschenk 2014.
10. Suttmann-Lea forthcoming. But these measures do not guarantee less *biased* turnout, especially when savvy campaigns adapt to them.
11. Rosenstone and Hansen 2002.
12. Schlozman, Verba, and Brady 2012, 124, 134, definition at 123n9.
13. Citrin, Schickler, and Sides 2003. See also Wolfinger and Rosenstone 1980, Highton and Wolfinger 2001.
14. Schlozman, Verba, and Brady 2012, 126–33.
15. Leighley and Nagler 2013, 158–69.
16. See Timpone 1998.
17. Rigby and Springer 2011, Springer 2014.
18. Sides et al. 2015; Blais 2006. But see Selb and Lachat 2009.
19. Wang 2012. On rarity of voter fraud, see Levitt 2014.
20. Kimball, Kropf, and Battles 2006; Overton 2007; Wang 2012.
21. Manza and Uggen 2006. On how whole neighborhoods are affected, see Burch 2013.
22. G. Powell 1986.
23. Downs 1957, esp. chaps. 5 and 6.
24. We suspect—though it would be difficult to prove—that misinformation may create more distortions in collective voting choices than in collective policy preferences. Electoral choices may be subject to more intense efforts to deceive that are less often contradicted by direct experience.
25. Downs argued that rational ignorance and uncertainty themselves *inevitably* lead to large power disparities (1957, 94). Perhaps. But we would emphasize the importance of whether *institutions* and *incentives* motivate and permit elites to mislead the citizenry. The proper arrangement of institutions and incentives (such as limits on private spending for political advertising) can, we believe, greatly reduce the distorting effects that misinformation has on democracy.
26. Geer 2006.
27. Bennett 2015.

28. Chong and Druckman 2007.
29. Erikson, MacKuen, and Stimson 2002; Page and Shapiro 1983.
30. The major exception is the work of Larry Bartels (2016), whose earlier studies of Senate roll call voting pioneered analyses of the independent influence of average and affluent citizens. On foreign policy, see Jacobs and Page 2005; Page and Bouton 2006.
31. See Gilens 2012, chap. 2; Gilens and Page 2014, 568–70.
32. See Gilens and Page 2014. Earlier, Gilens (2012) used alternative statistical approaches to explore the influence of different income groups on policy making.
33. Klein 2014.
34. Soroka and Wlezien 2008, 2010; Kelly and Enns 2010; Enns 2015. For our counterview, see Gilens 2009, 2015, 2016; Gilens and Page 2016.
35. Page, Bartels, and Seawright 2013. The truly wealthy, who may be the most influential people within the affluent group in our data, disagree with average citizens much more markedly than the merely affluent do.
36. Hacker and Pierson 2010, 83–87.
37. A. Smith (1776) 1976, book 5, chap. 1.
38. Pigou 1912.
39. See R. Musgrave and P. Musgrave 1980, chap. 3. Pure public goods are defined by entirely nonrival and nonexcludable consumption.
40. Beyond pure public goods, there are arguments for government action in cases of increasing returns to scale (rather than completely nonrival consumption) and in cases of *costly* (rather than completely infeasible) exclusion from consumption.
    A few conservative economists maintain that the costs of government action (red tape, loss of freedom) usually or always exceed the losses from underproduced public goods. We know of no systematic evidence that such is the case.
41. Barry-Jester 2016.
42. Gillis 2017. As Homan Jenkins (2015) points out, temperatures in 2005, 2010, and 2014 were too similar to each other to be sure which was the hottest year. But over many decades of record keeping, all ten of the earth's highest-temperature years have occurred since 1997. The years 2014, 2015, and 2016 each set new record highs.
43. *NYT*/Stanford/RFF, 1/7–22/15. See Davenport and Connelly 2015, A1, A11.
44. A. Stone 2009.
45. Krosnick and MacInnis 2013.
46. Kaufman 2017. The 52–46 confirmation vote was largely along party lines in the Republican-controlled Senate. Democrats had made an unsuccessful attempt to delay the vote until more than two thousand e-mails related to Pruitt's ties with the coal and gas industries could be examined. Objections from numerous environmentalists—and eight hundred former EPA workers who had signed a letter opposing the nominee—were ignored.
47. J. Jones 2013.
48. Pew Research Poll Database 2015.
49. Krogstad and Passel 2015.
50. Anderson Robbins Research and Shaw and Company Research 2014; Blanton 2014.
51. Smeltz, McElmurry, and Kafura 2014; Smeltz et al. 2016. Upon taking office, President Trump sought to tighten immigration policy and increase deportations.
52. Ehrenfreund 2014.

53. As many Americans now die from gunshot wounds as from automobile accidents (U.S. Department of Health and Human Services 2016).
54. District of Columbia v. Heller, 554 U.S. 570 (2008).
55. Kristoff 2015.
56. Pew Research Center 2013.
57. Plumer 2012.
58. Voorhees 2013.
59. Bushaw and Calderon 2014; PDK/Gallup 2014; Howell, West, and Peterson 2011.
60. Project on Student Debt 2006; Baron 2013.
61. Lardner 2013.
62. See McCarty, Poole, and Rosenthal 2013; T. Ferguson, Jorgensen, and Chen 2016b; both sets of scholars link congressional votes on financial reform to campaign contributions from banks.
63. See Page and Simmons 2000, chap. 3.
64. See Kenworthy 2014; Bakija et al. 2016; both draw lessons for the United States from the experience of other countries.
65. Hayek 1944.
66. M. Friedman 1962, chap. 10.
67. Page and Jacobs 2009, 61–63; J. Jones 2013; Murray 2015.
68. Moore 2014; Molyneux 2015.
69. Bartels 2016, chap. 8.
70. Lowery 2014.
71. See Jacobs and King 2016.
72. O'Brien 2014. Current EITC benefit levels are given on the IRS website at https://www.irs.gov/uac/newsroom/earned-income-tax-credit-do-i-qualify.
73. Slaughter 2015.
74. Hedberg 2015.
75. K. Davis et al. 2014.
76. Page and Jacobs 2009, 66.
77. DiJulio, Firth, and Brodie 2015b.
78. Starr 1995, Jacobs and Skocpol 2010.
79. J. Cohn 2016. For similar findings from previous years, see Dalen, Waterbrook, and Alpert 2015; Kaiser Family Foundation 2011.
80. See Bouie 2013; CNN/ORC 2013. The individual mandate was crucial to both the passage of the act (bringing insurance companies on board) and to its financing (forcing currently healthy people to pay premiums that subsidized lower-cost coverage for those more likely to get sick). A universal "single-payer," government-run system—if politically feasible—might well have proven more popular.
81. Altman 2005.
82. National Priorities Project 2017.
83. Details on how Social Security works are given on the official website at https://www.ssa.gov. For an excellent summary, see Altman and Kingson 2015, 209–16. On reducing poverty, see Blank 1997, 228; Jencks 2015b.
84. Altman and Kingson (2015) provide detailed refutations of the most common attacks on Social Security.
85. Proportion of revenue "shortfall" calculated from Altman and Kingson 2015, 226–27. The projected 75-year shortfall is 2.88 percent of taxable payroll over that period. Gradually eliminating the tax "cap" while paying benefits (under a

progressive formula) on the new contributions would produce net revenue equal to 1.95 percent of currently taxable 75-year payroll: that is, 67.7 percent of the total shortfall (1.95/2.88 = 0.677.) On public support for raising the "cap" on payroll taxes, see Page and Jacobs 2009, 70, 127–28n59.

86. If at least as many people who say we are spending "*about* [italics added] the right amount" want a small increase as want a small decrease (a reasonable assumption), then in every General Social Survey since its inception, a majority has favored at least some increase in Social Security spending.

87. Tucker, Reno, and Bethell 2013.

88. Cook and Moskowitz 2014; Jacobs and Shapiro 1999. On support by the wealthy, see Page, Bartels, and Seawright 2013, 56, 58.

89. Altman and Kingson (2015, chap. 9) describe the "billionaires' war" against Social Security.

90. Studies indicate that giving lower-income workers meaningful power to switch among private investments would produce extremely high administrative costs that would eat up a large portion—as much as 40 percent—of their contributions. See United States Congressional Budget Office 2004, esp. Table 1-1.

91. Historically, Social Security has played no role whatsoever in creating budget deficits. Each year it has taken in more money than it has paid out, money that has been used—in effect—as a source of loans to fund other programs, such as military spending.

92. Page and Jacobs 2009, 85. This finding has remained essentially the same in repeated surveys over more than two decades.

93. Motel 2015; Page and Jacobs 2009, 86, 91. On attitudes toward proposals to "redistribute" income by taxing the rich, see Newport 2017.

94. Molyneux and Garin 2013.

95. Page and Jacobs 2009, 86. But less precise survey questions find support for "abolish[ing]" the estate tax; see Drum 2010. Misinformation about who pays how much probably plays a part; see Graetz and Shapiro 2006.

96. Page and Jacobs 2009, 87.

97. Hacker and Pierson 2010.

98. Huang and Debot 2016.

99. Graetz and Shapiro 2006.

100. Stiglitz (2012) shows in detail that many U.S. policies have *worsened*, rather than reduced, economic inequality. See also Reich 2015; Baker 2016.

CHAPTER FOUR

1. Bartels 2016.

2. See the discussions of downward spiral at the end of chapter 2 and in Kelly forthcoming.

3. See Gilens 2012, esp. chap. 2; Gilens and Page 2014, 568–70.

4. Here, and in Gilens and Page 2014, we measure the opinions of the "average citizen" in terms of the opinions of people in the middle (at the median) of the *income distribution*, as described in Gilens 2012. These people are conceptually distinct from, but empirically almost identical to, those at the medians of *opinion* distributions—that is, the Downsian "median voter" (Downs 1957).

5. To put this another way, in our analysis, the measured opinions of the affluent may be serving largely as an *indicator* of the opinions of the truly wealthy, which gen-

erally differ from ordinary citizens' opinions in the same direction—but by much greater amounts—than the affluents' opinions do.

6. Does this mean that the United States should be called a "plutocracy," or an "oligarchy"? We see the answer as depending both on how those terms are defined and on the results of future research. See Winters and Page 2009; Winters 2011.

7. Valelly 1989.

8. Wisconsin Elections Commission 2016. On rural resentment in Wisconsin, see Cramer 2016; Walsh 2004, 2007.

9. Willis 2015; National Institute on Money in State Politics Follow the Money Database 2017.

10. Isikoff 2015.

11. Wisconsin Democracy Campaign 2013.

12. Wines 2016; on policy preferences, see Blumenthal 2011.

13. Douglas-Gabriel 2015; Gabriel 2015.

14. D. Kaufman 2015.

15. Investigative reporter Nicholas Confessore (2015b) tells the remarkable story of how billionaire Ken Griffin and others in 2014 helped elect as Illinois governor the multimillionaire Bruce Rauner, who pursed an agenda similar to Scott Walker's.

16. Center for Responsive Politics 2017a.

17. Ornstein et al. 2017.

18. The U.S. tax "checkoff" system is moribund, providing too little money for presidential candidates to accept the cash and restrictions. As we will see, some states and localities do provide public money for their elections.

19. Bonica et al. 2013.

20. According to the Center for Responsive Politics (2017b), through April 30, 2016, Sanders had raised $129 million in under-$200 contributions and $80 million in over-$200 contributions, compared with Clinton's $40 million and $148 million, respectively.

21. Through April 2016, Sanders had raised $229 million and Clinton $335 million (*New York Times* 2016b).

22. These figures include all campaign, party, and outside spending on behalf of each candidate (Center for Responsive Politics 2017g).

23. Bowie and Lioz 2013.

24. Citizens United v. Federal Election Commission, 558 U.S. 310, 130 S. Ct. 876, 175 L. Ed. 2d 753, 187 LRRM 2961 (2010); SpeechNow.org v. Fed. Election Commission, 599 F.3d 686 (D.C. Circuit 2010). See Kennedy 2014.

25. Costa 2015.

26. An engaging biography of the Kochs is Schulman 2014. Excellent detail on the Kochs' and other wealthy families' political activities is given by Jane Mayer (2016; on the Kochs' regulatory tangles, see chap. 4). Papers on the Koch network by Theda Skocpol and her research group are available at http://www.scholarsstrategynetwork.org/. See also Skocpol and Hertel-Fernandez forthcoming.

27. Schulman 2014, 99–116; J. Mayer 2016, 53–59.

28. J. Mayer 2016, 57–58. Candidates Ed Clark and David Koch did not, however, fully embrace the hard-line Libertarian platform. Clark made friendly references to "low-tax liberalism" and to John F. Kennedy (Schulman 2014, 112–14).

29. J. Mayer 2016, chaps. 10–14; Bautista-Chavez and James 2016; Skocpol and Hertel-Fernandez 2016; Hertel-Fernandez and Skocpol 2016; Skocpol and Hertel-Fernandez forthcoming.

30. Confessore 2015a.
31. Alberta and Johnson 2016.
32. Confessore 2015a.
33. The Democrats had been favored to win several Senate seats from vulnerable Republicans in 2016, but they won only two (in Illinois and New Hampshire) out of the four needed for control, losing in the waning days in Wisconsin, Pennsylvania, Indiana, and Florida (as well as longer shots in Missouri, Iowa, and Arizona), after heavy advertising attacks on the Democratic candidates. But the left-leaning Majority Forward spent heavily too. See Light 2016.
34. P. Stone 2016. President Trump's initial cabinet appointees and policy decisions mostly followed conservative Republican orthodoxy.
35. Hertel-Fernandez and Skocpol forthcoming; see Hertel-Fernandez, Skocpol, and Lynch 2016. But the Kochs' effort to defund the Export-Import Bank—a darling of multinational corporations—ultimately lost (Hertel-Fernandez and Skocpol 2016). On the Democracy Alliance, see Sclar et al. 2016.
36. In Trump's detailed (but little-publicized) tax policy plans, however, equal treatment of "carried interest" was more than offset by sharp *cuts* in the taxes of all high-income earners, so that hedge fund managers would pay less in the end. See the Tax Policy Center report on Trump's revised tax plan (Nunns et al. 2016).
37. B. Davis and Hilsenrath 2016; Autor, Dorn, and Hanson 2016; Adamy and Overberg 2016.
38. The Libertarian Rand Paul was an exception, opposing hawkish foreign policy and also "corporate welfare." But Paul fell out of the race early.
39. A clever investigative reporter (Shane 2017) tracked down the identity of one inventive fabricator of fake news, who spread spurious stories to more than six million Americans concerning "tens of thousands" of fraudulent ballots marked for Clinton; the New York Police Department charging Bill Clinton for an underage sex ring; and protestors beating a homeless veteran to death. It is impossible to know what effect such false stories had, but they certainly did not help Clinton.
40. Schaffner 2016.
41. T. Frank 2016; MacGillis 2016; Khoury 2016.
42. See Gest 2016.
43. T. Ferguson 2016; Olen 2016.
44. On congressional elections see A. Gerber 1998; Jacobson 2013. T. Ferguson, Jorgensen, and Chen (2016a) show a particularly stark connection between money and outcomes, and they use a clever new technique to get at causation. On presidential elections, see Bartels 2016.
45. Confessore, Cohen, and Yourish (2015).
46. Ruy Tuxeira, quoted in Confessore, Cohen, and Yourish 2015, A24.
47. Page, Seawright, and Lacombe (2015). In the 2012 election cycle, 81 percent of the Forbes 400 billionaires made reportable donations to presidential or congressional candidates (Bonica and Rosenthal 2016). Others may have made dark money contributions to social welfare organizations or hidden their super PAC contributions through difficult-to-trace front organizations.
48. Adelson quoted in Bertoni 2012.
49. We are grateful to Tom Ferguson and Paul Jorgenson for sharing their carefully cleaned FEC data on 2011–12 contributions.
50. T. Frank 2016, chap. 10, esp. 203.
51. Debenedetti 2016. See also Saban's *New Yorker* profile in Bruck 2010.

52. Garofoli 2015.
53. T. Ferguson and Rogers 1986; Mizruchi 2013.
54. Reich 1997; Lizza 2012.
55. Page, Bartels, and Seawright 2013, 64. Multimillionaires polled in the Survey of Economically Successful Americans (SESA) were 58 percent Republican, 27 percent Democratic. This survey is discussed later in the text.
56. Sides et al. 2015, 371. Percentages of the 2012 presidential vote going to Obama over Romney were as follows: no high school, 64 percent; high school graduate, 51 percent; college graduate 47 percent; postgraduate, 55 percent.
57. *New York Times* 2016a, P9.
58. See T. Frank 2016.
59. In 2012, 61 percent of the citizenry agreed that officials "don't care much"; only 18 percent disagreed (Gilens 2015, 2).
60. Drutman 2015, 22. But we cannot be sure exactly how much bribery occurs. It is extremely hard to detect (anyone who engages in bribery has strong incentives to keep it secret) and equally hard to prove (the actors' intentions and the causal connections between the *quid* and the *quo* of quid pro quo are elusive.)
61. Lessig 2015, chaps. 2, 12; 2011, 15–20, 226–47; Teachout 2009, 2014.
62. Israel 2016. A leaked Democratic Congressional Campaign Committee "Model Daily Schedule" for incoming representatives included four hours of call time every day.
63. Lessig 2015, 19.
64. Jacobson 2013, 143–44.
65. Carnes 2013; Choma 2014. Most senators are multimillionaires.
66. Teachout 2014, 1–3.
67. Justice Kennedy quoted in *Citizens United*, 558 U.S. at § 3.B.2, also shown in Teachout 2014, 233. For detailed critiques of the *Citizens United* decision, see Post 2014.
68. We know about the conservatism of billionaires mainly from their *actions*, including contributions to candidates and issue-oriented groups. Most billionaires say nothing in public about their policy preferences, and it is impossible to interview them systematically.
69. Page, Bartels, and Seawright 2013; Cook, Page, and Moskowitz 2014, 385–88.
70. Thirty-two percent of SESA multimillionaires called deficits or excessive spending the "most important problem" facing the country. Only 11 percent said unemployment, and only 11 percent cited education. See Page, Bartels, and Seawright 2013.
71. As shown in table 4.1, about half (49 percent) of Americans also favored increasing—rather than decreasing or keeping the same—the Earned Income Tax Credit (EITC), which subsidizes the incomes of low-wage workers. But only 13 percent of millionaires favored increasing the EITC.
72. Gilens 2009, 2012.
73. But affluent and wealthy Americans have tended to be *more* liberal than the general public on some social/cultural/moral issues. On the top 4 percent or so of income earners, see Page and Hennessy 2011.
74. Page, Bartels, and Seawright 2013; Cook, Page, and Moskowitz 2014, 389–90.
75. Ansolabehere, de Figueiredo, and Snyder 2003. A limitation of this research: PAC Contributions provide handy data but are a small and atypical part of total financial contributions.

76. R. Hall and Wayman 1990.
77. Hall and Wayman 1990; Kalla and Broockman 2016.
78. West 2014, 11–15.
79. Hillary Clinton reportedly spent much of August 2016, just before her autumn campaign, hobnobbing in the Hamptons with Wall Street bankers and other wealthy acquaintances (Chozick and Martin 2016; Olen 2016). "Renaissance Weekend" is a secretive, annual, invitation-only retreat—much enjoyed by Bill and Hillary Clinton—at which prominent elites network and discuss world affairs.
80. Cook, Page, and Moskowitz 2014, 391–93.
81. Cook, Page, and Moskowitz 2014, 391–93, 394.
82. Hetherington and Rudolph 2015.
83. Hacker and Pierson 2016.
84. Domhoff 2014, chaps. 4, 5, esp. 76–79.
85. Domhoff 2014, chap. 4.
86. Domhoff 2014, 81–90.
87. Domhoff 2014, 89–91.
88. J. Mayer 2016.
89. J. Mayer 2016, chap. 2.
90. J. Mayer 2016, chap. 3, esp. 105, 107.
91. J. Mayer 2016, 107–20; Hollis-Brusky 2015; Teles 2008.
92. J. Mayer 2016, 112–19.
93. J. Mayer 2016, 87, and chaps. 5–6, esp. 149–55, 159–61.
94. J. Mayer 2016, 163–64, and chaps. 7–9. For further details, see the papers of the Skocpol research group and Skocpol and Hertel-Fernandez forthcoming.
95. Altman and Kingson 2015, chap. 9.
96. Hiltzik 2012.
97. Altman and Kingson 2015, chap. 9.
98. Altman and Kingson 2015, chap. 9. On p. 155 they present Sarah Anderson's and Scott Klinger's list of anti–Social Security CEOs, their estimated private pensions, and the enormous deficits in their own employee pension funds.
99. Altman and Kingson (2015, chap. 2) show in detail that Social Security works well and can continue to do so. Their extensive sources include reports by the Social Security Trustees and actuaries, Social Security Administration officials, the Congressional Budget Office, and academic experts.
100. T. Lieberman 2012.
101. See Kingson 2010.
102. Goodman 2017.

CHAPTER FIVE

1. Madison, *Federalist* paper no. 10, in Hamilton, Madison, and Jay (1787–88) 1999; Truman 1971, esp. 512.
2. Schattschneider 1960, 35.
3. Schlozman, Verba, and Brady 2012.
4. Schlozman, Verba, and Brady 2012, 321, 356.
5. Schlozman, Verba, and Brady 2012, 409.
6. Drutman 2015, 8–9.
7. Putnam 2000; Skocpol 2003, 90–91, 154–55.
8. Galbraith 1952.

9. G. Mayer 2004; Table A-1, 2015, in U.S. Bureau of Labor Statistics 2016. See also Skocpol 2003, 155. On the relationship between union decline and rising income inequality, see Kimball and Mishel 2015. Piazza (2002) discusses unions' efforts to go global.

10. Goldfield 1987; Lichtenstein 2013, esp. chaps. 4–6.

11. Warner 2013, 3.

12. Warner 2013, 6.

13. See Geoghegan 2004; Lichtenstein 2013, chaps. 7–8.

14. Baumgartner et al. 2009, chap. 10, esp. 202–12. Mark Smith's (2000) useful time-series analysis of U.S. Chamber of Commerce positions and policy results does not actually attempt to estimate the Chamber's influence; it analyzes under *what conditions* (chiefly a friendly public "mood") the Chamber's positions and actual policy tend to correspond.

15. Despite the rather crude nature of our interest group alignment measure, it correlates strongly with broader measures of interest group engagement and resources (Gilens 2012, 128). On our data and methods generally and on the precise way the alignment index was calculated, see Gilens 2012, chap. 2 and 127–35, 263; Gilens and Page 2014, 568–91. In the case of the ten industries that do not lobby through a collective industry-wide organization, we gathered information on the common positions of the constituent corporations.

16. Random errors in measurement of an independent variable produce a downward bias in estimates of its effects on a dependent variable.

17. Many relatively narrow policy decisions (such as special tax breaks or subsidies that affect only one firm) may be affected by one of the thousands of interest groups not included in our measure.

18. For groups' alignments and citizens' preferences, $r = .04$ (n.s.).

19. Correlation coefficients for individual groups and average citizens are given in Gilens 2012, 156–57.

20. For all membership groups and average citizens, $r = .12$***: significant but small.

21. Business-oriented and mass-membership groups had regression coefficients of .43 and .24, respectively.

22. For all business-oriented groups and average citizens, $r = -.10$***. On individual groups, see Gilens 2012, 156–57.

23. Truman 1971, 511–12. David Truman's theoretical assumption of frictionless formation of new groups, originally published in 1951, was decisively refuted by Mancur Olson (1965).

24. Businesses' and affluents' preferences: $r = -.02$ (n.s.).

25. Drutman 2015, 4–5, 23, 76.

26. Drutman 2015, 4–5, 86–87. In 2012, of the $2.57 billion in total business lobbying expenditures, $1.84 billion came from 3,587 *individual* corporations, with 372 firms spending at least $1 million each.

27. Burstein (2014) shows that most policy proposals considered by Congress are quite narrow, well below the radar of ordinary citizens, and not subject to opinion surveys.

28. Schattschneider 1960, chap. 1, esp. 3, 7,16; McConnell 1966, chap. 4; Drutman 2015. On policy made "in the dark," see Curry (2015), who emphasizes congressional leaders' resulting power over rank-and-file members of Congress.

29. Baumgartner et al. 2009, 2–6, 283.

30. It is also why we restrict our own analyses of policy making to the "public agenda" of issues that ordinary Americans might have at least some passing familiarity with (and which polling organizations consider important enough to warrant asking about on national surveys). See Gilens 2012, 50–56.
31. Manley 1970, 220–34.
32. Drutman 2015, 28–31.
33. Lipton and Moyer 2015, A1, A17.
34. Leech 2013, 120–22.
35. Leech 2013, 123–24.
36. Jacobs and King 2016, chap. 3, esp. 101, 113, 119–21.
37. Tripathi, Ansolabehere, and Snyder 2002.
38. On investments in politicians, see Snyder 1992. On roll-call vote studies showing inconsistent results, see Ansolabehere, de Figueiredo, and Snyder 2003; Stratmann 1998; Baldwin and Magee 2000. On contributions buying access, see Langbein 1986; L. Powell 2012; Kalla and Broockman 2016. On contributions buying behind-the-scenes efforts, see Hall and Wayman 1990.
39. Arnold 1990.
40. Hall and Wayman 1990, 810.
41. CBS News/New York Times 2009; Kaiser Family Foundation 2009. On driving down the cost of health care, see U.S. Congressional Budget Office 2013.
42. Center for Responsive Politics 2017c.
43. Kaiser Family Foundation 2009.
44. Kollman 1998.
45. Feuer 2016. The quoted researcher was Tarso Ramos.
46. T. Ferguson and Rogers 1986; Mizruchi 2013; Hacker and Pierson 2016.
47. Oreskes and Conway 2010.
48. Domhoff 2014, chaps. 4, 5.

CHAPTER SIX
1. See Brass 2013; Plumer 2013.
2. Reuters 2013.
3. Federalist paper no. 51, in A. Hamilton, Madison, and Jay (1787–88) 1999. Madison argued (incorrectly, we believe) that the resulting status quo bias would not privilege elites against the masses (Federalist paper no. 57). But he acknowledged that it could impede affirmative policy making (Federalist paper no. 62).
4. A presidential veto can sometimes be overridden by hard-to-obtain supermajorities in both chambers of Congress. Supreme Court decisions can be overturned by Constitutional amendments, which are extremely difficult to enact. Presidents can sometimes act on their own, particularly in foreign policy (see Howell 2003). But there is no way to override a House or Senate no vote—or inaction—on legislation.
5. Mansbridge 2012; Federalist papers no. 10, 51, in A. Hamilton, Madison, and Jay (1787–88) 1999.
6. Hacker 2004; Hacker and Pierson 2010.
7. Mansbridge 2012.
8. Binder 2003; Mann and Ornstein 2012. Moreover, multiple bills are now often packed together into "omnibus" bills or resolutions, which reduce opportunities for democratic control and tend to lead to inefficiency and waste. Very few legislators or staffers are able to read thousand-page bills given to them the night before a vote.

9. If, for example, one party controlled all branches of government but pursued policies sought by its donors and activists against the wishes of most Americans, the Senate filibuster might conceivably protect democracy rather than thwarting it.

10. Since the time that Ronald Reagan came to office (1981) through 2016, we have had divided party government three-quarters of the time.

11. Mayhew 1991.

12. Poole and Rosenthal 2007, 2014; McCarty, Poole, and Rosenthal 2009.

13. Uslaner 1993; Ahuja 2008, 14–15; L. Hamilton 2009, 45.

14. Harbridge (2015) shows that many House members continue to cosponsor bills introduced by members of the other party. Party polarization is more extreme on roll call votes (as in our figure 6.2) because party leaders often prevent votes on bipartisan proposals. But Harbridge acknowledges in her conclusion that cosponsorship has declined since 2006.

15. Aldrich 1983; Brady, Han, and Pope 2007.

16. Matthews 1960, esp. 116–17. Evan Bayh, on leaving the Senate, painted a striking picture of the loss of collegiality since the time when his father (also a Democratic senator from Indiana) had friends in both parties (Bayh 2010).

17. Jacobson 2004; Theriault 2008.

18. Ahuja 2008, 42, 51. See also Bernhard and Sulkin 2017.

19. See Ornstein et al.2013; Desilver 2013; Benen 2014.

20. See the simple models in Downs 1957, chaps. 4, 8. Other chapters introduce much more complexity.

21. Fiorina 1981; Achen and Bartels 2016.

22. Aldrich 1983, 2011.

23. McClosky, Hoffman, and O'Hara 1960; M. Barber 2016a and 2016b; Aldrich 2011, 194, 313–14; Jacobson 2000; Fiorina, Abrams, and Pope 2005; G. Miller and Schofield 2003; Sinclair 2006, 22, 34.

24. Bump 2014; Peterson and Hook 2014; Gabriel 2014.

25. Jacobson 2013, 36.

26. Jacobson 2005; McDonald 2006.

27. Chen and Rodden (2013). Carson et al. (2007), by contrast, argue strongly that gerrymandering causes polarization. Mann (2006, 265–66) and McCarty, Poole, and Rosenthal (2009) disagree. Gerber and Lewis (2006) point out that even within the same district, members of Congress from different parties tend to have quite different ideologies. Sinclair (2006) notes that the Senate has polarized as much as the House, so that something else—probably party activists—must be at work. We agree with Sinclair about activists. But as to the Senate, a number of states are not electorally competitive. And politicians usually have to make it through noncompetitive elections for state legislatures or Congress, or sometimes both, before running for the Senate.

28. Chen and Rodden (2013), focusing on "electoral bias" (partisan advantage), use simulations to show that—because of residential segregation, "natural," nongerrymandered contiguous district boundaries would lead to virtually as much partisan clustering and electoral bias as gerrymandering does. Bill Bishop (2008) argues that sociopolitical migration contributes to clustering.

29. Chen and Rodden 2013; Jacobson 2013, 17–19; N. Cohn 2014.

30. Aldrich 2000; Sundquist 1983, 297, 357; Karol 2009, 103.

31. Bond and Fleisher 2000; S. Smith 2007; Levendusky 2010.

32. McCarty, Poole, and Rosenthal 2006; M. Barber and McCarty 2015.

33. See Stiglitz 2002.

34. T. Ferguson and Rogers 1986. On the economic conservatism of wealthy individuals, see Page, Bartels, and Seawright 2013; chapter 4 of this volume.

35. Hacker and Pierson 2016.

36. See Solt, Habel and Grant 2011; Solt 2014.

37. Abramowitz 2010; Levendusky 2010; Fiorina, Abrams, and Pope 2005.

38. Jacobson 2012; Carmines and Stimson 1989; Hetherington 2001.

39. Gerber and Morton 1998; Jacobson 2012; Brady, Han, and Pope 2007. However, Hirano et al. (2010) disagree.

40. Bafumi and Herron 2010.

41. Brady, Ferejohn, and Harbridge 2008.

42. Newport 2013.

43. Manchin 2013.

44. Koger 2010, 4, 224; Schatz 2009.

45. Udall 2013.

46. On the reading of children's stories by Rand Paul, see Memmott 2013; on similar tactics as employed by Ted Cruz, see O'Keefe and Kane 2013.

47. Koger 2010, 121. On the use of the filibuster to stop civil rights legislation, see Riker 1986, chap. 8.

48. Koger 2010, chap. 8.

49. Koger 2010, 21; Grim, Stein, and Siddiqui 2014.

50. Koger 2010, 173; Ornstein et al. 2013, Table 6-7; Binder 2003, 2013b.

51. Exceptions to the sixty-vote Senate now include most appointments (except to the Supreme Court) and "budget reconciliation" measures.

52. Binder 2013a. There was an uptick in district court confirmation success in the 112th Congress, however, and the Senate's easing of requirements for closing debate on judicial nominees should eventually lead to higher success rates and fewer unfilled vacancies in the judiciary—though it certainly did not do so in 2016, when virtually all action ground to a halt.

53. Koger 2010, 173–78; W. Oleszek 2011; W. Oleszek 2014, 256–57.

54. Dahl 2001, 15–20; Levinson 2006, 49–62.

55. U.S. Const., art. I, § 3.

56. Levinson 2006, 49.

57. U.S. Bureau of the Census 2013. For earlier figures, see Levinson 2006, 50–51.

58. Beutler 2012; F. Lee and Oppenheimer 1999; Levinson 2006, 25–26, 57, 60.

59. Mann and Ornstein 2012; Sinclair 2006, chap. 2.

60. Reason-Rupe Public Opinion Survey 2013; National Employment Law Project 2017.

61. Named after former Speaker of the House Dennis Hastert; see Sherman and Allen 2011; Milbank 2014.

62. As few as 26 percent: $.51 \times .51 = .2601$.

63. See Krehbiel 1998.

64. See Cox and McCubbins 2005. "Semiclosed" rules, permitting only a few specified amendments, can have much the same effect.

65. Pearson and Schickler 2009, 1239. A successful petition requires signatures from more than half (218) of all representatives. Members, especially those belonging to the majority party, tend to fear retribution from their leaders if they sign.

66. McCloskey 2010, chaps. 5, 6. Justice Roberts, the key switcher, may have been motivated by legitimacy concerns (McKenna 2002).

67. Balkin 2001.

68. Roosevelt quoted in Kramer 2004, esp. 247–48.

CHAPTER SEVEN

1. American National Election Studies 2015.

2. Weber 1999, 625–26; Primo and Milyo 2006, 34; Leighley and Nagler 2013, 133–35.

3. Heymann et al. 2009; R. Jones et al. 2015.

4. Singer 2011; Center for Media and Democracy et al. 2016.

5. Center for Media and Democracy et al. 2016.

6. Spaulding 2014.

7. U.S. Const., art. XII, XV, XVI, XVII, XIX, XXIII, XXIV, and XXVI.

8. D. Phillips 1906; Lessig 2015.

9. Dahl 1971, 1–2.

10. Scarrow 2007, 197, 202.

11. Federalist paper no. 10, in A. Hamilton, Madison, and Jay (1787–88) 1999; Lessig 2012; Lessig 2015, chap. 13.

12. Teachout 2009, 2014; Lessig 2015. See also Hasen 2016; Lioz 2015.

13. Lioz 2015.

14. Dahl 1957; McGuire and Stimson 2004; Clark 2010.

15. Center for Media and Democracy et al. 2016.

16. To qualify for public financing, candidates must first raise a specified amount from private contributions of no more than $100 each (the amount differing for the various offices covered by the Clean Election laws). See Brickner 2008.

17. The idea is that there are *declining marginal returns* to money spent on campaigns— each extra dollar has a little less impact than the dollar before. So if a substantial amount of public money is available, even if private-money Candidate A raises more than public-money Candidate B, Candidate A's advantage should not be great.

18. Malbin, Brusoe, and Glavin 2012; Center for Governmental Studies 2003; Mahlotra 2008; Levin 2006; Migally and Liss 2010.

19. Government by the People Act of 2014, U.S. House, H.R. 20, 113th Cong. (2014). See Lioz 2014 for an overview. As of February 2016, the Government of the People Act had 166 Democratic cosponsors and—unfortunately—only one Republican.

20. Deductions strongly favor people in high tax brackets, where deductions are more valuable. Small refundable tax credits are more equalizing but neglect people who do not file income taxes (such as those whose incomes are below the threshold requiring one to file) and leave the way open for large supplementary contributions by the affluent. Making equal-size vouchers available to every eligible citizen would be easier and more universal.

21. Lessig 2011, chap. 16; 2015, chap. 4. Lessig would allow small, supplemental private contributions, but we believe that that would tend to undermine political equality and contribute to party polarization. Earlier voucher-type proposals include Hasen's (1996) "coupons" and Ackerman and Ayres's (2002) "patriot dollars."

22. Wealthy self-funding candidates present a particular problem for some types of

campaign finance regulation, but Democracy Vouchers could be conditioned on agreement not to spend the *candidate's own* private money (or anyone else's.)

23. For presidential general elections, the moribund tax checkoff system could be revived, simply by increasing the amount of money each taxpayer could allocate to one of the parties well above the current $3. But it would be extremely difficult to expand such a system to multiple candidates at other levels or to primary elections at any level.

24. A Gallup Poll conducted in 2013 suggests that only a slim majority of the public, about 50 percent, supports public financing of federal elections (Saad 2013b).

25. On the Connecticut poll (by Zogby) and the 2015 backlash, see Common Cause 2010; Maine Citizens for Clean Elections 2013; Hartford *Courant* 2015.

26. Ballotpedia 2015.

27. Groups not required to disclose their donors include 501(c)4 and 501(c)6 organizations. See Center for Responsive Politics 2017d.

28. Public Citizen 2015. The proposed executive order would apply to 70 percent of the Fortune 100 companies (Center for Media and Democracy et al. 2016, 11).

29. Kennedy and McElwee 2014.

30. On outside spending, see Center for Responsive Politics 2017f.

31. Bowie and Lioz 2013.

32. Federalist paper no. 10, in A. Hamilton, Madison, and Jay (1787–88) 1999.

33. Bertrand, Bombardini, and Trebbi 2011.

34. Drutman 2015, 230–32.

35. On rules against gifts, see the 2007 "Honest Leadership and Open Government Act" amendments to the Lobbying Disclosure Act of 1995.

36. Ziobrowski et al. 2004.

37. La Pira and Thomas 2017.

38. White 2005. Not just members of Congress. The Open Secrets website counts 143 revolving-door *staffers* who worked for the House and Senate Finance committees alone (Center for Responsive Politics 2017e).

39. Individuals (including former members of Congress and their staff) who are hired to influence government policy can avoid registering as lobbyists if they do not devote more than 20 percent of their time to any one client.

40. Drutman 2015, 225–27.

41. Levinthal 2009.

42. Kosar 2015.

43. Drutman 2015, 232–34.

44. Drutman 2015, 228–30.

45. Drutman 2015, 230.

46. On "deliberative panels," see Fishkin 2009.

47. Voice of the People. led by Steven Kull, at vop.org. See also Fishkin 2009.

48. Federalist paper no. 10, in A. Hamilton, Madison, and Jay (1787–88) 1999.

49. Wallerstein 1999.

50. In these and other cases, unions have served as both progressive and conservative forces, depending on historical circumstances and on the perceived interests of union members and nonunion workers. See Marmor 2000; Lichenstein 2013; Bloch 1993.

51. R. Freeman 2011.

52. Goldfield 2007; Rogers 2014; R. Freeman 2011.

53. In addition to reversing the deunionization trend, union-like political organizing could be facilitated by "unbundling" unions' collective bargaining from their political activities: see Sachs 2013.

54. Schlozman, Verba and Brady 2012; Gallego 2010; Jackman 1987; Kasara and Suryanarayan 2014.

55. Pateman 2012; Barber 2004; Dewey 1927 and his work on education.

56. Manza and Uggen 2006; Burch 2013.

57. U.S. Bureau of the Census 2017.

58. Palmer 2014; Roth 2014; Brennan Center for Justice 2013, 2014; Bentele and O'Brien 2013.

59. Alvarez, Baily, and Katz 2007. "Voter fraud," the ostensible reason for these laws, appears to be mostly a myth. See Minnite 2010; Levitt 2007; Wang 2012.

60. Klar and Krupnikov 2016.

61. See G. Powell 1986.

62. On ranked choice or instant runoff voting, see Tolbert et al. 2014; FairVote 2014.

63. Dēmos 2017; Brennan Center for Justice 2017.

64. CCEP Policy Brief 2013; Cha and Kennedy 2014. See Hamner 2009; Tolbert et al. 2008.

65. Kasdan 2013; Gronke, Galanes-Rosenbaum, and Miller 2008.

66. Knack 1995; Hill 2003; Brown and Wedeking 2006.

67. Cha 2013; League of Women Voters 2014.

68. Springer 2014; Rigby and Springer 2011; Brians and Grofman 2001

69. CCEP Policy Brief 2013.

70. Berinsky, Burns, and Traugott 2001; A. Gerber, Huber, and Hill 2013.

71. Berinsky 2005; Burden et al. 2014; Burden and Gains 2015; Duverger 1972.

72. Suttmann-Lea forthcoming.

73. Burden et al. 2014; Rigby and Springer 2011; Suttmann-Lea forthcoming.

74. Sentencing Project 2017; Burch 2013. See also Manza, Brooks, and Uggen 2004; Manza and Uggen 2006; Prison Policy Initiative 2017.

75. Independent studies indicate that fraudulent voting by individuals is rarely a problem. Much more common are cases in which eligible voters are improperly discouraged or prevented from voting (Levitt 2007, 2014; Minnite 2010). Advocates of universal voter registration, whose websites provide pro and con arguments and information about specific proposals, include FairVote: For a More Perfect Union (http://www.fairvote.org); the Brennan Center for Justice (http://www.brennancenter.org); Dēmos (http://www.demos.org); and Election Protection (http://www.866ourvote.org/). See Weiser, Waldman, and Paradis 2008.

76. Malkin 2008. For a reply, see Trope 2009.

77. On the history and rationales of efforts to restrict voting, see Keyssar 2009; Wang 2012.

78. Shineman 2016; Gutmann 2004.

79. Page and Shapiro 1992; Gilens 2012. Recall the discussion in chapter 1.

CHAPTER EIGHT

1. We imagine a continuum of increasing *procedural* difficulty that goes from changing informal practices (the easiest), to changing rules, to changing laws, and finally to amending the Constitution (the hardest). *Political* difficulty can be another matter.

2. Modest efforts to make some Senate holds public were adopted in 2007 and 2011 (M. Oleszek 2015).

3. In 1908, amid a financial crisis, Senator Robert La Follette filibustered for eighteen hours against a banking bill that he considered to be a gift to the financial elite. The bill passed anyhow, but his filibuster inspired the public and solidified La Follette's reputation as a Progressive hero (Koger 2010, 4).

4. See Beth and Heitshusen 2014.

5. Koger 2010, 197–99. A return to the attrition strategy would probably only work along with some supplemental measures, such as restricting quorum calls and unanimous consent requirements, and perhaps by "benching" filibusterers who violate decorum.

6. Schickler 2001. See also Wawro and Schickler 2006; Peters 2013.

7. See Binder 2010.

8. See Karol 2015.

9. In the 2012 Cooperative Congressional Election Survey, 61 percent of respondents who reported donating more than $1,000 to a political candidate or group identified themselves as either a "strong Democrat" or a "strong Republican," compared with 54 percent of those giving between $25 and $1,000, 51 percent of those giving less than $25, and 43 percent of nongivers who reported the highest level of interest in government and public affairs. (The latter group contains those who would be the most likely to join the ranks of contributors under campaign finance systems that encourage, subsidize, or pay the full cost of small contributions.) The comparable figure for all survey respondents combined was 39 percent. On small donors, see Malbin 2013; on donors compared with nondonors, see Bafumi and Herron 2010; M. Barber 2016a and 2016b.

10. Andrew Hall (2014) argues that the adoption of public funding in Maine and Arizona led to greater polarization in their state legislatures, while Masket and Miller (2014) find no difference in partisan extremism between representatives in these states who opted into their public financing system and those who used private contributions to fund their campaigns. Analyzing a broader array of states, La Raja and Schaffner (2015, 104) find that a state's adoption of contribution limits on either individual donations or party fund-raising tends to result in more polarized legislatures, while limits on interest group donations have no impact on polarization. Examining the level, rather than the presence or absence of contribution limits, Michael Barber (2016a) finds that stricter limits on individual contributions *reduce* polarization, while stricter limits on political action committee (PAC) donations *increase* polarization. These and other studies are limited by the incompleteness of existing reforms. Substantial depolarization may require multiple reforms. To examine any one of them in isolation may provide little insight into the consequences of simultaneous reforms to campaign finance, redistricting laws, ballot access, etc.

11. On candidates having become more extreme, see A. Hall 2016. On voters preferring moderates, see A. Hall 2016; Canes-Wrone, Brady, and Cogan 2002; Ansolabehere, Snyder, and Stewart 2001.

12. Bawn et al. 2012; Masket 2009; Thomsen 2014.

13. Levitt 2017.

14. Carson, Crespin, and Williamson 2014; Grainger 2010; Lindgren and Southwell 2013. In contrast, Cottrill (2012) finds weak and inconsistent differences between legislative and commission-based districting, and McCarty, Poole and Rosenthal

(2009) find only modest differences between existing congressional polarization and their hypothetical simulation of random (nongerrymandered) districting.

15. Article I, Section 4 of the U.S. Constitution provides that Congress may by law regulate the "times, places, and manner" of holding House elections. Federal authority over *state* legislative districts might be justified as enforcing the equal protection of the laws, under the Fourteenth Amendment.

16. Chen and Rodden 2013.

17. For example, if highly clustered, urban-dwelling racial and ethnic minorities are partly blended with suburban voters—increasing the number of representatives influenced by minority constituents—districts can retain substantial (say, 60 percent, rather than the former 90 or 95 percent) proportions of minorities, so that minority candidates have a good shot at winning and providing descriptive representation in Congress. See Swain 2006; Whitby 1997; Mansbridge 1999.

18. See Tolbert et al. 2014; FairVote 2014. Relatedly, Adams (1996) shows evidence that multimember districts tend to produce more moderate candidates.

19. Bullock and Clinton 2011; McGhee et al. 2014, fig. 4. See also E. Gerber and Morton 1998; Hirano et al. 2010.

20. Ahler, Citrin, and Lenz 2015.

21. A. Hall 2015, 2016.

22. McGhee 2014. McGhee mentions various "safety valve" options involving the possibility of additional choices in the general election.

23. Presidential primaries suffer similar problems of low and biased turnout but to a lesser extent. The problem is mitigated by high national stakes, actively competing candidates, and high media attention. We address the presidential nominating system in a later section.

24. Lijphart 2015, 74–75.

25. We are aware that this procedure is not impervious to strategic behavior or Arrow-type social choice problems. But the practical likelihood of seriously undemocratic outcomes seems remote.

26. Since the individual states have initial responsibility for regulating federal as well as state and local elections within their boundaries, a federal law may be required to ensure widespread or universal use of instant runoffs.

27. See Lijphart 2012, chap. 8.

28. Lijphart (2012, 276–77) shows these relationships for full "consensus democracy," of which PR is an important element.

29. Lijphart 2012, 150–51.

30. Duverger 1954, 1972.

31. U.S. Const., art. I, § 6, para. 2.

32. If proportional representation were not required in all states, some one-party states might skip it and deny fair representation to their minority party, thus undemocratically tilting the national balance between parties in Congress. The same problem might well occur with independent districting commissions, if they were not required in all states.

33. About half of the U.S. states send six or fewer members to the House of Representatives. For them, a single statewide district would be perfectly feasible. For states with larger numbers of representatives, multiple megadistricts with, perhaps, five or six representatives each, would keep the number of winner slots low enough that most voters should be able to rank that many candidates.

34. Dahl 2001, 15–20; Levinson 2006, 49–62.
35. U.S. Const., art. I, § 3, para. 1.
36. U.S. Const., art. V.
37. If the idea of giving California Senate votes in proportion to its population seems startling, consider that at present, the twenty-one smallest states—whose combined population is less than California's—get fully forty-two out of one hundred senators, a much bigger share than the 12 percent of Senate votes that California would have, based on fair representation of its population. See Gelman 2004.
38. Ansolabehere and Snyder 2008.
39. U.S. Const., art. V. Despite these obstacles, the U.S. Constitution has been amended seventeen times since the Bill of Rights was adopted (with a total of twenty-seven amendments): about once every fourteen years, on average.
40. Lessig 2011, chap. 20; 2012; 2015, chap. 13.
41. Lessig 2011, 292–93; Goldman 1952, 40, 60, 175.
42. Lessig 2011, chap. 20; 2015, chap. 13. Lessig's website, http://www.lessig.org/, includes calls to action and information about how people can become more involved in reform efforts.
43. As schoolteachers are fond of pointing out, there is actually no "college," no personal meeting among electors. Each state records its electors' votes and transmits the signed, certified, and sealed list of these votes to the President of the Senate in Washington, DC. See U.S. Const., art. II, § 1; U.S. Const., amend. XII.
44. In a 2013 Gallup poll, 63 percent of respondents favored doing away with the electoral college and basing the election on the national popular vote (29 percent opposed doing away with it, and 8 percent had no opinion); see Saad 2013a.
45. National Popular Vote 2017.
46. A *superdelegate* is a creation of the Democratic Party, someone chosen by the party (rather than elected as a delegate through state primaries or caucuses), who is free to vote for any candidate he or she wishes at the party's nominating convention (*Merriam-Webster OnLine*, s.v. "superdelegate," accessed March 2, 2017, https://www.merriam-webster.com/dictionary/superdelegate). Superdelegates may include "notable party figures" such as elected officials, current and former presidents, and "select leaders of organizations affiliated with the Democratic National Committee" (Fain 2016). In the 2016 election, there were 712 superdelegates in addition to more than 4,000 elected delegates at the Democratic convention (Fain 2016; Greve 2016). The Republicans in 2016 also had superdelegates, but they made up a smaller proportion of delegates and did not have unrestricted voting power (Greve 2016).
47. McCloskey 2010, chaps. 5, 6.
48. Majorities of Americans supported each of these policies. See Hemenway, Azrael, and Miller 2001; DiJulio, Firth, and Brodie 2015a; Dutton et al. 2015; Survey by MoveOn.org., conducted by Greenberg Quinlan Rosner Research, April 29–May 3, 2010, accessed at Roper Center iPoll: USGREEN.10COURT.R43.
49. Kramer 2004, 249. We might also change the way we think and talk about the Supreme Court. As noted in chapter 6, there is something to be said for the idea that "the people themselves" should have the ultimate say about what the Constitution means. But how? Perhaps only through their democratically elected representatives, using the tools we mention.
50. Dahl 1957.

CHAPTER NINE

1. Wilentz 2016.
2. Brands et al. 2009, chap. 25; Lindert and Williamson 2016. See also chapter 2.
3. D. Phillips 1906.
4. McCloskey 2010, chap. 5, 6.
5. Sundquist 1983, chap. 7.
6. Bartels 2016; Reich 2007; Hacker and Pierson 2010; K. Phillips 1990.
7. Goodwyn 1978. On the size of the Farmers' Alliance, see Schwartz 1977.
8. People's Party 1892.
9. People's Party 1892.
10. People's Party 1892.
11. See Fredman 1968.
12. Sanders 1999, 410.
13. Goodwyn (1978 and 1976 [the unabridged version]) offers a sympathetic por-
    trait of the Populists based on extensive primary sources. The influential account
    by Hofstadter (1955) ignored the progressive Omaha platform and the Populists'
    cooperative, democratic roots in the Farmers' Alliance. Focusing instead on the
    ephemeral "free silver" episode, Hofstadter painted a much more negative picture.
14. Lause (2001) argues that diverse coalitions like the Populists' can become
    incoherent.
15. McGerr 2003; Lears 2009; Hofstadter 1955.
16. Hofstadter 1955, sec. 4. Hofstadter's analysis of the Progressives is more solid than
    his caricature of the Populists.
17. Hofstadter 1955, 148–54; Wiebe 1967, chap. 6; McGerr 2003, chaps. 2, 3.
18. Hofstadter 1955, 186–98.
19. Mowrey 1958; E. Morris 2001; Blum 1954.
20. A. Link 1954.
21. Keyssar 2009, chap. 5, esp. 103–4. See also Burnham 1970 on the sharp decline in
    voting turnout after 1896.
22. E. Gerber 1999; Cronin 1989; Lewis, Schneider and Jacoby 2015.
23. Fox 2012, 30–35; D. Smith and Tolbert 2004, 78; Frankel and Dye 1991; Yellin
    2013.
24. For arguments against the Seventeenth Amendment (which we do not find convinc-
    ing), see Hoebeke 1995.
25. The brief popular account by Zinn (1999, 397–401) is generally consistent with
    that of recent historians. See Lichtenstein 2013.
26. Piven and Cloward (1977) argue, however, that labor made its strongest gains
    from early spontaneous action; the Wagner Act brought stability more than worker
    gains.
27. Ferejohn and Rosenbluth (2017) describe a broad historical pattern in which mass-
    mobilization wars tend to compel elites to accept increased democracy. See also
    Keyssar 2009. Scheidel (2017) analyzes wars as economic "levelers."
28. Hacker and Pierson 2016.
29. See Table 13 in U.S. Bureau of the Census 1976.
30. U.S. Const., amend. XV.
31. Sullivan 1991; NAACP 2017. On the continuing political importance of black
    churches, see Harris 1994, 1999; Calhoun-Brown 1996.
32. Many craft unions excluded blacks (Schickler 2016).

33. R. Lieberman 1998; Katznelson 2013.
34. Schickler 2016, 133.
35. Schickler 2016, 174.
36. Myrdal 1944; Wilentz 2016; Klinker and Smith 1999.
37. Snow and Benford 1992.
38. The following ideas are generally consistent with Robert Reich's suggestions on "how to make a movement" (Reich 2012, 109–18).
39. Tarrow 2011; Smelser 1962, 102; Melucci 1996; Castells 2012.
40. Susan B. Anthony's centennial speech is available from the Elizabeth Cady Stanton and Susan B. Anthony Papers project, at http://ecssba.rutgers.edu/docs/decl.html. On the struggle for suffrage, see Banaszak 1996; on later phases of the women's movement, see J. Freeman 1975; Mansbridge 1986.
41. Not all successful social movements share these characteristics. The environmental and antiwar movements, for example, did not draw on strong preexisting social identities; the environmental, women's, and civil rights movements did not have a sole policy goal but backed broad agendas relevant to an array of public and private entities.
42. Sides et al. 2014, 389. Public financing of election campaigns, for example—if not properly explained—can be viewed as a giveaway of taxpayer money to disliked politicians. Understandable public cynicism can be countered by state-level reform successes.
43. McAdam 1982, 1988; A. Morris 1984.
44. Flacks 1988.
45. Banaszak 1996; McCammon et al. 2001; A. Morris and Staggenborg 2004.
46. Sierra Club 2017.
47. McGerr 2003, 40–43; Hofstadter 1955, 143–46.
48. Wiebe 1989.
49. Oberschall 1973.
50. McCarthy and Zald 1977.
51. Mayday PAC 2014.
52. Silver 1998; Strolovitch 2007. Compromise may often be unavoidable, but this means that some members of a large reform coalition are likely to get more than others. As Strolovitch (2007) points out, unless care is taken, the most disadvantaged members can be the ones who get left behind.
53. Kriesi and Wisler (1999) speak of the need for some degree of "elite congruence."
54. Piven and Cloward 1977; McAdam, Tarrow, and Tilly 2001, 318–20.
55. Amenta 2006, 219; McCammon et al. 2001, 65; McConnaughy 2013.
56. McAdam 1982; Chong 1991, 239. On the power base in the northern Democratic Party, see Schickler 2016.
57. McAdam, Tarrow, and Tilly 2001; Tarrow 2011.
58. Southern Democrats were mostly opposed. See GovTrack 2017a, 2017b, 2017c, 2017d.
59. See Lessig 2011, chaps. 4–7, 12; 2015, chap. 10.
60. Goldwater 1960, 39.
61. Burden et al. 2014.
62. On conditions for the success of social movements, see Smelser 1962; Alinksy 1971; C. Tilly, L. Tilly, and H. Tilly 1975; Gamson 1975; Piven and Cloward 1977; J. Jenkins and Perrow 1977; McAdam 1982; Snow et al. 1986; Chong 1991;

Banaszak 1996; McCammon et al. 2001; Snow et al. 2004; Amenta 2006; and Tarrow 2011, among others. Alinsky's (1971) "rules for radicals" can be useful to nonradical reformers as well.

CHAPTER TEN

1. For Bernie Sanders, see Facebook post July 19, 2016, https://www.facebook.com /senatorsanders/posts/10154972709207908; for Hillary Clinton, see A. Phillips 2015; for Jeb Bush, see Date 2015; for Ted Cruz, see Fox News 2015; for Donald Trump, see Politico 2016.
2. Stohr 2015. Arguably, the *Speech Now* decision that gave birth to super PACs has had a larger impact on contemporary campaign contributions, but *Citizens United* appears to have become something of a shorthand for the recent series of Supreme Court decisions on campaign finance.
3. Quoted in Ornitz and Struyk 2015.
4. Rubio 2015.
5. Hillary for America 2016.
6. In the end, federal action will almost certainly be necessary. States where corporations and the wealthy have the strongest grip on government—where reforms are the most needed—are also the least likely to act on their own.
7. M. Miller 2014.
8. D. Ferguson 2017.
9. Brater 2016.
10. Brennan Center for Justice 2017.

REFERENCES

Abramowitz, Alan I. 2010. *The Disappearing Center: Engaged Citizens, Polarization, and American Democracy*. New Haven, CT: Yale University Press.

Achen, Christopher H., and Larry M. Bartels. 2016. *Democracy for Realists: Why Elections Do Not Produce Responsive Government*. Princeton, NJ: Princeton University Press.

Ackerman, Bruce A., and Ian Ayres. 2002. *Voting with Dollars: A New Paradigm for Campaign Finance*. New Haven, CT: Yale University Press.

Adams, Greg D. 1996. "Legislative Effects of Single-Member vs. Multimember Districts." *American Journal of Political Science* 40 (1): 129–44.

Adamy, Janet, and Paul Overberg. 2016. "Rapid Change Aids Trump." *Wall Street Journal*, November 2, A1, A10.

Ahler, Douglas, Jack Citrin, and Gabriel S. Lenz. 2015. "Why Voters May Have Failed to Reward Proximate Candidates in the 2012 Top Two Primary." *California Journal of Politics and Policy* 7 (1).

Ahuja, Sunil. 2008. *Congress Behaving Badly: The Rise of Partisanship and Incivility and the Death of Public Trust*. Westport, CT: Praeger.

Alberta, Tim, and Eliana Johnson. 2016. "Exclusive: In Koch World 'Realignment,' Less National Politics." *National Review*, May.

Aldrich, John H. 1983. "A Downsian Spatial Model with Party Activism." *American Political Science Review* 77:974–90.

———. 2000. "Southern Parties in State and Nation." *Journal of Politics* 62 (3): 643–70.

———. 2011. *Why Parties? A Second Look*. Chicago: University of Chicago Press.

Alinsky, Saul D. 1971. *Rules for Radicals: A Practical Primer for Realistic Radicals*. New York: Vintage Books.

Aljazeera. 2013. "Iran Celeb rates Rouhani's Presidential Win." June 16. http://www.aljazeera.com/news/middleeast/2013/06/201361523312748181.html.

Althaus, Scott L. 2003. *Collective Preferences in Democratic Politics: Opinion Surveys and the Will of the People*. New York: Cambridge University Press.

Altman, Nancy J. 2005. *The Battle for Social Security: From FDR's Vision to Bush's Gamble*. New York: Wiley.

Altman, Nancy J., and Eric R. Kingson. 2015. *Social Security Works! Why Social Security Isn't Going Broke and How Expanding It Will Help Us All*. New York: New Press.

Alvarez, Michael R., Delia Bailey, and Jonathan Katz. 2007. "The Effect of Voter Identification Laws on Turnout." VTP Working Paper 57, Version 2, Caltech/MIT Voting
Technology Project.

Amenta, Edwin. 2006. *When Movements Matter: The Townsend Plan and the Rise of
Social Security*. Princeton, NJ: Princeton University Press.

American National Election Studies (ANES). 2015. "The ANES Guide to Public Opinion and Electoral Behavior." November 11. http://www.electionstudies.org/nesguide
/toptable/tab5b_3.htm.

American Political Science Association. 1950. "Toward a More Responsible Two-Party
System: A Report of the Committee on Political Parties." *American Political Science
Review* 44 (3).

Anderson Robbins Research and Shaw and Company Research. 2014. "Fox News
Poll: Voters Express Concern about Obamacare, ISIS, Immigration Overreach."
Fox News. http://www.foxnews.com/politics/interactive/2014/12/10/fox-news-poll
-voters-express-concern-about-obamacare-isis-immigration-overreach/.

Ansolabehere, Stephen, John M. de Figueiredo, and James M. Snyder. 2003. "Why
Is There So Little Money in US politics?" *Journal of Economic Perspectives* 17
(1):105–30.

Ansolabehere, Stephen, and James M. Snyder. 2008. *The End of Inequality: One Person,
One Vote and the Transformation of American Politics*. New York: Norton.

Ansolabehere, Stephen, James M. Snyder, and Charles Stewart III. 2001. "Candidate Positioning in US House Elections." *American Journal of Political Science* 45
(1):136–59.

Anzia, Sarah F. 2012. "Partisan Power Play: The Origins of Local Election Timing
as an American Political Institution." *Studies in American Political Development*
26:24–49.

Arnold, R. Douglas. 1990. *The Logic of Congressional Action*. New Haven, CT: Yale
University Press.

Arrow, Kenneth J. 1963. *Social Choice and Individual Values*. 2nd ed. New York: Wiley. First published 1951.

Atkinson, Anthony B. 2015. *Inequality: What Can Be Done?* Cambridge, MA: Harvard
University Press.

Auten, Gerald, Geoffrey Gee, and Nicholas Turner. 2013. "Income Inequality, Mobility,
and Turnover at the Top in the US, 1987–2010." *American Economic Review* 103
(3): 168–72.

Autor, David H., David Dorn, and Gordon H. Hanson. 2016. "The China Shock:
Learning from Labor-Market Adjustment to Large Changes in Trade." *Annual Review of Economics* 8:205–40.

Bafumi, J., and M. C. Herron. 2010. "Leapfrog Representation and Extremism: A Study
of American Voters and Their Members in Congress." *American Political Science
Review* 104 (3): 519–42.

Bailey, Martha J., and Sheldon Danziger, eds. 2013. *Legacies of the War on Poverty*.
New York: Russell Sage.

Bajika, Jon, Lane Kenworthy, Peter Lindert, and Jeff Madrick. 2016. *How Big Should
Our Government Be?* Berkeley: University of California Press.

Baker, Dean. 2016. *Rigged: How Globalization and the Rules of the Modern Economy
Were Structured to Make the Rich Richer*. Washington, DC: Center for Economic
and Policy Research.

Baldwin, Robert E., and Christopher S. Magee. 2000. "Is Trade Policy for Sale? Congressional Voting on Recent Trade Bills." *Public Choice* 105 (1–2): 79–101.

Balkin, Jack M. 2001. "Bush v. Gore and the Boundary between Law and Politics." *Yale Law Journal* 110 (8): 1407–58.

Ballotpedia. 2015. "Maine 'Clean Elections' Initiative, Question 1 (2015)." https:// ballotpedia.org/Maine_%22Clean_Elections%22_Initiative,_Question_1_(2015).

Banaszak, Lee Ann. 1996. *Why Movements Succeed or Fail: Opportunity, Culture, and the Struggle for Woman Suffrage.* Princeton, NJ: Princeton University Press.

Barber, Benjamin R. 2004. *Strong Democracy: Participatory Politics for a New Age.* Twentieth-Anniversary Edition. Oakland, CA: University of California Press.

Barber, Michael J. 2016a. "Ideological Donors, Contribution Limits, and the Polarization of American Legislatures." *Journal of Politics* 78 (1): 296–310.

———. 2016b. "Representing the Preferences of Donors, Partisans, and Voters in the US Senate." *Public Opinion Quarterly* 80 (S1): 225–49.

Barber, Michael J., and Nolan McCarty. 2015. "Causes and Consequences of Polarization." In Persily, *Solutions to Political Polarization in America,* 15–58.

Baron, Kathryn. 2013. "Make Student Loans More Affordable, Says Sen. Elizabeth Warren." EdSource. October 9. http://edsource.org/2013/make-student-loans-less -interest-ing-says-sen-elizabeth-warren/40151#.VK8Lk6b1u8A.

Barry-Jester, Anna Maria. 2016. "What Went Wrong in Flint." FiveThirtyEight. January 26. http://fivethirtyeight.com/features/what-went-wrong-in-flint-water-crisis -michigan/.

Bartels, Larry M. 2016. *Unequal Democracy: The Political Economy of the New Gilded Age.* Rev. ed. New York: Russell Sage Foundation and Princeton University Press. First published 2008.

Bartels, Larry M., Joshua D. Clinton, and John G. Geer. 2016. "Representation." In *The Oxford Handbook of American Political Development,* edited by Richard M. Valelly, Suzanne Mettler, and Robert C. Lieberman, 399–424. New York: Oxford University Press.

Baumgartner, Frank R., Jeffrey Berry, Marie Hojnacki, David C. Kimball, and Beth L. Leech. 2009. *Lobbying and Policy Change: Who Wins, Who Loses, and Why.* Chicago: University of Chicago Press.

Bautista-Chavez, Angie M., and Sarah James. 2016. "Beyond Their Comfort Zone: Koch Network Outreach to Latinos and Millennials." Paper presented at the Annual Meeting of the Midwest Political Science Association, Chicago, April 8.

Bawn, Kathleen, Martin Cohen, David Karol, Seth Masket, Hans Noel, and John Zaller. 2012. "A Theory of Political Parties: Groups, Policy Demands and Nominations in American Politics." *Perspectives on Politics* 10 (3): 571–97.

Bayh, Evan. 2010. "Why I'm Leaving the Senate." *New York Times,* February 20.

Benen, Steve. 2014. "Obama Blasts 'Least Productive Congress in Modern History.'" *Maddow Blog.* April 10. http://www.msnbc.com/rachel-maddow-show/obama -blasts-least-productive-congress.

Bennett, W. Lance. 2015. *News: The Politics of Illusion.* 9th ed. Chicago: University of Chicago Press.

Bentele, Keith, and Erin E. O'Brien. 2013. "Jim Crow 2.0? Why States Consider and Adopt Restrictive Voter Access Policies." *Perspectives on Politics* 11 (4): 1088–1116.

Berelson, Bernard R., Paul F. Lazarsfeld, and William N. McPhee. 1954. *Voting: A Study of Opinion Formation in a Presidential Campaign.* Chicago: University of Chicago Press.

Berinsky, Adam J. 2004. *Silent Voices: Opinion Polls and Political Participation in America*. Princeton, NJ: Princeton University Press.

———. 2005. "The Perverse Consequences of Electoral Reform in the United States." *American Politics Research* 33: 471–91.

Berinsky, Adam J., Nancy Burns, and Michael W. Traugott. 2001. "Who Votes by Mail? A Dynamic Model of the Individual-level Consequences of Voting-by-Mail Systems." *Public Opinion Quarterly* 65 (2): 178–97.

Bernhard, William, and Tracy Sulkin. 2017. *Legislative Style*. Chicago: University of Chicago Press.

Bertoni, Steven. 2012. "Billionaire Sheldon Adelson Says He Might Give $100M to Newt Gingrich or Other Republican." *Forbes*, February.

Bertrand, Marianne, Matilde Bombardini, and Francesco Trebbi. 2011. "Is It Whom You Know or What You Know? An Empirical Assessment of the Lobbying Process." *National Bureau of Economic Research Working Paper 16765*. National Bureau of Economic Research, Cambridge, MA. February. http://www.nber.org/papers /w16765.pdf.

Berzon, Alexandra, and Richard Rubin. 2016. "Trump's Father Helped GOP Candidate with Numerous Loans." *Wall Street Journal*, September 23.

Beth, Richard S., and Valerie Heitshusen. 2014. *Filibusters and Cloture in the Senate*. Congressional Research Service report RL30360, December 24.

Beutler, Brian. 2012. "The Map That Proves Red Staters Use the Safety Net Too." Talking Points Memo. February 22. http://talkingpointsmemo.com/dc/the-map-that -proves-red-staters-use-the-safety-net-too.

Binder, Sarah A. 2003. *Stalemate: Causes and Consequences of Legislative Gridlock*. Washington, DC: Brookings Institution Press.

———. 2010. "Boehner Claims He'll Clean Up the House. But Don't Count On It." *New Republic*, November 19.

———. 2013a. "GOP Opposition to Judicial Nominations: What's the Precedent?" *Monkey Cage* (blog), June 13.

———. 2013b. "What Senate Cloture Votes Tell Us about Obstruction." *Monkey Cage* (blog), November 12.

Bishop, Bill. 2008. *The Big Sort: Why the Clustering of Like-Minded America Is Tearing Us Apart*. Boston: Houghton Mifflin.

Bishop, George F. 2005. *The Illusion of Public Opinion: Fact and Artifact in American Public Opinion Polls*. Lanham, MD: Rowman and Littlefield.

Bivens, Josh. 2013. "Using Standard Models to Benchmark the Costs of Globalization for American Workers without a College Degree." Economic Policy Institute Briefing Paper No. 354, March 22.

Blais, Andre. 2006. "What Affects Voter Turnout?" *Annual Review of Political Science* 9:111–25.

Blank, Rebecca M. 1997. *It Takes a Nation: A New Agenda for Fighting Poverty*. New York: Russell Sage and Princeton University Press.

Blanton, Dana. 2014. "Fox News Poll: Voters Worry about Checks and Balances after Obama Immigration Action." Fox News. December 10. http://www.foxnews.com /politics/2014/12/11/fox-news-poll-obama-immigration-overreach-worry-about -checks-and-balances/.

Bloch, Farrell E. 1993. "Political Support for Minimum Wage Legislation: 1989." *Journal of Labor Research* 14 (2): 187–90.

Blumenthal, Mark. 2011. "Polls: Wisconsin Polarized But Leaning toward Unions." *Huffington Post*, May 25.

Blum, John Morton. 1954. *The Republican Roosevelt*. Cambridge, MA: Harvard University Press.

Bond, Jon R., and Richard Fleisher. 2000. "Partisanship and the President's Quest for Votes on the Floor of Congress." In Bond and Fleisher, *Polarized Politics*, 154–85.

———, eds. 2000. *Polarized Politics: Congress and the President in a Partisan Era*. Washington, DC: CQ Press.

Bonica, Adam, Nolan McCarty, Keith T. Poole, and Howard Rosenthal. 2013. "Why Hasn't Democracy Slowed Rising Inequality?" *Journal of Economic Perspectives* 27 (3): 103–23.

Bonica, Adam, and Howard Rosenthal. 2016 "The Wealth Elasticity of Political Contributions by the Forbes 400." August 19. doi: http://dx.doi.org/10.2139/ssrn.2668780.

Borjas, George J. 2014. *Immigration Economics*. Cambridge, MA: Harvard University Press.

Bouie, Jamelle. 2013. "Americans Are Clear: Obamacare Just Isn't Liberal Enough." *Daily Beast*. December 23. http://www.thedailybeast.com/articles/2013/12/23/americans-are-clear-obamacare-just-isn-t-liberal-enough.html.

Bowie, Blair, and Adam Lioz. 2013. *Billion-Dollar Democracy: The Unprecedented Role of Money in the 2012 Elections*. January. New York City: Dēmos. http://www.demos.org/sites/default/files/publications/billion.pdf.

Brady, David W., John Ferejohn, and Laurel Harbridge. 2008. "Polarization and Public Policy: A General Assessment." In Nivola and Brady, *Red Nation and Blue Nation?* 2:185–216.

Brady, David W., Hahrie Han, and Jeremy C. Pope. 2007. "Primary Elections and Candidate Ideology: Out of Step with the Primary Electorate?" *Legislative Studies Quarterly* 32 (1): 79–107.

Brands, H. W., T. H. Breen, R. Hal Williams, and Ariela J. Gross. 2009. *American Stories: A History of the United States*. New York: Pearson Longman.

Brass, Clinton T. 2013. *Shutdown of the Federal Government: Causes, Processes, and Effects*. CRS Report RL34680. Congressional Research Services. Washington, DC: Library of Congress.

Brater, Jonathan. 2016. "Automatic Voter Registration in Oregon a Huge Success." Brennan Center for Justice (blog). April 8. https://www.brennancenter.org/blog/automatic-voter-registration-oregon-huge-success.

Brennan Center for Justice. 2013. "Voting Laws Roundup 2013." December 19. http://www.brennancenter.org/analysis/election-2013-voting-laws-roundup.

———. 2014. "Voting Laws Roundup 2014." December 18. http://www.brennancenter.org/analysis/voting-laws-roundup-2014.

———. 2017. "Bipartisan Support for Voter Registration Modernization," March 10. https://www.brennancenter.org/analysis/voter-registration-modernization-support.

Brians, Craig Leonard, and Bernard Grofman. 2001. "Election Day Registration's Effect on U.S. Voter Turnout." *Social Science Quarterly* 82 (1): 170–83.

Brickner, T., with Naomi Mueller. 2008. *Clean Elections: Public Financing in Six States, Including New Jersey's Pilot Projects*. Eagleton Institute of Politics at Rutgers University. http://www.eagleton.rutgers.edu/research/newjersey/documents/CE-PublicFinancinginSixStates09-08.pdf.

Brown, Robert D., and Justin Wedeking. 2006. "People Who Have Their Tickets But Do Not Use Them: 'Motor Voter,' Registration, and Turnout Revisited." *American Politics Research* 34 (4): 479–504.

Bruck, Connie. 2010. "The Influencer." *New Yorker*, May 10. http://www.newyorker.com/magazine/2010/05/10/the-influencer.

Bryce, James. 1995. 2 vols. *The American Commonwealth*. Indianapolis: Liberty Fund. First published in 1888; major update in 1910.

Bullock, Will, and Joshua D. Clinton. 2011. "More a Molehill than a Mountain: The Effects of the Blanket Primary on Elected Officials' Behavior from California." *Journal of Politics* 73 (3): 915–30.

Bump, Phillip. 2014. "The Remarkably Small Percentage of People It Took to Oust Eric Cantor." *Washington Post*, June 11. http://www.washingtonpost.com/blogs/the-fix/wp/2014/06/11/the-remarkably-small-percentage-of-people-it-took-to-oust-eric-cantor/.

Burch, Traci. 2013. *Trading Democracy for Justice: Criminal Convictions and the Decline of Neighborhood Political Participation*. Chicago: University of Chicago Press.

Burden, Barry C., David T. Canon, Kenneth R. Mayer, and Donald P. Moynihan. 2014. "Election Laws, Mobilization, and Turnout: The Unanticipated Consequences of Election Reform." *American Journal of Political Science* 58 (1): 95–109.

Burden, Barry C., and Brian J. Gains. 2015. "Presidential Commission on Election Administration: Absentee and Early Voting: Weighing the Costs of Convenience." *Election Law Journal* 14 (1): 32–37.

Burnham, Walter Dean. 1970. *Critical Elections and the Mainsprings of American Politics*. New York: Norton.

———. 2007. "Triumphs and Travails in the Study of American Voting Participation Rates, 1788–2006." *Journal of the Historical Society* 7 (4): 505–604.

Burnham, Walter Dean, Thomas Ferguson, and Louis Ferleger. 2010. *Voting in American Elections: The Shaping of the American Political Universe since 1788*. Washington, DC: Academica Press.

Burstein, Paul. 2014. *American Public Opinion, Advocacy, and Policy in Congress*. New York: Cambridge University Press.

Bushaw, William J., and Valerie J. Calderon. 2014. "The 46th Annual PDK/Gallup Poll of the Public's Attitudes toward the Public Schools." Phi Delta Kappa International. 2 parts, September and October. http://pdkintl.org/noindex/PDK_Poll46_2014.pdf; http://pdkintl.org/noindex/PDKGallupPoll_Oct2014.pdf.

Calhoun-Brown, Allison. 1996. "African American Churches and Political Mobilization: The Psychological Impact of Organizational Resources." *Journal of Politics* 59 (4): 935–53.

Canes-Wrone, Brandice, David W. Brady, and John F. Cogan. 2002. "Out of Step, Out of Office: Electoral Accountability and House Members' Voting." *American Political Science Review* 96 (1): 127–40.

Carmines, Edward G., and James A. Stimson. 1989. *Issue Evolution: Race and the Transformation of American Politics*. Princeton, NJ: Princeton University Press.

Carnes, Nicholas. 2013. *White Collar Government: The Hidden Role of Class in Economic Policy Making*. Chicago: University of Chicago Press.

Carson, Jamie L., Michael H. Crespin, Charles J. Finocchiaro, and David W. Rohde. 2007. "Redistricting and Party Polarization in the U.S. House of Representatives." *American Politics Research* 35 (6): 878–904.

Carson, Jamie L., Michael H. Crespin, and Ryan D. Williamson. 2014. "Reevaluating the Effects of Redistricting on Electoral Competition, 1972–2012." *State Politics and Policy Quarterly* 14 (2): 165–77.

Castells, Mannuel. 2012. *Networks of Outrage and Hope: Social Movements in the Internet Age.* Cambridge, UK: Polity Press.

CBS News/New York Times. 2009. "CBS News/New York Times Monthly Poll, September 2009 (ICPSR 27805)." Institute for Social Research, University of Michigan. http://www.icpsr.umich.edu/icpsrweb/ICPSR/studies/27805.

CCEP Policy Brief. 2013. "Online Voter Registration: Impact on California's 2012 Election Turnout, by Age and Party Affiliation." *California Civic Engagement Project, UC Davis Center for Regional Change*, no. 4. https://ccep.ucdavis.edu/s/UCDavis _CCEP_Brief_-4_Online_Voter_Turnout_Final.pdf.

Center for Governmental Studies. 2003. "Investing in Democracy: Creating Public Financing of Elections in Your Community." http://research.policyarchive.org /231.pdf.

Center for Media and Democracy, Common Cause, Dēmos, Every Voice, People For the American Way, Public Citizen, ReThink Media, and U.S. PIRG. 2016. *Our Voices, Our Democracy: Victories since "Citizens United" and the Road Ahead; Empowering Voters over Wealthy Interests.* Dēmos. February. http://www.demos.org/sites /default/files/publications/Our%20Voices%20Our%20Democracy%20FINAL.pdf.

Center for Responsive Politics. 2017a. "Cost of Election." Accessed February 23. https://www.opensecrets.org/overview/cost.php.

———. 2017b. "Election Overview: Top Individual Contributors." Accessed February 23. https://www.opensecrets.org/overview/topindivs.php.

———. 2017c. "Insurance: Money to Congress; All Senators." Accessed March 28. https://www.opensecrets.org/industries/summary.php?ind=F09&cycle=2006& recipdetail=S&mem=Y.

———. 2017d. "Outside Spending by Disclosure, Excluding Party Committees." Accessed February 28. http://www.opensecrets.org/outsidespending/disclosure.php ?range=tot.

———. 2017e. "Revolving Door." Accessed February 28. https//www.opensecrets.prg/ revolving/.

———. 2017f. "Total Outside Spending by Election Cycle, Excluding Party Committees." Accessed February 28. https://www.opensecrets.org/outsidespending/cycle _tots.php?cycle=2016&view=Y&chart=N#summ.

———. 2017g. "2012 Presidential Race." Accessed February 23. https://www .opensecrets.org/pres12/.

Cha, J. Mijin. 2013. "Registering the Millions: The Success and Potential of the National Voter Registration Act at 20." Dēmos. http://www.demos.org/registering -millions-success-and-potential-national-voter-registration-act-20.

Cha, J. Mijin, and Liz Kennedy. 2014. "Millions to the Polls: Practical Policies to Fulfill the Freedom to Vote for All Americans." Dēmos. http://www.demos.org/millions -polls.

Chen, Jowei, and Jonathan Rodden. 2013. "Unintentional Gerrymandering: Political Geography and Electoral Bias in Legislatures." *Quarterly Journal of Political Science* 8 (3): 239–69.

Chen, Stefanos. 2015. "Los Angeles Spec House with Beauty Salon Sells for $30 Million." *Wall Street Journal*, January 23, M2.

Chetty, Raj, David Grusky, Maximilian Hell, Nathaniel Hendren, Robert Manduca, and Jimmy Narang. 2016. *The Fading American Dream: Trends in Absolute Income Mobility since 1940.* Working Paper No. 22910. Cambridge, MA: National Bureau of Economic Research.

Chetty, Raj, Nathaniel Hendren, Patrick Kline, and Emmanuel Saez. 2014. "Where Is the Land of Opportunity? The Geography of Intergenerational Mobility in the United States." *Quarterly Journal of Economics* 129 (4): 1553–1623.

Choma, Russ. 2014. "Millionaires' Club: For First Time, Most Lawmakers Are Worth $1 Million-Plus." *OpenSecrets* (blog). January 9. https://www.opensecrets .org/news/2014/01/millionaires-club-for-first-time-most-lawmakers-are-worth-1 -million-plus/.

Chong, Dennis. 1991. *Collective Action and the Civil Rights Movement.* Chicago: University of Chicago Press.

Chong, Dennis, and James N. Druckman. 2007. "Framing Public Opinion in Competitive Democracies." *American Political Science Review* 101 (4): 637–55.

Chozick, Amy, and Jonathan Martin. 2016. "Clinton Uses Access to Woo the Ultra-rich." *New York Times*, September 9, A1, A20.

Citrin, Jack, Eric Schickler, and John Sides. 2003. "What if Everyone Voted? Simulating the Impact of Increased Turnout in Senate Elections." *American Journal of Political Science* 47 (1): 75–90.

Clark, Tom S. 2010. *The Limits of Judicial Independence.* New York: Cambridge University Press.

CNN/ORC. 2013. "Healthcare Poll: December 16–19, 2013." http://i2.cdn.turner.com /cnn/2013/images/12/23/cnn.orc.poll.health.care.pdf.

Cohn, Jonathan. 2016. "Poll: Only One-Fourth of Americans Actually Want Full Obamacare Repeal." Huffington Post. December 1. http//www.huffingtonpost.com /entry/obamacare-repeal-poll_us_583f3b6fe4b017f37fe2607f.

Cohn, Nate. 2014. "Why Democrats Can't Win." *New York Times*, September 7, SR 1, 7.

Common Cause. 2010. "Poll Shows 79% Support the Citizens' Election Program in Connecticut." News release, January 27. http://www.ct.gov/seec/lib/seec/citizens _election_program_/common_cause_press_release_01272010.pdf.

Confessore, Nicholas. 2015a. "Koch Brothers' Budget of $889 Million for 2016 Is on Par with Both Parties' Spending." *New York Times*, January 27, A1.

———. 2015b. "Rich Governor and Allies Tilt Illinois' Future." *New York Times*, November 30, A1, A14.

Confessore, Nicholas, Sarah Cohen, and Karen Yourish. 2015. "From Only 158 Families, Half the Cash for '16 Race." *New York Times*, October 11, A1, A24.

Converse, Philip E. 1964. "The Nature of Belief Systems in the Mass Public." In *Ideology and Discontent*, edited by David E. Apter, 206–61. New York: Free Press.

Cook, Fay Lomax, and Rachel L. Moskowitz. 2013. "The Great Divide: Elite and Mass Opinions about Social Security." In *The New Politics of Old Age Policy*, edited by Robert Hudon, pp. 69–98. Baltimore, MD: John Hopkins Press.

Cook, Fay Lomax, Benjamin I. Page, and Rachel L. Moskowitz. 2014. "Political Engagement by Wealthy Americans." *Political Science Quarterly* 129 (3): 381–98.

Cooper, Betsy, Daniel Cox, Rachel Lienesch, and Robert P. Jones. 2015. "Anxiety, Nostalgia, and Mistrust: Findings from the 2015 American Values Survey." Public Religion Research Institute. November 17. http://www.prri.org/research/survey-anxiety -nostalgia-and-mistrust-findings-from-the-2015-american-values-survey/.

Corak, Miles. 2013. "Income Inequality, Equality of Opportunity, and Intergenerational Mobility." Institute for the Study of Labor (IZA) Discussion Paper No. 7520, July.

Costa, Robert. 2015. "GOP Donor Foster Friess Launches New Effort to Boost Rick Santorum." *Washington Post*, January 14.

Cottrill, James B. 2012. "The Effects of Non-Legislative Approaches to Redistricting on Competition in Congressional Elections." *Polity* 44 (1): 32–50.

Cox, Gary W., and Mathew D. McCubbins. 2005. *Setting the Agenda: Responsible Party Government in the U.S. House.* New York: Cambridge University Press.

Coy, Peter. 2014. "The Richest Rich Are in a Class by Themselves." Bloomberg Businessweek, April 3. https://www.bloomberg.com/news/articles/2014-04-03/top-tenth-of-1-percenters-reaps-all-the-riches.

Cramer, Katherine J. 2016. *The Politics of Resentment: Rural Consciousness in Wisconsin and the Rise of Scott Walker.* Chicago: University of Chicago Press.

Cronin, Thomas E. 1989. *Direct Democracy: The Politics of Initiative, Referendum, And Recall.* Cambridge, MA: Harvard University Press.

Curry, James M. 2015. *Legislating in the Dark: Information and Power in the House of Representatives.* Chicago: University of Chicago Press.

Dahl, Robert A. 1956. *A Preface to Democratic Theory.* Chicago: University of Chicago Press.

———. 1957. "Decision-Making in a Democracy: The Supreme Court as a National Policy-Maker." *Journal of Public Law* 6:279–95.

———. 1971. *Polyarchy: Participation and Opposition.* New Haven, CT: Yale University Press.

———. 2001. *How Democratic Is the American Constitution?* New Haven, CT: Yale University Press.

Dalen, James E., Keith Waterbrook, and Joseph S. Alpert. 2015. "Why Do So Many Americans Oppose the Affordable Care Act?" *American Journal of Medicine* 128 (8): 807–10.

Date, S. V. 2015. "Why Jeb Bush Is Talking about Income Inequality." *National Journal*, April 30. https://www.nationaljournal.com/s/27667.

Davenport, Coral, and Marjorie Connelly. 2015. "Most in G.O.P. Say They Back Climate Action." *New York Times*, January 31, A1, A11.

Davis, Bob, and Jon Hilsenrath. 2016. "How the China Shock, Deep and Swift, Spurred the Rise of Trump." *Wall Street Journal*, August 11, A1, A5.

Davis, Karen, Kristof Stremikis, David Squires, and Cathy Schoen. 2014. "Mirror Mirror on the Wall: How the Performance of the U.S. Health Care System Compares Internationally." Commonwealth Fund. June. http://www.commonwealthfund.org/publications/fund-reports/2014/jun/mirror-mirror.

Davis, Otto A., Melvin J. Hinich, and Peter C. Ordeshook. 1970. "An Expository Development of a Mathematical Model of the Electoral Process." *American Political Science Review* 64 (June): 426–48.

Debenetti, Gabriel. 2016. "Team Clinton's Favorite Billionaire." *Politico*, November 4.

Delli Carpini, Michael X., and Scott Keeter. 1996. *What Americans Know about Politics and Why It Matters.* New Haven, CT: Yale University Press.

Dēmos. 2017. "What Is Same Day Registration? Where Is It Available?" http://www.demos.org/publication/what-same-day-registration-where-it-available.

Desilver, Drew. 2013. "Congress Ends Least-Productive Year in Recent History." Pew Research Center. December 23. http://www.pewresearch.org/fact-tank/2013/12/23/congress-ends-least-productive-year-in-recent-history/.

Dewey, John. 1927. *The Public and Its Problems*. New York: Henry Holt.

DiJulio, Biana, Jamie Firth, and Mollyann Brodie. 2015a. "Kaiser Health Tracking Poll: April 2015." Henry J. Kaiser Family Foundation. April 21. http://kff.org/health -costs/poll-finding/kaiser-health-tracking-poll-april-2015/.

———. 2015b. "Kaiser Health Tracking Poll: August 2015." Henry J. Kaiser Family Foundation. August 20. http://kff.org/health-costs/poll-finding/kaiser-health -tracking-poll-august-2015/.

Domhoff, G. William. 2014. *Who Rules America? The Triumph of the Corporate Rich*. 7th. ed. New York: McGraw-Hill.

Douglas-Gabriel, Danielle. 2015. "Scott Walker's Real Record on Higher Education in Wisconsin." *Washington Post*, August 12.

Downs, Anthony. 1957. *An Economic Theory of Democracy*. New York: Harper and Row.

Drum, Kevin. 2010. "What's the Deal with the Estate Tax?" *Mother Jones*, December 15. http://www.motherjones.com/kevin-drum/2010/12/whats-deal-estate-tax.

Drutman, Lee. 2015. *The Business of America Is Lobbying: How Corporations Became Politicized and Politics Became More Corporate*. New York: Oxford University Press.

Dutton, Sarah, Jennifer De Pinto, Anthony Salvanto, and Fred Backus. 2015. "Have the Goals of the Civil Rights Movement Have Been Achieved?" CBS News. March 4. http://www.cbsnews.com/news/have-the-goals-of-the-civil-rights-movement-have -been-achieved/.

Duverger, Maurice. 1954. *Political Parties, Their Organization and Activity in the Modern State*. London: Methuen.

———. 1972. "Factors in a Two-Party and Multiparty System." In *Party Politics and Pressure Groups: A Comparative Introduction*, 23–32. New York: Crowell.

Ehrenfreund, Max. 2014. "Your Complete Guide to Obama's Immigration Executive Action." *Washington Post*, September 20. http://www.washingtonpost.com/news /wonkblog/wp/2014/11/19/your-complete-guide-to-obamas-immigration-order/.

Ehrenreich, Barbara. 2008. *Nickel and Dimed: On (Not) Getting By in America*. New York: Henry Holt.

Enns, P. K. 2015. "Relative Policy Support and Coincidental Representation." *Perspectives on Politics* 13 (4): 1053–64.

Erikson, Robert S., Michael B. MacKuen, and James A. Stimson. 2002. *The Macro Polity*. New York: Cambridge University Press.

Esser, Ingrid, Tommy Ferrarini, Kenneth Nelson, Joakim Palme, and Ola Sjoberg. 2013. "Unemployment Benefits in EU Member States." EU European Commission Report, July.

Fain, Tom. 2016. "Will Somebody Please Explain . . . What Is a Superdelegate?" Utica, NY, *Observer-Dispatch*, July 25. http://www.uticaod.com/will-somebody-please -explain-superdelegate.

FairVote: Center for Voting and Democracy. 2014. "What Is RCV?" http://archive3 .fairvote.org/reforms/instant-runoff-voting/what-is-irv/.

FairVote: For a More Perfect Union. 2017. "Campaign Civility: Ranked Choice Voting and Civil Campaigning." Accessed March 1. http://www.fairvote.org/research _rcvcampaigncivility.

Ferejohn, John A., and Frances McCall Rosenbluth. 2017. *Forged through Fire*. New York: Liveright.

Ferguson, Dana. 2017. "S.D. Senate Strikes Voter-Approved Ethics Law." *Argus Leader*, February 1. http://www.argusleader.com/story/news/politics/2017/02/01 /sd-senate-strikes-voter-approved-ethics-law/97333962/.

Ferguson, Thomas. 1995. *Golden Rule: The Investment Theory of Party Competition and the Logic of Money-Driven Political Systems*. Chicago: University of Chicago Press.

———. 2016. "'Wall Street Plus Identity Politics' Formula Is Over for the Democrats." Real News Network. November 9. http://therealnews.com/t2/index.php?option=com_content&task=view&id=767&Itemid=74&jumival=17643.

Ferguson, Thomas, and Jie Chen. 2005. "Investor Blocs in American History." *Journal of the Historical Society* 5 (4): 503.

Ferguson, Thomas, Paul Jorgensen, and Jie Chen. 2016a. "How Money Drives U.S. Congressional Elections." Working Paper No. 48, August 1. Institute for New Economic Thinking, New York.

———. 2016b. "The Surge and Its Aftermath: High Finance, Political Money, and the U.S. Congress." Working Paper, November 8.

Ferguson, Thomas, and Joel Rogers. 1986. *Right Turn: The Decline of the Democrats and the Future of American Politics*. New York: Hill and Wang.

Feuer, Alan. 2016. "The Ideological Roots of the Oregon Standoff." *New York Times*, January 10, SR3.

Fiorina, Morris P. 1981. *Retrospective Voting in American National Elections*. New Haven, CT: Yale University Press.

Fiorina, Morris P., Samuel J. Abrams, and Jeremy Pope. 2005. *Culture War? The Myth of a Polarized America*. 2nd ed. New York: Pearson Longman.

Fishkin, James S. 2009. *When People Speak: Deliberative Democracy and Public Consultation*. New York: Oxford University Press.

Flacks, Richard. 1988. *Making History: The Radical Tradition in American Life*. New York: Columbia University Press.

"The Forbes 400." 2016. Special Issue, *Forbes*, October 25. Comparable issues in October of previous years.

Ford, Martin. 2015. *Rise of the Robots: Technology and the Threat of a Jobless Future*. New York: Basic Books.

Fox, Cybelle. 2012. *Three Worlds of Relief: Race, Immigration, and the American Welfare State from the Progressive Era to the New Deal*. Princeton, NJ: Princeton University Press.

Fox News. 2015. "Sen. Ted Cruz Slams Obama's State of the Union Talking Points." January 21. http://www.foxnews.com/transcript/2015/01/21/sen-ted-cruz-slams-obama-state-union-talking-points/.

Frankel, Noralee, and Nancy Schrom Dye. 1991. *Gender, Class, Race, and Reform in the Progressive Era*. Lexington: University Press of Kentucky.

Frank, Robert. 2007. *Richistan: A Journey through the American Wealth Boom and the Lives of the New Rich*. New York: Three Rivers.

———. 2015. "For the New Superrich, Life is Much More than a Beach." *New York Times*, June 21, BU3.

Frank, Thomas. 2016. *Listen, Liberal; or, What Ever Happened to the Party of the People?* New York: Henry Holt.

Fredman, Lionel E. 1968. *The Australian Ballot: The Story of an American Reform*. East Lansing: Michigan State University Press.

Freeland, Chrystia. 2012. *Plutocrats: The Rise of the New Global Super-Rich and the Fall of Everyone Else*. New York: Penguin.

Freeman, Jo. 1975. *The Politics of Women's Liberation: A Case Study of an Emerging Social Movement and Its Relation to the Policy Process*. New York: McKay.

Freeman, Richard B. 2011. "What Can We Learn from the NLRA to Create Labor Law for the Twenty-First Century?" *ABA Journal of Labor and Employment Law* 26 (2): 327–43.

———. 2014. "Who Owns the Robots Rules the World." IZA World of Labor. May. http://wol.iza.org/articles/who-owns-the-robots-rules-the-world/long.

Friedman, Milton. 1962. *Capitalism and Freedom.* With the assistance of Rose D. Friedman. Chicago: University of Chicago Press.

Friedman, Thomas L. 2007. *The World Is Flat: A Brief History of the Twenty-First Century.* New York: Picador.

Gabriel, Trip. 2014. "Cantor Forgot Virginia Roots, Voters Contend." *New York Times,* June 12, 2014, A1, A17.

———. 2015. "Scott Walker, Set for a Bigger Stage, Faces G.O.P. Revolt in Wisconsin." *New York Times,* June 24, A1.

Galbraith, John Kenneth. 1952. *American Capitalism: The Concept of Countervailing Power.* New York: Houghton Mifflin.

Gallego, Aina. 2010. "Understanding Unequal Turnout: Education and Voting in Comparative Perspective." *Electoral Studies* 29 (2): 239–48.

Gamson, William A. 1975. *The Strategy of Social Protest.* Homewood, IL: Dorsey Press.

Garofoli, Joe. 2015. "Tom Steyer Says Effort to End Inequality Isn't Political Move." *San Francisco Chronicle,* August 11. http://www.sfchronicle.com/business/article /Tom-Steyer-says-effort-to-end-inequality-isn-t-6438690.php.

Geer, John. 2006. *In Defense of Negativity: Attack Advertising in Presidential Campaigns.* Chicago: University of Chicago Press.

Gelman, Andrew. 2004. "Overrepresentation of Small States/Provinces, and the USA Today Effect." *Statistical Modeling, Causal Influence, and Social Science* (blog). October 15. http://andrewgelman.com/2004/10/15/overrepresentat/.

Geoghegan, Thomas. 2004. *Which Side Are You On? Trying to Be for Labor When It's Flat on Its Back.* With a new afterword. New York: New Press. First published 1991.

Gerber, Alan. 1998. "Estimating the Effect of Campaign Spending on Senate Election Outcomes Using Instrumental Variables." *American Political Science Review* 92 (2): 401–11.

Gerber, Alan S., Gregory A. Huber, and Seth J. Hill. 2013. "Identifying the Effects of Elections Held All-Mail on Turnout: Staggered Reform in the Evergreen State." *Political Science Research and Methods* 1 (1): 91–116.

Gerber, Elizabeth. 1999. *The Populist Paradox: Interest Group Influence and the Promise of Direct Legislation.* Princeton, NJ: Princeton University Press.

Gerber, Elizabeth, and Jeffrey Lewis. 2004. "Beyond the Median: Voter Preferences, District Heterogeneity, and Political Representation." *Journal of Political Economy* 112 (6): 1364–83.

Gerber, Elizabeth, and Rebecca Morton. 1998. Primary Election Systems and Representation. *Journal of Law, Economics, and Organization.* 14: 304–24.

Gest, Justin. 2016. *The New Minority: White Working Class Politics in an Age of Immigration and Inequality.* New York: Oxford University Press.

Gilens, Martin. 2009. "Preference Gaps and Inequality in Representation." *PS: Political Science and Politics.* 42 (2): 335–41.

———. 2012. *Affluence and Influence: Economic Inequality and Political Power in America.* New York: Russell Sage Foundation and Princeton University Press.

———. 2015. "The Insufficiency of 'Democracy by Coincidence': A Response to Peter K. Enns." *Perspectives on Politics* 13 (4): 1065–71.

———. 2016. "Simulating Representation: The Devil's in the Detail." *Research and Politics* 3 (2).

Gilens, Martin, and Benjamin I. Page. 2014. "Testing Theories of American Politics: Elites, Interest Groups, and Average Citizens." *Perspectives on Politics* 12 (3): 564–80.

———. 2016. "Critics Argued with Our Analysis of U.S. Political Inequality. Here Are 5 Ways They're Wrong." *Washington Post*, May 23.

Gillis, Justin. 2017. "Earth Sets a Temperature Record for the Third Straight Year," *New York Times*, January 18. https://www.nytimes.com/2017/01/18/science/earth-highest-temperature-record.html?_r=0.

Giugni, Marco, Doug McAdam, and Charles Tilly, eds. 1999. *How Social Movements Matter*. Minneapolis: University of Minnesota Press.

Gladwell, Malcolm. 2008. *Outliers: The Story of Success*. New York: Little, Brown.

Goldfield, Michael. 1987. *The Decline of Organized Labor in the United States*. Chicago: University of Chicago Press.

———. 2007. "The Impact of Globalization and Neoliberalism on the Decline of Organized Labour in the United States." In *Labor, Globalization and the State: Workers, Women, and Migrants Confront Neoloberalism*, edited by Debdas Banerjee and Michael Goldfield, 121–59. New York: Routledge.

Goldman, Eric Frederick. 1952. *Rendezvous with Destiny: A History of Modern American Reform*. New York: Knopf.

Goldman, Jonah. 2011. "Voter Registration: Assessing Current Problems." *Testimony of Jonah H Goldman, Director, National Campaign for Fair Elections, Lawyer's Committee for Civil Rights Under Law, Before the Senate Committee on Rules and Administration*. 112th Cong.

Goldwater, Barry M. 1960. *The Conscience of a Conservative*. Shepherdsville, KY: Victor.

Goodman, Peter S. 2017. "Amidst Populist Fury, Elite Mull Inequity, but Avoid Talk of Sacrifice." *New York Times*, January 19, B1, B4.

Goodwyn, Lawrence. 1976. *Democratic Promise: The Populist Moment in America*. New York: Oxford University Press.

———. 1978. *The Populist Moment: A Short History of the Agrarian Revolt in America*. New York: Oxford University Press. (Abridged version of Goodwyn 1976.)

Gordon, Robert J. 2016. *The Rise and Fall of American Growth: The U.S. Standard of Living since the Civil War*. Princeton, NJ: Princeton University Press.

GovTrack. 2017a. "H.R. 7152: Civil Rights Act of 1964." Accessed March 3. https://www.govtrack.us/congress/votes/88-1964/h182.

———. 2017b. "H.R. 7152: Passage." Accessed March 3. https://www.govtrack.us/congress/votes/88-1964/s409.

———. 2017c. "To Agree to Conference Report on S. 1564, the Voting Rights Act." Accessed March 3. https://www.govtrack.us/congress/votes/89-1965/h107.

———. 2017d. "To Pass S. 1564, the Voting Rights Act of 1965." Accessed March 3. https://www.govtrack.us/congress/votes/89-1965/s78.

Graetz, Michael, and Ian Shapiro. 2006. *Death by a Thousand Cuts*. Princeton, NJ: Princeton University Press.

Grainger, Corbett A. 2010. "Redistricting and Polarization: Who Draws the Lines in California?" *Journal of Law and Economics* 53 (3): 545–67.

Greenberg, Edward S., Leon Grunberg, Sarah Moore, and Patricia B. Sikora. 2010. *Turbulence: Boeing and the State of American Workers and Managers*. New Haven, CT: Yale University Press.

Greve, Joan. 2016. "What Are Superdelegates? And Yes, Republicans Have Them, Too." *Washington Week* (blog). July 12. http://www.pbs.org/weta/washingtonweek /blog-post/what-are-superdelegates-and-yes-republicans-have-them-too.

Grim, Ryan, Sam Stein, and Sabrina Siddiqui. 2013. "Harry Reid, Mitch McConnell Reach Filibuster Reform Deal." Huffington Post. January 24. http://www .huffingtonpost.com/2013/01/24/harry-reid-mitch-mcconnell-filibuster_n_2541356 .html.

Gronke, Paul, Galanes-Rosenbaum, and Peter A. Miller. 2008. "Early Voting and Voter Turnout." In Cain, Donovan, and Tolbert, *Democracy in the States*, 68–82.

Gutmann, Amy. 2004. *Why Deliberative Democracy?* Princeton, NJ: Princeton University Press.

Hacker, Jacob. 2004. "Privatizing Risk without Privatizing the Welfare State: The Hidden Politics of Social Policy Retrenchment in the United States. " *American Political Science Review* 98 (2): 243–60.

Hacker, Jacob S., and Paul Pierson. 2010. *Winner-Take-All Politics: How Washington Made the Rich Richer — And Turned Its Back on the Middle Class*. New York: Simon and Schuster.

———. 2016. *American Amnesia: How the War on Government Led Us to Forget What Made America Prosper*. New York: Simon and Schuster.

Hall, Andrew B. 2014. *How the Public Funding of Elections Increases Candidate Polarization*. Stanford University. January 13. http://www.campaignfreedom.org/wp -content/uploads/2014/07/Hall-2014-Tax-Financing-And-Polarization.pdf.

———. 2015. "What Happens When Extremists Win Primaries?" *American Political Science Review* 109 (1): 18–42.

———. 2016. "Who Wants to Run? How the Devaluing of Political Office Drives Polarization." Stanford University. Unpublished manuscript.

Hall, Richard L., and Frank W. Wayman. 1990. "Buying Time: Moneyed Interests and the Mobilization of Bias in Congressional Committees." *American Political Science Review* 84 (3): 797–820.

Halpern-Meekin, Sarah, Kathryn Edin, Laura Tach, and Jennifer Sykes. 2015. *It's Not Like I'm Poor: How Working Families Make Ends Meet in a Post-Welfare World*. Oakland: University of California Press.

Hamilton, Alexander, James Madison, and John Jay. (1787–88) 1999. *The Federalist Papers*. Edited by Clinton Rossiter. New York, NY: Mentor.

Hamilton, Lee. 2009. *Strengthening Congress*. Bloomington: Indiana University Press.

Hamner, Michael. 2009. *Discount Voting: Registration Reforms and Their Effects*. New York: Cambridge University Press.

Harbridge, Laurel. 2015. *Is Bipartisanship Dead? Policy Agreement and Agenda-Setting in the House of Representatives*. New York: Cambridge University Press.

Harris, Frederick C. 1994. "Something Within: Religion as a Mobilizer of African American Political Activism." *Journal of Politics* 56 (1): 42–58.

———. 1999. *Something Within: Religion in African-American Political Activism*. Cary, NC: Oxford University Press.

Hartford *Courant*. 2015. "House, Senate Democrats Back Off on Campaign Finance Cuts" November 29.

Hasen, Richard L. 1996. "Clipping Coupons for Democracy: An Egalitarian/Public Choice Defense of Campaign Finance Vouchers." *California Law Review* 84 (1): 1–59.

———. 2016. *Plutocrats United: Campaign Money, the Supreme Court, and the Distortion of American Elections*. New Haven, CT: Yale University Press.

Haug, Christoph. 2013. "Meetings." In Snow et al., *Wiley-Blackwell Encyclopedia of Social and Political Movements.*

Hayek, Friedrich A. 1944. *The Road to Serfdom.* Chicago: University of Chicago Press.

Healy, Andrew, and Gabriel S. Lenz. 2014. "Substituting the End for the Whole: Why Voters Respond Primarily to the Election-Year Economy." *American Journal of Political Science* 58:31–47.

Hedberg, Kathy. 2015. "CCC Camps Crucial Amid Depression." *Idaho Statesman,* July 29, D3.

Heerwig, Jennifer A., and Katherine Shaw. 2014. "Through a Glass, Darkly: The Rhetoric and Reality of Campaign Finance Disclosure." *Georgetown Law Journal* 102 (1443): 1443–1500.

Hemenway, D., D. Azrael, and M. Miller. 2001. "National Attitudes Concerning Gun Carrying in the United States." *Injury Prevention* 7:282–85.

Hertel-Fernandez, Alexander, and Theda Skocpol. 2016. "Billionaires Against Big Business: Growing Tensions in the Republican Party Coalition." Paper presented at the Annual Meeting of the Midwest Political Science Association, Chicago, April 8.

Hertel-Fernandez, Alexander, Theda Skocpol, and Daniel Lynch. 2016. "Business Associations, Conservative Networks, and the Ongoing Republican War over Medicaid Expansion." *Journal of Health Politics, Policy and Law* 41 (2).

Hetherington, Marc J. 2001. "Resurgent Mass Partisanship: The Role of Elite Polarization." *American Political Science Review* 95 (3): 619–31.

Hetherington, Marc J., and Thomas J. Rudolph. 2015. *Why Washington Won't Work: Polarization, Political Trust, and the Governing Crisis.* Chicago: University of Chicago Press.

Heymann, Jody, Hye Jin Rho, John Schmitt, and Alison Earle. 2009. "Contagion Nation: A Comparison of Paid Sick Day Policies in 22 Countries." Center for Economic and Policy Research. May. http://cepr.net/documents/publications/paid-sick -days-2009-05.pdf.

Highton, Benjamin, and Raymond E. Wolfinger. 2001. "The Political Implications of Higher Turnout." *British Journal of Political Science* 31 (1): 179–92.

Hillary for America. 2016. "Factsheets: Hillary Clinton's Proposals to Restore Integrity to American Elections." *The Briefing.* https://www.hillaryclinton.com/briefing /factsheets/2015/09/08/restore-integrity-to-elections/.

Hill, David. 2003. "A Two-Step Approach to Assessing the Composition Effects of the National Voter Registration Act." *Electoral Studies* 22:703–20.

Hiltzik, Michael. 2012. "Unmasking the Most Influential Billionaire in U.S. Politics." *Los Angeles Times,* October 2.

Hines, Joseph. 2014. "It Takes Nearly $8 Million to Join the Wealthiest One Percent." *Dēmos Policyshop* (blog). September 19. http://www.demos.org/blog/9/19/14/it -takes-nearly-8-million-join-wealthiest-one-percent.

Hirano, S., J. M. Snyder, S. Ansolabehere, and J. M. Hansen. 2010. "Primary Elections and Partisan Polarization in the US Congress." *Quarterly Journal of Political Science* 5 (2): 169–91.

Hochschild, Arlie Russell. 2016. *Strangers in Their Own Land: Anger and Mourning on the American Right.* New York: New Press.

Hochschild, Jennifer. 1981. *What's Fair? Americans' Beliefs about Distributive Justice.* Cambridge, MA: Harvard University Press.

Hoebeke, Christopher H. 1995. *The Road to Mass Democracy: Original Intent and the Seventeenth Amendment.* New Brunswick, NJ: Transaction Publishers.

Hoffman, Beth. 2013. "Who Receives 'Food Stamps'? And Why It Is Critical To Continue Their Support." Forbes.com, September 23. https://www.forbes.com /sites/bethhoffman/2013/09/23/who-receives-food-stamps-and-why-it-is-critical-to -continue-their-support/#50e2dc645e49.

Hofstadter, Richard. 1955. *The Age of Reform: From Bryan to F.D.R.* New York: Random House.

Holbrook, Thomas M., and Aaron C. Weinschenk. 2014. "Campaign, Mobilization, and Turnout in Mayoral Elections." *Political Research Quarterly* 67 (1): 42–55.

Hollis-Brusky, Amanda. 2015. *Ideas with Consequences: The Federalist Society and the Conservative Counterrevolution.* New York: Oxford University Press.

Howell, William G. 2003. *Power without Persuasion: The Politics of Direct Presidential Action.* Princeton, NJ: Princeton University Press.

Howell, William G., Martin R. West, and Paul E. Peterson. 2011. "The Public Weighs In on School Reform." *Education Next* 11 (4). http://educationnext.org/the-public -weighs-in-on-school-reform/.

Huang, Chye-Ching, and Brandon Debot. 2016. "Ten Facts You Should Know about the Federal Estate Tax." *Center on Budget and Policy Priorities.* Updated September 8. http://www.cbpp.org/research/ten-facts-you-should-know-about-the-federal -estate-tax.

Hulse, Carl. 2014. "Lawmakers' Modest Proposal: To Pass Spending Bills on Time." *New York Times,* May 30, 14.

Isikoff, Michael. 2015. "Secret $1.5 Million Donation from Wisconsin Billionaire Uncovered in Scott Walker Dark-Money Probe." Yahoo! News, March 23. https:// www.yahoo.com/news/wisconsin-gov-scott-walker-photo-charlie-114429739886 .html.

Israel, Steve. 2016. "Confessions of a Congressman." *New York Times,* January 9, A19.

Jackman, Robert W. 1987. "Political Institutions and Voter Turnout in the Industrial Democracies." *American Political Science Review.* 81 (2): 405–23.

Jacobs, Lawrence R., and Desmond King. 2016. *Fed Power: How Finance Wins.* New York: Oxford University Press.

Jacobs, Lawrence R., and Benjamin I. Page. 2005. "Who Influences U.S. Foreign Policy?" *American Political Science Review* 99 (1): 107–23.

Jacobs, Lawrence R., and Robert Y. Shapiro. 1999. *Myths and Misunderstandings about Public Opinion toward Social Security: Knowledge, Support, and Reformism.* New York: Century Foundation.

Jacobs, Lawrence R., and Theda Skocpol. 2010. *Health Care Reform and American Politics: What Everyone Needs to Know.* New York: Oxford University Press.

Jacobson, Gary C. 2000. "Party Polarization in National Politics: The Electoral Connection." In Bond and Fleisher, *Polarized Politics,* 9–30.

———. 2004. "Explaining the Ideological Polarization of the Congressional Parties since the 1970s." *Social Science Research Network,* April.

———. 2005. "Competition and U.S. Congressional Elections." In McDonald and Samples, *Marketplace of Democracy,* 27–52.

———. 2007. *A Divider, Not a Uniter: George W. Bush and the American People.* New York: Pearson Education.

———. 2012. "The Electoral Origins of Polarized Politics: Evidence from the 2010 Cooperative Congressional Election Study." *American Behavioral Sciences* 56 (12): 1612–630.

————. 2013. *The Politics of Congressional Elections.* 8th ed. New York: Pearson.

Jaffe, Alexandra. 2014. "Biggest Super Tuesday Casualty?" *Hill,* June 3.

Jencks, Christopher. 2015a. "The War on Poverty: Was It Lost?" *New York Review,* April 2, 82–85.

————. 2015b. "Did We Lose the War on Poverty?—II." *New York Review,* April 23, 37–40.

Jenkins, Homan W. Jr. 2015. "Climate Reporting's Hot Mess." *Wall Street Journal,* January 21.

Jenkins, J. Craig, and Charles Perrow. 1977. "Insurgency of the Powerless: Farm Worker Movements (1946–1972). *American Sociological Review* 42 (2): 249–68.

Johnston, David Cay. 2016. *The Making of Donald Trump.* Brooklyn: Melville House.

Jones, Jeffrey M. 2013. "Americans Widely Back Government Job Creation Proposals." Gallup. March 20. http://www.gallup.com/poll/161438/americans-widely-back -government-job-creation-proposals.aspx.

Jones, Robert P., Daniel Cox, Betsy Cooper, and Rachel Lienesch. 2015. "Anxiety, Nostalgia, and Mistrust: Findings from the 2015 American Values Survey." Public Religion Research Institute. November 17. http://publicreligion.org/site/wp-content /uploads/2015/11/PRRI-AVS-2015.pdf.

Kaiser Family Foundation. 2009. "Chartpack: Kaiser Health Tracking Poll—September 2009." September 1. http://kff.org/health-costs/poll-finding/chartpack-kaiser-health -tracking-poll-september-2009.

————. 2011. "Kaiser Health Tracking Poll: December 2011." December. https:// kaiserfamilyfoundation.files.wordpress.com/2013/03/8265-c.pdf.

Kalla, Joshua L., and David E. Broockman. 2016. "Campaign Contributions Facilitate Access to Congressional Officials: A Randomized Field Experiment." *American Journal of Political Science* 60 (30): 545–58.

Kammer, Anthony, and Liz Kennedy. 2013. "The Explainer: Who Decides When a Corporation Spends Money on Politics?" Dēmos. May. http://www.demos.org/sites /default/files/publications/Explainer-CorporateExplainer2-4.pdf.

Karol, David. 2009. *Party Position Change in American Politics: Coalition Management.* New York: Cambridge University Press.

————. 2015. "Party Activists, Interest Groups, and Polarization in American Politics." Chapter 3 in *American Gridlock: The Sources, Character, and Impact of Political Polarization,* edited by James A. Thurber and Antoine Yoshinaka. New York: Cambridge University Press.

Kasara, Kimuli, and Pavithra Suryanarayan. 2014. "When Do the Rich Vote Less Than the Poor and Why? Explaining Turnout Inequality across the World." *American Journal of Political Science* 59 (3): 613–27.

Kasdan, Diana. 2013. *Early Voting: What Works.* Brennan Center for Justice at New York University School of Law, Democracy Program. http://www.brennancenter.org /sites/default/files/publications/VotingReport_Web.pdf.

Katznelson, Ira. 2013. *Fear Itself: The New Deal and the Origins of Our Time.* New York: Liveright.

Kaufman, Alexander C. 2017. "Scott Pruitt Confirmed as EPA Chief Despite Firestorm over Emails." Huffington Post, February 17. http://www.huffingtonpost.com/entry /scott-pruitt-confirmed-epa_us_58a71504e4b07602ad53f023.

Kaufman, Dan. 2015. "Scott Walker and the Fate of the Union." *New York Times Magazine,* June 12, MM41.

Keates, Nancy. 2015. "The Bedroom Boom." *Wall Street Journal*, June 26, M1, M7–9.

Kelly, Nathan J. 2009. *The Politics of Income Inequality in the United States*. New York: Cambridge University Press.

———. Forthcoming. *America's Inequality Trap: How Economic Inequality Feeds on Itself and Why It Matters*. Chicago: University of Chicago Press.

Kelly, Nathan J., and Peter K. Enns. 2010. "Inequality and the Dynamics of Public Opinion: The Self-Reinforcing Link between Economic Inequality and Mass Preferences." *American Journal of Political Science* 54 (4): 855–70.

Kennedy, Liz. 2014. "Dollars and Sense: How Undisclosed Money and Post-McCutcheon Campaign Finance Will Affect the 2014 Election and Beyond." *Testimony of Liz Kennedy, Counsel at Demos, Submitted to the United States Senate Committee on Rules and Administration*. 113th Cong. http://www.demos.org/publication/dollars -and-sense-how-undisclosed-money-and-post-mccutcheon-campaign-finance-will -affect.

Kennedy, Liz, and Sean McElwee. 2014. "Do Corporations and Unions Face the Same Rules for Political Spending?" Dēmos. July 23. http://www.demos.org/publication /do-corporations-unions-face-same-rules-political-spending.

Kenworthy, Lane. 2014. *Social Democratic America*. New York: Oxford University Press.

Kessler, Glenn. 2016. "Trump's False Claim He Built His Empire with a 'Small Loan' from His Father." *Washington Post*, March 3.

Keyssar, Alexander. 2009. *The Right to Vote: The Contested History of Democracy in the United States*. Rev. ed. New York: Basic. First published 2000.

Key, V. O. Jr. 1961. *Public Opinion and American Democracy*. New York: Knopf.

Khoury, Rana. 2016. *As Ohio Goes: Life in the Post-Recession Nation*. Kent, OH: Kent State University Press.

Kimball, David C., Martha Kropf, and Lindsay Battles. 2006. "Helping America Vote? Election Administration, Partisanship, and Provisional Voting in the 2004 Election." *Election Law Journal* 5 (4): 447–61.

Kimball, Will, and Lawrence Mishel. 2015. "Unions Decline and the Rise of the Top 10 Percent's Share of Income." Economic Policy Institute, February 3. http://www .epi.org/publication/unions-decline-and-the-rise-of-the-top-10-percents-share-of -income/.

Kingson, Eric R. 2010. "A Tale of Three Commissions: The Good, the Bad, and the Ugly." *Poverty and Public Policy* 2 (3).

Klar, Samara, and Yanna Krupnikov. 2016. *Independent Politics: How American Disdain for Parties Leads to Political Inaction*. New York: Cambridge University Press.

Klein, Ezra. 2014. "The Most Terrifying Graph on Democracy is a Flat Line." Vox. May 14. http://www.vox.com/2014/5/14/5718080/the-most-terrifying-graph-about -democracy-is-a-straight-line.

Klinkner, Philip A., and Rogers M. Smith. 1999. *The Unsteady March: The Rise and Decline of Racial Equality in America*. Chicago: University of Chicago Press.

Knack, Stephen. 1995. "Does 'Motor Voter' Work? Evidence from State-Level Data." *Journal of Politics* 57 (3): 796–811.

Kochhar, Rakesh, and Richard Fry. 2014. "Wealth Inequality has Widened along Racial, Ethnic Lines since End of Great Recession." Pew Research Center, December 12. http://www.pewresearch.org/fact-tank/2014/12/12/racial-wealth-gaps-great -recession/.

Koger, Gregory. 2010. *Filibustering: A Political History of Obstruction in the House and Senate*. Chicago: University of Chicago Press.

Kollman, Ken. 1998. *Outside Lobbying: Public Opinion and Interest Group Strategies*. Princeton, NJ: Princeton University Press.

Kosar, Kevin R. 2015. "Why I Quit the Congressional Research Service." *Washington Monthly*, January/February.

Kramer, Larry. 2004. *The People Themselves: Popular Constitutionalism and Judicial Review*. New York: Oxford University Press.

Krehbiel, Keith. 1998. *Pivotal Politics: A Theory of U.S. Lawmaking*. Chicago: University of Chicago Press.

Kriesi, Hanspeter, and Dominique Wisler. 1999. "The Impact of Social Movements on Political Institutions: A Comparison of the Introduction of Direct Legislation in Switzerland and the United States." In Giugni, McAdam, and Tilly, *How Social Movements Matter*, 42–65.

Kristoff, Nicholas. 2015. "A New Way to Tackle Gun Deaths." *New York Times*, October 4, SR9.

Krogstad, Jens Manuel, and Jeffrey S. Passel. 2015. "Five Facts about Illegal Immigration in the U.S." Pew Research Center. November 3. http://www.pewresearch.org/fact-tank/2016/11/03/5-facts-about-illegal-immigration-in-the-u-s/.

Krosnick, Jon A. and Bo MacInnis. 2013. *Does the American Public Support Legislation to Reduce Greenhouse Gas Emissions?* American Academy of Arts and Sciences. http://climatepublicopinion.stanford.edu/wp-content/uploads/2013/05/GW-Deadalus-Published.pdf.

Lamarche, Gara. 2014. "Is Philanthropy Bad for Democracy?" *Atlantic*, October 30.

Landemore, Helene. 2013. *Democratic Reason: Politics, Collective Intelligence, and the Rule of the Many*. Princeton, NJ: Princeton University Press.

Langbein, Laura I. 1986. "Money and Access—Some Empirical-Evidence." *Journal of Politics* 48 (4): 1052–62.

LaPira, Timothy M., and Herschel F. Thomas. 2017. *Revolving Door Lobbying: Public Service, Private Influence, and the Unequal Representation of Interests*. Lawrence: University Press of Kansas.

La Raja, Raymond J., and Brian F. Schaffner. 2015. *Campaign Finance and Political Polarization: When Purists Prevail*. Ann Arbor: University of Michigan Press.

Lardner, Jim. 2013. "Americans Agree on Regulating Wall Street." *U.S. News and World Report*, September 16. http://www.usnews.com/opinion/blogs/economic-intelligence/2013/09/16/poll-shows-americans-want-more-wall-street-regulation-five-years-after-the-financial-crisis.

Lause, Mark A. 2001. *The Civil War's Last Campaign: James B. Weaver, the Greenback-Labor Party and the Politics of Race and Section*. Lanham, MD: University Press of America.

League of Women Voters. 2014. "League Urges Administration to Fully Implement the NVRA at ACA Health Benefit Exchanges." http://www.lwv.org/content/league-urges-administration-fully-implement-nvra-aca-health-benefit-exchanges.

Lears, T. J. Jackson. 2009. *Rebirth of a Nation: The Making of Modern America, 1877–1920*. New York: HarperCollins.

Leech, Beth L. 2013. *Lobbyists at Work*. New York: Apress/Springer.

Lee, Frances E., and Bruce Ian Oppenheimer. 1999. *Sizing Up the Senate: The Unequal Consequences of Equal Representation*. Chicago: University of Chicago Press.

Lee, M. J. 2016. "Resetting Red and Blue in the Rust Belt." CNN Politics, April 25. http://www.cnn.com/2016/04/25/politics/rust-belt-voters-trump-clinton-sanders /index.html.

Leighley, Jan E., and Jonathan Nagler. 2013. *Who Votes Now? Demographics, Issues, Inequality, and Turnout in the United States.* Princeton, NJ: Princeton University Press.

Lessig, Lawrence. 2011. *Republic, Lost: How Money Corrupts Congress — and a Plan to Stop It.* New York: Hachette.

———. 2012. "Calling for a Convention." *American Prospect*, January 4. http:// prospect.org/article/calling-convention.

———. 2015. *Republic Lost: The Corruption of Equality and the Steps to End It.* Rev. ed. New York: Hachette. Major revision of 2011 work.

Levendusky, Matthew. 2010. *The Partisan Sort: How Liberals Became Democrats and Conservatives Became Republicans.* Chicago: University of Chicago Press.

Levin, Steven M. 2006. Keeping It Clean: Public Financing and American Elections. Center for Governmental Studies. http://users.polisci.wisc.edu/kmayer/466/Keeping _It_Clean.pdf.

Levinson, Sanford. 2006. *Our Undemocratic Constitution: Where the Constitution Goes Wrong (And How We the People Can Correct It).* New York: Oxford University Press.

Levinthal, Dave. 2009. "Lobbyists Terminating Their Federal Registrations at Accelerated Rate." *OpenSecrets* (blog). November 2. https://www.opensecrets.org/news /2009/11/lobbyists-terminating-their-fe/.

Levitt, Justin. 2007. *The Truth about Voter Fraud.* Brennan Center for Justice at New York University School of Law. http://www.brennancenter.org/sites/default/files /legacy/The%20Truth%20About%20Voter%20Fraud.pdf.

———. 2014. "A Comprehensive Investigation of Voter Impersonation Finds 31 Credible Incidents Out of One Billion Ballots Cast." *Washington Post*, August 6.

———. 2017. "All about Redistricting: Professor Justin Levitt's Guide to Drawing the Electoral Lines." Loyola Law School. Accessed March 1. http://redistricting.lls.edu /who.php.

Lewis, Daniel C., Saundra K. Schneider, and William G. Jacoby. 2015. "The Impact of Direct Democracy on State Spending Priorities." *Electoral Studies* 40:531–38.

Lichtenstein, Nelson. 2013. *State of the Union: A Century of American Labor.* Rev. and Expanded ed. Princeton, NJ: Princeton University Press.

Lieberman, Robert C. 1998. *Shifting the Color Line: Race and the American Welfare State.* Cambridge, MA: Harvard University Press.

Lieberman, Trudy. 2012. "How the Media Has Shaped the Social Security Debate." *Columbia Journalism Review*, April 18.

Light, John. 2016. "Outside Spenders Make Final Push to Win Congress." Moyers and Company. November 4. http://billmoyers.com/story/big-spenders-make-final-push/.

Lijphart, Arend. 2012. *Patterns of Democracy: Government Forms and Performance in Thirty-Six Countries.* 2nd ed. New Haven, CT: Yale University Press.

———. 2015. "Polarization and Democratization." In Persily, *Solutions to Political Polarization in America*, 73–82.

Lindert, Peter H., and Jeffrey C. Williamson. 2016. *Unequal Gains: American Growth and Inequality since 1700.* Princeton, NJ: Princeton University Press.

Lindgren, Eric, and Priscilla Southwell. 2013. "The Effect of Redistricting Commissions on Electoral Competitiveness in U.S. House Elections, 2002–2010." *Journal of Politics and Law* 6 (2): 13–18.

Link, Arthur S. 1954. *Woodrow Wilson and the Progressive Era: 1910–1917*. New York: Harper and Row.

Link, William A., and Susannah J. Link, eds. 2014. *The Gilded Age and Progressive Era: A Documentary Reader*. Malden, MA: Wiley-Blackwell.

Lioz, Adam. 2014. *The Government by the People Act: Legislation to Curb the Power of Wealthy Donors and Put Government Back in the Hands of Voters*. Dēmos. February. http://www.demos.org/sites/default/files/publications/Demos -GovByThePeopleAct.pdf.

———. 2015. *Breaking the Vicious Cycle: Rescuing Our Democracy and Our Economy by Transforming the Supreme Court's Flawed Approach to Money in Politics*. Dēmos. December 15. http://www.demos.org/publication/breaking-vicious-cycle-rescuing -our-democracy-and-our-economy-transforming-supreme-court

Lippmann, Walter. (1922) 1965. *Public Opinion*. New York: Macmillan.

Lipton, Eric, and Liz Moyer. 2015. "Lobbyists Shield a Tax Loophole Worth $1 Billion." *New York Times*, December 21, A1, A17.

Lizza, Ryan. 2012 "The Obama Memos: The Making of a Post-Post-Partisan Presidency." *New Yorker*, January 30.

Lowery, Wesley. 2014. "Senate Republicans Block Minimum Wage Increase." *Washington Post*, April 30. http://www.washingtonpost.com/news/post-politics/wp/2014/04 /30/senate-republicans-block-minimum-wage-increase-bill/.

Lublin, Joann S. 2015. "Parsing the Pay and Performance of Top CEOs." *Wall Street Journal*, June 25, B1, B4.

MacGillis, Alec. 2016. "Revenge of the Forgotten Class." *ProPublica*, November 10.

Mackie, Gerry. 2003. *Democracy Defended*. New York: Cambridge University Press.

Mahlotra, Neil. 2008. "The Impact of Public Financing on Electoral Competition: Evidence from Arizona and Maine." *State Politics and Policy Quarterly* 8 (3): 263–81.

Maine Citizens for Clean Elections. 2013. "Critical Insights on Maine Tracking Survey: Spring 2013." May. https://www.mainecleanelections.org/sites/default/files/polling /130516_MCCE_Polling_CI_TopLineResults.pdf.

Malbin, Michael J. 2013. "Small Donors: Incentives, Economies of Scale, and Effects." *Forum* 11 (3): 385–411.

Malbin, Michael J., Peter W. Brusoe, and Brendan Glavin. 2012. "Small Donors, Big Democracy: New York City's Matching Funds as a Model for the Nation and States." *Election Law Journal* 11 (1):3–20.

Malkin, Michelle. 2008. "Universal Voter Registration?" *Michelle Malkin* (blog). November 10. http://michellemalkin.com/2008/11/10/universal-voter-registration/ #comments.

Manchin, Joe. 2013. "Manchin Statement on the 'Public Safety and Second Amendment Rights Protection Act.'" News release, April 17. http://www.manchin.senate .gov/public/index.cfm/2013/4/manchin-statement-on-the-public-safety-second -amendment-rights-protection-act.

Manley, John F. 1970. *The Politics of Finance: The House Committee on Ways and Means*. Boston: Little, Brown.

Mann, Thomas E. 2006. "Polarizing the House of Representatives: How Much Does Gerrymandering Matter?" In Nivola and Bracy, *Red and Blue Nation?* 1:263–83.

Mann, Thomas E., and Norman J. Ornstein. 2012. *It's Even Worse Than It Looks: How the American Constitutional System Collided with the New Politics of Extremism.* New York: Basic Books.

Mansbridge, Jane J. 1986. *Why We Lost the ERA.* Chicago: University of Chicago Press.

———. 1999. "Should Blacks Represent Blacks and Women Represent Women? A Contingent 'Yes.'" *Journal of Politics* 61 (3): 628–57.

———. 2003. "Rethinking Representation." *American Political Science Review* 97 (4): 515–28.

———. 2012. "The 2011 James Madison Lecture: On the Importance of Getting Things Done." *PS: Political Science and Politics* 45 (1): 1–8.

Manza, Jeff, Clem Brooks, and Christopher Uggen. 2004. "Public Attitudes toward Felon Disenfranchisement in the United States." *Public Opinion Quarterly* 68 (2): 275–86.

Manza, Jeffrey, and Christopher Uggen. 2006. *Locked Out: Felon Disenfranchisement and American Democracy.* New York: Oxford University Press.

Marmor, Theodore R. 2000. *The Politics of Medicare.* 2nd ed. Hawthorne, NY: Aldine Transaction.

Martin, John P. 2014. "Activation and Active Labour Market Policies in OECD Countries: Stylized Facts and Evidence on Their Effectiveness." Institute for the Study of Labor Policy Paper Series No. 84, June.

Masket, Seth E. 2009. *No Middle Ground : How Informal Party Organizations Control Nominations and Polarize Legislatures.* Ann Arbor: University of Michigan Press.

Masket, Seth E., and Michael G. Miller. 2015. "Does Public Election Funding Create More Extreme Legislators? Evidence from Arizona and Maine." *State Politics and Policy Quarterly* 15 (1): 24–40.

Matthews, Donald R. 1960. *U.S. Senators and Their World.* Chapel Hill: University of North Carolina Press.

May, Kenneth O. 1952. "A Set of Independent Necessary and Sufficient Conditions for Simple Majority Decisions." *Econometrica* 20 (4): 680–84.

Mayday PAC. 2014. "67,547 Donations for over $10,947,947 from Across the Nation." https://v1.mayday.us/your-donations/.

Mayer, Gerald. 2004. *Union Membership Trends in the United States.* Washington, DC: Congressional Research Service.

Mayer, Jane. 2016. *Dark Money: The Hidden History of the Billionaires behind the Rise of the Radical Right.* New York: Doubleday.

Mayhew, David. 1991. *Divided We Govern: Party Control, Lawmaking, and Investigations.* New Haven, CT: Yale University Press.

McAdam, Doug. 1982. *Political Process and the Development of Black Insurgency, 1930–1970.* Chicago: University of Chicago Press.

———. 1988. *Freedom Summer.* New York: Oxford University Press.

McAdam, Doug, Sidney G. Tarrow, and Charles Tilly. 2001. *Dynamics of Contention.* Cambridge: Cambridge University Press.

McCall, Leslie. 2013. *The Undeserving Rich: American Beliefs about Inequality, Opportunity, and Redistribution.* New York: Cambridge University Press.

McCammon, Holly J., Karen E. Campbell, Ellen M. Granberg, and Christine Mowery. 2001. "How Movements Win: Gendered Opportunity Structures and U.S. Women's Suffrage Movements, 1866 to 1919." *American Sociological Review* 66 (1): 49–70.

McCarthy, John D., and Mayer N. Zald. 1977. "Resource Mobilization and Social Movements: A Partial Theory." *American Journal of Sociology* 82 (6): 1212–41.

McCarty, Nolan M., Keith T. Poole, and Howard Rosenthal. 2006. *Polarized America: The Dance of Ideology and Unequal Riches.* Cambridge, MA: MIT Press.

———. 2009. "Does Gerrymandering Cause Polarization?" *American Journal of Political Science* 53 (3): 666–80.

———. 2013. *Political Bubbles: Financial Crises and the Failure of American Democracy.* Princeton, NJ: Princeton University Press.

McCloskey, Robert G. 2010. *The American Supreme Court.* 5th. ed. Revised by Sanford Levinson. Chicago: University of Chicago Press.

McClosky, Herbert, Paul Hoffman, and Rosemary O'Hara. 1960. "Issue Conflict and Consensus among Party Leaders and Followers." *American Political Science Review* 54 (2): 406–72.

McClosky, Herbert, and John Zaller. 1984. *The American Ethos: Public Attitudes toward Capitalism and Democracy.* Cambridge, MA: Harvard University Press.

McConnaughy, Corrine M. 2013. *The Woman Suffrage Movement in America : A Reassessment.* New York: Cambridge University Press.

McConnell, Grant. 1966. *Private Power and American Democracy.* New York: Random House.

McDonald, Michael P. 2006. "Redistricting and Competitive Elections." In McDonald and Samples, *Marketplace of Democracy,* 222–44.

McDonald, Michael P., and John Samples, eds. 2006. *The Marketplace of Democracy: Electoral Competition and American Politics.* Washington, DC: Brookings Institution.

McGerr, Michael. 2003. *A Fierce Discontent: The Rise and Fall of the Progressive Movement in America, 1870–1920.* New York: Oxford University Press.

McGhee, Eric. 2014. "Voter Turnout in Primary Elections." *Public Policy Institute of California.*

McGhee, Eric, Seth Masket, Boris Shor, Steven Rogers, and Nolan McCarty. 2014. "A Primary Cause of Partisanship? Nomination Systems and Legislator Ideology." *American Journal of Political Science* 58 (2): 337–51.

McGuire, Kevin T., and James A. Stimson. 2004. "The Least Dangerous Branch Revisited: New Evidence on Supreme Court Responsiveness to Public Preferences." *Journal of Politics* 66 (4): 1018–35.

McKenna, Marian C. 2002. *Franklin Roosevelt and the Great Constitutional War: The Court-Packing Crisis of 1937.* New York: Fordham University Press.

Melucci, Alberto. 1996. *Challenging Codes: Collective Action in the Information Age.* Cambridge: Cambridge University Press.

Memmott, Mark. 2013. "Nearly 13 Hours Later, Sen. Paul Ends His Filibuster; Here's The Video." *National Public Radio,* March 7. http://www.npr.org/sections/thetwo -way/2013/03/07/173693133/nearly-13-hours-later-sen-paul-ends-his-filibuster -heres-the-video.

Meyer, David S. 1990. *A Winter of Discontent: The Nuclear Freeze and American Politics.* New York: Praeger.

Migally, Angela, and Susan Liss. 2010. *Small Donor Matching Funds: The NYC Election Experience.* Brennan Center for Justice. http://www.brennancenter.org /page/-/Small%20Donor%20Matching%20Funds-The%20NYC%20Election %20Experience.pdf.

Milbank, Dana. 2014. "Dana Milbank: Republicans' Gagging Hypocrisy." *Washington Post,* June 9.

Miller, Gary, and Norman Schofield. 2003. "Activists and Partisan Realignment in the United States." *American Political Science Review* 97 (2): 245–60.

Miller, Michael Gerald. 2014. *Subsidizing Democracy: How Public Funding Changes Elections and How It Can Work in the Future.* Ithaca, NY: Cornell University Press.

Minnite, Lorraine. 2010. *The Myth of Voter Fraud.* Ithaca, NY: Cornell University Press.

Mishel, Lawrence. 2012. "The 10-year Decline in Wages for most College Graduates." Economic Policy Institute, October 3. www.epi.org/publication/10-year-decline -wages-college-graduates/.

———. 2015. "Top Compensation Soars, and Why We Do Not Look at 'Average CEOs.'" *Economic Policy Institute Worki ng Economics Blog.* June 22. www.epi .org/blog/top-ceo-compensation-soars-and-why-we-do-not-look-at-average-ceos/.

Mishel, Lawrence, Josh Bivens, Elise Gould, and Heidi Shierholz. 2012. *The State of Working America.* 12th ed. Ithaca, NY: Cornell University Press.

Mizruchi, Mark S. 2013. *The Fracturing of the American Corporate Elite.* Cambridge, MA: Harvard University Press.

Molyneux, Guy. 2015. "Support for a Federal Minimum Wage of $12.50 or Above." Hart Research Associates. January 14. http://www.nelp.org/content/uploads/2015 /03/Minimum-Wage-Poll-Memo-Jan-2015.pdf.

Molyneux, Guy, and Geoff Garin. 2013. "Americans' Budget Priorities." Hart Research Associates. January 29. http://www.americansfortaxfairness.org/files/Hart-Memo -on-Fiscal-Cliff-Poll.pdf.

Moore, Peter. 2014. "Poll Results: Minimum Wage." YouGov. January 29. https:// today.yougov.com/news/2014/01/29/poll-results-minimum-wage/.

Morris, Aldon D. 1984. *The Origins of the Civil Rights Movement: Black Communities Organizing for Change.* New York: Free Press.

Morris, Aldon D., and Suzanne Staggenborg. 2004. "Leadership in Social Movements." In *The Blackwell Companion to Social Movements*, edited by David A. Snow, Sarah Anne Soule and Hanspeter Kriesi. Malden, MA: Blackwell Publishing.

Morris, Edmund. 2001. *Theodore Rex.* New York: Random House.

Motel, Seth. 2015. "F Facts on How Americans View Taxes." Pew Research Center. April 10. http://www.pewresearch.org/fact-tank/2015/04/10/5-facts-on-how -americans-view-taxes/.

Mowrey, George E. 1958. *The Era of Theodore Roosevelt 1900–1912.* New York: Harper.

Mueller, John. 2001. *Capitalism, Democracy, and Ralph's Pretty Good Grocery.* Princeton, NJ: Princeton University Press. First published 1999.

Murray, Patrick. 2015. "National: DC's Negative Impact on Americans." Monmouth University Polling Institute. July 9. http://www.monmouth.edu /assets/0/32212254770/32212254991/32212254992/32212254994/32212254995 /30064771087/c743d069-96d6-4f89-a378-e368c19a8639.pdf.

Musgrave, Richard A., and Peggy B. Musgrave. 1980. *Public Finance in Theory and Practice.* 3rd ed. New York: McGraw-Hill.

Myrdal, Gunnar. 1944. *An American Dilemma.* New York: Harper.

NAACP. 2017. "Oldest and Boldest." Accessed March 2. http://www.naacp.org/pages /naacp-history.

National Employment Law Project. 2017. "History of the Minimum Wage." Raise the Minimum Wage. Accessed February 27. http://raisetheminimumwage.com/history/.

National Institute on Money in State Politics Follow the Money Database. 2017. "Individuals' Contributions to Walker, Scott K." February 8. http://www.followthemoney.org/show-me?c-t-eid=4656950&d-et=2#[{1|gro=c-r-id,d-eid,f-s.

National Popular Vote. 2017. "Agreement among the States to Elect the President by National Popular Vote." Accessed March 2. http://www.nationalpopularvote.com/written-explanation.

National Priorities Project. 2017. "Federal Spending: Where Does the Money Go?" Accessed February 20. https://www.nationalpriorities.org/budget-basics/federal-budget-101/spending/.

Newport, Frank. 2013. "Americans Wanted Gun Background Checks to Pass Senate." Gallup. April 29. http://www.gallup.com/poll/162083/americans-wanted-gun-background-checks-pass-senate.aspx.

———. 2017. "Americans Continue to Say U.S. Wealth Distribution Is Unfair." Gallup. Accessed February 21. http://www.gallup.com/poll/1714/taxes.aspx.

New York Times. 2016a. "How the Presidential Election Took a U-Turn in 2016." November 10, P1, P9–P12.

———. 2016b. "Which Presidential Candidates Are Winning the Money Race." June 22. http://www.nytimes.com/interactive/2016/us/elections/election-2016-campaign-money-race.html.

Nivola, Pietro S., and David W. Brady. 2006–8. *Red and Blue Nation? Consequences and Corrections of America's Polarized Politics.* 2 vols. Washington, DC: Brookings Institution.

Nivola, Pietro S., and William A. Galston. 2008. "Toward Depolarization," in Nivola and Brady, *Red and Blue Nation?* 2:235–84.

Nunns, Jim, Len Burman, Ben Page, Jeff Rohaly, and Joe Rosenberg. 2016. *An Analysis of Donald Trump's Revised Tax Plan.* Tax Policy Center research report, October 18.

Oberschall, Anthony. 1973. *Social Conflict and Social Movements.* Englewood Cliffs, NJ: Prentice-Hall.

O'Brien, Matthew. 2014. "Republicans Support Expanding the EITC—Just Not if It Costs Money." *Atlantic.* March 5. http://www.theatlantic.com/business/archive/2014/03/republicans-support-expanding-the-eitc-just-not-if-it-costs-money/284247.

OECD and Jelle Visser. 2013. "ICTWSS database (Institutional Characteristics of Trade Unions, Wage Setting, State Intervention and Social Pacts, 1960–2010), version 3.0." Organisation for Economic Co-operation and Development. https://stats.oecd.org/Index.aspx?DataSetCode=UN_DEN.

O'Keefe, Ed, and Paul Kane. 2013. "Sen. Cruz Ends Anti-Obamacare Talkathon after More Than 21 Hours." *Washington Post*, September 25.

Olen, Hellaine. 2016. "Clinton Lost the Economic Argument: It Was the Only Way She Could Have Eased Trump Voters' Racism, and She Blew It." *Slate*, November 9.

Oleszek, Mark J. 2015. "'Holds' in the Senate." Congressional Research Service Report R43563.

Oleszek, Walter J. 2011. *Proposals to Reform "Holds" in the Senate.* Congressional Research Service Report RL31685.

———. 2014. *Congressional Procedures and the Policy Process.* 9th ed. Thousand Oaks, CA: CQ Press.

Olson, Mancur Jr. 1965. *The Logic of Collective Action: Public Goods and the Theory of Groups.* Cambridge, MA: Harvard University Press.

Oreskes, Naomi, and Erik M. Conway. 2010. *Merchants of Doubt: How a Handful of Scientists Obscured the Truth on Issues from Tobacco Smoke to Global Warming.* New York: Bloomsbury.

Ornitz, Jill, and Ryan Struyk. 2015. "Donald Trump's Surprisingly Honest Lessons about Big Money in Politics." ABC News, August 11. http://abcnews.go.com/Politics/donald-trumps-surprisingly-honest-lessons-big-money-politics/story?id=32993736.

Ornstein, Norman J., Thomas E. Mann, Michael J. Malbin, and Andrew Rugg. 2013. *Vital Statistics on Congress: Data on the U.S. Congress — A Joint Effort from Brookings and the American Enterprise Institute.* Washington, DC: Brookings Institution and American Enterprise Institute.

Ornstein, Norman J., Thomas E. Mann, Michael J. Malbin, and Molly E, Reynolds. 2017. *Vital Statistics on Congress*, chapter 3. Brookings. www.brookings.edu/vitalstats.

Overton, Spencer. 2007. *Stealing Democracy: The New Politics of Voter Suppression.* New York: Norton.

Page, Benjamin I. 1978. *Choices and Echoes in Presidential Elections: Rational Man and Electoral Democracy.* Chicago: University of Chicago Press.

———. 1996. *Who Deliberates? Mass Media in Modern Democracy.* Chicago: University of Chicago Press.

———. 1997. "Trouble for Workers and the Poor: Economic Globalization and the Reshaping of American Politics." Evanston, IL: Joint Center for Poverty Research, Northwestern University and University of Chicago.

———. 2007. "Is Public Opinion an Illusion?" *Critical Review* 19 (1) 35–45.

Page, Benjamin I., Larry M. Bartels, and Jason Seawright. 2013. "Democracy and the Policy Preferences of Wealthy Americans." *Perspectives on Politics* 11 (1): 51–73.

Page, Benjamin I., with Marshall M. Bouton. 2006. *The Foreign Policy Disconnect: What Americans Want from Our Leaders but Don't Get.* Chicago: University of Chicago Press.

Page, Benjamin I., and Cari Lynn Hennessy. 2011. "What Affluent Americans Want from Politics." Working Paper No. WP-11-08. Institute for Policy Research, Northwestern University.

Page, Benjamin I., and Lawrence R. Jacobs. 2009. *Class War? What Americans Really Think about Economic Inequality.* Chicago: University of Chicago Press.

Page, Benjamin I., Jason Seawright, and Matthew B. Lacombe. 2015. "Stealth Politics by U.S. Billionaires." Paper presented at the annual meeting of the American Political Science Association, San Francisco, September 3–6.

Page, Benjamin I., and Robert Y. Shapiro. 1983. "Effects of Public Opinion on Policy." *American Political Science Review* 77 (1): 175–90.

———. 1992. *The Rational Public: Fifty Years of Trends in Americans' Policy Preferences.* Chicago: University of Chicago Press.

Page, Benjamin I., and James R. Simmons. 2000. *What Government Can Do: Dealing with Poverty and Inequality.* Chicago: University of Chicago Press.

Palmer, Kim. 2014. "Cleveland Democrat Challenges New Ohio Early Voting Limits." Reuters. February 27. http://www.reuters.com/article/us-usa-ohio-politics-idUSBREA1Q2A520140227.

Pateman, Carole. 2012. "Participatory Democracy Revisited." *Perspectives on Politics* 10 (1): 7–19.

PDK/Gallup. 2014. 'The PDK/Gallup Poll of the Public's Attitudes towards Public

Schools." *Phi Delta Kappa International.* http://www.pdkintl.org/files/2014-PDK -Gallup-Poll-Presentation.pdf.

Pearson, Kathryn, and Eric Schickler. 2009. "Discharge Petitions, Agenda Control, and the Congressional Committee System, 1929–76." *Journal of Politics* 71 (4): 1238–56.

People's Party. 1892. "National People's Party Platform." In W. Link and S. Link, *Gilded Age and Progressive Era,* 183–88.

Persily, Nathaniel, ed. 2015. *Solutions to Political Polarization in America.* New York: Cambridge University Press.

Peters, Jeremy W. 2013. "In Landmark Vote, Senate Limits Use of the Filibuster." *New York Times.* http://www.nytimes.com/2013/11/22/us/politics/reid-sets-in-motion -steps-to-limit-use-of-filibuster.html.

Peterson, Kristina, and Janet Hook. 2014. "Tea Party Upsets GOP No.2 Cantor." *Wall Street Journal,* June 12, A1, A4.

Pew Research Center. 2013. "Broad Support for Renewed Background Checks Bill, Skepticism about Its Chances." May 23. http://www.people-press.org/2013/05/23/broad -support-for-renewed-background-checks-bill-skepticism-about-its-chances/2/.

Pew Research Poll Database. 2015. "Pew Research Center for the People & the Press Political Survey, Jan. 2015." January 11. http://www.people-press.org/2015/01/11 /january-2015-political-survey.

Phillips, Amber. 2015. "7 Ways Bernie Sanders Will Run against Hillary Clinton." *Washington Post,* May 26. https://www.washingtonpost.com/news/the-fix/wp/2015 /05/26/bernie-sanders-hillary-clinton/?utm_term=.9679c917db86.

Phillips, David Graham. 1906. "The Treason of the Senate." *Cosmopolitan Magazine* 40 (March): 4. Reprinted in book form by Academic Reprints, Stanford, California, n.d.

Phillips, Kevin. 1990. *The Politics of Rich and Poor.* New York: Harper Collins.

Piazza, James A. 2002. *Going Global: Unions and Globalization in the United States, Sweden, and Germany.* Lanham, MD: Lexington Books.

Pigou, A. C. 1912. *Wealth and Welfare.* London: MacMillan.

Piketty, Thomas. 2014. *Capital in the Twenty-first Century.* Translated by Arthur Goldhammer. Cambridge, MA: Harvard University Press.

———. 2015. "A Practical Vision of a More Equal Society." *New York Review of Books,* June 25, 26–29.

Pintor, Rafael Lopez, Maria Gratschew, and Kate Sullivan. 2002. "Voter Turnout Rates from a Comparative Perspective." In *Voter Turnout since 1945: A Global Report,* edited by Rafael Lopez Pintor and Maria Gratschew. Stockholm: Institute for Democracy and Electoral Assistance.

Piven, Frances Fox, and Richard A. Cloward. 1977. *Poor People's Movements: Why They Succeed, How They Fail.* New York: Pantheon Books.

Plumer, Brad. 2012. "Everything You Need to Know about the Assault Weapons Ban, in One Post." *Washington Post Wonkblog.* December 17. http://www.washingtonpost .com/news/wonkblog/wp/2012/12/17/everything-you-need-to-know-about -banning-assault-weapons-in-one-post/.

———. 2013. "Absolutely Everything You Need to Know about How the Government Shutdown Will Work." *Washington Post,* September 30.

Polgreen, Lydia. 2015. "From Ferguson to Charleston, Anguish about Race Keeps Building." *New York Times,* June 21, A17.

Politico. 2016. "Full Transcript: Donald Trump NYC Speech on Stakes of the Election." June 22. http://www.politico.com/story/2016/06/transcript-trump-speech-on-the-stakes-of-the-election-224654.

Poole, Keith. 2017. "Political Polarization: House 1879–2015; Party Means on Liberal–Conservative Dimension." K7MOA Legacy Voteview. Accessed February 25. http://www.voteview.com.

Poole, Keith T., and Howard Rosenthal. 2007. *Ideology and Congress*. 2nd ed. New Brunswick, NJ: Transaction. Originally published 1997 as *Congress: A Political-Economic History of Roll Call Voting*.

———. 2014. "The Polarization of the Congressional Parties." Voteview, January 19. http://voteview.com/political_polarization.asp.

Popper, Nathaniel, and Jessica Silver-Greenberg. 2015. "JP Morgan Chase and Goldman Sachs Chiefs to Get a Sweeter Pay Package." *DealB%k* (blog). January 22. https://dealbook.nytimes.com/2015/01/22/jpmorgan-chase-keeps-jamie-dimons-compensation-unchanged/?_r=0.

Post, Robert C. 2014. *Citizens Divided: Campaign Finance Reform and the Constitution*. Cambridge, MA: Harvard University Press.

Powell, G. Bingham Jr. 1986. "American Voter Turnout in Comparative Perspective." *American Political Science Review* 80 (1): 17–43.

Powell, Lynda W. 2012. *The Influence of Campaign Contributions in State Legislatures: The Effects of Institutions and Politics*. Ann Arbor: University of Michigan Press.

Primo, David M., and Jeffrey Milyo. 2006. "Campaign Finance Laws and Political Efficacy: Evidence from the States." *Election Law Journal* 5 (1): 23–39.

Prison Policy Initiative. 2017. "Felony Disenfranchisement." Last modified March 1. http://www.prisonpolicy.org/research/felon_disenfranchisement/.

Project on Student Debt. 2006. "Survey: Americans Want Relief from Rising Student Debt." Pew Charitable Trusts. May 6. http://www.pewtrusts.org/en/about/news-room/press-releases/2006/05/04/survey-americans-want-relief-from-rising-student-debt.

Public Citizen. 2015. "Groups Bring One Million Signatures to White House Urging President Obama to Curb Dark Money." December 16. http://www.citizen.org/pressroom/pressroomredirect.cfm?ID=5765.

Putnam, Robert D. 2000. *Bowling Alone: The Collapse and Revival of American Community*. New York: Simon and Schuster.

Ranney, Austin. 1962. *The Doctrine of Responsible Party Government, Its Origin and Present State*. Champaign: University of Illinois Press.

Reason-Rupe Public Opinion Survey. 2013. "December 2013 National Telephone Survey." http://reason.com/assets/db/13867177334087.xls.

Reich, Robert B. 1997. *Locked in the Cabinet*. New York: Knopf.

———. 2007. *Supercapitalism: The Transformation of Business, Democracy, and Everyday Life*. New York: Alfred A. Knopf.

———. 2012. *Beyond Outrage: What Has Gone Wrong with Our Economy and Our Democracy, and How to Fix It*. New York: Vintage.

———. 2015. *Saving Capitalism: For the Many, Not the Few*. New York: Knopf.

Reid, T. R. 2010. *The Healing of America: A Global Quest for Better, Cheaper, and Fairer Health Care*. New York: Penguin.

Remini, Robert V. 1963. *The Election of Andrew Jackson*. New York: J. B. Lippincott.

Reuters. 2013. "Fitch Places United States' 'AAA' on Rating Watch Negative." October 15.

Rigby, Elizabeth, and Melanie J. Springer. 2011. "Does Electoral Reform Increase (or Decrease) Political Equality?" *Political Research Quarterly* 64 (2): 420–34.

Riker, William H. 1982. *Liberalism against Populism: A Confrontation between the Theory of Democracy and the Theory of Social Choice*. San Francisco: W. H. Freeman.

———. 1986. *The Art of Political Manipulation*. New Haven, CT: Yale University Press.

Rogers, Joel. 2014. "Why 'Harris v. Quinn' Has Labor Very, Very Nervous." *Nation*, March 27. http://www.thenation.com/article/why-harris-v-quinn-has-labor-very -very-nervous/.

Rosenstone, Steven J., and John Mark Hansen. 2002. *Mobilization, Participation, and American Democracy*. Reprint, New York, NY: Pearson. First published 1993.

Roth, Zachary. 2014. "Wisconsin is the Latest Swing State to Target Early Voting." MSNBC. March 13. http://www.msnbc.com/msnbc/wisconsin-gop-early-voting.

Rubio, Marco. 2015. Interview by Steve Inskeep, National Public Radio, April 13. http://www.npr.org/sections/itsallpolitics/2015/04/13/399415802/transcript-nprs -full-interview-with-sen-marco-rubio.

Saad, Lydia. 2013a. "Americans Call for Term Limits, End to Electoral College." Gallup. January 18. http://www.gallup.com/poll/159881/americans-call-term-limits -end-electoral-college.aspx.

———. 2013b. "Half in U.S. Support Publicly Financed Federal Campaigns." Gallup. June 24. http://www.gallup.com/poll/163208/half-support-publicly-financed -federal-campaigns.aspx.

Sabl, Andrew. 2015. "The Two Cultures of Democratic Theory: Responsiveness, Democratic Quality, and the Empirical-Normative Divide." *Perspectives on Politics*: 13 (2): 345–65.

Sachs, Benjamin. 2013. "The Unbundled Union: Politics without Collective Bargaining." *Yale Law Journal* 123 (1): 148–207.

Samuelson, Paul A. 1948. "International Trade and the Equalisation of Factor Prices." *Economic Journal* 58 (230): 163–84.

———. 1949. "International Factor-Price Equalization Once Again." *Economic Journal* 59 (234): 181–97.

———. 1950. "The Gains from International Trade." In *Readings on the Theory of International Trade*. Edited by H. S. Ellis and L. A. Metler. Homewood, IL: Irwin.

Sanders, Elizabeth. 1999. *Roots of Reform: Farmers, Workers, and the American State, 1877–1917*. Chicago: University of Chicago Press.

Scarrow, Susan E. 2007. "Political Finance in Comparative Perspective." *Annual Review of Political Science* 10:193–201.

Schaffner, Brian. 2016. Vox. "White Support for Donald Trump Was Driven by Economic Anxiety, but also by Racism and Sexism." November 16. http://www.vox .com/mischiefs-of-faction/2016/11/16/13651184/trump-support-economic-anxiety -racism-sexism.

Schattschneider, E. E. 1960. *The Semisovereign People: A Realist's View of Democracy in America*. New York: Holt.

Schatz, Joseph J. 2009. "Senate Scales Back Its Stimulus." *Congressional Quarterly Weekly*, February 9, 306–8.

Scheiber, Noam, and Dalia Sussman. 2015. "Inequality Troubles Americans across Party Lines, a Poll Finds." *New York Times*, June 4, A1, B8.

Scheidel, Walter. 2017. *The Great Leveller: Violence and the History of Inequality from the Stone Age to the Twenty-first Century*. Princeton, NJ: Princeton University Press.

Scheve, Kenneth F., David Stasavage, and Russell Sage Foundation. 2016. *Taxing the Rich: A History of Fiscal Fairness in the United States and Europe*. Princeton, NJ: Princeton University Press.

Schickler, Eric. 2001. *Disjointed Pluralism: Institutional Innovation and the Development of the U.S. Congress*. Princeton, NJ: Princeton University Press.

———. 2016. *Racial Realignment: The Transformation of American Liberalism, 1932–1965*. Princeton, NJ: Princeton University Press.

Schlozman, Kay Lehman, Sidney Verba, and Henry E. Brady. 2012. *The Unheavenly Chorus: Unequal Political Voice and the Broken Promise of American Democracy*. Princeton, NJ: Princeton University Press.

Schulman, Daniel. 2014. *Sons of Wichita: How the Koch Brothers Became America's Most Powerful and Private Dynasty*. New York: Grand Central.

Schumpeter, Joseph A. 1950. *Capitalism, Socialism and Democracy*. New York: Harper and Row. First published 1942.

Schwartz, Michael H. 1977. "An Estimate of the Size of the Southern Farmers' Alliance 1884–1890." *Agricultural History* 51 (4): 759–69.

Schwarz, Hunter. 2014. "Voter Turnout in Primary Elections This Year Has Been Abysmal." *Washington Post* (blog). July 23. http://www.washingtonpost.com/blogs/govbeat/wp/2014/07/23/voter-turnout-in-primary-elections-this-year-has-been-abysmal/.

Sclar, Jason, Alexander Hertel-Fernandez, Theda Skocpol, and Vanessa Williamson. 2016. "Donor Consortia on the Left and Right: Comparing the Membership, Activities, and Impact of the Democracy Alliance and the Koch Seminars." Paper presented at the Annual Meeting of the Midwest Political Science Association, Chicago, April 8.

Searcey, Dionne. 2015. "Home Pricey Home: In a Tepid Market, Builders Cater to the Desires of the Well-Off." *New York Times*, February 25, B1, B8.

Selb, Peter, and Romain Lachat. 2009. "The More, the Better? Counterfactual Evidence on the Effect of Compulsory Voting on the Consistency of Party Choice." *European Journal of Political Research* 48 (5): 573–97.

Sentencing Project. 2017. "Felony Disenfranchisement." Accessed March 1. http://www.sentencingproject.org/issues/felony-disenfranchisement/.

Shane, Scott. 2017. "How to Make a Masterpiece in Fake News." *New York Times*. January 19, A1, A17.

Sherman, Jake, and Jonathan Allen. 2011. "Boehner Seeks 'Majority of the Majority.'" *Politico*, July 30. http://www.politico.com/story/2011/07/boehner-seeks-majority-of-the-majority-060296?jumpEdition.

Shineman, Victoria Anne. 2016. "If You Mobilize Them, They Will Become Informed: Experimental Evidence that Information Acquisition Is Endogenous to Costs and Incentives to Participate." *British Journal of Political Science*. https://doi.org/10.1017/S0007123416000168.

Sides, John, Daron Shaw, Matt Grossman, and Keena Lipsitz. 2014. *Campaigns and Elections: Rules, Reality, Strategy, Choice*. 2012 Election Update. New York: W. W. Norton.

———. 2015. *Campaigns and Elections: Rules, Reality, Strategy, Choice*. 2nd ed. New York: Norton.

Sierra Club. 2017. "Democracy." Accessed March 28. https://web.archive.org/web/20170210001027/http://www.sierraclub.org/democracy.

Silver, Ira. 1998. "Buying an Activist Identity: Reproducing Class through Social Movement Philanthropy." *Sociological Perspectives* 41 (2): 303–21.

Sinclair, Barbara. 2006. *Party Wars: Polarization and the Politics of National Policy Making*. Norman: University of Oklahoma Press.

———. 2008. "Spoiling the Sausages? How a Polarized Congress Deliberates and Legislates." In Nivola and Brady, *Red Nation and Blue Nation?* 2:55–87.

Singer, Stephen. 2011. "Connecticut 1st State to Require Paid Sick Time." *Washington Post*, July 5. https://www.washingtonpost.com/business/economy/connecticut-1st -state-to-require-paid-sick-time/2011/07/05/gIQAU9S1zH_story.html

Skocpol, Theda. 2003. *Diminished Democracy: From Membership to Management in American Civic Life*. Norman: University of Oklahoma Press.

Skocpol, Theda, and Alexander Hertel-Fernandez. 2016. "The Koch Network and the Rightward Shift in U.S. Politics." Paper presented at the Annual Meeting of the Midwest Political Science Association, Chicago, April 8.

———. Forthcoming. *The Koch Effect*. Chicago: University of Chicago Press.

Slaughter, Anne-Marie. 2015. "A Toxic Work World." *New York Times*, September 20, SR 1, 6.

Smelser, Neil J. 1962. *Theory of Collective Behavior*. London: Routledge and Kegan Paul.

Smeltz, Dina, Ivo Daalder, Karl Friedhoff, and Craig Kafura. 2016. "America in the Age of Uncertainty." Chicago Council on Global Affairs. October 6. https://www .thechicagocouncil.org/publication/america-age-uncertainty.

Smeltz, Dina, Sra McElmurry, and Craig Kafura. 2014. "Holding Steady: Public Opinion on Immigration." Chicago Council on Global Affairs. October. http://www .thechicagocouncil.org/sites/default/files/Immigration_Survey_Brief.pdf.

Smith, Adam. (1776) 1976. *An Inquiry into the Nature and Causes of the Wealth of Nations*. Edited by Edwin Cannan. Chicago: University of Chicago Press.

Smith, Daniel A., and Caroline J. Tolbert. 2004. *Educated by Initiative: The Effects of Direct Democracy on Citizens and Political Organizations in the American States*. Ann Arbor: University of Michigan Press.

Smith, Mark A. 2000. *American Business and Political Power: Public Opinion, Elections, and Democracy*. Chicago: University of Chicago Press.

Smith, Steven S. 2007. *Party Influence in Congress*. Cambridge: Cambridge University Press.

Snow, David A., and Robert D. Benford. 1992. "Master Frames and Cycles of Protest." In *Frontiers in Social Movement Theory*, edited by Aldon D. Morris and Carol McClurg Mueller. New Haven, CT: Yale University Press.

Snow, David A., Donatella della Porta, Bert Klandermans, and Doug McAdam, eds. 2004. *The Wiley-Blackwell Encyclopedia of Social and Political Movements*. Malden, MA: Blackwell.

Snow, David A., E. Burke Rochford Jr., Steven K. Worden, and Robert D. Benford. 1986. "Frame Alignment Processes, Micromobilization, and Movement Participation." *American Sociological Review* 51 (4): 464–81.

Snyder, James M. 1992. "Long-Term Investing in Politicians—or, Give Early, Give Often." *Journal of Law and Economics* 35 (1): 15–43.

Solt, Fredrick. 2014. "Reversing the Arrow? Economic Inequality's Effect on Religiosity." In *Religion and Inequality in America: Research and Theory on Religion's Role in Stratification*, edited by Lisa A. Keister and Darren E. Sherkat, 337–53. New York: Cambridge University Press.

Solt, Fredrick, Philip Habel, and J. Tobin Grant. 2011. "Economic Inequality, Relative Power, and Religiosity." *Social Science Quarterly* 92 (2): 447–65.

Somin, Ilya. 2013. *Democracy and Political Ignorance: Why Smaller Government Is Smarter*. Stanford, CA: Stanford University Press.

Soroka, Stuart N., and Christopher Wlezien. 2008. "On the Limits to Inequality in Representation." *PS: Political Science and Politics* 41 (2): 319–27.

———. 2010. *Degrees of Democracy: Politics, Public Opinion, and Policy*. New York: Cambridge University Press.

Spaulding, Stephen. 2014. *"The New Nullification" at Work: Executive Branch Nominations and the Tactics of Obstruction*. Common Cause: Holding Power Accountable. http://www.commoncause.org/research-reports/the-new-nullification.pdf.

Springer, Melanie J. 2014. *How States Shaped the Nation: American Electoral Institutions and Voter Turnout, 1920–2000*. Chicago: University of Chicago Press.

Stanley, Harold W. 1988. "Southern Partisan Changes: Dealignment, Realignment or Both?" *Journal of Politics* 50 (1): 64–88.

Starr, Paul. 1995. "What Happened to Healthcare Reform?" *American Prospect*, Winter. http://prospect.org/article/what-happened-health-care-reform.

Stewart, James. 2008. "The Birthday Party: How Stephen Schwarzman Became Private Equity's Designated Villain." *New Yorker*, February 11. http://www.newyorker.com/magazine/2008/02/11/the-birthday-party-2.

Stiglitz, Joseph E. 2002. *Globalization and Its Discontents*. New York: W. W. Norton.

———. 2012. *The Price of Inequality*. New York: W. W. Norton.

Stohr, Greg. 2015. "Bloomberg Poll: Americans Want Supreme Court to Turn Off Political Spending Spigot." September 28. https://www.bloomberg.com/politics/articles/2015-09-28/bloomberg-poll-americans-want-supreme-court-to-turn-off-political-spending-spigot.

Stone, Andy. 2009. "Green Bill's Biggest Test Awaits in the Senate." *Forbes*, June 27. http://www.forbes.com/2009/06/27/clean-energy-act-carbon-congress-business-washington-energy-bill.html.

Stone, Peter. 2016. "How a Network Led by the Billionaire Koch Brothers Is Riding the Trump Wave." *Guardian*, December 7.

Stratmann, T. 1998. "The Market for Congressional Votes: Is Timing of Contributions Everything?" *Journal of Law and Economics* 41 (1): 85–113.

Strolovitch, Dara Z. 2007. *Affirmative Advocacy: Race, Class, and Gender in Interest Group Politics*. Chicago: University of Chicago Press.

Sullivan, Patricia. 1991. "Southern Reformers, the New Deal, and the Movement's Foundation." In *New Directions in Civil Rights Studies*, edited by Armstead L. Robinson and Patricia Sullivan, 81–102. Charlottesville: University Press of Virginia.

Sundquist, James L. 1983. *Dynamics of the Party System: Alignment and Realignment of Political Parties in the United States*. Washington, DC: Brookings Institution.

Surowiecki, James. 2004. *The Wisdom of Crowds: Why the Many are Smarter than the Few and How Collective Wisdom Shapes Business, Economics, Societies, and Nations*. New York: Doubleday.

Suttmann-Lea, Mara. Forthcoming. "Convenience at a Cost: The Unintended Consequences of Early Voting for American Politics." PhD diss., Northwestern University.

Swain, Carol M. 2006. *Black Faces, Black Interests: The Representation of African Americans in Congress*. Lanham, MD: University Press of America.

Szymanski, Ann-Marie E. 2003. *Pathways to Prohibition: Radicals, Moderates, and Social Movement Outcomes*. Durham, NC: Duke University Press.

Tarrow, Sidney G. 2011. *Power in Movement: Social Movements, Collective Action, and Politics*. 3rd ed. Cambridge: Cambridge University Press. First published 1994.

Taub, Stephen. 2015. "The 2015 Rich List: The Highest Earning Hedge Fund Managers of the Past Year." Institutional Investors Alpha, May 5. http://www.institutionalinvestorsalpha.com/Article/3450284/The-2015-Rich-List-The-Highest-Earning-Hedge-Fund-Managers-of-the-Past-Year.html.

———. 2016. "The 2016 Rich List of the World's Top-Earning Hedge Fund Managers." Institutional Investor's Alpha, May 10. http://www.institutionalinvestorsalpha.com/Article/3552805/The-2016-Rich-List-of-the-Worlds-Top-Earning-Hedge-Fund-Managers.html.

Teachout, Zephyr. 2009. "The Anti-Corruption Principle." *Cornell Law Review* 94 (2): 341–414.

———. 2014. *Corruption in America: From Benjamin Franklin's Snuff Box to Citizens' United*. Cambridge, MA: Harvard University Press.

Teles, Steven M. 2008. *The Rise of the Conservative Legal Movement: The Battle for Control of the Law*. Princeton, NJ: Princeton University Press.

———. 2015. "The Scourge of Upward Redistribution." *National Affairs* 25. http://www.nationalaffairs.com/publications/detail/the-scourge-of-upward-redistribution.

Temin, Peter. 2016. "The American Dual Economy: Race, Globalization, and the Politics of Exclusion." *International Journal of Political Economy* 45 (2): 85–123.

Thal, Adam. 2016. "Class Isolation and Affluent Americans' Perception of Social Conditions." *Political Behavior*. doi:10.1007/s11109-016-9361-9.

Thelen, Kathleen. 2014. *Varieties of Liberalization and the New Politics of Social Solidarity*. New York: Cambridge University Press.

Theriault, Sean M. 2008. *Party Polarization in Congress*. New York: Cambridge University Press.

Thompson, Derek. 2015. "A World without Work." *Atlantic*, July/August.

Thomsen, Danielle M. 2014. "Ideological Moderates Won't Run: How Party Fit Matters for Partisan Polarization in Congress." *Journal of Politics* 76 (3): 786–97.

Tilly, Charles, Louise Tilly, and Richard H. Tilly. 1975. *The Rebellious Century, 1830–1930*. Cambridge, MA: Harvard University Press.

Timpone, Richard J. 1998. "Structure, Behavior, and Voter Turnout in the United States." *American Political Science Review* 97 (1): 145–58.

Tocqueville, Alexis de. (1835) 2000. *Democracy in America*. Edited and translated by Harvey C. Mansfield and Delba Winthrop. Chicago: University of Chicago Press.

Tolbert, Caroline, Todd Donavan, Kellen Gracey, and Cary Wolbers. 2014. "Experiments in Election Reform: Voter Perceptions of Campaigns under Preferential and Plurality Voting." Paper presented at the conference on Electoral Systems Reform, Stanford University, March 15–16.

Tolbert, Caroline, Todd Donovan, Bridgett King, and Shaun Bowler. 2008. "Election Day Registration, Competition, and Voter Turnout." In *Democracy in the States: Experiments in Election Reform*, edited by Bruce Cain, Todd Donovan, and Caroline Tolbert, 83–89. Washington, DC: Brookings Institution Press.

Trading Economics. 2017. "China Average Yearly Wages: 1952–2017." http://www.tradingeconomics.com/china/wages.

Tripathi, Mickey, Stephen Ansolabehere, and James M. Snyder. 2002. "Are PAC Contributions and Lobbying Linked? New Evidence from the 1995 Lobby Disclosure Act." *Business and Politics* 4 (2): 131–55.

Trope, Adam. 2009. "Inconvenienced by Democracy: Dismantling the Argument Against Universal Voter Registration." March 6. *FairVote* (blog). http://www .fairvote.org/research-and-analysis/blog/inconvenienced-by-democracy-dismantling -the-argument-against-universal-voter-registration/.

Truman, David B. 1971. *The Governmental Process: Political Interests and Public Opinion.* 2nd ed. New York: Knopf. First published 1951.

Tucker, Jasmine V., Virginia P. Reno, and Thomas N. Bethell. 2013. Strengthening Social Security: What Do Americans Want? Washington, DC: National Academy of Social Insurance. https://www.nasi.org/sites/default/files/research/What_Do _Americans_Want.pdf.

Udall, Tom. 2013. "Udall Calls for Reform to Fix Broken Senate." News release, July 15. http://www.tomudall.senate.gov/?p=press_release&id=1365.

United States Bureau of the Census. 1975. *Historical Statistics of the United States, Colonial Times to 1970, Bicentennial Edition, Part 1.* Washington, D.C.: U.S. Government Printing Office.

———. 1976. *Consumer Income: Money Income in 1974 of Families and Persons in the United States.* Current Population Reports Series P-60, no.101, January. https:// www2.census.gov/prod2/popscan/p60-101.pdf.

———. 2013. "2010 Population Finder." Last modified August 6. http://www.census .gov/popfinder/.

———. 2017. "Voting and Registration: Percent Voted in 2014." Accessed February 28. http://thedataweb.rm.census.gov/TheDataWeb_HotReport2/voting/voting.hrml.

United States Bureau of Labor Statistics. 2017. "Union Members Summary." News release, January 26. https://www.bls.gov/news.release/union2.nro.htm.

United States Congressional Budget Office. 2004. "Administrative Costs of Private Accounts in Social Security." March 1. https://www.cbo.gov/publication/15467.

———. 2013. "Add a 'Public Plan' to the Health Insurance Exchanges." November 13. https://www.cbo.gov/budget-options/2013/44890.

———. 2016. "The Distribution of Household Income and Federal Taxes, 2013." June 8. https://www.cbo.gov/publication/51361.

United States Department of Health and Human Services. 2016. *National Vital Statistics Report 65* (4).

United States Election Project. 2017. "2016 November General Election Turnout Rates." Accessed February 20. http://www.electproject.org/2016g.

United States House of Representatives, Office of the Clerk. 2013. *Statistics of the Congressional Election of November 6, 2012.* Washington, DC: Government Printing Office.

United States Senate. 2017. "Senate Action on Cloture Motions." Accessed February 27. www.senate.gov/pagelayout/reference/cloture_motions/clotureCounts.htm.

Uslaner, Eric M. 1993. *The Decline of Comity in Congress.* Ann Arbor: University of Michigan Press.

Valelly, Richard M. 1989. *Radicalism in the States: The Minnesota Farmer-Labor Party and the American Political Economy.* Chicago: University of Chicago Press.

Van Mechelen, Natascha, and Jonathan Bradshaw. 2013. "Child Poverty as a Government Priority: Child Benefit Packages for Working Families, 1922–2009." In *Work and Welfare in Europe: Minimum Income Protection in Flux,* edited by Ive Marx and Kenneth Nelson, 81–107. London: Palgrave Macmillan.

Voorhees, Josh. 2012. "Gun Control Compromise Fails to Clear GOP Filibuster." *Slat-

est (blog). April 17. http://www.slate.com/blogs/the_slatest/2013/04/17/manchin _toomey_gun_control_amendment_compromise_lacks_votes_to_avoid_gop.html.

Wallerstein, Michael. 1999. "Wage-Setting Institutions and Pay Inequality in Advanced Industrial Societies." *American Journal of Political Science* 43 (3): 659–80.

Walsh, Katherine Cramer. 2004. *Talking about Politics: Informal Groups and Social Identity in American Life.* Chicago: University of Chicago Press.

———. 2007. *Talking about Race: Community Dialogues and the Politics of Difference.* Chicago: University of Chicago Press.

Wang, Tova Andrea. 2012. *The Politics of Voter Suppression: Defending and Expanding Americans' Right to Vote.* Ithaca, NY: Cornell University Press.

Warner, Kris. 2013. "The Decline of Unionization in the United States." *Labor Studies Journal* 38 (2): 110–38.

Wawro, Gregory J., and Eric Schickler. 2006. *Filibuster: Obstruction and Lawmaking in the U.S. Senate.* Princeton, NJ: Princeton University Press.

Weber, Ronald E. 1999. "Presidential Address: The Quality of State Legislative Representation; A Critical Assessment." *Journal of Politics* 61 (3): 609–27.

Weick, Karl E. 1979. *The Social Psychology of Organizing.* Reading, MA: Addison-Wesley.

Weiser, Wendy, Michael Waldman, and Renée Paradis. 2008. "Universal Voter Registration: Policy Summary." *Brennan Center for Justice.* http://www.brennancenter .org/page/-/publications/UVR.Proposal.pdf.

West, Darrell M. 2014. *Billionaires: Reflections on the Upper Crust.* Washington, DC: Brookings Institution.

Whitby, Kenny J. 1997. *The Color of Representation: Congressional Behavior and Black Interests.* Ann Arbor: University of Michigan Press.

White, Brad. 2005. *Congressional Revolving Doors: The Journey from Congress to K Street.* Washington, DC: Public Citizen.

Wiebe, Robert H. 1967. *The Search for Order: 1877–1890.* New York: Hill and Wang.

———. 1989. *Businessmen and Reform: A Study of the Progressive Movement.* Reprint, Chicago: Ivan R. Dee. First published 1962.

Wilentz, Sean. 2005. *The Rise of American Democracy: Jefferson to Lincoln.* New York: W. W. Norton.

———. 2016. *The Politicians and the Egalitarians: The Hidden History of American Politics.* New York: W. W. Norton.

Willis, Derek. 2015. "To Understand Scott Walker's Strength, Look at His Donors." *New York Times,* February 12, A18.

Wines, Michael. 2016. "Judges Find Wisconsin Redistricting Unfairly Favored Republicans." *New York Times,* November 21, A1.

Winters, Jeffrey A. 2011. *Oligarchy.* New York: Cambridge University Press.

Winters, Jeffrey A., and Benjamin I. Page. 2009. "Oligarchy in the United States?" *Perspectives on Politics* 7 (4): 731–51.

Wisconsin Democracy Campaign. 2013. "Recall Race for Governor Cost $81 Million." January 31. http://www.wisdc.org/pro72512.php.

Wisconsin Elections Commission. 2016. "Wisconsin Voter Turnout Statistics. Accessed February 22. http://elections.wi.gov/elections-voting/statistics/turnout.

Wolfinger, Raymond E., and Steven J. Rosenstone. 1980. *Who Votes?* New Haven, CT: Yale University Press.

Yellin, Eric Steven. 2013. *Racism in the Nation's Service: Government Workers and* the *Color Line in Woodrow Wilson's America*. Chapel Hill: University of North Carolina Press.

Yerak, Becky. 2015. "Prairie Payday." *Chicago Tribune*, June 21, sec. 2, 1–3.

Zaller, John R. 1992. *The Nature and Origins of Mass Opinion*. Cambridge, MA: Cambridge University Press.

Zinn, Howard. 1999. *A People's History of the United States: 1492–Present*. New York: Harper Collins. First published 1980.

Ziobrowski, Alan J., Ping Cheng, James W. Boyd, and Brigitte J. Ziobrowski. 2004. "Abnormal Returns from the Common Stock Investments of the U.S. Senate." *Journal of Financial and Quantitative Analysis* 39 (4): 661–76.

INDEX

AARP, 136

access to officials, 120–23

accountability, political: full disclosure of election spending and, 193; stealth politics and, 107

accountants, hard hit by technology, 42–43

Achen, Christopher, 277n10

acronyms, 9

active labor market policies, 45–46, 283n89

activists, responsibility of, for party polarization, 165. *See also under* parties

Adams, Jane, 255

Adelson, Sheldon: contributions of, to Newt Gingrich, 97; contributions of, to Scott Walker, 93; major funder of Donald Trump, 98; net worth of, 33; silence of, about taxes and Social Security, 106; on "socialist-style economy," 106; stealth politics by, 105–6

affluent Americans: evidence on policy influence by, 91–92; income level of, 92; increases in affluence at the top, 30–32; independence of, from business groups, 138–39, 292n24; policy preferences of, 118

Affordable Care Act (ACA), 83–85; efforts to repeal, 85; killing the public option in, 145; mixed popularity of, 84; opposition to "individual mandate" in, 84, 286n80; passage and effects of, 83–84; public support

for expanding, 84; public support for specific provisions of, 84; voter registration through, 206

AFL-CIO, 136, 259

African Americans: civil rights movement and, 247–51; clustering of, in one-party districts, 161–62; disenfranchisement of, 207; loss of voting power by, due to district clustering, 161–62; Supreme Court's mixed record on, 15; wealth of African American families, 32

agenda control, House standing committees and, 175

aggregation, of individuals' preferences, 10–11, 277n1

AIG, lobbying expenditures by, 140

Ailes, Roger, 126

air, clean, 73

aircraft production, decline of workers in, 41–42

alienation, 181–82

all-mail elections, 206–7

Althaus, Scott, on fully informed preferences, 278n20

Altman, Nancy J., 291n99

Altria, lobbying expenditures by, 140

American Bar Association (ABA), 132

American Dream: decline of economic mobility and, 29–30; realizable in 1950s and 1960s, 27; wage stagnation and, 41

American Enterprise Institute, 125